The Dorsey Series in Psychology

Advisory Editors

Wendell E. Jeffrey
University of California, Los Angeles

Salvatore R. Maddi
The University of Chicago

Bruce Ekstrand
University of Colorado, Boulder

PRINCIPLES OF PSYCHOLOGICAL RESEARCH

JOEL A. GOLD
University of Maine, Orono

1984

THE DORSEY PRESS   Homewood, Illinois 60430

© THE DORSEY PRESS, 1984

ISBN 0-256-02858-3

Library of Congress Catalog Card No. 83-72619

Printed in the United States of America

1 2 3 4 5 6 7 8 9 0 ML 1 0 9 8 7 6 5 4

To Becky and Ted

Preface

This book, as the title implies, is a general introduction to the principles of psychological research. Since research in psychology is diverse in terms of topics and methods, I felt that a text dealing with research methods in psychology should attempt to present a balanced approach, covering various methods and employing examples from different content areas within the field. Having taught a course in research methods for 15 years, I felt that most of the texts seemed to emphasize experimental designs at the expense of correlational techniques. Therefore, I have given equal weight to experimental and correlational approaches and employed studies from social, clinical, developmental, and experimental psychology to illustrate the various methods.

The book is organized into three general parts. Part 1 contains an introductory chapter dealing with psychology as a science, comparing the differences and similarities between scientific and nonscientific approaches. Chapter 2 introduces the concept of variability, and more specifically, that of variance. The explanations are totally verbal and presume no previous statistical background. My feeling was that concepts should be the important focus of this text and not computations. For those who are interested in computations, footnotes refer the reader to the appendix which contains computational examples for most of the major statistical techniques discussed in the text. The concept of accounting for variance is carried throughout the book and serves as a unifying theme underlying the various methods of research. Chapter 3 covers the topic of measurement in psychology, providing specific emphasis on reliability. Measurement through surveys and through observation is also discussed.

Part 2 deals with the basic issues involved in experimental and correlational research. Chapter 4 introduces the correlation coefficient and explains linear regression. Chapter 5 defines the nature of an experiment and explains independent and dependent variables. It concludes with a section on single-subject experimental designs. Chapters 6 and 7 explain the basics of statistical inference. As in previous chapters, formulas and computations are avoided, and all presentations are handled on a verbal, conceptual level. Chapter 6 discusses the nature of chance and defines the concept of a sampling distribution. Chapter 7 extends this discussion to sampling distributions of differences between means and the nature of

Type I and Type II errors. Chapter 8 deals with questions of the internal and external validity of experimental data and includes a discussion of ethical issues in research. Chapter 9 explains the nature of quasi-experimental designs, emphasizing cohort and time-series approaches.

Part 3 deals with complex experimental and correlational approaches. Chapter 10 explains factorial experiments using between- and within-subjects factors and discusses the designs which employ both manipulated and nonmanipulated variables. Chapter 11 covers multiple correlation and regression, partial correlation, and factor analysis. Again, in both Chapter 10 and Chapter 11, all statistical issues are handled on a verbal level. Multiple regression is depicted through the use of Venn diagrams.

Finally, Part 4 includes a discussion in Chapter 12 of construct validity in both experimental and correlational situations, much of which is carried out through presentation of research studies that exemplify aspects of the construct validation process. Chapter 13 is a step-by-step movement through an actual experiment in order to demonstrate the complexities and difficulties involved in the research process.

This book was begun on a sabbatical at Arizona State University. I wish to express my appreciation to the University of Maine for extending that sabbatical period and to the psychology department at Arizona State University for their support during my stay in Tempe. Special notes of gratitude are due Sandy Braver and Nancy Eisenberg, who read and commented upon early drafts of the manuscript. I am also indebted to Marian Perry, Eva Benson, and Anne Theriault for their heroic work in deciphering my handwriting and producing the numerous drafts of the manuscript. Finally, I would like to thank my reviewers who have made this an interesting and even pleasant experience.

Joel A. Gold

Contents

An Alternative Experimental Approach: *Treatment Removal. Multiple-Baseline.* Group versus Single Subject Designs.

**Part 3
UNDERSTANDING MORE OF THE VARIANCE**

Part 4
UNDERSTANDING PSYCHOLOGICAL CONSTRUCTS

PRINCIPLES OF
PSYCHOLOGICAL
RESEARCH

Part 1

THE UNDERLYING
PRINCIPLES

Chapter 1

Introduction

The scene is a coffee shop in a building at a university. Two people enter; one is a female graduate research assistant, and the other is a male student who is a subject in a psychological experiment. There has been a break in the experimental session, and the assistant has taken the student to the coffee shop to wait for the study to resume. The assistant and the student sit down at a table with a woman dressed in a loose fitting lab coat and wearing a rather severe hair style and no makeup. The graduate assistant then excuses herself for a moment in order to make a phone call. The student, left alone with the woman, engages her in conversation, compliments her during the conversation, and offers to pay for her drink—behaviors toward a member of the opposite sex that could generally be considered to reflect romantic interest.

Later that day, the same graduate assistant brings another male student to the coffee shop during the experimental break, and again they sit at the table with the same plain looking woman. The assistant, as before, excuses herself to make a phone call, leaving the subject alone with the woman. This student does not engage her in conversation, offers no compliments, nor does he attempt to pay for her drink. Whereas the first subject interacted positively (i.e., approached the woman), the second subject shows no trace of the positive interaction and in fact seemed to avoid her.

The following morning, the events of the previous day are repeated except that the plain looking woman with whom the assistant and the subject sit is now very attractive. Her clothes are form-fitting, her hair is done attractively, and she is wearing makeup. As in the second case the previous day, the subject, when left alone with the woman, seems to avoid her, showing no behaviors which could be construed to be romantic. Finally, that same afternoon, another subject left alone with the attractive woman engages her in conversation, compliments her, and even asks for her telephone number.

If we kept watching these encounters, we would see that half of the subjects meet the woman when she is plain looking, while the other half meet her when she looks very attractive. We would also see that some of the students who meet the attractive woman engage in approach behaviors toward her while others seem to avoid her. The same phenomenon occurs with the plain looking woman: some of the subjects interact positively with her, while the others emit very few behaviors which could be classified as positive. Is this difference between the subjects who do and do not act positively toward the woman when she appears plain and when she is attractive an accidental difference, or is there some reason for the difference? All that we know from watching the students is that there are differences in their behavior; that is, they vary as to the manner in which they respond to the attractive or plain woman. If this variability in the behavior of the students is accidental or random, that is, if there is not a pattern or method to it, then the reason for it cannot be understood. We could describe each event that occurs, but no understanding of the differences between events would be possible. On the other hand, there may be an explanation for the variability we see; that is, there may be some reason why certain students approach the attractive woman while others approach the plain woman.

An explanation of the variability of the behavior would probably involve determining the "things" that produced or are related to the differences we observe between the subjects. Psychologists call any aspect of the environment or any response of interest that can vary in some measurable way a *variable,* as opposed to a *constant,* which has only one value. Since all the students who were maneuvered to the table in the coffee shop sat down with the woman, this behavior, which showed no variability, would be a constant. Their objective then is to see if the individual differences in one variable—engaging in romantic behaviors— are related to the individual differences in some other variable.

In the case of these students, there is a variable which is systematically related to engaging in positive actions toward the woman when she is plain looking and when she is attractive. That variable has to do with the events which preceded the meeting in the coffee shop. Specifically, before going to the coffee shop with the graduate assistant, the subjects took a bogus intelligence test. Half of them were told that they had performed very well, while the other half were told that they had done poorly. Half of the subjects in each feedback group then were maneuvered into an encounter with either the attractive or the plain looking woman in the coffee shop.

Is there then a systematic relationship between the variable of positive actions and the positive or negative feedback on the bogus intelligence test? The answer is that those students who were told they did well on the test engaged in a high number of positive actions toward the attractive woman and few positive actions toward the plain looking woman. On the other hand, those students who were told they performed poorly on the test engaged in more positive actions toward the plain than toward the attractive looking woman. The outcome is shown in Table 1–1. It should be noted that within each group in the study, subjects showed some variability in behavior. For example, not all subjects who received positive feedback showed exactly the same number of positive actions toward the attractive woman. They varied, but on the average, those subjects who

TABLE 1–1
Relationship between test feedback, attractiveness of the female, and subjects' behavior toward the female

	Feedback on Test	
Female Confederate	*Positive*	*Negative*
Attractive	More positive behaviors	Fewer positive behaviors
Plain	Fewer positive behaviors	More positive behaviors

received positive feedback showed more positive actions toward the attractive than toward the plain woman, while the opposite tendency occurred for the negative feedback subjects. Thus, the differential behaviors of the subjects to the women was related to the preceding events.

SCIENTISTS AND NONSCIENTISTS—THE SIMILARITY

The important point is that we attempt to understand the individual differences in a specific behavior by seeing if those differences are related in systematic ways to individual differences in previous experiences or other behaviors. That is, we always attempt to make sense of one variable by relating it to other variables. For example, if we observed a group of high school students, we would soon see variability in their degree of interaction with the opposite sex. Some of the students would be extremely popular, involved in a "social whirl," others would interact moderately, while some would hardly ever be seen with a member of the opposite sex. It probably would not take long for us to observe that another variable seemed to be consistently related to social interaction— that variable being physical attractiveness. If the most attractive people tended to be the most socially involved and the least attractive people tended to be the least involved, then some understanding of the basis of social involvement would be achieved. Although this judgment about the relationship between social interaction and attractiveness would be an informal process, not based on scientific procedures and statistical considerations, it would, nonetheless, probably be made.

In the sense that all of us attempt to understand the variability around us, make guesses or hypotheses about the reasons for that variability, and look for evidence to support our guesses, we are all acting as scientists. Also, to the extent that we draw conclusions without any empirical evidence, we are behaving like nonscientists. We are continuously evaluating and categorizing the behavior of others, judging the reasons for the behaviors, and collecting the evidence in support of those judgments. The order of the process may change in that we sometimes first observe two behaviors which systematically vary together and then conclude that one is the basis for the other; but in any case, we explain one type of variability with another. In other words, all of us are motivated to understand and account for the variability in the behaviors that surround us.

The formal process of the scientist is very much the same as the informal process of the nonscientist. The difference between the two lies in the scientist's adherence to certain rules and procedures within the general process. But the task is identical: to explain individual differences (variability) in one variable by relating it to a second variable that may be systematically related to the first. The point is that, for the scientist or the layman, nothing can be understood by itself. Behaviors are only understandable in their context with other behaviors. The viewpoint of this text will be that *research is aimed at understanding variation among individuals*. A number of very different methods will be examined in the course of this book, but all will have one thing in common—the explanation of a behavior's variability via one or more other behaviors.

SCIENTISTS AND NONSCIENTISTS—THE DIFFERENCE

So far, I have emphasized the similarities between the scientist and the nonscientist in their attempts to achieve understanding of the world around them. We will now look at the rules and procedures that differentiate the observations of the scientist from those of the layman. The purpose of these rules and procedures is to prevent bias. Bias is related to the tendency of people to look for evidence that supports their beliefs about the world, while ignoring evidence that contradicts those beliefs. All of us have beliefs or opinions about the events that occur in the world around us. Sometimes these beliefs come from respected authorities, such as parents or teachers, and sometimes they are arrived at through our own experience. Whichever way the belief is formed, it often becomes *the* way of seeing the world—it becomes truth. We tend to see clearly those events that confirm the belief and overlook or discount those events that question the validity of the belief. Just watch people describe their favorite political candidate and then listen to someone on the other side of the political fence describe that same candidate. Very often, both will be biased by their views and both will have collected evidence, either favorable or unfavorable, that supports those views. Unfortunately, each either will have failed to notice the evidence that does not support their view or will have discounted it as being irrelevant.

Not only do we tend to gather only confirming evidence for our beliefs, but we also seek out others who hold beliefs that are highly similar to our own. The reason for this seeking of similar others is that they do not challenge our beliefs and, consequently, our ability to understand and deal with the world.

Scientists are subject to the same biases as other mortals. They hold beliefs about the nature of reality, and they attempt to gather evidence and recruit support for those beliefs. Unlike the layman, the scientist is bound by rules and procedures that specify the prescribed manner in which the ideas or beliefs are tested. The rules and procedures ensure that the beliefs can be tested fairly and verified, and also that the studies can be repeated by others who may or may not hold similar beliefs. If a belief is verified using the scientific method and if the verification can be repeated by others, particularly those not holding the belief, the belief gains a great deal of credence.

Since science specifies the manner in which a belief is verified, scientific argument is not so dependent upon the man making the argument. Obviously, a well-expressed idea will be attended to and have more impact on others than one poorly expressed. All other things being equal, bright, articulate individuals will have more success getting their ideas across than their dull, inarticulate counterparts; but the bottom line, even for highly articulate scientists, is whether they propound their ideas in a testable manner and then proceed to verify them according to the rules of science. Sometimes an explanation of reality is based almost solely upon the verbal skill of the individual providing the explanation. For example, novelists often achieve acceptance of their ideas based upon their skill in verbally stating the ideas, rather than achieving acceptance based upon actual data supporting the ideas. I once had a colleague, a theoretical physicist, who was bright, highly verbally skilled, and quite witty. G. (as I will call him) would expound at length on various topics, and his verbal skill, coupled with a slight European accent, made him a highly influential individual. At first, I was awed by the sheer beauty and logical consistency of his arguments, but as he began to wander into my "backyard," that is, into my area of knowledge, I would sit and listen as usual, walk out of his office overpowered with the brilliance of the argument, and then realize that not only had he failed to offer a shred of evidence in support of his viewpoint, but he had failed to realize that there was research that provided evidence supporting a contradictory view. I would then tromp back to his office and hit him with the opposing facts. At this point, he would hesitate a moment, say "alright, then how about this," and proceed to offer a whole new and equally compelling viewpoint. As you can see, I was influenced by the man making the arguments but only as long as he didn't infringe on my own expertise. In the long run, his eloquence lost in competition with scientific evidence.

OBJECTIVITY

In order to collect unbiased evidence, a clear statement of the problem under investigation is a necessity in any scientific endeavor. This means that the concepts involved must be clearly defined and must be non-contradictory; i.e., the theoretical ideas must be internally consistent. While novelists are able to deal solely with abstractions, scientists must at some point tie their concepts to concrete entities, since ultimately they must provide evidence for their ideas or conjectures. This linkage between concepts and the concrete representations of those concepts comes about through *operational definitions*. Providing operational definitions of the concepts being investigated means that, for the purpose of the investigation, the scientist has supplied not only a verbal definition, but also a definition based upon the actual techniques of measurement employed in the study. Take, for example, the case of the variability in social interaction of high school students. If we wished to determine whether physical attractiveness was related to the amount of social interaction engaged in by students, we would need to gather evidence on both attractiveness and amount of interaction. In order to do this, we would have to operationally define both terms. Attractiveness might be operationally defined as the average rating given by three independent judges on a 10-point scale of physical attractiveness, and social interaction might be defined as the number of dates per month. We could then see if higher scores on the attractiveness scale coincided with a greater number of dates per month. Other scientists then would be able to understand the concepts, agree or disagree with them, and more importantly, be able to employ the same operations in either replicating the research or testing it further.

Operational definitions permit us to define abstract concepts in terms of the operations that specify their presence or absence, or the extent of their presence. They are the translation of an idea into a concrete reality, and because translations can vary in quality, operational definitions can also vary in the adequacy with which the concrete operation reflects the abstract concept. Consider again the study discussed earlier dealing with positive actions toward the attractive and plain looking women. The investigators were interested in whether people try to match themselves in terms of attraction to a member of the opposite sex. In other words, do individuals perceive their own value and then attempt to match that value in another person? Specifically, do individuals who are high in self-esteem feel that they are able to match themselves with an attractive member of the opposite sex and thus should show more romantic actions toward her, while low self-esteem individuals believe they must settle for a less attractive person? In this study, the positive and negative feedback were designed to produce high and low self-esteem, respectively. Thus, the states of high and low self-esteem were operationalized by the feedback procedures employed in the study. Matching should be reflected in romantic actions toward the opposite sex person, and these were defined in terms of such behaviors as complimenting the woman, paying for her drink, and asking for her telephone number.

While the operations employed seem reasonable, each is only one of a number of possible similar operations which could have been employed. For example, high and low self-esteem could have been manipulated by an operation employing previous interest in or rejection of the subject by a member of the opposite sex. Also, romantic actions could have been operationally defined by nonverbal behaviors, such as increased eye contact or lessened distance between the subject and the woman.

We can see from this example that any single operational definition will not fully reflect the more abstract concept which it represents. If it did, then only success and failure on a test would define the conditions which raise and lower self-esteem, and only compliments, paying for drinks, and asking for a telephone number would define romantic actions. Under a model of strict operationism, our concepts would have no generality. In fact, a number of different operations, all having some common element and producing parallel results, is the key to meaningful definitions of concepts. Providing operational definitions of the concepts, descriptions of the subject population used, the apparatus employed, and the way in which the behavior is measured allows others in the field to judge the concepts in terms of their operational definitions. Thus, the adequacy of the procedures designed to test a problem can be evaluated. Finally, a decision can be made as to whether the data collected—the evidence—supports the propositions of the researchers.

Once we have satisfactory operational definitions, we must still be concerned with other areas of potential bias in the collection of our data. For example, all data must be allowed in, not just cases which confirm the researchers' expectations. The chips are allowed to fall where they may. The achievement of objectivity is difficult and depends upon such factors as the randomness of the sample, employing data collectors and analyzers who are ignorant as to the hypotheses of the study, and the inclusion of observations that permit the testing of alternative explanations. Whereas the layman states a belief and gives supporting evidence, the biased manner in which the evidence is collected often throws doubt on the assertion. Evidence is often chosen which supports the proposition, and evidence which might be counter to the individual's assertion is often ignored. Thus, cases are handpicked by individuals, and nonconfirming evidence is conveniently overlooked or forgotten. An excellent demonstration of this process of bias comes from a study done a number of years ago by Hastorf and Cantril (1954). Dartmouth and Princeton, traditional rivals, had played their annual football game which the press had depicted as being very rough and dirty. Hastorf and Cantril showed a film of the game to groups of students from each of the schools and had them simply count the number of infractions of the rules they saw each team commit. Students from both schools saw fewer infractions committed by their own team than the opposing team. Thus, Dartmouth students saw the Princeton team as playing dirtier, while Princeton students saw the Dartmouth team as breaking the rules more often. The point is that both groups were biased data collectors, seeing those incidents which confirmed their prior beliefs and overlooking those which challenged those beliefs. Since the scientist, as a human being, is vulnerable to this same type of bias, the necessity for the objectivity criterion in the scientific method is obvious. If objective procedures are used, they guard against bias by guaranteeing all the evidence its day in court. The specific techniques for attaining objectivity while carrying out psychological research will be an important thrust of this book.

ASKING ANSWERABLE QUESTIONS

Not all questions or statements are open to scientific investigation. For example, mystical or spiritual assertions are simply not open to scientific corroboration. The statement that natural disasters are a punishment by God for the decadence of the American people is not one that is open to scientific verification.

Even if we could agree on an operational definition of decadence and relate it to disasters that occurred at times when decadence was high, we could not demonstrate God's hand in bringing about this relationship. Questions calling for value judgments also are not open to scientific test. For example, the statement that it is better to be open than closed-minded is a value judgment and, as such, is accessible to philosophical discussion but not scientific test. On the other hand, the propositions that open-minded individuals are more efficient problem solvers, are more demo-cratic in their orientation, and are less personally rigid are ones that are open to scientific investigation. You might personally believe that it is better to be a more efficient problem solver, more democratic, and less rigid, but the scientific proposition simply states the relationship between open and closed-mindedness and three other variables. There is nothing in the proposition that states that open-minded individuals are better than closed-minded individuals; that is, there is no good-bad dimension. The important point is that science is valueless; its aim is to understand the world—not judge it.

Although questions dealing with value judgments and those which are metaphysical in nature are not answerable through the scientific method, this still leaves a great many questions to ask and to attempt to answer through the scientific method. How do scientists come up with the appropriate questions? In other words, where do scientists look to get ideas for questions? The answer is virtually everywhere. Some ideas and questions spring from everyday observation of the surrounding world, while others arise as a function of the knowledge already accumulated in a given area of research. Where the idea begins is unimportant. What is important is that it can be investigated through the scientific method.

PSYCHOLOGY AS A SCIENCE?

If you were enrolled in a course in biology, physics, or chemistry, the above title would probably never appear in your text, and if by some remote chance it did appear, it certainly would not be phrased as a question.

It seems as though every undergraduate psychology course begins with a section that proceeds, at some length, to justify dealing with psychology as a science. Are we trying to convince our students of the truth of this, or are we trying to convince ourselves? Both are probably true. Many students are skeptical about psychology being a member of the same league as physics, chemistry, and biology, and many psychologists tend to be defensive and unsure of the place of psychology in the scientific universe. Is the skepticism on the part of students and the insecurity on the part of psychologists justified? Both may be justified in that both are based, to a degree, on the reality of the state of the field at the present time.

Psychology is generally defined in most introductory texts as the scientific study of behavior. This statement is certainly true since behavior can be defined so as to include almost anything happening within or among organisms. At the same time, this definition also reflects the enormous breadth of the field. A look at the contents of an introductory text reveals the study of problems, ranging from measurement of the electrical potential of a nerve cell to the use of scream therapy to alleviate some type of emotional problem. The orientations of people in the field of psychology are extremely divergent. For instance, it is a fact that some individuals within the field see psychology more as an art than a science and argue against the use of scientific methods; even among those psychologists who do view psychology as a science, the orientations, the problems studied, and the methods employed to study the problems differ. While some psychologists run tightly controlled experiments, others deal with test and questionnaire data via fancy statistical procedures. All are psychologists, and except for those who do not employ scientific methods, all are scientists.

Given the tremendous divergence in orientations, content studied, and methodologies, and the fact that some psychologists even reject the scientific method, it is no wonder that students are skeptical and psychologists insecure. With all of the above verbiage, I still have not answered the question for you—is psychology a science? The answer to the question of whether psychology is a science is yes and no. If psychologists employ the techniques of their discipline which are aimed at objectivity, then for those individuals psychology is a science.

Science, first of all, is not a particular method or technique. That, upon reflection, should be obvious from examination of the techniques of two of the disciplines that most people would agree are science: chemistry and astronomy. Chemists mix precise amounts of chemicals in order to test for different effects. In other words, they are able to manipulate the world and control it in order to discover the way it works. On the other hand, astronomers can only observe and record the activities of the universe through telescopic observation. They are not able to move or change planetary bodies or create astronomical conditions in order to test their ideas. Not only are chemists and astronomers studying different areas of content, they are also studying those content areas in different ways. Other disciplines we call science vary from one another as much as chemistry and astronomy. The biologist may study the workings of the circulatory system or the respiratory system, the physicist may study the acceleration of particles in a cyclotron, a zoologist may research the ecological habits of wild dogs, and the geologist may survey glaciers in the Antarctic, to cite just a few of the disparate problems attacked by some of the disciplines we call science. Each of these problems is also studied via the particular techniques developed by and appropriate to the specific discipline. If the problems studied and the techniques of studying the problems have little in common, then what allows us to treat all of these various fields as science? That is, what do these very different disciplines have in common? The answer is that they all share an approach to achieving understanding: First, they rely upon empirical evidence, and second, they try to collect the evidence so as to maximize objectivity, which means that the evidence can be verified by any who doubt it.

THEORY IN SCIENCE

In most psychology courses that you have taken or will take, a great deal of emphasis is placed upon theory. For example, most psychology departments teach a whole course in theories of personality, which details the major theoretical works on personality, such as psychoanalytic theory, behavioral theory, or humanistic theory. Or in social psychology courses, theories such as cognitive dissonance, attribution, or social learning are presented. Some of the theories, such as psychoanalytic theory, are broad, attempting to encompass almost all of human behavior, while others, such as dissonance theory, are concerned with only specific aspects of behavior. All of them are imperfect in some way. That is, on the one hand, their concepts may be too abstract and impossible to operationalize, or on the other hand, they may be so narrow that they account for only a very limited range of behavior under very specific conditions.

Why the emphasis on theory? Why not simply present the relationships between variables which have been supported by the research? What is the role of theory? Theory has two functions: integration and explanation. Theory organizes existing information into meaningful conceptual categories. It links research findings together on the basis of commonalities. This is the integrative function. The second function of theory is that of explanation. Theory gives us the rationale behind the observed relationships. It provides the basis of the relationship by positing either the reason for or the manner in which the relationship occurs. Empirical data are just that—a group of observed events. The organization among those events and the accompanying explanation for the organization is what theory provides.

The scientist examines the relationship between variables and proceeds to put some sort of structure upon those relationships. That is, relationships are categorized and interpreted in some consistent framework or theory. It should be remembered that any time that elements are grouped together under a single conceptual label, those elements are alike only on the basis of some particular criterion for grouping. This, of course, means that those same elements differ from one another on other criteria. This logical linking of the concepts is the explanatory function of the theory. Each concept describes a relationship between variables. It is the tying together of the various relationships that provides explanation or rationale for those relationships. Scientists impose explanations upon the relationships. It is their perceptions of the manner in which the events in the world can be understood. The scientist has constructed a system that attempts to describe and link certain regularities in the world, and since it is a man-made construction, it is not true or false. A theory never accounts for all of the data or all of the relationships, but until a better explanation is posited, it is the accepted account of reality.

Theories, then, attempt to account for the observed regularities in the world. How does one then choose one theory over another? The theory that is more general, that is, the theory that is able to adequately explain a broader range of phenomena, is generally chosen over the more restricted theory. Keep in mind that breadth alone is not the criterion, but rather breadth with precision; that is, the theory must adequately account for the data. Psychoanalytic theory, for example, certainly has generality since it attempts to explain the total human personality; but its concepts are vague and, thus, difficult to operationalize. This vagueness stands in the way of adequate testing of the theory against other positions.

If two theories have the same generality and precision, then the criterion of parsimony holds as a test between them. That is, the theory with the fewest assumptions and the greatest ease of prediction is the theory of choice. For example, my physicist friends inform me that Ptolemaic theory, which stated that the earth was the center of the solar system, could account for the same data as Copernican theory, which states that the earth and the other planets revolve around the sun. In order to account for the same data, many more assumptions and involved calculations are necessary when Ptolemaic theory is employed, and thus it is a much less parsimonious explanation of the universe.

THEORY IN PSYCHOLOGY

Psychological theories are judged by the same standards as theories in other disciplines, but often the choice among various theoretical positions in psychology is more difficult than in the other sciences. This difficulty is related to the fact that the data base for various theoretical positions is not as well established in psychology as in the other sciences. The strong lawful relationships that exist in chemistry and physics do not exist very often in psychology. The lack of lawful relationships is due, I feel, to the great variability in the behavior of organisms, especially humans.

This, of course, returns us to the starting point of this chapter—individual differences or variability. Human behavior is extremely varied and is influenced by a myriad of variables. The psychologist can only study relatively few of these variables at a time and, thus, only part—and often this is a small part—of the individual differences can be determined. A colleague of mine in the biochemistry department studies the intestines of chickens. He takes a group of chickens and treats the intestines of some in one manner, those of others in a second manner, and then determines if there are differences in the intestines of the two groups. The intestines of chickens apparently show very few individual differences, and therefore all of the intestines given treatment A respond almost identically, and those given treatment B respond alike. Thus, any difference between the

A and B groups becomes readily apparent. In typical psychological experiments, on the other hand, individuals in group A are given one treatment, such as rewards, while those in group B are not given this treatment, and then performance on some task is recorded. When the performances are examined, it is found that within each of the two groups, people respond differently; that is, there is a great variability. Some subjects given rewards show highly skilled performance while others perform at a mediocre level, and the same is true of those given no reward. On the average, group A may outperform group B, but some people in A do worse than some of those in B. This variability is due to a whole complex of variables not under control or under study in the experiment. People come to the study with differing backgrounds, motivational levels, and ability levels, and those pre-experimental differences produce differences in their performances. This, of course, clouds the effects of the treatment, and thus, the differences due to reward versus no reward are not as apparent as the treatment differences for the biochemist. Psychologists often study behaviors and causes of those behaviors which are quite complex. This means that subjects will vary a great deal in how they respond to any treatment and also that any specific treatment will be only one part of the total causal condition for the behavior. There are some more restricted situations studied by psychologists which are akin to those studied by my colleague in biochemistry. For example, studies dealing with brain functions in rats show few individual differences. Accurate electrical stimulation of a given lower brain center will produce the same response in all rats to whom it is applied. As the cause or treatment becomes more abstract and complex, variability in the responses of the subjects increases. Psychologists are not the only researchers who find a great amount of variability in what they study. Any research dealing with complex causes and responses has the same problem. For instance, medical researchers dealing with the effects of saccharin or cancer or the control of pain through aspirin run into the same increased variability problems as do psychologists who study complex behaviors and their causes.

This complexity of behavior, that is, the great variability, very often precludes the finding of simple and straightforward lawful relationships. This means that psychological theory is often built upon a shaky base. This is a problem, of course, but that is the state of the art. If one wants to study something which has a broad factual base and straightforward procedures, that person probably should not study behavior, especially human behavior.

WHY STUDY THE PRINCIPLES OF PSYCHOLOGICAL RESEARCH?

Most university psychology departments offer or even require a research methods and principles course for undergraduate majors. It is understandable that a doctoral student who expects to follow a career of research in psychology would need such a course. What is the purpose of exposing undergraduate students to research methods when they may not pursue graduate education in psychology? Why not simply require only courses in specific content areas, such as social, physiological, or abnormal psychology?

There are, I feel, two main reasons for requiring an undergraduate course in research methods. The first reason is that the primary strength of psychology lies not in the bank of facts which have been discovered but in the research techniques that have been developed for uncovering facts. Many of the physical sciences have, over the years, produced a broad and valid data base with resultant lawful relationships. In this regard, psychology is in its infancy. Although psychologists certainly have discovered a great many facts about behavior and have proposed and tested a number of interesting theories, the generality of those facts and the validity of the theories is in a very limited state. In other words, psychology is still at an early stage of development, with much work needed to produce the solid base already achieved in the physical sciences. Psychologists derive their primary value not as purveyors but as discoverers of knowledge. Thus, an understanding of the techniques and principles, the tools of the discovery process, would seem to be of central importance to a student of psychology.

The above emphasis upon the methods of research should not be taken to indicate that method alone is enough. Methods are employed to investigate problems that arise in specific content areas. A knowledge of the issues and the past research in these areas is as critical to studying the problems as is knowledge of the proper research technique. Thus, students need a balance of content and method in order to fully appreciate the field of psychology.

The second reason for an undergraduate course in research methods relates to the development of a critical or doubting attitude. Comprehension of the principles of research involves an understanding of how questions are properly formulated, terms are defined, and methods employed that allow appropriate conclusions to be drawn. Hopefully, a critical approach to questions and issues in general will be developed by students at the same time they are applying these principles to psychological research. We are living in a world where we are constantly bombarded with information and conclusions about a multitude of issues. The principles discussed in this text can be useful in trying to evaluate many of these issues. To cite only a few examples: commercials are constantly claiming scientific evidence for the superiority of certain products, government agencies discuss the effectiveness of various programs they have instituted, and literary figures propose explanations of human behaviors on television talk shows. Unfortunately, all of these issues are presented in a rather one-sided manner. The audience very seldom has a chance to hear rebuttal or questions about either the facts themselves or the manner in which the facts were derived.

For example, advertisements claiming superiority for a given pain reliever may not specify what the product is superior to or may not define what they mean by effectiveness. A government agency that claims its antismoking campaign has reduced cigarette consumption may not show evidence that it is the campaign, rather than some other factor, which produced the change, or even that the change is greater than the typical changes in consumption that occur over time.

The critical approach to evaluating evidence, which comes along with an understanding of the principles of research, will serve the student well in judging evidence and claims from areas outside of psychology. Hopefully, passive acceptance will be replaced by active questioning about evidence and the manner in which evidence is gathered.

This book then will attempt to show some of the ways in which psychologists do study behavior. It will show the manner in which studies are designed, procedures are carried out, and conclusions are drawn. The testing of theory and the difficulties involved in this process will be examined. It is hoped the reader will gain an understanding of the difficulty of doing high-quality research and a respect for some of the excellent research programs which have broadened our understanding of behavior.

Chapter 2

A Closer Look
at Variability

As I stated in Chapter 1, understanding individual differences or variability is the main concern of psychologists. Chapter 2 will take a closer look at the meaning, interpretation, and assessment of variability. The discussion will begin with the psychologist's concept of error.

UNEXPLAINED VARIABILITY

Let us start with a situation most of you have experienced. You are sitting in your introductory psychology class when your instructor announces, "Today the class has a visitor who would like you to fill out an attitude scale." The visitor, an undergraduate political science major, arrives, asks for your cooperation, explains how to fill out the scale, asks you to indicate your age and sex, and asks you to rate your political orientation on a 10-point liberalism-conservatism scale. He then proceeds to distribute the questionnaire to the class. The items on the attitude scale deal with beliefs about a current candidate for president of the United States. After the scales are completed and collected, one of the students in the class asks the visitor why he gave the scale. The visitor states that he is interested in students' attitudes about the presidential candidate. He says that scores on the scale can range from high to low reflecting, respectively, highly favorable to highly unfavorable attitudes. He states that since the students in the class are probably a good reflection of most undergraduates, he is interested in how variable they are in their attitudes.

The student, being bright and also somewhat skeptical, acknowledges the fact that people will vary on their attitudes toward the candidate and possibly that the class may represent undergraduates in general, but asks what the variability or differences in attitude mean. The visitor states that obviously the differences reflect liberal-conservative political orientation; that is, liberals are favorable and conservatives unfavorable toward the candidate. Being a persistent sort, the student asks how the visitor knows that. The visitor replies that it is obvious, at which point the student retorts that the only obvious thing is that it is not obvious. The student states that he believes the differences are related to gender. His argument is that the candidate is a rather handsome man and that women will be attracted to him and men threatened by him and thus the favorable attitudes will be held by women and the unfavorable ones by men. The visitor, being a political science and not a psychology major, states that the student's idea is ridiculous, ends the debate, and leaves the room.

Is the visitor correct, or is the student correct? Is the variability in attitudes toward the candidate related to liberal-conservative political orientation, or is it related to gender or both or neither? The answer is that at this point, there is no way of determining who is correct. All we know is that there are individual differences in attitude, but what those differences reflect is unknown. We are in a state of ignorance since a variable (in this case, attitudes toward the candidate) cannot be understood by itself. If gender and measures of political orientation had been obtained, we could see whether each relates to attitudes toward the president, but without that information the variability in attitudes toward the president is what psychologists term unexplained variability. The aim of research is to achieve understanding or to reduce unexplained variability. The only way to do this is to relate the variability in one variable (e.g., attitudes toward the candidate) to the variability in another variable (e.g., gender). *To the extent that they are related, the unexplained variability is reduced and understanding of the individual differences is achieved.* In short, it is variability that we do not understand that constitutes the basic task of our science—we are trying to account for the variability in the behavior of people.

By employing the term *understanding,* I have chosen a loaded word. I do not use this term to mean only causal explanations, although sometimes the understanding we achieve is of a causal nature. By understanding, I mean anything that allows us to reduce our ignorance by showing systematic relationships among variables. Thus, if attitudes toward the candidate were related to liberal-conservative political attitudes, we could not conclude that being liberal caused the favorable attitudes toward the candidate, but we would have at least achieved an understanding of what the differences in attitudes toward the candidate were related to. The depth and type of understanding achieved depends upon the question being asked and the method chosen to answer the question.

THE MEASURE OF VARIABILITY

Before discussing the ways in which we can see how one variable reduces or accounts for the variability in another variable, a measure of individual differences is needed. Variability refers to the degree of dispersion of a group of scores; the more the scores differ from one another, the greater the variability. In order to assess the degree of spread in a group of scores, we need to find a constant point of reference from which we can measure the spread. The point of reference that is typically used is the arithmetic *mean* of the distribution of scores.

The reason for choosing the mean as the reference point is that it has certain valuable properties. First of all, it is the center of the distribution in terms of its distance from the scores. That is, if we subtract the mean from each score in the distribution and total those differences, called deviations, they will add to zero. The mean is then a balancing point in the distribution since the summed deviations on one side of the mean will be equal to the summed deviations on the other side. As an example, take the following scores: 24, 20, 18, 12, 10, 6. The mean of these scores is 15. Now if 15 is subtracted from each of the scores, we have the following six distances from the mean: 9, 5, 3, -3, -5, -9. Fifteen, the mean, is a balancing point in the sense that the distances of the scores above it (9 + 5 + 3) are balanced by the distances of the scores below it $[(-3) + (-5)$

+ (-9)]. The second property of the mean is that the sum of the squared deviations of the scores from the mean will be a minimum. That is, if we subtract each score from the mean, square that difference, and add all of the squared differences, the sum that we get will be a smaller sum than we could get if we had chosen any value other than the mean as the reference point. The sum of squared deviations around the mean, termed the *sum of squares* for short, is then a sort of statistical bottom line. Calculating the sum of squares for a distribution means that we have described the variability of the distribution, and no other measure of variability could have been calculated, using the squares of the deviations of scores from some point other than the mean, which could yield a lower value. The reason for squaring the deviations from the mean will be clear if you will recall the first property of the mean—it is the point around which the deviations sum to zero. If adding the deviations from the mean always produces a sum of zero, differences in variability would not be seen by simply summing the deviations. If the variability was assessed by simply summing the deviations, distributions with a great deal of variability and those with little variability would always show the same degree of variability—zero. Thus, squaring each deviation gets around this problem and allows for variability comparisons. In other words, a distribution with greater individual differences will have a larger sum of squares than a distribution with fewer individual differences, if both distributions have the same number of scores.

One problem with dealing with the sum of squares as the measure of variability is that the size of the sum of squares is dependent upon the number of scores with which we are dealing. The more squared deviations that are added, the larger the sum of squares. If two groups are being compared and both have the same number of scores, comparing their variability via the sum of squares is no problem. On the other hand, if group A has 20 scores and group B has 100 scores, comparisons of the sums of squares will be meaningless. Even if group A is much more variable than group B, the sum of squares for group B will probably be larger since adding 100 squared numbers will produce a greater sum than adding only 10 squared numbers. In order to get around this problem, we simply divide each sum of squares by the number of scores that produced the sum. This produces a measure that tells us the mean squared deviation from the mean; that is, the average distance in squared units each score lies away from the mean. This measure is called the *variance* (or the mean square) of the distribution of scores. If the square root of the variance is calculated, we have a measure of variability called the standard deviation. It reflects the average distance a score lies from the mean in unsquared units. The computational procedures for the mean, sum of squares, variance, and standard deviation are demonstrated in section II of the appendix.

There are other ways to describe variability besides calculating the variance.[1] The problem with employing measures of variability other than the variance is that they are not open to many of the more powerful and complex statistical techniques which have been developed. Most of these techniques depend upon the mean and variance since both of these measures involve the actual values of the scores in a distribution. Therefore, in attempting to understand the concept of variability, we will concentrate on the variance as the most powerful measure of individual differences.

COMPONENTS OF VARIANCE

The understanding of variance is the goal of psychological research, and as I stated before, in order to understand the variance in one variable, we need to relate that variance to the variance of another or other variables. The specific methods employed for achieving this relationship are the topics covered in the subsequent chapters of this book. Whatever method is used, the aim is to analyze or divide the variance observed on some variable into two basic parts. These two components are *systematic* and *unsystematic variance*.

Systematic Component

The systematic component refers to that part of the variance which is related to or can be accounted for by another variable. If we go back to the scale regarding attitudes toward the president, an example will demonstrate this concept. In Table 2-1a, there are scores for the hypothetical attitudes toward the presidential candidate for 20 people. Inspection of the table reveals that, in this case, people were either highly favorable (a score of 40) or highly unfavorable (a score of 10). Even though there are only two different values in this distribution of 20 scores, there is a great deal of variance since the scores are so far apart. The mean of this distribution is 25, and one can see that if all of the 40s and 10s were subtracted from the mean, squared, added, and divided by 20 to calculate the variance, it would be quite a large number—225 to be exact.

Without any other information, we have no idea what the variance is due to; that is, why half of the people scored only 10 and the other half scored 40. But let us say that all the people who scored 10 were males and all those who scored 40 were females, as shown in Table 2-1a by the Ms and Fs in parentheses next to the subject numbers. In that case, sex would

---

[1] If, for example, a distribution is badly skewed, the few extreme scores will have too much influence on the remaining scores. This will cause the mean to be an inaccurate representation of the central tendency of the scores. In order to get around this problem, the median—the point dividing the upper and lower 50 percent of the cases—is used to represent the scores. In the case where the distribution is skewed and the median is used to describe central tendency, a measure of variability called the *interquartile deviation* is used to represent the variability of the distribution. It is basically a measure of the range of the middle 50 percent of the scores and is not sensitive to the actual values of the scores.

TABLE 2–1

**Hypothetical attitude toward the presidential candidate scores for 20
male and 20 female subjects where all variance is systematic (a)
and variance is both systematic and unsystematic (b)**

a.

Subject Number		Score	Subject Number		Score
1.	(F)	40	11.	(M)	10
2.	(F)	40	12.	(M)	10
3.	(M)	10	13.	(F)	40
4.	(F)	40	14.	(F)	40
5.	(M)	10	15.	(M)	10
6.	(M)	10	16.	(F)	40
7.	(F)	40	17.	(M)	10
8.	(F)	40	18.	(M)	10
9.	(M)	10	19.	(F)	40
10.	(M)	10	20.	(F)	40

b.

Subject Number		Score	Subject Number		Score
1.	(F)	40	11.	(M)	20
2.	(F)	40	12.	(M)	20
3.	(F)	40	13.	(M)	20
4.	(F)	40	14.	(M)	20
5.	(F)	40	15.	(M)	20
6.	(F)	30	16.	(M)	10
7.	(F)	30	17.	(M)	10
8.	(F)	30	18.	(M)	10
9.	(F)	30	19.	(M)	10
10.	(F)	30	20.	(M)	10

be perfectly related to attitudes toward the president, and the variance in
the attitude scores would be totally predictable (accounted for) through
knowledge of the subject's sex. The variance in the scores would be
completely systematic; that is, it would be completely accounted for by
another variable—subject sex. In other words, you could sensibly try to
persuade people that the psychology student's hypothesis about the presidential candidate's attractiveness was correct.

Unsystematic Component

To illustrate this component, let us again return to the attitude toward the
candidate scale and the hypothetical data presented in Table 2–1b. Again,
we have the scores of the 20 subjects on the scale and the sex of the subject
(M or F) designated in the table, but this time all of the scores are not either
10s or 40s. This time the scores are 10s, 20s, 30s, and 40s, all represented
equally. The males still are the lowest, scoring 10 and 20, and the females
the highest, scoring 30 and 40. Some of the variance, then, is still systematic. That is, there is still a relationship between sex and attitude toward the
candidate, but there is now some variance still remaining that is unsystematic. Within each sex, the scores vary. Some females score 40 and some 30,
while some males score 10 and some 20. Since we have no idea why these

differences within the sexes occur, they constitute error. We are able to understand part but not all of the variance in attitudes. This second case, where we fail to account for all of the variance, is the usual situation in psychological research. Behavior is highly complex, and seldom can we completely account for this complexity.

The unsystematic component refers to that part of the variance that is unrelated to the variable employed in the study. It is that part of the total variance that still remains after attempting to explain the total variance by relating it to another variable. This part of the variance is termed error, and *error is ignorance or lack of understanding.* Thus, we begin with a variable, observe the total amount of variance in that variable, relate that variable to another variable, and term that part of the total variance that relates systematic, and that part which doesn't relate unsystematic or error variance. Error has a very specific meaning. Keep in mind that it refers to ignorance or lack of understanding; it is not error in the sense of a mistake.

RATIOS OF VARIANCES

Since we seldom account for all of the variance in one variable through another or other variables, we need to make judgments about the amount of variance we actually do account for. These judgments take two forms. The first deals with whether we account for a significant amount of systematic variance. The question of significance is a question of chance or probability. We answer this question by calculating the ratio of systematic variance to error variance. Keep in mind that the systematic variance in one variable is a function of another variable that is related to it. If the amount of unsystematic variance was larger or even almost as large as the amount of systematic variance, then it could not be said with any assurance that the results were attributable to the variable we brought in to account for the variance. This ratio, termed F (after Sir Ronald Fischer who devised the ratio concept), can be evaluated through statistical tables to see whether it is significant. If the ratio of systematic to error variance is significant, it means that the results of the study were not a chance occurrence. The question of how this is actually tested will be explained in more detail in Chapter 7. The important point here is that the ratio of explained to unexplained variance can be tested to see whether the relationship between the variables is a real or chance phenomenon.

If the ratio of systematic to error variance is significant, then a second judgment is often called for. This second judgment deals with the degree of strength of the relationship between the variables. The ratio of systematic to total variance yields the basis for this judgment. For example, if the total variance of a variable was 200 and the systematic variance was 100, then the ratio between the two would be .50. The direct interpretation of this ratio is that 50 percent of the variance in one variable can be accounted for by the second variable.

OBSERVING VARIANCE: DATA AND MEASUREMENT

In order to calculate the variance of a variable, relate it to another or other variables, divide it into its component parts, and form ratios among the components, it is necessary to transform the responses of subjects into numbers. Whatever the variable under study, the data are the behaviors of the subjects of the study put into some symbolic form. The symbols, usually numbers, are gathered with some sort of measuring instrument (e.g., an attitude scale, a test, or a reaction timer) and provide a quantitative measurement of the behavior under study, just as the ruler with its numbers provides a measurement of length. It should be noted that a great deal of psychological research is devoted to devising measuring "tools" for behavior and that measuring length with a ruler is a lot easier than finding a psychological yardstick on which people will agree. Because of differences in the way in which we define units of measurement among the various measurement instruments we use, the numbers sometimes differ in the amount of information they convey. Therefore, the instruments or scales we use may be classified in terms of the level of measurement they provide. These levels, termed *scales of measurement,* provide more powerful information at each succeeding higher level. The scales of measurement, proceeding from highest to lowest level, are called ratio, interval, ordinal, and nominal.

Ratio Scales

With ratio scales, we know the rank ordering of subjects, the distances between subjects' scores, and the distance of each score from a zero point. Judgments can then be made that: (1) subject A scores better than subject B who outscores subject C, (2) the distance between A's score and B's score is so many times greater than the distance between B's score and C's score, and (3) the ratio of A to B's score is of some value. This last judgment of ratios between scores distinguishes ratio from interval scales—the next measurement level. Ratio scales have a meaningful zero or reference point, and the distances of scores from this zero point can be assessed. If we are comparing heights, for example, the absolute zero or reference point is obvious (e.g., the floor), and the distance from this zero point can then be measured. Thus, if we have three people, A, B, and C, who are six, five, and four feet tall, respectively, we know that the six-foot person is 1½ times as tall as the four-foot person.

Interval Scales

Whereas ratio scales possess a meaningful zero point, this point is unknown with interval scales. We are able to judge the distance of scores from each other or from some arbitrary reference point, but not from zero. For example, if the heights of the three people were measured, not from the floor, but from a table top, and the height of the table was unknown, we would have interval scale measurement. Let us say that from the table top the three heights were A = 3, B = 2, and C = 1 foot, but that the height of the table was unknown. We would have no zero point, but we would have an arbitrary reference—the table top. Given this, we could rank the subjects on height in terms of distance from the table top, and we could say that the distance between A and B is equal to the distance between B and C, but we could not state the ratio between the three subjects. That is, since the height of the table is unknown, we could not say that A is three times as tall as C. In fact, given that we measured the three people from the top of another table which was one foot shorter than the first table, the three heights from this second table top would have been A = 4, B = 3, and C = 2 feet. The distance in height between A and B is still equal to the distance between B and C, but the ratios between the three subjects have changed. Whereas the ratio between A and C from the first table top was 3:1, the ratio from the second table top is 2:1. In fact, given that the table is three feet high and A, B, and C are six, five, and four feet tall, respectively, (from zero), A is not three times as tall as C but only 1½ times as tall.

In most psychological research, we are working from a table top and have no idea of the height of the table. Intelligence, for example, is a variable where no meaningful zero exists. A zero on the test simply means no questions correctly answered but certainly does not imply zero intelligence. Someone who failed every question but could tie their shoes when told to do so would have some intelligence. Given no real zero point, direct comparisons between intelligence scores are also meaningless. Does a score of 140 reflect twice as much intelligence as one of 70? Since a person scoring 140 is probably quite capable of handling doctoral level material and a person scoring 70 is probably barely educable, the difference between them in intelligence is probably not two to one, but some astronomical number. Thus, rather than judging how far scores fall from zero, we use an arbitrary reference point comparing the scores in terms of their distance from this reference point. Quite often, this reference point is the mean of the group, and scores are compared in terms of their respective distances from the mean.

Ordinal Scales

With ordinal scales, we not only have no real zero point, but the distances between scores are also unknown. We have only the relative ordering of individuals; that is, only rankings. Let us say, for example, that 50 students are ranked on a test with the best performance given a rank of 50 and the lowest performance a rank of 1. Let us assume that the test consisted of 100 points and that the best performance was 100, the second highest was 90, and the third highest was 88. The student receiving the 100 receives a rank of 50, the 90 performance a 49, and the 88 a rank of 48. Although there is an actual 10 point score difference between the top two students, there is a difference between their ordinal positions of only one rank while the second and third students have only a two-point score difference and also show a one-point rank difference. All of the differences in magnitude among the original scores are lost in the ordinal scale. Sometimes the data in a study are available only at an ordinal scale level. For example, if subjects in a study were ranked as to their aggressiveness, then the data would be ordinal scale level. On the other hand, scores of subjects on a performance task are sometimes gathered and then changed to ranks, reducing an interval scale to an ordinal scale. This changing to an ordinal scale may be carried out because the researcher believes that the assumptions of an interval scale cannot be met. For example, the researcher might not want to assume that equal distances between scores reflect equal distances in the attribute being measured.

Nominal Scales

These scales are simply labels and categories. When 100 subjects in a study are given the identification numbers of 001 to 100, these numbers are intended to serve merely as labels that identify the subject. Nominal categories are groupings of subjects on the basis of some property, and the numbers employed are intended to simply label the categories. The numbers are not meant to convey information about magnitude. That is, when males are given a one and females a two, the ones and twos simply label those subjects who report themselves as male and female. Any other two numbers would serve just as well in maintaining the distinctiveness of the categories. For example, males could have been assigned the number 50 and females the number 25 since the numbers only serve as identification for grouping purposes and indicate nothing about magnitude. Variables which are assigned numbers that only represent presence or absence in a category (ones and zeros, for example) and yield no information about magnitude are called *dummy variables*. Thus, subject sex scored one for female and zero for male or political party affiliation scored one for Democrat and zero for Republican would both be dummy variables. Categorization does yield information in that comparisons can be made of the frequencies with which subjects fall into the categories. For example, we could gain useful information from category level scales in the case where we observed the frequencies of males and females who voted for a certain candidate. Although categories and their accompanying frequency comparisons are often useful, they are not very sensitive ways of assessing behavior.

What level scales do we have in psychology? Well, very seldom do we achieve ratio scales. As in the case of intelligence, as described previously, most psychological variables have no meaningful zero point. We do attain interval scale measurement, or at least we treat many of our measurements as being interval scales. We generally make judgments which relate to the distance scores fall from the mean and compare scores in terms of their respective distances from the mean. With interval scale measurement, all the powerful and complex statistical techniques are open to us. Our only limit is in making absolute judgments about the magnitude of scores.

While it is true that many of our measurements are treated as interval scales and that the previous discussion of variance is relevant to interval scale measures, many research projects in social science in general and psychology in particular deal with only nominal scale data. For example, most of the opinion survey work done by pollsters deals only with nominal scale variables. If a sample of men and women are asked to respond to the statement: "The Equal Rights Amendment should be ratified," and they answer "agree," "disagree," or "no opinion," these data would be treated only as nominal scale measurements. That is, the researchers would simply tally the frequencies of each sex who agreed, disagreed, or had no opinion on the matter, probably testing to see whether men and women differed significantly in their frequency of agreement and dis-agreement with the statement. Most survey results are of this type in that two nominal scale variables (e.g., political preference and area of the country or race and sex) are cross tabulated. Thus, while many of the examples employed in this book will deal with interval scale measurement and the concepts of variance are based upon interval scale data, this is not the only scale of measurement which is employed in research or which yields fruitful results.

Reliability

Whatever measurement level we achieve in a study, we are interested in whether the data are accurate; that is, whether they are free from measure-ment error. *Reliability refers to consistency of measurement.* If we mea-sure a variable through some sort of test or scale, that measurement must be relatively accurate before it would be useful to attempt to understand its variance by relating it to another variable. If, in the previous example, the attitude toward the presidential candidate scale contained a large amount of measurement error, we could only relate that part of the variance which was free of error to another variable. That part of the variance which is unreliable cannot relate to other variables and thus becomes part of the unsystematic or error component of variance. Consistency generally refers to freedom from error. Sometimes a measure is unreliable because it does not assess the behavior in question consistently over time. If the students' attitudes toward the candidate were remeasured the following day and scores changed a great deal, then the scale would be unreliable in terms of consistency over time. It could also be the case that the scale would be unreliable at even the first measurement. In this case, the inconsistency would be within the scale; that is, the scale would be internally inconsist-ent. Both of these types of reliability, internal consistency and consistency over time, will be discussed in more detail in Chapter 3. The important point here is that the less reliable our measures, the greater will be our difficulty in attaining understanding of the variables in which we are interested.

Validity

Given that we do have relatively reliable measures, the question then centers on the meaning of those measures. Are they assessing what we intend to assess? This is the question of *validity*. Sometimes in more practical or applied cases, this question can be answered through rather straightforward methods. In other situations, where more abstract theoretical issues are involved, simple answers to the validity question are not possible. The more complicated questions are quite difficult to answer and are at the heart of most of the research dealing with theoretical issues. In these cases, the road to validity is slow and complex. In Chapter 3, we will deal with some of the more straightforward methods of validation, while the more complex validity questions will be discussed in later chapters.

OBSERVING VARIANCE: METHODS OF STUDYING BEHAVIOR

As I stated previously, the aim of research is to understand individual differences by relating the variance in one variable to the variance in other variables. There are a number of ways to achieve this understanding, each way providing different types and amounts of understanding. These ways are the various methods of studying behavior. The methods fall into two broad categories: those which involve little or no interference by the researchers and those involving direct interference. In the first category are those techniques which attempt to measure behavior (observe variance) of subjects as it occurs without affecting or changing that behavior. These methods are called *correlational* approaches. The second category consists of techniques whereby the researcher actually attempts to manipulate the environment in some manner in order to see if the manipulation affects the desired behavior. The *experiment* is the sole proprietor of this second class. Generally, the less interference, the less artificial and more generalizable the results become, but at a price. That price is a decrement in control which precludes understanding of the direction and causal nature of the relationships found. Whereas experimental methods yield evidence of causality and provide more precise knowledge about the conditions under which behaviors occur, they often suffer from the artificiality of the laboratory and the inability to manipulate enough relevant variables.

Thus, the question is not which is the best approach, but rather which approach is most appropriate for answering a certain question. There are times when the most appropriate way to address a complex question is to begin by naturally observing behavior and then proceeding to the laboratory for closer scrutiny of the causal linkages. Alternatively, one might proceed by employing correlational studies followed by experimental procedures. There is also a third possibility which is gained by combining interference and noninterference. A manipulation of the environment may be introduced into a natural setting or a correlational variable; sex, for example, may be mixed with an experimental variable. There are numerous possibilities. The appropriateness of any particular method or mixture of methods is dictated by the specific problem or question being addressed. In subsequent chapters, these methods and combinations of methods will be presented along with their assets and liabilities and guidelines to their appropriate uses.

Chapter 3

Measurement:
Assessing Behavior

In order to understand or account for variance, we first have to measure the behavior of interest. Sometimes in psychological research, that measurement is quite straightforward. For example, if we were interested in the speed with which people respond to a critical situation, we could assess this by measuring the time it took them to throw a switch or press a button. If we were interested in measuring the degree of approach behavior to snakes shown by individuals with snake phobia, we could measure the distances that these individuals moved toward a snake at the end of a room. Both of these would be direct physical assessments of behaviors, and methods of measuring these behaviors would be readily available: An electronic timer which would record reaction time in milliseconds, and a tape measure which would assess distance in feet and inches, and both would be ratio scales, the ideal. Unfortunately, many of the problems and concepts of interest to psychologists do not lend themselves to the well-developed physical measurements of length and time. Rather, a great many of the concepts in psychology are abstract and must be operationalized and assessed through psychological measuring devices designed specifically for this purpose. Concepts such as intelligence, anxiety, open- and closed-mindedness, college aptitude, and racial attitudes, to name only a few, are generally assessed through these psychometric measuring instruments, which, for lack of a better term, are called *tests*.

Most of these measuring instruments consist of a series of questions or items, the responses to which are added together or combined in some fashion to yield a total score. This test score then reflects an individual's position on some psychological attribute. Relative differences in total scores are taken to represent relative differences between individuals on the attribute. These individual differences constitute the variable we are trying to understand. Some tests, termed *maximum performance tests,* have correct and incorrect responses and are designed to assess the highest level of performance individuals are able to achieve. Intelligence tests, aptitude tests such as the SATs, and more specific ability tests, such as artistic and musical ability tests and problem solving tests, are all of this type. Other tests, termed *typical performance tests,* have no correct or incorrect answers and are designed to assess the typical response of individuals. Attitude scales, interest inventories, and personality tests are of this second type.

RELIABILITY OF MEASUREMENT

Reliability refers to consistency of measurement. The more consistently we are able to measure anything, whether it is length, speed, or some psychological variable such as attitudes, the more precise will be our conclusions about those variables. For example, let us say that you were interested in measuring the length and width of a room for a carpet. Since once you order the carpet and it's cut and bound, you cannot return it, you would want your measurement to be as precise as possible. You proceed to carefully measure the room, finding the length to be 15 feet 3¼ inches and the width to be 10 feet 4½ inches. Wanting to be sure of your numbers before ordering the carpet, you again measure the room, finding the length to be 15 feet 3⅜ inches and the width 10 feet 4⅝ inches. A third attempt produces a third set of numbers differing slightly from the first two. Each set of numbers or measurements that you calculate is called an *obtained score*. The question is, which one is the real room size? Choosing any particular one would be dangerous. So you decide to take the average of the three measurements, and this is probably the best solution. In fact, if you had measured the room more than three times and averaged these, an even better or more precise judgment of the size would have been achieved. The average of an infinite number of measurements would have given you the true size of the room, which is called the *true score*. Each measurement was slightly inaccurate, that is, it departed from the true size, but averaging the three produced a more reliable assessment. In other words, each measurement, the obtained score, was equal to the actual size of the room, the true score, plus an *error of measurement*.

Even for physical measurements such as length, weight, and speed, there is some degree of unreliability. That is, the obtained score does not equal the true score. With psychological measurement, the problem of consistency also exists, and specific techniques have been developed to assess the accuracy of psychological measurements. These techniques stem from sophisticated mathematical and statistical theories of measurement. Although the mathematics are beyond the scope of this text, the basic notions behind the techniques can be understood.

The Domain of Content

The developer of a test is interested in a *psychological concept, termed a construct,* which may be, for example, some type of ability, a personality trait such as self-esteem or anxiety, or an attitude. For any construct, there is a theoretical *domain or universe of content*. The domain consists of all of the possible test items relevant to the construct. The test items could be either written statements or questions about various aspects of the construct or actual behavioral skills reflecting the construct. For example, the construct of knowledge of introductory psychology would consist of a domain of items or questions about all aspects of the content taught in an introductory psychology course. In writing the questions for a final exam in introductory psychology, the test developer would be drawing or sampling items from this domain. In the case of some constructs such as typing skill, the domain would consist of all possible typing behaviors engaged in by a typist. The test developer would, in this case, sample a series of these by making up a typing test that consisted of a number of these different behaviors, such as typing letters, addresses, and reports;

making corrections; and performing under various time restrictions. The final exam in the introductory psychology course would be only a sample of all of the possible questions which could be asked, and the typing test would consist of only a sample of all of the possible typing behaviors in the domain.

Obtained and True Scores

Since any particular set of items will not cover a whole domain of content, any particular test will not perfectly measure a construct. Hypothetically, if the whole domain of items for a given construct was available, these items would cover all aspects of the construct, and if individuals were to respond to all of these items, we would have their exact scores on the construct. In reality, they only answer some items; that is, those items that have been written for the test. Thus, their test scores, termed *obtained scores,* are not their exact scores on the construct. The scores that individuals would achieve if they responded to the entire domain of items are termed *true scores.* The more the sample of items in a test reflects the domain of all possible items, the closer the obtained test score is to the true score. The problem for the test developer, then, becomes one of taking the best sample of items; that is, the sample that will most clearly reflect the entire domain.

The Reliability Coefficient

How do test developers know when they have a test that gives a precise enough measure of the true score? This judgment comes from the *coefficient of reliability,* which is a number that can vary between zero and one. A reliability coefficient of one indicates perfect reliability or a perfect estimate of the true score from the test. A reliability coefficient of zero indicates that the test is totally undependable as a measure of the construct, and coefficients that fall between these points indicate varying degrees of precision of measurement of the construct. Thus, the higher the reliability coefficient, the more accurately scores on the test (obtained scores) reflect scores on the entire domain (true scores) and the less they contain errors of measurement. Gaining high reliability depends on two factors: the relationship of items to each other and the number of items on the test. *The more strongly the items on a test are related to each other and the more items there are on a test, the higher the reliability of the test will be.*

If two things are related, they have something in common, and to the extent that the items on a test are interrelated, they share some concept in common; that is, to some degree they are measuring the same construct. For example, if we asked people to rate (1) how confident they feel at social gatherings, (2) how adept they are at speaking in front of a group of people, and (3) how confident they are that they are able to carry out most tasks, we would probably find that these three items were interrelated since they all seem to reflect the construct of self-confidence. On the other hand, if none of the items on a test were related to each other, each item would be measuring something totally independent of the other items, and each would be drawn from a different domain. For example, if a test designed to measure knowledge of psychology contained items or questions about English history, electricity, politics, astronomy, and abnormal behavior, there would be little or no relationship among the items since they would be drawn from vastly different domains of content. Since individuals who could answer one type of question may or may not be able to answer the others, there would be no systematic relationship between the items. Adding the items to get an obtained score on the test would be like adding flowers, trucks, houses, and toenails to yield a single score which would reflect nothing. A test that consisted of unrelated items would be internally inconsistent in measuring a construct. Also, the larger the number of these interrelated items a test contains, the higher the reliability. Larger samples always give more precise estimates than smaller samples, and the same is true for tests. The higher the relationship among the items on the tests, the more we have sampled the domain, and thus the better our judgment of true scores. This type of reliability is called *internal consistency.*

The actual calculation of an internal consistency reliability coefficient follows directly from the above discussion. The degree of relationship among the items on the test is calculated through a statistic called the *correlation coefficient,* which is an index of the relationship between two sets of scores. The correlation coefficient is a measure of the degree to which two variables (that is, two sets of scores) are related. (A more precise explanation of the correlation coefficient will be given in the following chapter.) Each item on the test is correlated with each other item, and then all of these correlations are averaged. This average correlation among the items, along with the number of items on the test, is then employed in a formula producing a measure of reliability called *Coefficient Alpha.* The closer Coefficient Alpha is to one, the more internally consistent the test; that is, the more reliable the test. The closer Coefficient Alpha is to zero, the less internally consistent the test and consequently the poorer the test as an estimate of true scores.

Obviously, any test, such as the "Knowledge of Psychology" test, which consists of items tapping totally different things, will not be internally consistent. At the other extreme would be a test containing items all tapping the same thing. For example, if an "Attitude Toward the Taste of Chicken Soup" test consisted of items such as, "I enjoy eating chicken soup," "chicken soup tastes very good," and "I often enjoy a bowl of chicken soup," the correlations among the items would probably be close to perfect. In this case, the domain of content is so narrow that only a very few items would be needed to produce our internally consistent test since each item written would differ only slightly from any other item. Thus, at one end of the spectrum, we have very narrow domains of content which are quite easy to assess reliably but which may have limited theoretical importance. Toward the other end, we have tests that attempt to tap very broad and abstract domains, and therefore the items will show low relationships to each other. In fact, if the correlations are too low, the researcher should possibly consider redefining his construct into a number of different constructs, each tapped by an internally consistent set of items, since he is probably drawing from a number of domains of content. For example, the Scholastic Aptitude Test (SAT) consists of two domains of items, verbal and quantitative, each internally consistent. In essence, a narrow domain will take only a few items to achieve a high Coefficient Alpha, whereas a broader domain with its lower intercorrelations among items will take many more items to achieve internal consistency.

True and Obtained Score Variance

Coefficient Alpha can be interpreted as a proportion. In order to understand this, we must reexamine the definition of an individual score on a test, namely, the obtained score. The obtained score can be thought of as being made up of two parts: a true score, the score the person would receive on a perfect measurement, and an error score, the amount by which the obtained score misses the true score because there is error in measurement. In the case of internal consistency, the true score would be the score the person would receive if he responded to all of the items in the domain. The error score would be the amount that his score on a sample of items misses the true score. If we calculated the variance of the obtained scores, we would have a measure of the individual differences among people who took the test. Some of the variance in the obtained scores would be due to differences in the true scores, but some of the individual differences would be due to error. That is, the variance of the obtained scores would be made up of two parts: the true score variance and the error score variance. In other words, obtained variance = true variance + error variance.

If we were able to calculate the true score variance and divide it by the obtained score variance, the ratio would indicate the proportion of true score variance in obtained scores. If the ratio was 1.00, then we would know that all of the obtained score variance was true score variance and that we have estimated the true scores without error. But if the ratio was .50, then it would indicate that only half of the obtained score variance was true score variance. The reliability coefficient is defined as the ratio of true to obtained score variance; thus, Coefficient Alpha, being a reliability coefficient, indicates the proportion of true to obtained score variance.

CONSTRUCTING A TEST

Let us return to the topic of self-confidence in order to see how construction of a scale and testing of reliability might proceed. First of all, the scale developer would outline the domain of content involved in feelings of self-confidence. It might be decided that it should include items about social events, competency in dealing with strangers, belief in one's abilities, public speaking, leadership, and interactions with the opposite sex. Items would then be written in a form that people could answer by choosing an appropriate response from the alternatives provided. The response alternatives could be simply agree and disagree, or they could be a variety of alternatives such as strongly agree, slightly agree, neutral, slightly disagree, and strongly disagree.

If all of the items are worded the same way so that an agree response indicates a favorable and a disagree response an unfavorable attitude, response sets can develop that interfere with the measurement of the scale. *Response sets* are tendencies to respond in a fixed manner to a scale regardless of the content of the items on the scale. In the case of the self-confidence scale, wording of all of the items in the same direction might produce an agreeing or disagreeing tendency that would occur regardless of the content of the items themselves. For example, a person might agree with the first few items, and since all items are worded in the same direction, they might respond "agree" to the remaining items even though they don't actually agree with all of them. In other words, the wording of the scale would produce an agreeing set—a bias to agree more than you really did. Test developers often design their tests so that both favorably and unfavorably worded items are included. That is, some items are worded so that an agree response indicates a favorable and a disagree response an unfavorable attitude, and others are written so that an agree response reflects an unfavorable and a disagree response a favorable attitude. Then for a favorable item, an agree response could be scored one and a disagree zero, or strongly agree to strongly disagree could be scored from five to one, respectively. If the item was unfavorable, the scoring would be reversed. That is, agree responses could be scored zero and disagree responses one, or strongly agree to strongly disagree scored from one to five, respectively. Thus, agreement with favorable items or disagreement with unfavorable items would produce higher scores, so that those individuals who had positive attitudes would obtain high scores regardless of how the items were phrased.

A total score would be calculated for each individual by adding their scores for all of the items. Before calculating the reliability of the scale, an item analysis would be carried out. This is a procedure designed to choose only appropriate items for the scale and to discard any inappropriate items. Generally, this is done by correlating each item with the total score. If an item correlates with the total score, it means that the item is related to the total score and contributes to it. In other words, individuals who score high on the item are also high on the total score for the test. Items uncorrelated with the total score are not measuring whatever the other items are measuring and should be discarded. Coefficient Alpha would then be calculated from the knowledge of the average correlation among the remaining items and the number of items. If it were high enough, the scale would be considered internally consistent and an adequate measure of self-confidence, that is, an adequate estimate of true scores for this construct.

Very often, reliability has been calculated by what is termed the *split-half method,* which is an approximation to Coefficient Alpha. Rather than intercorrelating all of the items on a test and finding the average of these correlations, researchers would often simply split the test into two equal parts, calculate a single correlation between the scores on the two parts, and estimate reliability on the basis of this correlation. For example, the two parts could be the odd- and even-numbered items on the test since odd or even numbering is usually a random designation. Then, each person who took the test would have an odd score calculated by summing their scores on the odd-numbered items and an even-item score would result from summing the scores on the even-numbered items. It is these two scores which would be correlated. Thus, a high correlation would reflect the fact that persons who scored well on the odd items also scored well on the even items and that low even and odd scores went together, and consequently the two parts of the test are related. In other words, rather than splitting a 20-item test into 20 parts, as is done with Coefficient Alpha, the test is split into only two parts saving a great deal of time and effort. When calculations were all done by hand, the use of the split-half method was routine, but with the availability of computers, there is really no reason to employ it any longer. Since it does not employ the items individually and since different split halves would yield slightly different correlation coefficients, it only approximates Coefficient Alpha, which employs all of the information available. Therefore, it is not as accurate a measure of the internal consistency of a test as Coefficient Alpha.

Internal consistency reliability, calculated with Coefficient Alpha, is a necessity for any measuring instrument composed of items designed to tap or reflect a psychological construct. The items must hang together; that is, they must measure the same construct. The important point is that tests are composed of items designed to tap a psychological construct. Whether that construct is a problem-solving ability or an attitude toward the president, reliable measurement is necessary and is achieved by producing an internally consistent test—one that accurately assesses true scores.

STABILITY OF TESTS

Internal consistency is the first and most important type of reliability needed for most psychological measuring instruments, but there are other types of reliability which may be of interest in particular cases. One of these types deals with the *stability of the test over time*. That is, when the test is given to a group of people and then readministered at a later time, do people score relatively the same on both testings? If those individuals who scored high at time one score high again at time two, and those individuals who scored low at time one score low at time two, then the test is stable over that time period. In other words, scores at time one are correlated with scores at time two to see if the test is stable. Reliability of this type is called *test-retest reliability*. Test-retest reliability is of interest in those cases where the construct should have stability over time. For example, since intelligence is assumed to be something that endures over long periods, intelligence tests should have high test-retest reliability. On the other hand, many attitudes would not be expected to stay stable over long time periods. Events which intervene between the two testings can change attitudes and thus reduce the correlation between the two testings. This reduction would not be due to the unreliability of the measuring instrument, but rather to an actual change in the attitudes of the people. For example, attitudes toward the president's economic plan might change over a six-month period due to changes in the nation's economy. Coefficient Alpha might be high for both the test and the retest given six months later, showing that both are consistently measuring the attitude, which has changed over time, and produced a low test-retest correlation.

SURVEYS

Surveys generally consist of a series of items that attempt to gain information or judgments of various sorts from individuals. Generally, each of the items poses a distinct question to the respondents and asks them to choose their preferred alternative from a set of two or more possible alternatives. Many of the results reported on television news programs are derived from surveys given to a sample of individuals. Thus, one item on a survey dealing with the presidential candidate might ask for a judgment of views on the economy (correct, incorrect, or unsure), while another might ask whether you would vote for him if the election were held the next day (yes, no, or undecided). Each survey question typically permits alternative responses written specifically for that question. Also, many of the items on surveys deal with demographic information; that is, information about social attributes and vital statistics such as sex, age, income, and race.

Generally, the data derived from surveys are treated as only nominal scale measurement. That is, each question or item is listed along with the percentage of people choosing each response alternative. Thus, on the question about the candidate's views on the economy, the responses might be: 45 percent correct, 32 percent incorrect, and 23 percent unsure. The point is that generally each item is treated individually; items are not added together in order to give different scores to individuals. Often the demographic information is put together or cross tabulated with each item in order to present a better understanding of how opinion is divided. For example, the ratings of the candidate's views might be presented by cross tabulating the sex of the respondent with the response alternatives as shown in Table 3–1.

Thus, although for the total sample, the correct category receives the highest and the unsure category the lowest percentage of choices, this is due primarily to the high percentage of females rating his views as correct and the low percentage who are unsure. The males, on the other hand, are about equally divided in their opinion of his performance. These types of cross tabulations of demographic and opinion items can reveal important opinion differences in various segments of the society.

Market research frequently employs surveys to provide information about the public's reaction to or need for various products. By cross tabulating the demographic and opinion items, information can be gathered that shows the reaction of different occupational, socioeconomic, or ethnic groups to various products. Most questionnaire items, rather than being designed to measure a theoretical construct, are designed to elicit a response to a very specific situation. The interest is often not in estimating a domain of content, and thus, internal consistency reliability does not arise as a question for these measures.

On the other hand, the questions asked in surveys could be considered as items from a possible domain of content. For example, an overall judgment of the candidate's views on the economy seems to be only one question from a large domain of possible questions dealing with his views. First of all, the economy consists of various areas such as inflation, labor, employment, taxes, etc. Thus, the response to the single questionnaire item may be a much less accurate indication of an individual's opinion about the candidate's economic view than a series of responses to items tapping various aspects of his views. Since, as discussed previously, reliability is dependent on the correlation among items and the number of items on a test, surveys which often attempt to assess attitudes and opinions about issues from single questions can suffer from unreliability.

Why then ask only single items? One answer is a practical one in that surveys often are carried out on large samples taken randomly from the population. The individuals sampled will often have only a limited amount of time available to fill out the survey or answer questions over the telephone. This means that either it is not possible to ask a large number of items on the telephone or that the individuals in the sample may not

TABLE 3–1

Cross tabulation of sex and opinion of the candidate's views

	Candidate's Views			
Sex	Correct	Incorrect	Unsure	Total
Female	28%	16%	6%	50%
Male	17	16	17	50
Total	45%	32%	23%	100%

want to bother filling out a lengthy written questionnaire. They may slip it into the "round file" (wastebasket) rather than fill it out and return it. Thus, researchers may trade off internal consistency for a higher response rate. A second answer is that researchers are often only interested in a general feeling about an issue. In other words, they are not concerned about various beliefs about different facets of the issue, but rather they seek information about peoples' affective responses to a topic or product. In a sense, they are interested in only a narrow domain of responses, and narrow domains can be sampled with only a few or perhaps only a single item.

MEASUREMENT BY OBSERVATION

In many research situations, a construct is measured not by asking people structured questions with fixed alternatives for responding, but by observing them interact in a specific situation. For example, if one were interested in whether children imitate aggressive models who are either rewarded or punished for their aggression, it would be necessary to measure the level of aggression the children displayed after they viewed the models. An observer could watch each child play after the child had viewed the rewarded or punished model and judge each of the child's behaviors as to whether or not they imitated the aggressive model. For example, the observer could simply designate a behavior as aggressive or not by rating it on a scale of aggression from five, very aggressive, to one, not at all aggressive. The problem is that we would be dependent solely upon the accuracy of that one rater for our evaluation of aggressiveness. In fact, a behavior that one person may see as aggressive another may not. Similarly, a behavior rated as highly aggressive by one person may be seen as only slightly aggressive by another. In order to get around this problem, more than one rater is usually used. So that one rater will not influence the other, each independently rates the behaviors. This independence is achieved by either videotaping the behaviors and having the raters carry out their ratings alone or by isolating the raters from each other. If they agree to a high degree on their judgments, we would have more faith in the judgments than if only one rater's judgments were used. If only a judgment of aggressive or not aggressive is called for, the proportion of agreements between the raters in classifying the behaviors is a measure of reliability. On the other hand, if they rate the behaviors on a scale, then the correlation between their ratings would indicate the degree of reliability. This type of accuracy is termed *interjudge or interrater reliability*.

This judging or rating procedure applies not only to overt physical behavior but to verbal behavior as well. In some research situations, subjects are asked to write essay-type answers to questions, rather than respond to objective questions. These essays can then be judged in terms of some sort of content, such as the number of aggressive themes, or rated as to some variable, such as overall aggression in the essay. Again, the agreement between independent readers of the essay would be an indication of the reliability of measuring aggression. Similarly, spoken responses are often judged as to some property. For example, tape-recorded therapy sessions could be judged as to the level of empathy (the ability to take another's position and feel what they feel) that is exhibited by different therapists. Agreement among independent raters as to the degree of the therapists' empathy would provide evidence of the reliability of the measurement of empathy.

In order to enhance accuracy, raters are very often trained with pilot tapes or essays. These are materials designed for training rather than those from the actual study. The definitions of the target behaviors, e.g., what constitutes empathy, and specific responses on the pilot tapes and essays are pointed out to the raters and discussed in the training procedure. In the actual study, the raters make all judgments individually, with no communication between raters, in order to ensure independence of judgments. If they agree in their judgment, then a reliable assessment of the behavior has been achieved.

WHAT IS BEING MEASURED?

The above discussions of reliability, whether dealing with internal consistency, test-retest, or interjudge agreement of observed responses, only relate to whether or not the measurement of a construct is consistent but not to whether the measuring instrument actually measures the construct of interest to the researcher. A rather silly example may bring this point home. Let's say that a person was told to measure the length of a room in order to purchase the correct amount of molding for the baseboard that runs the length of the room. Let us assume that this individual, being a visitor from another planet, had no idea what *length* means. He then looked around the room and found a box on the wall which had markings and the word *degrees* next to them. So he observed the box and recorded where the needle pointed—71.5 degrees. Although knowing nothing about length, he did know about reliability and proceeded to measure the length two more times to get an accurate assessment. On the next two measurements, he observed the needle at 72 and 72.5 degrees, respectively. Wanting to be highly accurate and to make sure he was correct, he asked a friend (also a visitor from another planet) to measure the wall. The visitor also observed the box three times and read the needle at 71, 72, and 73, degrees respectively. He then averaged these figures and reported that a molding of 72 degrees was needed for the length of the room. His measurement had high reliability, but obviously it wasn't measuring length.

Although this example is silly, it is intended to illustrate the difference between reliability and validity of measurement. *Validity refers to whether the measure is assessing the construct of interest.* There are several types of validity, each determined by different methods. The simplest type of validity is called *face validity*. This refers to whether the measure looks as though it is measuring what it is supposed to measure. Face validity is not based on empirical evidence but rather on a logical judgment about the content of the measure, and for this reason, it is sometimes called *faith validity*. The other methods, criterion validity, known-groups validity, and construct validity, all depend on empirical research. Sometimes determining the validity of a measure is a straightforward procedure. Aptitude tests, for example, are valid when they predict some specific future ability. A measure of college aptitude would be valid to the extent that it was related to college grades. If individuals who scored well on the test given before entering college also received high grades after going to college, the aptitude test would be valid. This type of validity is termed *predictive* or *criterion validity* since the evidence for it rests in the ability of the test to predict a future criterion. Evidence of predictive validity is often gathered for tests used in practical or applied situations as opposed to basic research situations. For instance, the question of whether an aptitude for college test was valid would be answered simply by whether or not it predicted college performance. If aptitude for college was measured not by a test but by counting the number of hairs per square centimeter (HPSC) on the head, and further, if this predicted college grades, then this measure of college aptitude would have predictive validity. We might then ask about grades as a valid reflection of college performance, but if we accepted grades as the criterion, then the HPSC measure would have predictive validity. To take another example, if a therapist developed a measure to screen clients for whether or not they would benefit from therapy, the validity of the measure would lie in its ability to predict improved functioning following therapy. In both of the above cases, there is a need for an instrument that serves a practical purpose, and if the instrument developed fulfills this specific purpose, it is valid. Even in these cases where the validity is determined by the ability of the test to predict a criterion, validity is not an all-or-none proposition. A test that relates to a criterion to some degree but not perfectly is called partially valid. In other words, predictive validity, as well as any other type of validity, is a relative attribute of a test. The greater the amount of variance in the criterion that can be predicted by the test, the more valid the test.

Another rather straightforward approach to validity is through the *known-groups* method. This method entails establishing the validity of a measure by seeing if it can discriminate between groups known to hold divergent points of view on the topic. For example, a group of patients identified as depressives by clinical psychologists should score higher on a scale of depression than a group of patients identified as nondepressives or a group of individuals from the general population. A second example might be the validation of a measure of liberal-conservative political attitude by administering the scale to known politically left- and right-wing groups, such as members of a socialist party and members of the John Birch Society, an ultraconservative organization. Showing that known extreme groups score differently on the scale would give some indication that the scale is assessing what it was intended to assess.

However, this is a rather gross way of establishing validity since it only shows that the scale is able to differentiate between known groups at the extremes. The method could be extended to provide a more sensitive test of validity by employing a number of groups, rather than only two extremes. For instance, hospitalized patients identified clinically as being highly depressed could be compared with patients who are identified as being depressed but are not hospitalized, and both of these groups could be compared with a sample from the general population. If the hospitalized patients score the highest, the nonhospitalized patients score in the middle, and the general population group scores lowest, this would be taken as evidence of the scale's ability to discriminate among various levels of depression. This same logic could be employed with the liberalism-conservatism measure. Groups might consist of communists, socialists, liberal Democrats, moderate Republicans, conservative Republicans, and members of an ultraconservative group such as the John Birch Society. If the scores of these groups on the scale lined up from highest (liberal) to lowest (conservative) in the same order as their known political orientation, this would be an indication of the measure to sensitively discriminate among positions along the political spectrum.

One problem with the known-groups method is the identification of appropriate known groups. In the case of the liberal-conservative scale, the issue is straightforward, but in the case of many abstract psychological variables (such as anxiety, stress, dogmatism, personal control, etc.), the task of finding appropriate groups is much more difficult. Thus, this is a useful method but appropriate only where obviously agreed-upon known groups can be identified.

In psychological research, most of the concepts of interest are theoretical and abstract. Thus, it is not always or even often intuitively obvious that a given measure is testing or assessing what it is supposed to assess. The previous example of the judgment of empathy levels in therapists will illustrate the problem. Empathy is an abstract theoretical concept, and therefore, one cannot point directly to it. A researcher could say that certain types of behaviors, physical and verbal, would be indicators of empathy and then could train judges to observe these behaviors. If the judges agree in their ratings of the behaviors, the researcher would be reliably measuring whatever they agreed upon. But if the responses they were taught to look for and agree on were not manifestations of empathy but of something else (such as the ability to present oneself as concerned), then the researcher would not be measuring empathy, but rather the ability to present oneself as concerned.

The question is, how does the researcher know what is being measured? The techniques for assessing reliability are well developed and fairly straightforward, but the methods for determining validity are much more complicated. Basically, the task is to see whether empathy, as measured, relates to the things it is supposed to relate to in the manner in which it is supposed to relate. The expected relationships are given by a theory of empathy either developed by others or by the researcher who is doing the measuring. What if the measure of empathy does not relate to these things as the theory predicts? Is the measurement invalid, or is the theory incorrect in the relationships it posits? Well, if alternative methods of assessing empathy tend to be related to the researcher's method but do not follow the theoretical predictions, then the theory is probably invalid. On the other hand, if other methods of assessing empathy do follow the theoretical predictions, then the researcher is probably measuring something other than empathy. The road to validation of psychological constructs, termed *construct validity,* is long and difficult, generally being achieved not with one study but by means of a multitude of studies. In fact, the question of *construct validity* is what much psychological research is all about. The techniques described throughout the remaining chapters of the book are all aimed at understanding behavior, and many are ways of providing validity for psychological constructs.

THE BASIC APPROACHES:
SIMPLE CORRELATIONAL
AND EXPERIMENTAL
PROCEDURES

Chapter 4

An Introduction to the
Correlational Method

It was emphasized in the first two chapters that in order to account for the variance of a variable, we relate it to other variables. Sometimes this is done through *experimentation* where the researcher manipulates one or more variables, termed *independent variables,* and examines the effect of this manipulation on another variable, termed the *dependent variable.* The study discussed in Chapter 1 dealing with self-esteem and romantic behaviors was of this type. The experimenter manipulated the type of feedback subjects received on a test and the attractiveness of the woman they encountered, the independent variables, and assessed their responses toward the woman, the dependent variable. In carrying out this type of research, the experimenter attempts to control all extraneous variables; that is, all variables not directly of interest. The focus of experimental research, then, is on manipulation and control, and much psychological research is of this type. But many times, researchers are not able to manipulate variables of interest or to gain control over extraneous variables. Consider, for example, a situation where the researcher is interested in the relationship between liberal-conservative political attitudes and social class. Neither variable is able to be manipulated by the experimenter since both variables are beyond the researcher's control. Often, problems do not lend themselves well to the experimental method. In these instances, the researcher finds it necessary to study variables as they occur rather than bringing about their occurrence through direct manipulation.

In this case, the strategy is to examine the relationship between two or more variables in order to see whether they have some systematic relationship to each other without manipulating or interfering with the variables. *This general approach of examining interrelationships among variables without manipulating and controlling is termed the correlational method.* The survey research approach discussed earlier is a correlational method since responses to various items and questions are simply interrelated. Much of the work on clinical populations is also correlational in nature, examining the relationships between various classifications of mental patients and other variables, such as social class or intelligence. Finally, natural observation, a technique where organisms are simply observed in their natural environment with no involvement on the part of the researcher, is a correlational method. The feature common to all of these examples is that no manipulation and control on the part of the researcher takes place.

THE CORRELATION COEFFICIENT

The most widely used statistic for describing the relationship between two variables is the Pearson Product Moment correlation coefficient—called simply, the *correlation coefficient.* This index of relationship is the building block of highly sophisticated techniques that allow us to gain answers to complicated questions. But before we attempt to understand these complex methods, let us examine more thoroughly the nature of the correlation coefficient itself.

The correlation coefficient, symbolized as *r,* is a measure of the degree to which two variables—that is, two sets of scores—covary. *To covary means "to vary together";* that is, there is some systematic relationship between the scores individuals receive on one variable and the scores they receive on the other variable. For example, if there is a tendency for individuals who have high scores on the attitude toward the presidential candidate scale to also have high incomes and for low-scoring individuals to have low incomes, then we could say that attitudes toward the presidential candidate and income covary positively. If individuals scoring high on the attitude toward the candidate scale have low incomes and individuals scoring low have high incomes, then the two variables covary negatively. Finally, if some of the high-scoring individuals on the attitude variable have high incomes and some of the high scorers have low incomes and the low scorers have both high and low incomes, then the variables do not covary. These three situations, positive, negative, and no covariation, respectively, are depicted graphically in Figure 4–1. These figures are termed *scatterplots.* The horizontal axis contains the various income levels, the vertical axis contains the attitudes, and the points represent the scores of the subjects plotted in relationship to both axes. Figure 4–1a, depicting a positive relationship, shows that the points form a pattern which moves from the lower-left to the upper-right portion of the graph. In Figure 4–1b, the negative relationship, the points move from the upper-right to the lower-left portion of the graph. Finally, in Figure 4–1c, the points form no particular pattern but are scattered throughout the graph, an indication of no covariation between the variables.

The correlation coefficient is an index of the covariance between two variables. It ranges between $+1.0$ and -1.0, with a positive correlation indicating that the two variables covary positively and a negative correlation indicating negative covariance. An $r = .00$ means that the variables do not covary—they are unrelated. The sign of the correlation coefficient tells the direction of covariation, positive or negative, whereas the number tells the degree or strength of the relationship. For example, an $r = -.40$ indicates the same degree but an opposite direction of relationship as an $r = +.40$. The importance of r is that it can be readily interpreted since its limits are defined as $+1.0$ and -1.0, and that it serves as the basis for more complicated statistical techniques which allow us to examine complex research questions. But the correlation coefficient, like other statistical tests we will discuss later, is suitable only when the data meet certain conditions. For example, only if two variables have a linear relationship can a correlation coefficient be interpreted. Linear relationships are those where increases in one variable are accompanied by corresponding increases in the other (or decreases in the case of a negative relationship). These relationships would best be graphically described by a straight line, for example, the relationships depicted in Figure 4–1a and b. There are

FIGURE 4–1

Scatterplots depicting positive (a), negative (b), and zero relationships between income and attitude toward the presidential candidate

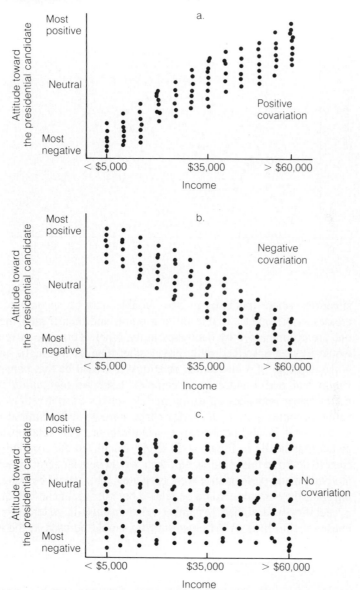

FIGURE 4–2
Hypothetical curvilinear relationship between motivation and performance

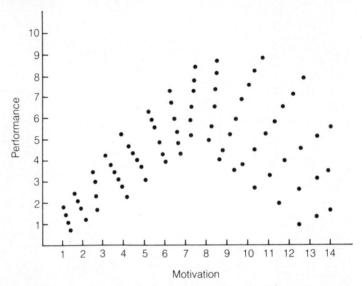

situations where increases in one variable may be accompanied by increases in the other variable up to a point, and then further increases in one are accompanied by decreases in the other. This type of relationship would be best described by a curve rather than by a straight line.

An example of a curvilinear relationship would be that between motivation and performance on a complex task. As motivation increases, performance improves up to the middle ranges of motivation. As motivation becomes quite high, performance starts to suffer until at very high motivational levels, performance is quite poor. This relationship is depicted graphically in Figure 4–2. If one calculated the correlation coefficient to describe this relationship, the *r* would be near zero, indicating that motivation and performance were unrelated. This would be quite misleading since the variables would be related but not in a linear fashion. Since *r* is specifically designed for linear relationships, it underestimates nonlinear relationships. A different statistic should be used in these cases.

CORRELATION AND PREDICTION

If two variables are highly correlated, then one variable is predictable from the other. Prediction is handled through a statistical technique called *linear regression*. Linear regression is a method whereby scores on one variable can be predicted from scores on the other variable. The variable we are trying to predict is called the *criterion variable,* and the variable that we are trying to predict from is called the *predictor variable*. The reader may recall that the issue of prediction has been raised previously in regard to predictive validity. A measure has criterion validity to the extent that the measure is able to predict a future criterion; i.e., the measure is correlated with the criterion. The strategy outlined below is the one that is followed when evidence for criterion validity is gathered.

Basically, the strategy is to gather data, usually from a fairly large number of individuals, on both a criterion and a predictor variable. For example, if we wanted to predict grades in college (GPA), the criterion variable, from Scholastic Aptitude Test (SAT) scores, the predictor variable, we would administer the SATs to a large group of high school seniors, wait four years, and collect their GPAs. If we examined their GPAs, we would find variance; that is, these students would show individual differences in their college grades. The question in regression analysis is whether we are able to account for this variance, or at least some of it, through knowledge of these students' SATs. The variance in the GPAs is the total amount of variance we are trying to account for. That part of the GPA variance related to SAT scores is called systematic, while that part not understandable through the SATs is called unsystematic or error variance.

Before we have the SATs to relate to the GPAs, all of the variance in the GPAs is unsystematic or error variance. Keep in mind that error does not refer to mistakes, but rather to ignorance or lack of understanding. Remember that a variable cannot be understood by itself; it can only be understood in terms of its relationship to other variables. Thus, the variance in the GPAs starts out as error in the sense that with only the GPAs by themselves, we have no understanding of the individual differences in GPAs. If, for example, someone showed you the grade point averages of five students and asked you what the individual differences in these grade point averages might be related to, you could only guess. One good guess would be that they would be related to college aptitude test scores, and another would be that they would be related to high school grades. In terms of evidence or lack of it, one guess is as good as the other. The point is that one would only know that the grade point averages vary. Any judgment about what might account for their variance would be speculative, and speculation can often be incorrect. Thus, with only the grades themselves, we are in a state of ignorance as to their variance, and thus the variance in the grades is all error variance in the sense that it is unaccounted-for variance.

If the SATs for the five students were made available and if we found them to be correlated with the GPAs, the error or lack of understanding of the individual differences in the GPAs would be reduced. If the correlation between the SATs and the GPAs were perfect, we would reduce the error to zero. If the correlation were less than perfect, the error would be reduced only to the extent of the relationship between the variables, and some error would still remain in the variance of the GPAs. Thus, just as ignorance or lack of understanding in everyday life is reduced by acquiring knowledge, the error in a criterion variable is reduced by acquiring knowledge of another or other variables which relate to that criterion. Just as the acquisition of knowledge in everyday life systematizes the world and makes it more comprehensible, the relationship of a predictor to a criterion variable makes the variance in the criterion more systematic and comprehensible.

The way we actually compute the systematic variance is to produce a *best-fitting straight line* from our knowledge of the relationship between the two variables. The line will contain all of the predictions of GPA from the SATs. It will be "best-fitting" in the sense that the actual GPAs achieved by the students will fall closer to this line than they would to any other straight line we could produce. Most of you will remember from your earlier mathematics that any specific straight line is defined by two values: the *slope of the line* and the *intercept*. The slope is the tilt of the line, and the intercept is the point where the line cuts the ordinate or vertical axis of the graph. For any given set of data points, there are an infinite number of straight lines that could be produced, each differing from the others in either its slope or intercept or both. Employing calculus, we are able to find the particular slope and intercept that give the best-fitting straight line for a given set of criterion and predictor scores. Figure 4–3 depicts a hypothetical scatterplot with a best-fitting straight line through the plotted points.

This best-fitting line is the line of prediction—the regression line; that

FIGURE 4–3
Best-fitting straight line

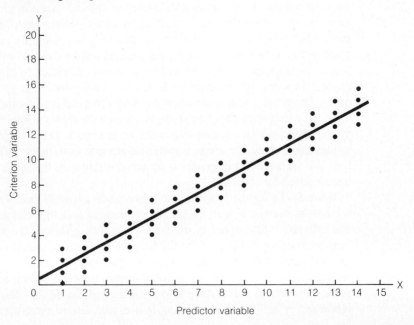

Predictor variable

is, we can predict a GPA, a score on the criterion, for every individual, and that predicted score will fall on the line. All of the actual GPAs will not fall on the line unless the criterion and predictor variables are perfectly related. To the extent that we predict a given GPA for someone and their actual GPA differs from that prediction, we have error. Again, this is not error in the sense of a mistake, but error due to the fact that the criterion and predictor variables are not perfectly related. If we took these errors, that is, the distances from the actual points to the regression line, and found their variance, we would have the unsystematic part of the total variance of the GPAs. Then, by subtracting this unsystematic variance from the total variance, we would find the systematic variance, which is that part of the total variance that can be understood or accounted for by our predictor variable, SAT scores.

Thus, the variance of a criterion variable can be broken up into a systematic component, that which is related to the predictor variable, and an unsystmatic or error component which is unrelated to the predictor. These components can be used in two different ways. First of all, we can gather information about the size of the relationship between the criterion and predictor variables. If we divided this systematic variance by the total variance, we calculate the proportion of the total variance which is systematic. This value is also the square of the correlation coefficient. For example, if $r = .50$, then $r^2 = .25$, which means that 25 percent of the variance in the criterion variable can be accounted for by the predictor variable. Thus, the square of the correlation coefficient is a ratio of the systematic to the total variance and always indicates the proportion of variance in one variable that can be accounted for by the other variable. The second use of the components of variance is to test whether or not the relationship between the variables is *statistically significant;* that is, whether or not it is due to chance. A full discussion of the concepts of statistical significance and chance will be undertaken in Chapter 6, and therefore the following is only a brief introduction. Since we calculate the relationship between the criterion and predictor variables on a sample taken from a population, the sample could show some relationship between the variables even though the variables are unrelated in the population. Therefore, we need to be able to test whether or not the relationship between the variables in our sample is just a chance deviation from a zero relationship or whether it reflects the fact that there is a relationship between the variables in the population. In order to carry out this test, we divide the systematic variance by the unsystematic variance, which yields a statistic called F. This statistic, $F,$ which can be looked up in a table, tests whether the relationship between the variables is due to chance or is a real phenomenon. In the case of the GPAs and SATs, if we determined that the relationship we observed was not due to chance, then we may want to go on to use the information we have found about the relationship of the variables to predict GPAs from the SATs.

Let us say that we have found that GPAs and SATs are strongly related.

We would then collect SATs from a new group of students applying to college and predict their GPAs using the slope and intercept found from our first groups. Each individual applying would then have an SAT score and a predicted GPA but no actual GPA. Decisions about admitting these people to college would be based upon their predicted GPAs. If it was predicted from an individual's SAT score that they would achieve a 1.2 GPA and a 2.0 GPA was needed to graduate, then they would be considered a bad risk and would probably not be accepted. The computation procedures for the correlation coefficient; the slope and intercept; predicted values; total, systematic, and unsystematic components of variance; and the F statistic are demonstrated in Section III of the appendix.

THE MEANING OF THE CORRELATION COEFFICIENT

The correlation coefficient is an index of the relationship between two variables, and its square gives the proportion of variance in one variable accounted for by the other variable. If variables are being studied through the correlational method, then a cause-and-effect judgment cannot be made about the relationship between the variables described by the correlation coefficient. It only reflects the degree to which two variables covary or share common variance. On the other hand, if the variables are being experimentally investigated so that one of the variables is manipulated and controlled by the researcher, then r can be given a cause-effect interpretation.

For example, assume a researcher was interested in whether the amount of reinforcement or reward one receives on a first task is related to the level of performance on a second task. If reward or reinforcement were manipulated so that subjects in an experiment received reinforcement on a task either 80, 60, 40, or 20 percent of the time and then performance was evaluated on a second task, we could examine the relationships between prior reinforcement rate and subsequent task performance by correlating the two variables. An r of .70 between the two would indicate that (1) prior reinforcement is related to task performance, (2) 49 percent of the variance in task performance can be accounted for through prior reinforcement, and (3) prior reinforcement differences cause differences in subsequent task performance. This last interpretation would not be based upon r itself but rather upon the method with which the relationship was studied. On the other hand, if the researcher had given subjects a first task and reinforced them for the correct responses they give, some subjects would have received high and some low reinforcement rates due to their differing abilities. If he then looked at performance on a second task, an r of .70 between the prior reinforcement rate and subsequent task performance would indicate that (1) prior reinforcement is related to task performance, and (2) 49 percent of the variance in task performance can be accounted for through prior reinforcement. However, no cause-effect statement could be made about the two variables. That is, the researcher could not state that prior reinforcement differences caused differences in task performance.

In the first situation, prior reinforcement was under the researcher's control and not the subject's. If subjects were assigned to the reinforcement rate groups randomly, then the groups should have differed only as to the reinforcement rate they received, and these performance differences could only have been produced by the reinforcement rate differences. On the other hand, in the second situation, reinforcement rate was beyond the researcher's control. If subjects were correct a great deal of the time, they received a high reinforcement rate, whereas if they were often incorrect, they received a low reinforcement rate. Since subjects who answered correctly a great deal of the time and received high rates of reinforcement may have been more intelligent or more highly motivated, differences in subsequent task performance may have been due to these intelligence and motivation differences rather than to reinforcement rate differences.

The important point here is that the correlational method is not the same as the correlation coefficient. The correlation coefficient is a statistic used to describe the relationship between variables. If the method of studying that relationship was the correlational method, then no cause-effect judgment can be made about the relationship, but if the method of study was experimental, then a cause-effect judgment is possible. Both methods could use the correlation coefficient to describe the relationship, but the meaning or interpretation of r would be different for the two methods.

This same logic applies to all other statistics. For example, assume that a researcher randomly assigns people to two groups. Subjects in group 1 take a test and are given feedback which indicates that they have performed well above average, while subjects in group 2 are given feedback indicating that they have performed well below average. Group 1 is the high and group 2 the low self-confidence group. All subjects then role-play a scene with an attractive member of the opposite sex and are rated by unseen judges as to the quality of their role-playing. The average ratings are then calculated for each group, and the group means are compared through a statistical test, called a t test, to determine whether the difference occurred by chance. The high self-confidence group is found to be rated higher in the quality of their role-playing than the low self-confidence group. Now, assume a second researcher gives a test of self-confidence and, on the basis of the scores, classifies subjects into high or low self-confidence groups. As in the example above, all subjects role-play a scene with an attractive member of the opposite sex and are then rated by judges as to the quality of their performances. The mean quality ratings for the two groups are then calculated and compared by means of a t test. As before, the high self-confidence group outscores the low self-confidence group.

Even though the results of both studies were evaluated through the same procedure, a comparison of the group means by a t test, the second was carried out through correlational method and the first through the experimental method. That is, in the first study, self-confidence was manipulated by the experimenter, whereas in the second study, subjects were simply classified as to being high or low in self-confidence on the basis of their test scores; the researcher had no control over their group assignment. As in the case of the correlation coefficient, the method and not the statistic determines the conclusion. Thus, in the case of the first study, the researcher can draw the conclusion that self-confidence differences cause differences in quality of role-playing. In the second study, no cause-effect judgment is possible. The point is that even though the results of the second study were not evaluated by the correlation coefficient, it is still a correlational study.

STRENGTH OF THE CORRELATIONAL METHOD

As stated previously, the correlational method is one where relationships between variables are observed without interfering or manipulating. As with all techniques, there are both advantages and disadvantages. One advantage of the correlational over the experimental method is that many important variables are not able to be experimentally manipulated and thus must be studied as they naturally occur. For example, sex or gender, which is often of great interest, cannot be manipulated. Researchers have no control over the assignment of their research subjects to male and female groups; that assignment has been previously determined through genetic coding. Developmental psychologists are often concerned with the relationship of age to other variables such as learning or social behavior, but there is no way of treating age experimentally. That is, they have no control over this variable since the age of their subjects is determined before their arrival at the research site. They cannot assign children randomly to any age group; they must either put them in the age groups to which they already belong or choose children of particular ages.

Sex, age, birth order, physical characteristics such as size or skin color are all variables which are determined at birth and are thus unchangeable parts of the organism. There are also psychological variables which have come to be a part of the organism through either experience alone or a combination of genetics and experience. For example, in order to study the relationship of intelligence to other variables, it is necessary to employ the correlational method since control over an individual's intelligence is out of the researcher's hands. Many personality variables, termed *traits,* are seen as enduring dispositions of the individual which are not easily changeable, at least through short-term interventions. Self-esteem, open- and closed-mindedness, and belief in personal control are traits individuals carry with them. It is true that people low in self-esteem could have their self-esteem raised or closed-minded individuals could be influenced to be more open-minded but probably only with great difficulty since these personality traits have been acquired over a number of years.

Let's take belief in personal control as an example. Individuals differ in their beliefs about the degree to which their behavior has an effect on the environment. Internal control individuals believe that they can affect or control the outcomes or events that happen to them through their actions, whereas external control individuals believe that their behavior has little or no effect; their outcomes are determined by chance or by powerful others. Individuals come to the research situation varying in degree of belief in personal control; that is, they are either internal or external to some degree. Thus, if one wanted to know whether belief in personal control was related to performance on some sort of skilled task, it would be necessary to answer this question by correlating scores on a measure of belief in personal control with scores on the task. The researcher does not determine the subject's degree of personal control, and so he must study this variable as it occurs.

This lack of control over variables is the usual case in many of the social sciences. For example, economists who study the relationship between economic indicators—such as wholesale prices or stock market trends—and the economic growth of the country must examine these variables as they occur. They are not able to manipulate or control either wholesale prices or the stockmarket in order to see what happens to the economy. Rather, they can only examine and describe the relationships between these variables and base their predictions on those variables that have been shown to have the most predictive power. Sociologists and political scientists are generally in the same situation. The variables of interest are usually beyond their control, and thus, the correlational method is the appropriate one for studying the relationships among these variables.

While it is true that some variables can *only* be studied through the correlational method, some variables which could be manipulated and controlled are still investigated with the correlational approach. If manipulation and control remove much of the ambiguity related to interpretation of causality and directional influence, why not always manipulate and control when it is possible to do so? One reason for choosing a correlational approach when an experimental one is possible is that experimental manipulations are often relatively weak, while naturally occurring events are very powerful. For example, let us suppose that we were interested in the relationship between self-confidence and attractiveness. That is, are individuals high in self-confidence more attractive to others than persons who are low in self-confidence? It is possible to manipulate self-confidence experimentally by providing positive or negative feedback to subjects about their personalities or abilities and to observe the effect of this manipulation on judgments of attractiveness. Since self-confidence would have been under the control of the researcher, the interpretation of the results would have been unambiguous. The feedback would have caused any differences in attractiveness between the high and low self-confidence groups.

The problem is that subjects would come to the study already high or low in self-confidence as a result of their abilities and past experiences, and it may be difficult to change those existing orientations through an experimental manipulation. The feedback provided by the experimenter to create high or low self-confidence may be insignificant compared to the compounded history of the subject. Obviously, with enough time and control over the subjects' environment, it would be possible to create large changes in self-confidence, but generally that time and control are not possible. Also, producing large and possibly long-lasting decreases in self-confidence would be considered by most people to be unethical. Therefore, the researcher may decide to investigate this problem by simply measuring self-confidence in subjects and having those subjects rated for attractiveness. The researcher foregoes the manipulation because of the probable weakness of that manipulation and trades clarity of interpretation for strength.

Very often, research on a question proceeds through a series of studies. The first step may be a correlational approach intended to achieve evidence of a relationship between variables. Often this first step achieves this evidence at low cost and describes what exists out in the world. Then, in order to more fully understand the causal nature of the relationship, the variables are examined experimentally through manipulation and control. Correlational methods here would serve an exploratory or discovery function.

WEAKNESS OF THE CORRELATIONAL METHOD

The major disadvantage of the correlational approach is ambiguity in terms of the interpretation of the results. Finding a relationship between variables in a correlational study says only that the variable are related. It implies nothing about the process behind the relationship. In the above example, by using the correlational method, one only knows that attractiveness and self-confidence are related. The experiment would have told you whether self-confidence influenced judgments of attractiveness. Finding that there is a relationship between two variables yields no information about whether variable X causes Y, or vice versa. Sometimes there is no causal relationship between the variables. Another variable entirely may be the cause of both of these variables. This would mean that the relationship between the original two variables is indirect and is due only to the fact that another variable influences both of them.

Let us say that researchers have found a relationship between the amount of pornographic materials in a society and the number of rapes. That is, as pornography has increased over the years, rape has increased. One possible interpretation of this result would be that pornography incites or causes rape. People read or see pornographic materials, become aroused, and carry out rapes. This is a possibility, of course, but there are other explanations as well. For example, the society has become more open in general over the years. One effect of this may have been to increase interest in sexual stimuli including pornography. Another effect may have been to increase the awareness of women toward more varied types of lifestyles. These would include living and traveling alone and working. If more women are living alone, more women are working, and more are traveling alone, there are more opportunities for rape to occur. Thus, as pornography would have increased, so would rape but not because they are directly related. Rather both would have increased due to a general change in societal attitudes. This is one possible interpretation, and with no other evidence, it is as viable as the first interpretation of pornography causing rape. This problem, the relationship being moderated by an outside variable as in the pornography-rape example, can be examined further through more sophisticated techniques. This moderator variable problem is tackled through a technique called *partial correlation,* which is discussed in Chapter 11.

The correlational method then has certain strengths and weaknesses. It is a useful technique for studying naturally occurring phenomena and for examining variables which are either not open to manipulation or are difficult to manipulate and control. The weakness of the correlational method lies in the ambiguity of the results it produces in that observed relationships may be a function of outside variables, rather than a function of a direct causal link between the variables being investigated.

Chapter 5

An Introduction
to the Experiment

WHAT IS AN EXPERIMENT?

Rather than beginning this chapter by presenting a technical and abstract definition of an experiment, let me pose a series of situations and accompanying questions.

1. In the fall of 1979, the Shah of Iran was allowed into the United States for medical treatment. Following his arrival here, the U.S. Embassy in Iran was seized and the occupants taken hostage.
   Question: Would the Iranians have seized the embassy and taken the hostages if the Shah had been denied entry into the United States?

2. In the fall of 1980, a world championship prizefight was held between the champion Roberto Duran and the challenger Sugar Ray Leonard, from whom Duran had won the title earlier in the year. In this rematch, Leonard seemed to be ahead in the early rounds, and then Duran did something quite remarkable in the history of professional boxing. He simply quit fighting in the middle of the eighth round; that is, without being knocked down or even hurt, he conceded the title to Leonard, later complaining that he had had cramps.
   Question: Would Leonard have won back the title if Duran had not quit in the middle of the eighth round?

3. On a more personal level, a student told me that she took the introductory psychology course from Dr. L. and that this course generated her interest in the field and caused her to major in psychology.
   Question: Would this student have majored in psychology even if she had taken a section of the introductory course taught by someone other than Dr. L.?

Each of the above questions could have at least two possible answers. If the Shah had not been admitted into the United States, the Iranians may not have been angered and seized the embassy. On the other hand, Iranian resentment toward the United States was probably based on past U.S. policy as much as on the particular situation of the Shah's entry into the United States, and the embassy seizure may have taken place even if the Shah had been excluded from this country. If Duran had not quit fighting, he may have come on strongly in the later rounds and won the fight. It is also possible that Leonard would have continued his early round supremacy and still have regained the championship. Even if the student had not taken Dr. L.'s section of the course, she may have decided to major in psychology. On the other hand, she may not have found the subject matter as interesting in another section and thus decided on a different major.

Unfortunately, it is impossible to determine the correct answer to each question. Since the Shah was allowed into the United States, there is no way of knowing the consequences of excluding him. Since Duran did quit fighting, we cannot know what would have happened if he had continued. Since the student has already taken Dr. L.'s section, there is no way of knowing what her choice of major would have been had she not taken this section. In a sense, life is a poor experiment, or more accurately, it is not an experiment at all.

If it were possible now to go back in time in each of the above situations and carry out the course of action which was not taken—that is, to have barred the Shah, to have Duran keep fighting, and to have the student take a different section of the introductory course—we could then compare these results with those which occurred following the courses of action that actually took place. Obviously we can't reconstruct history and play it again differently, but if we could, life would then be an experiment. It would be an experiment because we would be able to control the occurrence of events, and *control over the occurrence of events is the essence of an experiment.*

In other words, if it is in our power to both produce and prevent an event, we have the basis of an experiment. If we could go back in time, deny the Shah entry into this country, and then observe that the embassy was not seized, we would know that admitting him caused the seizure. In the same light, if Leonard had lost in replaying the fight, we would know that it was Duran's quitting that caused Leonard to regain the title. It should be noted that, along with the ability to control the occurrence of an event, we also need replication or repeatability since a single occurrence could be coincidental. In the above examples, in order to carry out a true experiment, we would have had to repeat each of the actual and the hypothetical circumstances a number of times. Thus, if a consequence occurs consistently when an event is produced but does not occur when the event is withheld, we know that the event's occurrence causes the consequence. This ability to determine causal agents makes the experiment a powerful tool for the scientist.

Obviously, at least in the case of the embassy seizure and the Duran-Leonard fight, there is no way of controlling the events or repeating them, and thus there is no definitive way of determining cause. Although there is also no way of determining whether Dr. L.'s course caused a particular student to major in psychology, we could determine whether Dr. L.'s section causes more students to major in psychology. We can control whether students who sign up for introductory psychology get Dr. L.'s section or another section of the course, and if those we assign to Dr. L. go on to major in psychology at a higher rate than those assigned to other sections, we could conclude that Dr. L.'s section causes more students to choose psychology as a major. In this case, we are able to have control over the occurrence of the event, exposure to Dr. L.'s section, and thus we are able to determine the causal nature of that event. Since control over the occurrence of an event means that the event can be both instituted and withdrawn, an experiment always involves a comparison between at least two conditions that differ or vary in one and only one respect. Situations that involve only a single condition are merely demonstrations and not true experiments.

Independent Variables

Those events that the researcher controls are termed independent variables. One sense in which these events are independent is that they are not under the control of the subjects in the study. They are, of course, under the control of the researcher in that he or she decides or controls which subjects will experience a given event and which will not. The events are variables because there are always at least two levels or intensities of the events. The levels of the independent variable may be only the simple presence and absence of the event, or they may include a number of different treatments.

Consider a situation where we are interested in the effects of exposure to uncontrollable events on subsequent performance. Assume that we decide to expose subjects to 50 trials of aversive loud noise that is either controllable or uncontrollable and then observe their performance on a subsequent task, such as solving anagrams. Anagrams are words with scrambled letters such as *leuqa* for the word *equal.* In the controllable condition, subjects will be able to terminate the noise, that is, escape from it, by pressing a series of buttons in the correct sequence. In the uncontrollable condition, there is no correct sequence of presses, and therefore no pattern of responding can be learned that will lead to escape. If we assign half of the subjects to the controllable or escapable noise condition while the other half is assigned to the uncontrollable or inescapable noise condition, we now have an independent variable (controllability) with only two levels (presence or absence). This, of course, would yield a comparison between subjects exposed to escapable noise and those exposed to inescapable noise. We could see if the escapable noise subjects performed better in solving the anagrams than the inescapable noise subjects. Since there was no group of subjects that simply solved the anagrams without being exposed to noise, we could not compare the effects of uncontrollability and controllability with no pretreatment.

On the other hand, if we had included a nonpretreated group, that is, one tested on the anagrams with no previous exposure to noise, we could make these comparisons and answer important questions. It would show us the effects of the two controllability conditions in comparison with no pretreatment. Thus, we could tell if inescapable noise lowers performance and whether escapable noise raises performance or simply produces performance equal to the no pretreatment group. The inclusion of the third condition, no pretreatment, enhances our understanding of the effects of the other conditions. When one of the conditions consists of an absence of any treatment, it is termed a *control condition.* This is the case for the no pretreatment group.

This three-group design using escapable and inescapable noise and a no pretreatment group has been widely employed in research on the topic of learned helplessness (Seligman, 1975). Seligman called this a *triadic design,* and it actually consists of a more powerful procedure than simply assigning subjects to the three groups. In this design, called a yoked control design, subjects in the escapable and inescapable conditions are run in "yoked" pairs. What this means is that the escapable and inescapable noise subjects receive exactly the same set of stimulus conditions except for controllability. Specifically, the noise comes on simultaneously for both subjects and terminates for both when the subject in the escapable noise condition presses the correct sequence of buttons. As described previously, there is no response that can be made by the subject in the inescapable noise condition which will result in termination of the noise. Therefore, in this yoked design, both subjects receive the same intensity and duration of noise. The only difference is that the subject in the escapable noise condition is able to learn a pattern of responding which will result in escape, while his inescapable noise partner does not have this possibility. This yoked control procedure allows one to conclude that it is the escapability variable and not simply differing amounts of exposure to noise which produces the subsequent performance differences.

Thus, the independent variable may consist of only two conditions, or it may consist of a number of conditions. In the above example dealing with controllability, the treatments differ or vary in kind. That is, the three conditions (escapable noise, inescapable noise, and no pretreatment) are qualitatively different. This is not always the case. Sometimes treatments vary on a quantitative scale; that is, they vary in degree. For example, if we were interested in the effects of various amounts of exposure to uncontrollability on subsequent performance, we could assign subjects to either 10, 30, 50, 70, or 90 trials of escapable or inescapable noise and then compare their anagram performance. Since the treatments would differ in magnitude, the independent variable would be quantitative in nature. The inclusion of a no pretreatment group (zero trials) in this experiment would constitute the control condition and would be quantitatively different from the other levels of noise exposure.

Dependent Variables

Up to this point, our discussion of the experimental method has centered on what the experimenter does. We have concentrated on the manipulation and control aspects of an experiment since these aspects distinguish the experimental method from other methods of study. Manipulating and controlling events is, of course, only part of the story. The other part concerns the effects of those manipulations. Controlling events is meaningless unless we are able to measure or assess the impact of the conditions we manipulate. *Dependent variables are the measured consequences which result from the manipulation of the independent variables.* In psychology, dependent variables are the measurements we make of a behavioral response of an organism, that is, a subject, in a treatment condition of the experiment. These responses are dependent in that they result from or depend upon the manipulations. That is, they may be dependent upon the independent variable. The experiment is carried out to find if the dependent variable is indeed dependent upon the independent variable. For example, are the number of anagrams solved dependent on the various controllability conditions, the independent variable? The responses of subjects are variable in that they are able to vary in intensity.

In the studies discussed above, we were interested in whether the various conditions (escapable noise, inescapable noise, and no pretreatment) produced different effects. Specifically, did exposure to inescapable noise result in poorer performance on the subsequent task than exposure to escapable noise or no exposure to noise? The subsequent task we discussed was solving anagrams, but we did not specify exactly how we were going to measure performance on this task. One way would be to simply present all subjects with a single anagram and then compare the conditions as to the number of subjects who solve it. This would seem to be one reasonable measure of the effects of the three conditions on subsequent performance. The dependent variable in this case would be assessed as a simple dichotomy: solve the anagram or fail to solve it. In other words, it would be measured on a nominal scale.

Although this appears to be a reasonable way of assessing subsequent performance, there may be a problem with it. Simply assessing whether or not subjects solve a single anagram may not be a very sensitive measurement of the effects of the independent variable. For example, if the single anagram chosen is too difficult, most subjects may fail, or if it is too easy, most may pass. A second possibility is that if the time given to solve the anagram is too short, most subjects may fail, or if it is too long, most may pass. Thus, giving only a single anagram and simply assessing success or failure to solve it may not provide an adequate measure of subsequent performance. Another alternative would be to provide a series of anagrams and then take the number of these solved as the dependent variable. We know from our discussion on reliability that as the number of items in a measure increases, the reliability of the measure increases. Thus, having subjects solve a number of anagrams would provide a more reliable measure of their performance than having them solve only a single anagram. A third approach might involve both counting the number of anagrams scored and assessing the time taken to solve each one. Thus, even if no differences appeared in the number of anagrams solved, differences among the conditions may appear in the time taken to arrive at the solutions. In other words, even though the escapable noise and no pretreatment groups may not differ from the inescapable noise group on the total number of anagrams solved, they may arrive at their solutions more quickly than the inescapable noise group. The point of this example is that the dependent variable is the evidence of the effects of the manipulations and ways of gathering that evidence can vary in complexity.

Random Assignment

As I pointed out previously, the distinguishing feature of the experimental method is manipulation. The definition of an independent variable is that it is under the control of the experimenter. It is the experimenter who exercises control, deciding which subjects will receive which treatment by assigning them to the respective conditions. Actually, the idea that it is the experimenter who decides who will receive a given condition of the independent variable is somewhat misleading. It is misleading to the extent that assignment of subjects to conditions is not based upon a personal decision of the experimenter. Rather, it is based upon chance. In a true experiment, subjects are assigned to the various treatment conditions on a random basis, which means that all subjects have an equal chance of being exposed to any of the treatments. We will see that *random assignment is a crucial aspect of the experimental method.*

In order to demonstrate the value of random assignment in experimental research, let us return again to the case of the influence of controllability on anagram performance. Keep in mind that the study involved the assignment of subjects to three conditions—escapable noise, inescapable noise, and no pretreatment. This assignment would be done on a random basis; that is, every subject would have an equal chance of being assigned to any condition. There are a number of ways this random assignment could actually be carried out. Let's examine three of them in order to correctly demonstrate the nature of random assignment. If there were 45 subjects available to participate in the experiment, we would want to assign 15 subjects to each of the three conditions. One way we could do this would be to type each subject's name on a small card, put all of the 45 cards into a large drum, spin the drum, and begin taking the cards from the drum. The first 15 names would be assigned to condition 1 (escapable noise), the second 15 to condition 2 (inescapable noise), and the third 15 to condition 3 (no pretreatment). A second method might involve using a table of random numbers for the assignment of subjects to conditions. These are tables of numbers in random order produced for the purpose of generating random sequences. The experimenter simply locates a point on the table with his or her finger and moves either down the column or across the row. Each time a number from 1 to 3 is encountered, it is assigned to a student until all of the 45 students have been assigned to the three conditions. A third method involves the random assignment of the three conditions to the various days and time periods in which the experiment will be run. In other words, rather than assigning all 45 subjects to the conditions before the experiment begins, the three conditions are randomly assigned among the 45 experimental sessions needed to complete the experiment. Table 5–1 shows a hypothetical listing of the dates and times for the first 15 experimental sessions, along with the conditions randomly assigned (through a random number table) to these

TABLE 5–1

**Hypothetical listing of the dates and times for the
first 15 randomly assigned conditions in the
escapable noise experiment**

1.	Sept. 30	8:00 A.M.	No pretreatment
2.	Sept. 30	9:00 A.M.	Inescapable noise
3.	Oct. 2	2:00 P.M.	No pretreatment
4.	Oct. 4	10:00 A.M.	Inescapable noise
5.	Oct. 5	1:00 P.M.	Escapable noise
6.	Oct. 9	8:00 A.M.	No pretreatment
7.	Oct. 9	9:00 A.M.	Escapable noise
8.	Oct. 11	2:00 P.M.	Escapable noise
9.	Oct. 13	10:00 A.M.	Inescapable noise
10.	Oct. 14	1:00 P.M.	Inescapable noise
11.	Oct. 17	8:00 A.M.	Escapable noise
12.	Oct. 17	9:00 A.M.	Inescapable noise
13.	Oct. 19	2:00 P.M.	Escapable noise
14.	Oct. 21	10:00 A.M.	No pretreatment
15.	Oct. 22	1:00 P.M.	No pretreatment

sessions. Thus, the subject who signs up for September 30, 8:00 A.M. will receive no pretreatment, whereas the subject who signs up for the 9:00 A.M. slot on the same day will receive inescapable noise, etc. It should be noted that if the previously described yoked design was used, the escapable and inescapable noise conditions would need to be run simultaneously since this design entails running subjects in pairs.

These methods all produce the same result. That is, all of them assign subjects to the conditions on a chance or random basis. What is the advantage of this assignment? Basically, it is an attempt to ensure that the conditions are alike before the actual treatment takes place. In order to see how this occurs, let us assume that we have randomly assigned the 45 students to the three conditions and we are ready to begin the experiment. Since the fact that any subject finds himself or herself in a particular condition is due to chance, each of the conditions will contain a mixture of students. For instance, some will be generally proficient at solving anagrams, and some will be rather mediocre. Some will believe that they have control over events in their life, while some will believe that they have little control.

Thus, within each condition, there will be quite a bit of variability among the subjects in terms of anagram ability, belief in control, and a great many other characteristics. This variability or heterogeneity will exist for each group and should be about the same for all of the groups. That is, although the subjects in the inescapable noise condition will vary a great deal, the subjects in the other two conditions will also vary—and in the same ways; e.g., in anagram proficiency and belief in control. In other words, if, before the treatments began, we had subjects solve a series of anagrams (different ones than those employed for the dependent variable) and assessed their belief in control over events in their lives, the average anagram performance and the average belief in control would be about the same across the three conditions. "About the same" means that any pretreatment differences would be small ones that could be due to chance.

Assume that the three conditions are now run and subjects are tested as to their anagram performance (number of anagrams solved). If the subjects in the escapable noise and no pretreatment conditions solve many more anagrams than those in the inescapable noise condition, this difference would have to be due to the effect of receiving inescapable noise. "Many more" would mean that the difference between the performances of the groups would be so large as to be unlikely to have occurred by chance. In other words, random assignment is an attempt to ensure equality before treatment so that any inequality after treatment can be attributed to the effects of the treatments.

In order to further explicate the role of random assignment, let us consider the consequences of assigning subjects to the various conditions of the experiment on some nonrandom bases. One possible way in which the study could have been carried out was to run all of the subjects in a condition in a block. For example, the first 15 sessions might all be no pretreatment sessions, the next 15 escapable noise sessions, and the final 15 inescapable noise conditions. Subjects would sign up for the days and time periods they wanted, they would be treated at the designated time with the scheduled treatment, and then tested on the dependent variable. If the subjects receiving inescapable noise performed more poorly than the subjects in the other two groups, can we conclude that the treatment differences produced this difference in performance? Absolutely not! Since the subjects selected the time slots and since the conditions were not randomly assigned to those time slots, some factor other than the treatments may have produced the performance differences. For instance, it is possible that the subjects who chose the later time slots were less interested in participating in research and thus would be less involved in the study. Since the inescapable noise sessions were scheduled for the final 15 sessions, these sessions would contain less involved students. Therefore, the poorer performance of the inescapable noise subjects may be due to the fact that they were initially less involved—meaning they would not pay as close attention or try as hard as the subjects in the other groups—rather than being due to the effects of the inescapable noise.

As a second example of nonrandom assignment, let us assume that the 45 subjects had all signed up for the study and that the experimenter was to assign them to the various conditions. He alphabetizes their last names and then assigns the first 15 on the alphabetized list to the inescapable noise condition, the second 15 to the no pretreatment condition, and the last 15 to the escapable noise condition. The conditions are scheduled in a random sequence so that subjects assigned to a given condition are run at different dates and times. Now, again assume that we find that the inescapable noise group performs more poorly than the escapable noise and the no pretreatment group. Can we now state that the inescapable noise produced the poorer performance? Again, we cannot draw this conclusion since it is possible that the last names of the subjects may have been the causal agent. In other words, not only do the three sections differ systematically with respect to the independent variable, they also differ systematically with respect to the last names of the subjects. The last name differences aren't as clear as a rival cause for the performance differences as the different time slots described above, but nevertheless they are a possible cause of the differences. For instance, last names can differ in terms of the national origin of the individuals, and it is possible that members of some nationalities are more proficient at tasks involving verbal skills. Therefore, the differences could be due not to the treatment differences but rather to last name differences which might actually reflect skill differences of different national backgrounds.

In both of the above cases, there is more than one variable operating in a systematic fashion: the independent variable and the variable of time differences in the first case and the variable of national origin (last name) in the second case. The study is confounded since the variable we are interested in, the independent variable, is not under the control of the experimenter. It is not really independent since it depends upon or is related to variables connected with the subjects; i.e., the times they sign up for and their last names. It may be that in these two cases, it was the inescapable noise that produced the performance differences, but it may have also been something else related either to the subjects who chose these time slots in the first case or to the names (national origins) of the subjects in the second case. The problem is that we can't untangle these two possible causes, and thus we cannot draw a firm conclusion about the effects of inescapable noise, which, of course, was the real purpose of the study.

The utility of random assignment should now start to become clear. The factors which confounded the results in the above two cases would not be operating where subjects are assigned randomly to conditions. Chance would dictate which subjects ended up in the various conditions, and by chance, the conditions should be pretty well equated as to individual differences which might be related to the dependent variable. Thus, if the conditions are equated as to different subject variables before the treatment and still show differences on the dependent variable after treatment, the differences can be clearly attributed to the treatments; that is, to the independent variable.

Again, I have spoken of random assignment equating the experimental conditions before treatment. As I stated previously, *random assignment assures that initial differences between groups are due to chance.* In actuality, although the goal of random assignment is to have the conditions or groups begin identically, this goal is seldom achieved. Let us say that we wanted to form two conditions using random assignment and that we wanted the two conditions to start out equally on the variable of intelligence. The subjects A and B arrive for the experiment in pairs, and assignment of each member of the pair to one of the two conditions is determined by a flip of the coin. The coin is flipped, A is assigned to condition 1, and B to condition 2. Since it is quite unlikely that A and B will be the same in intelligence, the two conditions are not the same at this point. For example, if A were brighter than B and A was assigned to condition 1, condition 2 would be lower than condition 1 on the variable of intelligence. Any difference between the two conditions must be due to chance since that is the basis on which the two subjects were assigned. Each succeeding pair is then assigned in the same way—a coin flip. The greater the number of pairs assigned, the more likely it is that we will end up with an equal distribution of intelligence within each group. That is, it is unlikely that each of the coin flips will result in the brighter member of the pair being assigned to group 1 and the duller to group 2. We would expect that, in the long run, the brighter member would be assigned to group 1 half of the time, and since each group would contain half of the brighter and half of the duller members of the pairs, the groups would be quite close together in intelligence.

The key to producing the equality between the conditions lies in the phrase "the long run." With only a few people assigned to each group, we could, by chance alone, end up with higher intelligence in group A than in group B. As the number of subjects per group increases, the probability of the groups being close together also increases. Thus, although random assignment does not guarantee initial equality between conditions, it does guarantee that, as more individuals are assigned, the closer the groups will come to equality.

As I stated previously, if subjects are assigned to conditions randomly, that is, on a chance basis, any differences between conditions after assignment must be chance differences. These differences could either be quite large if only a few subjects are assigned or quite small if the conditions contain large numbers of subjects; but in each case, any differences between conditions will be due to chance and not to any systematic variable such as self-selection. The importance of these initial (pretreatment) differences being due to chance is related to drawing conclusions about the effect of the treatments. If the conditions differ after treatment, the question arises as to whether these differences are no more than the chance differences which would occur through random assignment or whether these differences are greater than those expected by chance. If we could calculate the difference we would expect by chance and then compare this to the difference which actually occurred after treatment, we could decide if the difference which we observed was greater than that expected by chance. In fact, we are able to calculate the size of the difference we can expect by chance, and thus we are able to compare our result to this. The method by which we calculate the expected difference and the logic behind this process will be fully explained in the next chapter. At this point, it is sufficient to say that we are able to figure out what would happen by chance and compare the effects of our treatments to this criterion.

VARIABILITY AND THE EXPERIMENTAL METHOD

A central theme of this text is that psychological research attempts to account for or understand variability. The experimental method can be viewed as an attempt to understand the variability in the dependent variable through the manipulation of the independent variable. Experiments are carried out to find out what independent variables affect which dependent variables. An effective independent variable causes variability in the dependent variable. Therefore, we are trying to find the sources of variability in the dependent variable; i.e., to account for that variability. For demonstration purposes, let us return to our experiment in its simplest form: the independent variable consisting of two groups (escapable and inescapable noise) and the dependent variable being correct solution of a single anagram. Assume that we have randomly assigned 50 subjects equally between the two experimental conditions. The subjects are run, and their performance on the anagram is recorded.

We find that the results show that out of the 40 subjects in the two conditions, 20 have correctly solved the anagram, and 20 have failed. Thus, there is variability in the subjects' anagram solving behavior; that is, there is variability in the dependent variable. The question at issue is whether any of that variability is related to the independent variable. If we cast the hypothetical results in tabular form as in Table 5–2, we can gain a clearer picture of the variability.

First of all, if we examine the columns of the table, we see that of the 20 subjects who received escapable noise, 15 solved the anagram while 5 failed it. Of the 20 subjects who received inescapable noise, only 5 solved the anagram while 15 failed to solve it. Since the subjects were randomly assigned to the two conditions, it can be shown that by chance alone we could expect 10 from each section to have solved the anagram. A basic law of chance states that the probability of the joint occurrence of two independent events is the product of their separate probabilities. One event is being in a particular condition. The second event is solving the anagram. Since half of all of the students were in the escapable noise condition, the probability that a student would be in that condition was .5.

TABLE 5–2
Hypothetical cross tabulation of the results showing the relationship between escapability and success-failure in anagram solution

Anagram Performance	Escapable Noise	Inescapable Noise	Total
Success	15	5	20
Failure	5	15	20
Total	20	20	40

This, of course, was controlled at the beginning of the experiment by randomly assigning the subjects equally to the two conditions. Since half of all of the subjects solved the anagram, the probability that a subject would solve it was also .5. Thus, according to the above law, the probability that a subject would both be in the escapable noise condition and also solve the anagram is the product of the probabilities of the two separate events: .5 × .5, or .25. Since there are 40 subjects, we would expect that 25 percent, or 10 of them, would be in the escapable noise condition and solve the anagram. This same logic would apply to the inescapable noise condition, and we would expect 25 percent, or 10 subjects, from this condition to solve the anagram. The actual results as depicted in the table show that more subjects from the escapable noise condition and fewer subjects from the inescapable noise condition solved the anagram than would be expected by chance.

Thus there is a relationship between the dependent variable of anagram-solving behavior and the independent variable of escapable-inescapable noise. The relationship is not perfect since there are five subjects from the escapable noise condition who did not solve the anagram and five subjects from the inescapable noise condition who did solve the anagram. This variability within each condition cannot be accounted for by the independent variable because within each condition all subjects received the same condition of the independent variable. This *variability within the conditions is unsystematic or error variability*. It is error in the sense of ignorance in that we don't know what produced the variability within the conditions. On the other hand, the *variability between conditions in correct solutions is systematic variability* since it is related to the different treatments.

In the above situation, the dependent variable had only two levels—it was simply a dichotomy—solved or failed to solve the anagram. If the dependent variable had been more complex—for example, total number of anagrams solved out of 10 attempted—we would not be able to calculate so easily what would be expected by chance. Even so, the basic logic would be the same. There would be variability within each group in number of anagrams solved, and there would be variability between the groups shown in the average number of anagrams solved by each of the two groups. Again, the variability within the group would reflect error or unsystematic variability, while the difference between the means of the two groups would reflect variability which is systematic; that is, variability related to the independent variable.

In order to demonstrate systematic and error variability in this more complex situation, let us again assume that 20 subjects were randomly assigned to the escapable noise and 20 subjects were assigned to the inescapable noise condition. Each subject responded, after treatment, to 10 anagrams. The hypothetical results are shown in Table 5–3.

We see that within the escapable noise condition, the subjects vary in performance with six subjects solving all 10 anagrams, eight solving 9,

TABLE 5–3
Hypothetical relationship between escapability and number of anagrams solved

	Escapable Noise	Inescapable Noise
	8	5
	10	6
	9	4
	10	4
	9	4
	9	6
	10	6
	9	4
	8	5
	9	5
	10	6
	8	5
	10	6
	8	5
	9	4
	8	5
	9	5
	8	4
	10	6
	9	5
Mean	9.0	5.0

and six subjects solving 8 anagrams. There is also variability in perform-ace within the inescapable noise condition with six subjects solving six anagrams, eight solving five, and six subjects solving four anagrams. The average scores in the escapable and inescapable noise conditions are 9.0 and 5.0, respectively. The scores within each group are quite close to each other reflecting small error variability, while the group means are quite far apart reflecting comparatively large systematic variability. The variability between the means of the groups is a direct function of the manipulation. It reflects the fact that the treatments have moved the groups apart. In other words, the variability between the group means is variability we have created through the manipulation. In order to decide whether this created variability is large enough to be considered not due to chance, we need to compare it against a criterion of some sort. This criterion is the variability within the conditions. If the variability between the group means is greater than the within-group variability, that is, greater than would be expected by chance, we can conclude that the independent variable had an effect. This is an important concept, comparing the between- to the within-groups variability, and we shall examine it more closely at a later point in the text.

A CLOSER LOOK AT INDEPENDENT AND DEPENDENT VARIABLES

Many studies in psychology deal with theoretical variables called con-structs. These theoretical variables are not defined in terms of concrete entities or operations; they are abstractions. Operational definitions map abstract constructs into the world of concrete objects and behaviors. Thus, in manipulating a particular set of conditions, a researcher is operationalizing a conceptual independent variable by mapping it into a set of concrete operations. If, for example, one wanted to see the effects of increasing motivation on performance, motivation would need to be manipulated and performance then assessed. The problem is that both motivation and performance are abstractions. Since evidence about their relationship is gathered in the real world by manipulating concrete objects and observing concrete behavior, these theoretical constructs need to be defined in terms of concrete entities or operations.

One could deprive organisms of food for different amounts of time, expose organisms to differing amounts of shock or noise, or offer different inducements (rewards). All of these treatments would operationalize the abstract theoretical construct of motivation, and thus there is a choice of possible treatments which will represent a theoretical construct. Just as motivation can be operationally defined in various ways, the dependent variable of performance is also open to various definitions. Performance could be operationalized as number of correct choices in a maze, speed of escape from aversive stimulation, or number of errors found on a proofreading task, depending on the type of study and organism employed. Motivation and performance are conceptual independent and dependent variables, whereas level of shock and speed of escape would be the operational variables employed to represent the conceptual variables.

As a second example of this notion, consider again the study on controllability. As I stated previously, this study is representative of many carried out to investigate the theory of learned helplessness. Simply stated, the theory posits that organisms who are exposed to uncontrollable events form a generalized perception of uncontrollability and then behave in a helpless manner. More specifically, organisms exposed to situations where reinforcement is not contingent upon their responses show performance decrements in subsequent situations where reinforcement is contingent on their responses. In order to test this theory, one would need to manipulate the contingency of reinforcement in one situation and then examine performance in a second situation. The researchers decided to manipulate contingency through the use of escapable and inescapable noise. They could have employed other stimuli such as shock, or they could have used feedback on a test in the form of actual success and failure versus random success and failure as their representations of contingency and noncontingency—the independent variable. Thus, for any theoretical independent variable, there are a number of operations which can be used to define it.

The second abstraction in the theory is performance. In our example, we used anagram solution, and even here we saw that anagram solution can take different forms such as number correct or time taken to solve. Other measures could also have been employed such as a second escape

TABLE 5–4
Relationships among conceptual and operational independent and dependent variables

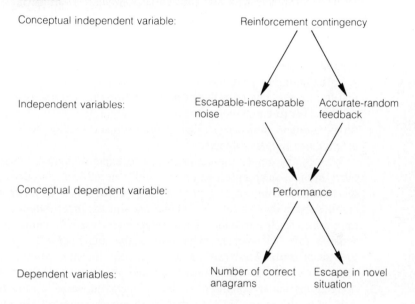

Conceptual independent variable: Reinforcement contingency

Independent variables: Escapable-inescapable   Accurate-random
noise   feedback

Conceptual dependent variable: Performance

Dependent variables: Number of correct   Escape in novel
anagrams   situation

situation or solving problems. Performance is a conceptual variable that is defined in a particular study by a specific set of operations. Table 5–4 depicts the relationships between the conceptual variables and their operations.

The point is that there is usually not a single operation which fully defines a theoretical concept, but rather a theoretical construct can be defined by any of a series of operations. Thus, there is always the question of adequately representing the independent and dependent variables through the operations chosen by the researcher. In other words, in most studies, the researcher will have to decide which operations would best define the conceptual independent and dependent variables. This problem of definition and the adequacy of operational definitions is the problem of construct validity. It is a complicated issue which we will try to illuminate at a later point in the text.

AN ALTERNATIVE EXPERIMENTAL APPROACH

This chapter has focused on the experimental paradigm as one in which subjects are randomly assigned to two or more conditions. In other words, the basis of the approach is that groups are equated through random assignment before a treatment is instated, and then the groups are compared on a dependent variable following the treatment. If the groups perform differently, on the average, this is taken as causal evidence of the effects of the different conditions. This process of comparing group performances is the typical manner in which experimental evidence is gathered, but it is not the only way. An alternative exists to the use of groups of subjects who are differentially treated. That alternative is the *single subject* approach to experimental research.

The single subject and the random groups design differ not only in their methods, as we shall see, but also in the philosophical principles on which they are based. The modern impetus for the single subject approach to research has come from the original and innovative work of B. F. Skinner and the experimenters in the operant conditioning laboratories who have followed his research model. Although much of their research has focused on nonhuman subjects, similar single subject methodology has been extended to human subjects.

What is the single subject approach to experimentation? It is, as the label implies, an approach employing only one subject who serves in all of the treatment conditions employed in the experiment. In other words, a single subject receives all of the conditions of the independent variable as opposed to each condition of the independent variable being given to a separate group of subjects. The basis of the single subject experiment is the use of *intrasubject replication.* In random groups experiments, each group is exposed to at most only a few and often only a single presentation of their particular condition of the independent variable, and therefore only a one-time response to that exposure is collected. In the single subject design, a subject is exposed not only to all conditions of the independent variable, but within each condition to a large number of trials. Therefore, the subject responds over and over to the same stimulus condition providing for replication of behavior under each condition.

The replication of responses under a given condition allows for a *stable* pattern of behavior to emerge and consequently an opportunity to observe changes in this pattern when a second condition of the independent variable is presented. The emphasis here is on the term *stable,* which refers to behavior that is not random but rather has either leveled out or has achieved a definite and unvarying pattern. To take an everyday example, consider a situation where you observe your dormitory roommate over a four-week period. You find that your roommate's behavior quickly stabilizes into a definite pattern of rising at 7:30 A.M., showering, eating breakfast in the cafeteria, and then leaving for a 9:00 A.M. class. There is little deviation from this pattern, except on weekends, in that the pattern and times for each event show little variation. If, after four weeks, your roommate breaks this pattern by sleeping later and omitting the shower and breakfast, you probably would quickly perceive this change in behavior. In fact, you would generally ask what had caused this change. In other words, you may search for an event that changed the stable pattern. Let us say that, after questioning your roommate, you discovered that he had begun to go out drinking in the evenings and that this activity had started just before the change in his morning behavior pattern. Although at this point, you could not unequivocally determine whether or not the nighttime drinking produced the change, you certainly could detect a change, and you would look for a causal event.

Suppose, on the other hand, that the behavior of your roommate in the first four weeks had not stabilized. Suppose that the rising times had varied and that sometimes he had showered and eaten breakfast and that at other times he had not done so, or that he had done one and not the other. Since no established or stable pattern of behavior had occurred, a change could not be detected. In both cases, he may have begun to go out drinking at night, but in the second case, the effects of his nighttime activities could not be detected, at least not through an observation of his morning behavior pattern. The point here is that stabilized behavior becomes an effective indicator of some intervening or impinging event when it changes from one pattern or level to another.

In the case of your roommate, the event must be guessed at through questioning and reconstruction of the events occurring over time. But what if the scenario had been very different? Suppose that you had observed your roommate's stable morning behavior and had been put off by its stable, or to you, rather compulsive nature. You decide to see if you can change this morning ritual by taking him out drinking in the evening. In other words, you decide to intervene in order to change the behavior. After a few nights on the town, any change in the morning behavior pattern should be easy to detect. If the change does occur, you would not need to search for the event that produced the change. Since you had intervened to produce the change, you would be quite sure that your intervention was the causal agent.

If, as soon as the morning behavior pattern changed, you ceased the nighttime activities, concluding that they had changed the behavior pattern, you could be drawing a false conclusion. A single deviation from even an established pattern could be a fluke and not due to your intervention. Therefore, you should keep up your intervention, allowing for a replication of the deviation from the sleeping late behavior. In other words, the new behavior in the presence of the intervention should stabilize. let us suppose this sequence happens: You observe the stable morning routine, intervene with the nighttime treatment, and observe a behavioral change that stabilizes. Now to ensure that your treatment is causing the change from the compulsive morning behavior to the sleeping late behavior, you remove your treatment. In other words, you cease the nighttime activities with your roommate and continue to observe his behavior. If the compulsive behavior returns and stabilizes when your treatment is removed, this is even more powerful evidence for the effects of the treatment.

Treatment Removal

In practice, the single subject approach usually takes the above sequence one step further and reintroduces the treatment a second time. This process of achieving a stable baseline, introducing the treatment and seeing the behavior change and stabilize at a new level, removing the treatment and seeing the behavior revert to the original level, and then reintroducing the treatment and seeing the behavior again change, is called an ABAB design. In this design, the A would indicate the periods where the treatment is absent while the Bs would indicate the periods where the treatment is present. There are some situations in which the initial period is a treatment rather than a baseline period. In this design, the treatment is initiated immediately and continued until a stable rate of behavior occurs. It is then removed until a change in behavior to a stable rate occurs, and finally the treatment is reinstated until the behavior returns to the stable level observed during the initial period. This treatment instatement, removal, and reinstatement is called a BAB design. BAB designs are often employed in situations where it is imperative that the treatment begin immediately. In these cases, there is also the problem of removing the treatment and returning the behavior to baseline. A second situation in which BAB designs are used concerns cases where the behavior does not exist before treatment begins. In other words, if the rate of behavior before treatment is close to zero, there is no sense gathering baseline data. Rather, one would simply begin the study with the instatement of the treatment.

As an example of an actual single subject design, consider a study by Azrin and Lindsley (1956) dealing with the reinforcement of cooperative behavior in children. The basic question the study attempted to answer was whether a reinforcing stimulus would act so as to develop and maintain cooperation in children. In this experiment, two children were seated across a table from one another and separated by a wire mesh screen. On the table in front of each child were three holes and a stylus or metal-tipped stick connected to an electrical wire. The children were first told to put the stylus into each of the holes. They were then told that some jelly beans would drop into the cup between the two children. The experimenter then left the room telling them that they could play any game they wished to play. If the children both placed their styli in opposite holes within 4 seconds of each other, a red light came on, and a single jelly bean fell into the cup.

The first period, a reinforcement period, was carried on for 15 minutes with each cooperative response being reinforced by a jelly bean. If, at the end of this period, a steady rate of cooperation was not achieved, reinforcement was continued until five minutes of steady cooperative responsing occurred. At this point, the second or *extinction* period ensued. Cooperative responses were not reinforced for 15 minutes and until a steady response rate occurred for five minutes. The final period was a reinstatement of reinforcement for cooperative responses until a stable rate of cooperation occurred for three minutes. There were 10 pairs of children who were run in this BAB design.

A comparison of the median number of cooperative responses occurring during the first three minutes of period 1 and the final three minutes of each of the periods shows a clear effect of reinforcement upon cooperation:

First three minutes initial reinforcement period: 5.5
Final three minutes initial reinforcement period: 17.5
Final three minutes extinction period: 1.5
Final three minutes second reinforcement period: 17.5

Thus, one can see that cooperation is low to begin with but developed by the end of the first reinforcement period. By the end of the extinction period, the removal of reinforcement reduced cooperation to the initial level, and its reinstatement in period 3 again raises the cooperative behavior to the level observed at the end of the first period. The ability to gain stable response rates with the instatement of the treatment (reinforcement), change that rate to a stable value with the removal of the treatment (extinction), and to again change the response rate when the treatment is reintroduced is strong causal evidence for the effect of the treatment.

Multiple-baseline

A second approach to single subject research involves the use of *multiple-baselines*. In these designs, baseline data are gathered on two or more behaviors, treatment designed to change only one of the behaviors is instated, and the behavior rates after intervention are compared. If the targeted behavior changes after treatment but the nontreated behavior remains at baseline, this is taken as evidence for the effectiveness of the treatment. At this point, the treatment is applied to the other behavior, and if this second behavior now also changes, this strengthens the judgment of the effectiveness of the treatment. Multiple baselines can be used in situations where behavior once changed cannot be reversed.

A single subject case study by Alford, Webster, and Sanders (1980) will serve to illustrate the multiple-baseline approach. In this study, the authors applied covert aversion conditioning procedures to two deviant sexual behaviors: obscene phone calling and exhibitionism. Their subject or patient was a 21-year-old married man with a satisfactory marital relationship who engaged in both obscene phone calling and exhibitionism. Their general approach was to gather a baseline assessment of physiological arousal and self-ratings of sexual urges, then to institute aversive conditioning for obscene phone calling and again assess the behaviors, and finally to initiate aversive conditioning for exhibitionism along with that for obscene phone calling and again assess the behaviors.

The specific procedure involved having the patient listen to different audiotapes depicting obscene phone calls, exhibitionism, and nondeviant sexual behavior. These tapes were played during the baseline phase, and assessments of physiological arousal in the form of penile erection were

gathered. The first treatment phase of 10 sessions consisted of presentation of audiotapes depicting scenes of obscene phone calling which were
aversive in nature in that nausea, suffocation, or arrest by the police were
involved in the scenes. Assessments were taken after the 5th and 10th
sessions. For the next 10 sessions, the aversive phone calling scenes were
continued, and the aversive exhibitionism audiotape scenes were also
added. Again, the behavioral assessments were gathered after the 5th and
10th sessions. It should be emphasized that at each assessment point the
subjects were measured in the presence of all three types of audiotapes
(obscene phone calling, exhibitionism, and nondeviant sexual behavior).
It should also be noted that the aversive tapes were similar but not
identical to the tapes used for the assessment. Following the final treatment, the patient was again assessed two times at three-day intervals in
order to see if the treatment generalized beyond the actual treatment
phase.

The results for penile erection are shown in Figure 5–1. In this presentation, the responses to the different scenes have been averaged, and only
the last assessment at each phase is shown. The first vertical double-
arrowed line indicates the point at which the aversive conditioning for the
obscene phone calling occurred, and the second double-arrowed vertical
line represents the occurrence of the aversive conditioning for exhibi-

FIGURE 5–1
Results of single subject multiple-baseline study

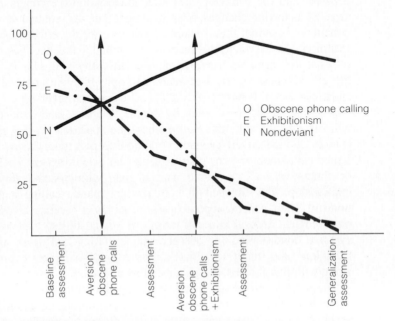

tionism being added. The large segmented line (O) reflects the percent of full penile erection in the presence of the obscene phone call audiotape scenes. The small segmented line (E) and the solid line (N) represent the same behavior in the presence of the exhibitionist and nondeviant audiotape scenes, respectively. The first point of each line represents baseline assessment, the second point represents the assessment after the aversive conditioning for obscene phone calls, the third point represents the assessment the aversive conditioning for exhibitionism, and the final point represents the assessment after treatment has ceased—a generalization assessment.

First of all, if one follows the O line, a large drop in response (penile erection) occurs after the first treatment, and a continued drop occurs following the second treatment. Keep in mind, that the second treatment consists of aversive conditioning for both obscene phone calling and exhibitionism. Examination of the E line also shows a drop from baseline to post-first treatment but a smaller one than that for the O line. The E line then shows a large drop from point 2 to point 3 after the second treatment has been implemented. Thus, the aversive conditioning for obscene phone calling lowered arousal for that behavior and also, to some extent, lowered the arousal for exhibitionism. This is not an unusual situation if the targeted behaviors have some interdependence. Apparently, obscene phone calling and exhibitionism were interdependent, at least for this subject.

The strength of a multiple baseline study lies in the change in targeted behavior and a lack of change in a nontargeted behavior. Since responsiveness to both obscene phone calling and exhibitionism changed as a function of the aversive conditioning of obscene phone calling (although the E line showed less change), the clarity of the results is affected. These authors did include a third behavior which was never directly treated in the form of responsiveness to nondeviant scenes. An examination of the N line shows that neither treatment affected responsiveness to nondeviant scenes. In a sense, this is the pure control which shows the clear effects of the treatment on the targeted behaviors.

The self-reported sexual urges data supported the findings for physiological arousal in that the pattern of results for the two measures was quite similar. In other words, sexual urge dropped strongly from baseline for obscene phone call scenes and slightly for exhibitionist scenes after the first treatment, and both continued to decline after the second treatment. On the other hand, sexual urges for the nondeviant scenes continued at a high level throughout the study. Thus, employing two different response measures, this multiple baseline study showed clear evidence of the effectiveness of the aversive conditioning treatment.

Another variation of the multiple baseline procedure is to employ different subjects rather than different variables. In this approach, two or more subjects are observed until a stable baseline is reached for each subject. The treatment is then applied to only one of the subjects. At this point, the treated subject shows behavioral changes while the untreated subject remains at baseline. The treatment is then applied to the previously untreated subjects whose behavior should now also change as a function of the treatment. Thus one subject, the initially untreated subject, acts as a control for the other, the initially treated subject. Usually, these single subject designs employ more than one subject in order to show that the treatment replicates across different subjects; that is, to see if the same pattern of results occurs. Thus, many studies will apply the treatment to two or three subjects, each of whom should show the same effects. In fact, in the experimental analysis of behavior (single subject) approach, the effects which are demonstrated for a single subject must then be replicable for every other subject in the experiment. This is a highly stringent criterion. In the experimental analysis of behavior approach, a change in the independent variable must produce a change in the behavior of every subject who has experienced the change.

GROUP VERSUS SINGLE SUBJECT DESIGNS

In most psychological experiments, every subject does not have to respond to the treatment. Rather, the group averages have to differ in order to conclude that the treatment was effective. Even though some subjects in the experimental group may show no change at all and some in the control group may change to some extent, the treatment would be judged effective if the mean of the experimental group was significantly greater than that of the control group. This usual practice of averaging results over groups of subjects undergoing a treatment has been criticized by the single subject researchers (Sidman, 1960). They argue that if the means of the groups differ, this difference usually only accounts for a portion of the individual differences (variance) among subjects, since within each of the groups, subjects still differ from one another. In other words, in groups experiments, only a portion of the variance, that reflected by the difference between the group means, is systematic, while a great deal of the variance, that within each group, remains unsystematic or error. By employing this method, they argue, group experiments result in the acceptance of a substantial degree of ignorance, since error variance is always variance due to unknown or unaccounted-for sources. Since each subject in a single subject design must show the effects from implementation of the treatment and its removal, there is no error in the sense that one subject responds to the manipulation while another subject does not.

There are some disadvantages or at least some criticisms of the single subject approach. First of all, its use depends directly upon repeated responding by the subject in each phase of the experiment. Since much of the work employing this approach was carried out with nonhuman subjects (pigeons, rats, etc.) in a highly restricted and controlled environment (the operant chamber or Skinner Box), gathering multiple responding was no problem. The responses of the subjects were narrowly defined in terms of rate of key pecking or bar pressing and fairly easily assessed. The responses of human subjects are often much more difficult to assess in a narrow manner, and many problems do not lend themselves to situations where repeated responding is possible. Thus, much of the single subject research with human subjects has focused upon clearly defined overt behaviors such as the cooperative behavior described in the Azrin study and the penile erection described in the case of the sexual deviant.

A second problem is that the patterns of behavior needed to justify a causal judgment of the effectiveness of the treatment are not always as clear as one would wish. In other words, the perfect outcome of the ABAB design is not always achieved. Subjects do not always reach a very stable baseline but rather show some fluctuation from trial to trial. This means that a change in behavior after the treatment is initiated is not always a clear departure from baseline. Rather it is open to the interpretation that it is only another random fluctuation in behavior. Since statistical criteria are not employed to judge the effectiveness of a treatment, a change in behavior from a somewhat unstable baseline could be due to a chance fluctuation but cannot be evaluated as to whether or not it is due to chance. Thus, as with all research techniques, there are advantages and disadvantages to employing a single subject approach. Some research problems lend themselves quite well to this approach, while others are more suitable for between group experiments.

Chapter 6

The Results of
a Study—Statistics I

Once a study has been planned and executed, the researcher is left with the task of deciding what has been found. In both correlational and experimental studies, the data are summarized into indices which reflect the results of the studies. These indices may be correlation coefficients, means, variances, or frequencies depending upon the type of study, the level of measurement employed, and the question which was investigated in the study.

The subjects in a study who generate the data upon which these indices are computed are usually simply representatives of a larger group in which the researcher is interested. The subjects in the study are a sample or subgroup of a larger population. In that sense, they are only a bridge to the larger group of interest. Their results are relevant only to the extent that they reliably reflect something about the population which they represent. The question of how reliably the results of a study reflect something beyond the subjects who actually generated those results is answered through the process of statistical inference.

THE ROLE OF CHANCE?

In order to understand how researchers make inferences from samples to populations, we need to first understand the concept of chance effects. Because samples, by definition, are subsets of the population and therefore do not contain all of the members of the population, the indices calculated upon them will not be identical to those calculated upon the whole population. For example, the correlation coefficient between two variables calculated on a sample will not be identical to the correlation coefficient calculated upon the whole population from which that sample is drawn. If we calculate the mean of a variable for a sample, that sample mean will not be identical to the population mean. If the members of the sample are drawn randomly from the population, then the fact that the correlation or mean of the sample does not exactly equal the correlation or mean of the population is a chance occurrence. In other words, sample values, termed *statistics,* will differ from population values, which are termed *parameters,* by chance alone.

If we could figure out how much difference between sample and population values would be expected by chance, we could decide whether or not any particular sample value deviated from a population value by chance or whether its deviation was so great that it would not be expected by chance. If the deviation was much greater then we would expect by chance, we could possibly conclude that chance did not produce this deviation. Rather, it was produced by something systematic. We would conclude that this sample must have come from some other population.

In order to demonstrate, let us consider a familiar event—a poker game. Although there is a great deal of skill involved in playing poker, the cards are distributed to the players on a chance basis; that is, the deck is well shuffled and the cards are dealt in order guaranteeing, under normal circumstances, that the cards drawn by the players are chance arrangements. Thus, we have a situation where good or bad hands are purely a result of chance.

Now, providing me with some pedagogic license, picture the following scene. The hero in this drama sits down to his weekly poker game with three friends and a stranger. The game is five card, no draw, nothing wild poker. The deck is shuffled, and each of the five players draws a card to see who will deal the first hand of poker. The stranger picks the highest card and wins the right to deal first. He then shuffles the cards and deals five cards to each of the players including himself. The betting starts and goes up extremely high until only the stranger and our hero are left in a head-to-head contest. Everything is now in the pot: money, deed to the house, keys to the car, and even the pet dog. This hand of poker has obviously become extremely important. Our hero has a full house, three kings and a pair of jacks and, feeling quite confident, calls and lays down his hand. The stranger then lays down his hand revealing ace, king, queen, jack, 10 of spades—a royal flush.

The stranger scoops up his winnings (money, house deed, car keys, and the pet sheepdog) and says that he is leaving. Our hero, tears in his eyes, having lost everything, turns to his friends and asks plaintively, "What should I do?" What should he do? Gambling carries with it risks of losing. If one does not want to lose, then one shouldn't gamble. Our hero was willing to risk losing, but something is now bothering him. It is not that he is a poor loser, unwilling to take the consequences of his bad luck, but rather he has doubts about whether or not bad luck was responsible for his loss. He strongly suspects that the stranger cheated, and he does not want to lose everything under dishonest conditions.

But why does he suspect cheating? He saw nothing dishonest happening. He has lost before, although never this much, but he has not suspected cheating. It is the hand which beat him that has produced the suspicion. Having played the game a great deal, he knows that the probability of being dealt a royal flush in spades from an honest deck is .0000004—a pretty rare event (it happens four times in every 10,000,000 hands). Putting this together with the facts that the winner was the dealer of the hand and is also a stranger has produced the feeling in our hero that he was cheated. It could be chance—royal flushes do occur—but the probability is so low and the circumstances so unusual that he rejects the idea that chance brought the hand to his opponent.

Therefore, what does he do? Well, he can either ask the stranger if he was cheating or he can tell the stranger directly that he was cheating and should put back the winnings. The stranger, of course, will deny that he was cheating. If he wasn't cheating, that is, if he won honestly, he will state that he didn't cheat. On the other hand, if he did cheat, he surely wouldn't admit it. Anyone who would cheat at cards would feel no guilt about lying about his deed. Our hero then is in a bind. He has no direct evidence of cheating, the stranger will not admit to cheating, and yet, due to the rarity of the event, he firmly believes that he was cheated.

Again let me stress that our hero is an ethical person. He would not ask for his belongings to be given back if he was not cheated, even though he lost everything. He is not just a sore loser, but he does demand a fair shake. What should he now do?

Let us say that he confronts the stranger, the stranger resists, and our hero physically subdues him and takes back the money. How can he know definitively that he has acted correctly? The answer is that he cannot. If the stranger did not cheat but rather was simply lucky, our hero has committed a grave injustice. He has accused an honest man of cheating, assaulted him, and taken from the man what is rightfully his. On the other hand, if the stranger did cheat, our hero acted correctly in giving the man what he deserved. Unfortunately, he does not know whether he made an error or acted correctly. If he had allowed the stranger to leave, he would be in the same bind. If the stranger had cheated, our hero would have lost everything unfairly, but if the stranger had played honestly, he would have acted correctly in allowing him to leave. Again, our hero would not know which had occurred—an error or a correct decision.

I have drawn this little example rather extremely and probably some-what absurdly in that: *(a)* the consequences were enormous—the loss of everything, *(b)* the situation was highly constricted—one hand of five cards and a complete stranger who deals the cards, and *(c)* the stranger had a spade royal flush. If only two or three dollars were in the pot, the winner would have been someone our hero knew well, had played with previously, and who had an honest history at the game, and if the winning hand would have been less rare, the decision to forcibly stop the stranger would not be an appropriate one. The gravity of the decision to stop the person forcibly or even to accuse him of cheating required extreme circumstances, including an extremely low probability of the event occurring by chance. If, for example, the stranger's hand had been a flush (any five cards of the same suit), the probability of this happening by chance would have been .002 rather than the probability of .0000004 for the royal flush. Approximately two chances in a thousand would not be extreme or rare enough to conclude that it was cheating that had produced the hand. Thus, the judgment that something other than chance was operating to produce the event (the winning hand), depended on (1) the probability of the event occurring by chance, (2) the consequences involved in the situation, and (3) the circumstances under which the event occurred.

This same logic applies to research situations. A study is carried out which yields certain results. These results could be simply chance findings, or they could be due to something systematic. Just as our hero had to decide whether or not the winning hand was a chance occurrence, a researcher must decide whether or not the result of a study is a chance occurrence. Our hero had to calculate the probability of the winning hand occurring by chance, examine the circumstances under which the hand occurred, and judge the consequences of deciding that the hand was or was not due to chance. A researcher also must calculate the probability of a given result occurring by chance, examine the conditions which were operating when the result occurred, and then judge the consequences of deciding that the result was either a chance finding or due to something systematic.

WHAT IS A RARE EVENT BY CHANCE?

In the case of the poker game, a spade high royal flush with a probability of .0000004 was considered rare enough to decide to stop the stranger, whereas a mere flush with a probability of .002 was not a rare enough event to take such a serious course of action. The rarity of the two events as differential criteria for the decisions was *based upon the gravity of the consequences of the decisions*. In research situations, the consequences of decisions are also important in determining how rare an event must be in order to decide whether or not it was due to chance. For instance, in some types of medical research, only a very rare result by chance would be considered evidence of a real effect since the consequences of deciding something was not chance might involve human lives.

As an example, let us consider another fictitious situation. Let us say that a researcher has developed a drug that is supposed to cure lung cancer. The research is at its final stages with the drug to be tested on a human population before being made available on the open market. The researcher decided to test it at a local medical center with 12 patients diagnosed as having lung cancer. He randomly assigns six of the patients to the drug group and six to a placebo group. A placebo is a substance which is known to have none of the intended effects. Neither the patients nor the nurses who administer the substances know whether or not they are getting or giving the placebo or the drug. This is a double blind technique which ensures that effects are due to the drug and not to extraneous factors. The substances are given four times daily for 30 days. At the end of this time, all of the patients in the study are thoroughly tested for their level of lung cancer.

The researcher has decided that if the drug group has an average level of cancer that is lower than the placebo group by an amount which could occur by chance only one time in a hundred, she will decide the drug works as a cancer cure. That is, she will decide that it was not chance that produced the difference since this could only have happened with a probability of .01 but that the difference was produced by the drug.

Was .01 a rare enough probability? Well, let's see what the consequences might be. If the drug really does work, that is, if she did not get the one in a hundred chance event, then the drug will help a great many people who suffer from lung cancer. All well and good. But what if she did get the one in a hundred shot; that is, what if the difference between the two groups was just chance and the drug actually had no effect? How could this happen—how could she have gotten a difference this large when the drug did not work? The answer is "by bad luck." For example, when she randomly assigned the patients to the two groups (drug and placebo), those patients, who were in better physical shape on some variable which was related to the progress of the disease ended up in the drug group in greater numbers than they ended up in the placebo group. This chance assignment would, of course, mean that the drug group, having patients with better prognoses, would show better results at the end of the 30-day test period. In fact, let us assume that the drug has no effect and that she found a chance occurrence. The drug is placed on the market. Let us further assume that, although it has no effect on cancer, it also does no harm to the body—it just does nothing.

Does the researcher have a problem? People will take the drug which does no good but also does no harm. Her mistake doesn't seem too serious. She took a one in a hundred chance and lost, but the consequences do not seem too bad—or are they? Well, the consequences will not only be bad; they will be disastrous. All of those people who take the drug in order to cure their lung cancer will probably give up other medical treatments. Since surgery is dangerous and radiation and chemotherapy are highly noxious, most of those people who would have undergone these treatments will forego them for this painless, supposedly "effective" drug. Most of these people will probably die without the other treatments. Thus, what seemed like an incorrect decision which had only minor consequences turns out to be one which has dire consequences.

What should the researcher have done in order to avoid making an incorrect decision when that decision is so serious? She should have accepted only results which were very rare by chance. A probability of .01 by chance is much too dangerous when the circumstances are that the drug will be marketed and people will die if it is not effective. This is analogous to accepting the flush, with a probability by chance of .002, as evidence of cheating, acting upon this, and taking the money back by force. Accusing someone of cheating when they didn't is a serious mistake, and taking their money by force when they won it honestly is robbery. On the other hand, if the drug would not be marketed after this test but subjected to a number of other tests before being marketed, then a .01 probability would have been more reasonable. The consequences of this one test would not have been nearly as great. Thus, the choice of a probability level is a complex matter depending upon the type of research and the implications of an incorrect decision.

So far, we have discussed only the cases of deciding an event was not due to chance when, in fact, it was chance that produced the results. In the case of the card game, a man was incorrectly accused of cheating, and in the case of the cancer drug, people died from the incorrect decision. But what of the situation where it is not chance that produces an effect, but the researcher concludes that it was a chance result. For example, what if the stranger had cheated with a spade flush and our hero had decided that this hand was due to chance? Or what if the drug had really worked, but the researcher had decided that it was chance that produced the difference in cancer levels? In the first case, our hero would have lost everything illegitimately, and in the second case, a cure for cancer would have been overlooked. Both of these outcomes would be due to the incorrect decisions that chance produced the result, and in both cases, the consequences would be quite drastic.

Thus, there are two types of incorrect decisions; that is, there are two types of errors that can occur. The first type, called a *Type I error, is a decision that a result is not due to chance when in fact it is chance that produced the result.* The second type, termed a *Type II error, is a decision that a result is due to chance when in fact the result has been produced by something systematic.* How are these two types of error related, and how do we guard against each of them? In order to answer these questions, we need to delve into the theory of statistical inference. The basis of this theory is the concept of the sampling distribution.

SAMPLING DISTRIBUTIONS

A sampling distribution is a distribution of random sample statistics. What does this definition mean? First, *a statistic is any index such as a mean, a variance, or a correlation coefficient calculated on a sample.* Second, the samples upon which these values are calculated are drawn randomly from a population. Thus, each sample statistic can be thought of as an estimate of that same index in the whole population. *The value or index in the population is called the population parameter.* Third, the term distribution implies that there are a number of these samples which have been calculated. That is, there are a number of samples which have been taken randomly from the population and a statistic calculated upon each of them. Since samples can be of different sizes, each sample size has its own sampling distribution. Thus, there are sampling distributions of the mean, sampling distributions of the variance, sampling distributions of the correlation coefficient, and sampling distributions of any other index or statistic. Further, *each statistic has as many different sampling distributions as there are different possible sample sizes.*

In order to demonstrate the concept of a sampling distribution in a more concrete manner, let us take the sampling distribution of the mean as an example. First, assume that there is a population for some variable of interest, such as attitude toward abortion, and that everyone in the population has a score on this variable. Let us further assume that these scores run from 1, indicating a strongly anti-abortion attitude, to 5, indicating a strongly favorable attitude toward abortion. If we added up all of these scores in the population and divided this sum by the number of people in the population, we would have the population mean, a parameter. Now we decide to sample from that population samples of size three. We put all of the scores in the population in a large drum, spin the drum, and draw out three of the scores. We then add up the three scores and divide the sum by three, giving us the mean of this first sample, a statistic.

We replace the three numbers, spin the drum, and draw out three more numbers. We then find the mean of this second sample. This same sequence of events is repeated thousands of time: spinning the drum, drawing three numbers, calculating the mean, and replacing the three numbers in the drum. There will be thousands of sample means calculated in this process. If we arranged these means from the highest to the lowest in value and counted the frequency with which each appeared, we would have a distribution of the means of sample size three drawn randomly from this population. We would have a sampling distribution of the mean. If we had decided to draw samples of a different size (e.g., 10), we would have produced another sampling distribution. The two sampling distributions would be alike in certain respects and would differ in certain ways.

They would be alike in that both distributions would have the same mean. In other words, if we went to the first sampling distribution where each sample mean was based upon three numbers, added up all of those sample means, and divided by the number of sample means, and then went to the second sampling distribution where each sample mean was based upon 10 cases and carried out the same procedure, the means of the two sampling distributions would be identical. Not only would the means of the two sampling distributions be the same, but they would also be identical to the mean of the population from which the samples were drawn. Sampling distributions of the mean based upon different size samples then are alike in that they have the same means, the mean of the population. On the other hand, sampling distributions based upon different size samples differ with respect to their variability. In the above example, the sampling distribution of the mean based upon samples of size 3 will be more variable than its counterpart based upon samples of size 10. Sampling distributions based upon larger-size samples are less variable than those based on smaller samples.

Sample Size

In order to demonstrate this phenomenon, let us consider two extreme situations: *(a)* a sampling distribution based upon samples of size 1 and *(b)* a sampling distribution based upon the size of the population. Let us take the case of sample size 1 first. As described previously, in order to actually produce a sampling distribution, we could put all of the values or scores in the population in a drum, spin the drum, draw out samples of a given size, compute statistics upon these samples, replace the scores in the drum, and repeat this procedure a large number of times. In the case of sample size 1, we would spin the drum and remove one score. If we were trying to estimate a population mean, that score would be our sample statistic. We would replace the score, spin the drum again, and draw out a second score, continuing this procedure hundreds of thousands of times. When we were finished we would have produced a sampling distribution of the mean based upon sample size 1. What would this distribution look like? Well, since the chances of drawing any score in the population are equal to the frequency of occurrence of that score in the population and with hundreds of thousands of samplings, our sampling distribution should look exactly like the population. It will have the same mean as the population and exactly the same variance.

Now let's take the other extreme—the size of each sample is equal to the size of the population. All of the scores in the population are placed in the drum, we spin the drum, draw out all of the scores, calculate the mean, replace the scores, and repeat this hundreds of thousands of times. Since we draw out all of the scores in the population for each sample, the mean of each sample will be the population mean. In other words, every value in our sampling distribution will be the same, the population mean, and thus there will be no variability in our sampling distribution. Every value in the sampling distribution would be perfectly accurate in estimating the population mean. In the case of samples based on the size of the population, there would be no error in our estimations.

At the other extreme, sample size 1, error would be at a maximum. Each of the scores in the population would be found on the sampling distribution, and each of the scores would be an estimate of the population mean. Obviously, using any specific score in a population to estimate the mean of a population would involve a great deal of error. At one end, sample size 1, the variability of the sampling distribution and error is at a maximum, and at the other end, sample size equal to population size, variability is zero and so is error. Between these two extremes comes our general principle: *As sample size rises, the variability of the sampling distribution falls and so does the error of estimating the population parameter.*

In order to demonstrate this important principle, let us assume that we have a population of 3 million people who have responded to a question by either agreeing, stating they are neutral, or disagreeing. These responses are scored respectively 3, 2, 1. Let us further assume that the population has responded equally to the three categories; that is, 1 million people in the population agreed, 1 million were neutral, and 1 million disagreed with the question. If we add up all of these scores, 1 million plus 2 million plus 3 million, we get 6 million; and if we divide this by 3 million, which is the size of the population, we get the population mean of 2. We now sample from this population samples of size 2. Table 6–1a shows the results of this sampling. The columns of the table indicate the possible numbers one could draw from the population as one score for each sample, and the rows indicate the second score that would be drawn to make sample size 2. The entries in the body of the table are the means of the two cases. Thus, at the intersection of the first row and first column

TABLE 6–1

Hypothetical sampling distributions of the mean for $N = 2$ (a) and $N = 3$ (b)

a.

	1st Case:	1	2	3
		1	1.0	1.5	2.0
2nd Case:	2	1.5	2.0	2.5
	3	2.0	2.5	3.0

b.

1st Case:		1			2			3		
2nd Case:		1	2	3	1	2	3	1	2	3
	1	1.0	1.333	1.667	1.333	1.667	2.0	1.667	2.0	2.333
3rd Case:	2	1.333	1.667	2.0	1.667	2.0	2.333	2.0	2.333	2.667
	3	1.667	2.0	2.333	2.0	2.333	2.667	2.333	2.667	3.0

is a 1, found by adding the 1 drawn as the first case, the 1 drawn as the second case, and dividing by 2, the sample size. In the second row and first column is a 1.5, found by adding the 1 drawn as the first case and the 2 drawn as the second case and dividing by 2.

The values in the table are all of the possible values of sample means, based on sample size 2, that could be drawn from this population. It can be seen that all of the values do not appear with the same frequency. That is, there are more 2.0s than 2.5s or 1.5s, and more of each of these than 1.0s or 3.0s. If we add up these nine means and divide by 9, we will have calculated the mean of the sample means, which is 2, the population mean. If we subtract 2.0, the mean of all of the means, from each of the means, square the differences, add these squares, and divide by 9, we will have calculated the variance of these sample means, which is the variance of this sampling distribution. The variance is .333. Readers may want to verify this for themselves.

Now let us see what would happen if we took samples of size 3 rather than size 2. The possible results of this are depicted in Table 6–1b, where the values in the table represent the means of three cases drawn from the population. Thus, the value at the intersection of the first row and first column is a mean equal to 1, the result of drawing a 1 for each of the three cases in the sample. The value at the intersection of the second row and fourth column is a mean equal to 1.667, the result of drawing a 2 for case 1, a 1 for case 2, and a 2 for case 3. If we add all of these 27 means and divide by 27, we will have the mean of this sampling distribution, which is again 2, the population mean. The reader may want to sum the 27 means and divide by 27 to verify this. Thus, both sampling distributions have the population mean as their mean.

Subtracting 2 from each of the 27 means, squaring and adding these differences, and dividing by 27, we find the variance to be .222. Thus, the second sampling distribution of means based upon sample size 3 has a smaller variance than the first sampling distribution of means based upon sample size 2. If we were to draw samples larger than three cases, the sampling distribution based upon this larger sample size would again have a mean equal to 2 but a variance smaller than either of the first two sampling distributions.

The basic principle is that as the size of the samples rises, the variance of the sampling distribution decreases. This decreasing variance means that the sample statistics fall closer to the mean of the sampling distribution, which is the population parameter. Thus, in a sampling distribution based upon very large samples, each sample statistic on the sampling distribution will be a close estimate of the population parameter.

Sampling distributions then are distributions of statistics calculated on samples taken from a population. Each sample statistic is an estimate of the population parameter, which is the value we would get if we used the entire population. There are sampling distributions for correlation coefficients, variances, medians, and other indices as well as for means.

Judgments about Chance

How are these sampling distributions employed in making judgments about chance? The answer lies in the calculation of the measure of variability of the sampling distribution, the variance. The variance of the sampling distribution is found by subtracting the mean of the sampling distribution from each of the sample statistics, squaring the differences, adding these squares, and dividing by the number of samples. The variance then is the average amount, in squared units, the sample statistics deviate from the mean of the sampling distribution. In order to get back to the unsquared units, we take the square root of the variance, which is called the standard deviation. *The standard deviation of a distribution tells us, on the average, how far values on a distribution fall from the mean of the distribution.* If the standard deviation is large, the values spread out a great deal from the mean. If it is small, the values fall in close to the mean.

For certain distributions, the percentage of values that lie between different points on the distribution can be calculated. For example, the percentage of cases which lie between a standard deviation above and a standard deviation below the mean can be calculated. Using this same logic, the number of standard deviations necessary to include a given percentage of cases can be calculated. On a normal distribution, for instance, exactly 1.96 standard deviations above and below the mean covers 95 percent of the cases, and conversely, 5 percent of the cases are out further than 1.96 standard deviations above and below the mean. Thus, if a sampling distribution is normal, then we know that 95 percent of the sample statistics lie within 1.96 standard deviations above and below the mean, and only 5 percent are beyond this. In fact, in the case of the mean, the sampling distribution is normal, and thus 95 percent of the sample means will lie within 1.96 standard deviations above and below the mean of the sampling distribution, which is the population mean. Thus, we can tell what kind of deviations of sample means from the population mean we would get by chance 95 percent of the time and what kind of deviations we would get only 5 percent of the time. *The standard deviation of a sampling distribution is called by a special name, the standard error.* Thus, the standard error of the mean is the standard deviation of the sampling distribution of means. Henceforth, all standard deviations of sampling distributions will be referred to as standard errors.

In order to demonstrate concretely how we might use a sampling distribution of the mean, let me present the following scenario. Assume for demonstration purposes that the mean intelligence test score for a population is 100. I ask my graduate assistant, Gordon Goldbrick, to take a random sample of 50 people from this population, give each person an intelligence test, measure their attitudes toward a number of political issues, and calculate the average intelligence test score for the sample. Assume that I not only know that the population mean for the intelligence test is 100, but also that the standard error of the mean for samples of 50 cases is 2.12. Since the sampling distribution of the mean is normal and consequently 95 percent of the means randomly sampled from a population will lie between 1.96 standard errors above and below the population mean, I can calculate where 95 percent of the means would lie on this sampling distribution. The standard error of the mean is 2.12, and thus 95 percent of the means should lie between 100, the population mean, plus the minus 2.12 times 1.96. That is, 95 percent of the means based upon 50 cases randomly sampled from a population with a mean of 100 should lie between 95.84 and 104.16. Now assume Gordon Goldbrick has given me a sample with a mean of 105.5, which is outside of these limits.

This, of course, could be just chance, since 5 times out of 100, means beyond 95.84 and 104.16 will be found by chance. On the other hand, I have always suspected that Mr. Goldbrick might behave in accordance with his name and that rather than sampling randomly, he chose his sample on some systematic basis. For example, he may have gone to a class of advanced students and asked for 50 volunteers, which, of course, would have been much easier than taking a random sample. I confront him with my suspicions, and he vehemently denies any wrongdoing. Therefore, I am in the same position as our hero in the poker game. What do I now do about this? I have a sample of students whose average intelligence deviates substantially from the population average. If this deviation is just chance, I should not blame Mr. Goldbrick, but if he has selected those individuals because of his own laziness, then a serious character flaw has been revealed. A graduate student who is lazy and irresponsible means that research conducted by this student will not be reliable. Just as our hero decided to stop the stranger from leaving, I decide to act against Mr. Goldbrick by dismissing him as my assistant and relating the incident to the other faculty members.

My decision in this matter is based on the knowledge of what I would expect to happen by chance; this knowledge derives directly from the sampling distribution of the mean. The sampling distribution has told me the probability of certain events occurring by chance, and my decision in regard to Mr. Goldbrick is based upon that probability. Again, as in the case of the poker game, my decision, if correct, will lead to appropriate action, but if I was incorrect and the result was just a chance occurrence, I have damaged Mr. Goldbrick wrongly.

In the case of Mr. Goldbrick, I was able to use my knowledge of the population mean and the standard error of the mean in order to calculate the probability of his sample mean occurring by chance. Hopefully, this served to demonstrate how sampling distributions are employed to make decisions. You may have said to yourself, "he may have known the population mean, but how in the world would he have known the standard error of the mean based on your samples of size 50, since the sampling distribution contains all of the possible sample means of a given size that can be drawn from the population?" Well, the standard error can be calculated without ever generating the sampling distribution itself. In the case of the mean, the standard error of the mean is a function of two values, the size of the samples in the distribution and the standard deviation of the population itself. That is, if we divide the standard deviation of the population by the square root of the sample size, we will have calculated the standard error of the mean. In other words, the standard error of the mean equals the population standard deviation divided by the square root of the sample size. Given that the standard deviation of the population was 15.0, dividing this by the square root of 50 yields 2.12. Thus, with the knowledge of the population mean and standard deviation, it was possible to calculate the standard error of the mean and consequently to make a decision about the role of chance.

Thus, one way that knowledge of sampling distributions can be used is in determining whether or not a given sample mean is likely to have been drawn from a population whose mean is known. Knowledge of sampling distributions also is important in situations where the population mean is unknown; in fact, the aim of the research is to estimate the population mean with the mean of the sample. In this case, the researcher draws a sample of a given size from the population and calculates the mean of the sample. This sample mean then will be one of all the possible sample means on the sampling distribution since the sampling distribution contains all possible sample means based on a given sample size.

If the population standard deviation is known, one may divide it by the square root of the sample size in order to calculate the standard error of the mean. If one then adds to and subtracts from the sample mean 1.96 times the standard error of the mean, one has an interval in which the population mean will fall with 95 percent probability. That is, there is a 95 percent chance that the population mean lies somewhere in the interval and only a

5 percent chance that it lies outside of the interval. This interval is known as the 95 percent confidence interval.

Let us say that a sample of size 25 is taken and the mean of the sample is calculated to be 100. Let us further assume that the population standard deviation is known to be 15, and therefore, the standard error of the mean is 3 (15 divided by the square root of 25). If we now multiple 3 by 1.96, the number of standard deviations that will include 95 percent of the cases, and add and subtract this product from 100, the sample mean, we will have produced an interval whose bounds are 105.88 and 94.12. We can now state that the probability is 95 percent, that the population mean is somewhere between 105.88 and 94.12. Conversely, the probability is only 5 percent that the population mean would be greater than 105.88 or less than 94.12. The interval we generate is termed a confidence interval since it tells us the level of confidence (i.e., 95 percent) that we can place in our statement.

In the above example, we used the population standard deviation to calculate the standard error of the mean and then generate a confidence interval for estimating the population mean. In most cases, if the population mean is unknown, the population standard deviation is also unknown. How then do we calculate the standard error of the mean? Well, although we don't know the population standard deviation, we can estimate it with the sample standard deviation,[1] divide this estimate by the square root of the sample size, and thus estimate the standard error of the mean. Using our estimate of the standard error of the mean, we can produce a confidence interval for the population mean.[2]

DECISION THEORY: THE LOGIC OF HYPOTHESIS TESTING

Much of the previous material in this chapter has dealt with hypothesis testing, albeit informally. The case of the poker game and the case of Mr. Goldbrick both involved the logic of hypothesis testing. Both cases involve a decision based upon the probability of an event occurring by chance, and both cases involved the possibility of an error on the part of the decision maker. In order to shed more light on the decision process, let us turn to a more formal exposition.

---

[1] Actually, the sample standard deviation is not an accurate estimate of the population standard deviation. It is biased by being too small in the long run. Therefore, a correction is applied in order to eliminate the bias. Rather than dividing the sum of the squared distances of the scores from the sample mean by the sample size, we divide by the sample size minus one. This inflates the sample variance and standard deviation.

[2] Since we have estimated the standard error of the mean, we employ a distribution called t rather than the normal distribution to calculate our probability. Generally, it will take a greater number of standard deviations to reach a given probability level on the t than on the normal distribution. Therefore, confidence intervals will be wider when t is used than when the normal distribution is used.

The Null Hypothesis

Statistical decision making begins with a statistical hypothesis on the part of the researcher. This hypothesis is called the *null hypothesis* since it basically states that there is nothing systematic occurring. That is, it is a hypothesis of chance effects. The null hypothesis for our hero in the case of the poker game was that chance was determining the cards. The null hypothesis in the case of Mr. Goldbrick was that any difference between the population and sample means was a chance effect. In both cases, the events that occurred, the spade royal flush and Mr. Goldbrick's extreme sample mean, were judged to be so rare by chance alone that the null hypothesis was judged to be untenable. That is, in both cases, the null hypothesis was rejected.

It is important for the reader to understand that this statistical hypothesis, the null hypothesis, is not the same as the research hypothesis being tested. In fact, the research hypothesis generally states that there is a systematic effect occurring; that is, it states the opposite of the null hypothesis. In order to illustrate this point, let us consider a well-known study—the famous fluoride toothpaste experiment. As shown on television, the experiment involved two groups of randomly assigned kids. One group received the toothpaste with fluoride added, while the other received the same toothpaste without fluoride. At the end of a period of time, the groups were compared as to the number of cavities they had. Since the researchers would not have been manipulating fluoride if they didn't have reason to believe it might be effective, the research hypothesis was that the fluoride group would have fewer cavities than the nonfluoride group. The null hypothesis was that fluoride would have no effect and that any difference between the two groups would be chance. In finding fluoride to be effective, the researchers rejected the null hypothesis and consequently accepted the research hypothesis.

The null hypothesis is rejected when results are significant; that is, when it is unlikely that they have occurred by chance. Thus, if a researcher feels that an event that occurs only 5 percent of the time or less by chance is an unlikely chance event, the null hypothesis may be rejected. If the decision to reject is made, it should be recognized that there is a 5 percent chance of that decision being erroneous. On the other hand, if the event occurs more than 5 percent of the time by chance and the null hypothesis is not rejected, there is also a chance that the decision is incorrect. Thus, when the null hypothesis is rejected, there is either a correct decision or an error, called a *Type I error;* and when the null hypothesis is not rejected, there is either a correct decision or an error, called a *Type II error.* The possible outcomes, decisions, and consequences of those decisions are depicted in Table 6–2. The columns of the table represent truth while the rows represent the conclusions one could draw. Using the poker example, we see that the truth is either that the stranger won honestly (column 1), did not cheat, or that he cheated

TABLE 6–2
Possible conclusions and consequences in the card game situation

	Truth	
Conclusion	Null Is True; The Stranger Did Not Cheat	Null Is False; The Stranger Did Cheat
The stranger did not cheat	Correct decision	Incorrect decision Type II error
The stranger did cheat	Incorrect decision Type I error	Correct decision

(column 2). These are the two possible truths. We also see that we can conclude either that he did not cheat (row 1), if the hand was insufficiently rare by chance, or that he did cheat (row 2), if the hand was rare enough. The cells of the table show the consequences of the decisions for each truth possibility. If the stranger won honestly and we conclude he did not cheat, we make a correct decision. If he won honestly and we conclude that he cheated, we make a Type I error. On the other hand, if he cheated and we conclude he did not cheat, we make a Type II error, whereas if he cheated and we conclude that he cheated, we make a correct decision. The chance or probability of a Type I error is fixed by the significance level chosen. In other words, if one chooses .05 as the level of rarity, the significance level, then there is a 5 percent chance of making a Type I error given that the null hypothesis is correct. Whereas the determination of the probability of a Type I error is straightforward, the determination of the probability of a Type II error is much more complex. In fact, it is usually impossible to exactly determine the probability of a Type II error. Even so, we are able to understand the nature of a Type II error and to use that knowledge to guard against making these errors.

In this chapter, we have introduced the idea of chance, defined the nature of sampling distributions, using the sampling distribution of the mean as an example, and have discussed the types of errors which are part of the decision process. In Chapter 7, we will delve more deeply into the nature of Type II errors and into the testing of hypotheses about differences between means.

The Results of
a Study—Statistics II

In this chapter, we will delve more deeply into the nature of Type II errors, looking at them from the standpoint of testing the difference between the means of two groups. We will begin by reexamining the decision process, this time employing the controllability experiment discussed in Chapter 5, with only two conditions—escapable and inescapable noise.

It will be recalled that subjects in one group (A) receive aversive noise which they can escape by pressing a correct sequence of buttons. Subjects in the other group (B) receive the same noise for the same duration but cannot escape by engaging in any particular behavior. Subjects are randomly assigned to the two groups. Following exposure to a number of noise trials, all subjects are given a series of 30 anagrams to complete. The research hypothesis is that exposure to inescapable aversive stimulation interferes with subsequent performance, and thus subjects in group A should solve more anagrams on the average than their counterparts in group B. The null hypothesis is that there is no difference between inescapable and escapable aversive stimulation in their effects upon subsequent anagram performance, and any difference evidenced between the two sample means will be due to chance. The null hypothesis thus states that there is only one population, whereas the research hypothesis states that there are two populations. If there is only one population, then there is a single sampling distribution of means from that population. If there are two populations, then each has a sampling distribution of the mean. The researcher's task is to decide whether the two sample means in the experiment come from the same sampling distribution or from two different sampling distributions.

Table 7–1, like Table 6–2, provides a description of the possibilities in the decision process. In this table, μ stands for a population mean and H_0 stands for the null hypothesis. The two columns of the table labeled A_1 and A_2 represent reality or truth in terms of the population. That is, either inescapable and escapable noise act in the same way and there is only one

TABLE 7-1
Possible conclusions and consequences in the escapable noise experiment

Possible conclusions from sample means		Reality	
		One population μ Escap. $=\mu$ Inescap. A_1	Two populations μ Escap. $\neq \mu$ Inescap. A_2
Not significantly different: μ Escap. $=\mu$ Inescap. Fail to reject H_0	B_1	Correct decision Probability $=$ 1-alpha	Incorrect decision Type II error Probability $=$ beta
Significantly different: μ Escap. $\neq \mu$ Inescap. Reject H_0	B_2	Incorrect decision Type I error	Correct decision Probability $=$ 1-beta

population (column A_1), or inescapable and escapable noise produce different effects and there are two populations (column A_2). The rows of the table represent the researcher's efforts to arrive at a conclusion. In the first row (B_1), the sample means are not significantly different, and the null hypothesis is not rejected. In the second row (B_2), the sample means are significantly different, and the null hypothesis is rejected. Each cell of the table represents the consequences of each conclusion.

TYPE I ERRORS

Let us focus first upon cells in column 1 (A_1), where there is only one population. Here the researcher, having adopted a given significance level called an *alpha level,* say .05, has tested the difference between the two sample means and found the result to occur more frequently than five in a hundred times by chance. He therefore fails to reject the null hypothesis that there is one population (B_1). In this case, since there is only one population (column A_1), he makes a correct decision. If, on the other hand, he tests the difference between the sample means and finds a difference so large it would occur fewer than five times in a hundred by chance, he rejects the null hypothesis. Since the reality of the situation is that there is only one population, he makes an error. This error of rejecting the null hypothesis when it is indeed true is called a Type I error. The probability of making this error is exactly equal to the significance level the researcher chooses, that is, alpha. Thus, if he chooses .05 as the significance level, the probability of a Type I error is .05. If the researcher had adopted .01 as the alpha level, then the probability of a Type I error would have been .01. Conversely, the probability of a correct decision when there is only one population is one minus alpha which is .95 or .99 in the above cases. Thus, in column 1 of the table, a mistake occurs by finding a significant difference, and a correct decision occurs when the difference is not significant.

TYPE II ERRORS

Now let us examine the second column of the table (A_2). Here the reality of the situation is that there are two populations; inescapable and escapable aversive stimulation do produce differential anagram performances. The researcher who now fails to reject the null hypothesis (row B_1) makes an error since he fails to conclude that there are two populations when, in fact, there are two. In this case, he has made a Type II error, which is failing to find a difference when one actually exists. *The probability of a Type II error is called beta,* and conversely, the probability of a correct decision in the situation where there are two populations is one minus beta. Unfortunately, the calculation of the probability of a Type II error is not as straightforward as a Type I error. The probability of a Type I error is set by the alpha level chosen by the researcher. The probability of a Type II error (beta) depends upon a number of factors which will be discussed below.

There is an important point to keep in mind, and that is that *a Type I error can only be made when there is one population* (both groups come from one population) and *a Type II error can be made only when there are two populations* (the groups come from two populations). Put another way, the probability of a Type II error when there is only one population is zero, as is the probability of a Type I error when two populations exist.

Let us now examine more closely the manner in which sampling distributions relate to the decision process. Under the condition where the null hypothesis is correct, there is one population and one sampling distribution of means from that population. If each of the means on that sampling distribution is subtracted from all of the other means and a frequency distribution of these differences is made, you would have a new kind of sampling distribution called the *sampling distribution of differences between two means*. This distribution would have an equal number of positive and negative differences, and the mean of all of these differences would be zero. The standard deviation of this sampling distribution would be called the *standard error of the difference between means*. With it, we could calculate the probability of specific differences occurring by chance. Just as we can calculate our estimate of the standard error of the mean using the sample standard deviation, we can calculate an estimate of the standard error of the difference between means using the standard deviations of the two samples.

In the experiment on inescapable versus escapable aversive stimulation, the researcher would (1) calculate the means and standard deviations of the two groups; he would then (2) calculate the difference between the two means, and (3) divide this difference by his estimate of the standard error of the difference as calculated from his two standard deviations. This would tell him how many standard errors apart his two means were from the mean of the sampling distribution, which is zero. If, for example, the escapable noise group scored 2.12 standard errors above the inescapable noise group, and this difference could only occur five times in a hundred or less by chance and his chosen alpha level was .05, he would conclude that this was not a chance difference. This conclusion would mean that he rejects the null hypothesis, stating that a difference this large is unlikely to have occurred between two means drawn from the same population. Thus, he is concluding that a difference this large was more likely to have resulted from comparing two means from separate populations.

The researcher has employed the sampling distribution of differences between means to evaluate the difference between his sample means and to come to a decision about the effects of escapable and inescapable aversive stimulation in the population. If there are two populations, that is, if escapable and inescapable aversive stimulation have different effects, then he has made a correct decision in rejecting the null hypothesis. On the other hand, if there is only one population, that is, if escapable and inescapable aversive stimulation work in the same way, he has made a Type I error. If the null hypothesis was correct, he had only a 5 percent chance of making an error; that is, he had only a 5 percent chance of finding a difference as large as the one that occurred between his sample means. In the above case, he would have been unlucky enough to have done just that, and a Type I error would have been committed. His random assignment, by chance alone, produced two groups drawn from the same population whose means were quite different. This only happens five times in a hundred, but he got one of those five events.

Figure 7–1 represents graphically the situation where the null hypothesis is correct; that is, there is only one population represented in curve *a*

FIGURE 7–1

A single population *(a)*, with accompanying sampling distributions of the mean *(b)*, and differences between means *(c)*

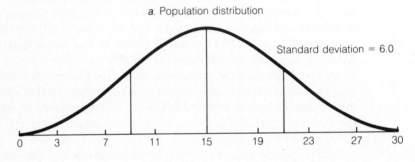

a. Population distribution

Standard deviation = 6.0

0   3   7   11   15   19   23   27   30

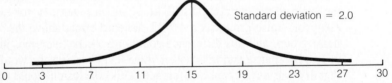

b. Sampling distribution of the mean for sample size 9

Standard deviation = 2.0

0   3   7   11   15   19   23   27   30

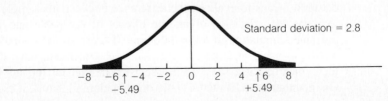

c. Sampling distribution of differences between means

Standard deviation = 2.8

-8   -6 ↑ -4   -2   0   2   4 ↑ 6   8
       -5.49   +5.49

of the figure. The mean of the population is 15, the standard deviation is 6, and the possible range of scores is from 0 to 30 anagrams correct. Curve *b* represents the sampling distribution of the mean, based upon sample size 9, from this population. The mean of this distribution is also 15, since the mean of the sampling distribution of means from a population is equal to the population mean. The standard deviation of this distribution is 2, which is the standard deviation of the population (6) divided by the square root of the sample size (9). Curve *c* is the sampling distribution of the differences between the means in curve *b*. The curve of differences between means all drawn from the same population has a mean of zero. Its standard deviation is based upon differences which involve two means and is a function of the two standard deviations. The standard deviation of curve *c* is 2.8. All three of these curves are normal, which means that 1.96 standard deviations above and below the mean will cover 95 percent of the cases. Thus, if our researcher finds the difference between the means of the escapable and inescapable noise groups to be at least 5.49 points apart, which is 2.8 (the standard error of curve *c*) times 1.96 (the number of standard errors needed to reach the .05 level of significance), he will reject the null hypothesis. That is, any difference which falls in the shaded areas of curve *c* will produce a rejection of the null hypothesis. For example, if the escapable noise group mean is 17.5 and the inescapable noise group mean is 12.0, a difference of 5.5 points, he will reject the null hypothesis.

If the difference falls in the nonshaded area, the null hypothesis will not be rejected. For example, if the escapable noise group mean is 17.5 and the inescapable noise group mean is 13—a difference of 4.5 points—he will not reject the null hypothesis. Since, in this case, there is one population, a difference in the nonshaded area of curve *c* will produce a correct decision, whereas a difference in the shaded area will produce a Type I error.

Figure 7–1 depicts the situation under the null hypothesis; that is, it depicts the first column of Table 7–1. The second column of Table 7–1, the case where there are two populations, is depicted in Figure 7–2. Panel *a* shows the two populations: inescapable on the left with a mean equal to 13 and escapable on the right with a mean equal to 17. Both have a standard deviation of 6. Panel *b* shows the two sampling distributions of the mean each with a mean equal to the mean of the population from which the samples were drawn and each with a standard deviation equal to 2. Notice that although the populations overlap a great deal, the sampling distributions overlap much less. This, of course, is due to the fact that the standard deviations of the sampling distributions are smaller than the standard deviation of the population. Panel *c* shows the sampling distribution of the differences between the means of the two sampling distributions. This sampling distribution of differences has a standard deviation of 2.8 but does not have a mean of 0. Rather the mean is 4, the difference between the means of the two populations. Thus, when there are two

FIGURE 7–2
**Two populations (a), with accompanying sampling distributions of the mean
(b), and differences between means (c)**

a. Population distributions

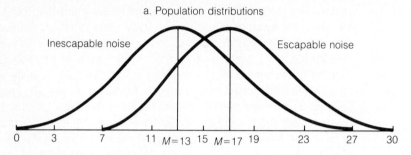

b. Sampling distributions of means

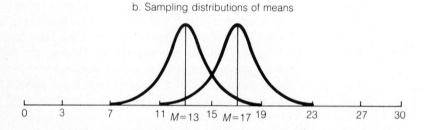

c. Sampling distributions of differences between means

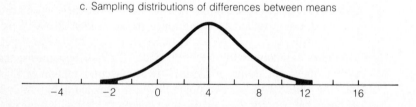

populations, each has a sampling distribution, and the sampling distribution of differences between means has a mean equal to the difference
between the two population means.

Now examine Figure 7–3 which shows the sampling distribution of
mean differences under the null hypothesis and under the condition where
there are two populations. The sampling distribution of differences has a
mean of 0 under the null hypothesis and a mean of 4, the actual differences between the two population means, under the condition where there
are two populations. The standard error of the difference for each curve is
2.8. Let us again assume that the researcher has chosen the .05 level of
significance. Given that the standard error of the difference between

FIGURE 7–3

Sampling distributions of the differences between means under the null hypothesis (one population: *M* = 0.0) and the alternative hypothesis (two populations: *M* = 4.0)

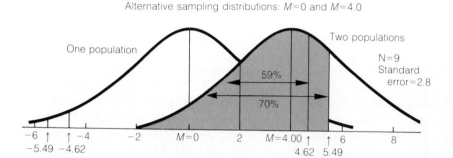

means is 2.8, a difference of 5.49 points (1.96 × 2.8) is needed to reach the .05 level and reject the null hypothesis. The researcher has to assume he is on the null hypothesis curve until he can reject that assumption. In other words, he doesn't know the two population curve of mean differences exists. If he knew this, he wouldn't be doing the research since he would already know the answer to his question. He also cannot start with the statistical hypothesis that there are two populations, since he would have to posit the size of the distance between the populations, which would entail a pure guess on his part. Therefore, he must posit that only one population exists, since he does know what would happen by chance if only one population does exist. In essence, he is stuck with the null hypothesis until he is able to show that the null hypothesis is untenable.

Unfortunately, although he believes that he is on the null hypothesis curve, he is actually on the two population curve since when there are two populations, the null curve doesn't exist. The researcher chose the .05 level of significance in order to take a 5 percent chance of making a Type I error, but since there are in fact two populations, the probability of a Type I error is zero. A Type I error is made when one rejects the null hypothesis, and of course, a rejection of the null hypothesis in this case, where there are two populations, is a correct decision. An error will be made only if he fails to reject the null hypothesis. This error will occur if his sample means differ by less than 5.49 points. That is, if the escapable noise group mean is 17.5 and the inescapable noise group mean is 13, a 4.5 point difference, he will fail to reject the null hypothesis, and he will make a Type II error. Thus, any difference on the two population curve to left of 5.49 will produce a Type II error. On the two population curve, the area to the left of 5.49 (the shaded area) is 70 percent of the total area of the curve. Thus, the probability of a Type II error in this case would be .70.

Let us look at the situation from an omniscient viewpoint. That is, let us assume that we could know the true situation that inescapable and escapable aversive stimulation represent two populations in terms of anagram performance. Further, let us assume that armed with this knowledge, we could observe the researcher pursue the question of the effects of inescapable and escapable aversive stimulation through his study with samples. Not knowing the answer to the question, he begins with the null hypothesis, chooses a 5 percent alpha level, carries out the study, and compares the two means finding a 4.50 point difference between them. He says to himself that he has only a 5 percent chance of making an incorrect decision. This, of course, would be true if there was only one population. But we know that there are two populations and that rather than having only a 5 percent chance of making an incorrect decision, he has a 70 percent chance. That is, he has only a 30 percent chance of deciding correctly that inescapable and escapable noise do have different effects.

REDUCING THE PROBABILITY OF A TYPE II ERROR

A 70 percent chance of an error seems very high. Could the researcher have done something differently and reduced the probability of a Type II error? We know that if he had wanted to reduce the probability of a Type I error, he could have chosen a more extreme alpha level; e.g., .01 instead of .05. But what could he have done to reduce the probability of a Type II error? Well, he could have done a number of possible things to reduce the probability of a Type II error. Each way works, but each has certain problems associated with it.

Change Alpha

First of all, he could have reduced the probability of a Type II error by choosing a less extreme alpha level. Recall that choosing an alpha level of .05 meant that he needed to go out 1.96 standard errors on the sampling distribution curve. Since each standard error was equal to 2.8, he needed his sample means to be 5.49 points apart (1.96 × 2.8). If he had chosen an alpha level of .10, he would have needed to go out only 1.65 standard errors, and the difference between his sample means would have had to have been only 4.62 points (1.65 × 2.8). Any difference to the left of 4.62 in Figure 7–3 would have produced a Type II error. This area is approximately 59 percent of the curve, and thus the probability of a Type II error is .59. Therefore, by choosing a less extreme alpha level, .10 rather than .05, he would have reduced the probability of a Type II error from .70 to .59.

This substantial reduction would be made at a cost to the researcher. If only one population exists, an alpha level of .10 means that he has a 10 percent chance of making a Type I error. Thus, when a researcher chooses a less extreme alpha level, he does reduce the probability of a Type II error if there are two populations, but he increases the probability of a

Type I error if there is only one population. The relationship between alpha level and the probability of a Type II error for the hypothetical data in Figure 7–3 is shown in Figure 7–4. In other words, Figure 7–4 depicts the relationship between alpha level and a Type II error where the difference between the two population means is 4 points and the standard error of the difference is 2.8. As the reader can see, as alpha increases, beta decreases, although the function is not linear. Going from an alpha of .05 to an alpha of .15 produces a sharper drop in beta than a change from .15 to .30. Nonetheless, the principle is that increasing alpha does reduce the probability of a Type II error. Keep in mind that the researcher does not know whether there are two populations or only one. If he does not want to increase his risk of a Type I error, he cannot change his alpha level.

Don't Hedge the Bet

Even though he cannot make his alpha level less extreme without increasing the risk of a Type I error, he can possibly use whatever level he chooses more efficiently. The reader will recall that on a normal curve, 1.96 standard deviations above and below the mean will cover 95 percent of the curve. That is, only 5 percent of the curve will fall beyond these points. This 5 percent is divided between the two ends or tails of the

FIGURE 7–4

Relationship between alpha level and probability of a Type II error when $M_1 - M_2 = 4$ and standard error = 2.8

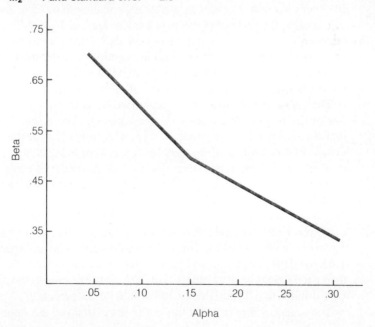

curve, leaving 2½ percent in each tail. On a sampling distribution curve of differences between means under the null hypothesis, half of the differences are positive and lie above and half are negative and lie below the mean. In Figure 7–3, the .05 level is at a difference between means of + 5.49 points, which is 1.96 standard errors above the mean, and − 5.49 points, which is 1.96 standard errors below the mean. Since the escapable noise population mean was 4 points above the inescapable noise population mean, the two population curve of mean differences is drawn on the positive side of the null hypothesis curve. It could also have been drawn on the negative side, indicating that the escapable noise population mean was lower than the inescapable noise population mean. In other words, if the null hypothesis is incorrect, if there are two populations, the difference between the population means could be positive or negative.

When the researcher chose an alpha level of .05 and employed 1.96 standard errors as his measure of whether that level had been reached, he implicitly decided to examine both ends of the null hypothesis curve. We know that if the escapable noise group had scored at least 5.49 points above the inescapable noise group, he would have rejected the null hypothesis and concluded that there were two populations. He would also have rejected the null hypothesis if the escapable noise group had fallen at least 5.49 points below the inescapable noise group. That is, in employing 1.96 standard errors on his measure of the .05 level, he was hedging his bet by splitting the 5 percent between the positive and negative ends of the curve. The researcher was making a *two-tailed test of significance*. In employing a two-tailed test, the null hypothesis is rejected when the difference between sample means reaches the required significance level in either direction. In order to be able to look at both positive and negative differences, the researcher has paid a price. He has divided his alpha level between the two tails of the curve and thus must go out further on the curve (more standard errors) in each direction in order to reject the null hypothesis. This, of course, makes it more difficult to reject the null hypothesis and raises the probability of a Type II error.

The alternative to this two-tailed procedure is to make a *directional or one-tailed test of significance*. In our example, the researcher believed that the escapable noise group would outperform the inescapable noise group. In other words, if inescapable noise were to have any effect at all, it would be a deleterious one. There was no reason to think that the inescapable noise group would outperform the escapable noise group. That is, from past research evidence and from a theoretical perspective, only a one-tailed prediction would be called for. Therefore, the researcher could place his total alpha level in one tail of the curve. In order to cut off 5 percent in one tail of the curve, he would need to go out approximately 1.65 standard deviations, and the difference between means that he would then need would be 4.62 points (2.8 × 1.65). The area to the left of 4.62 would indicate a Type II error and would be 59 percent.

The reader will notice that this is the same area and the same reduction in the probability of a Type II error that was attained when the confidence level was altered from .05 to .10. In the previous case, the researcher placed 5 percent of the curve in each tail giving a total confidence level of 10 percent. In the present case, he places 5 percent in only one tail and ignores the other end of the curve. This means that the null hypothesis can be rejected only if the escapable noise group mean is significantly greater than the inescapable noise group mean. A finding in the opposite direction, no matter how large, cannot result in a rejection of the null hypothesis. A one-tailed test then is a reasonable way to reduce the probability of a Type II error, given that the researcher expects to find only one outcome. That is, if a specific result is expected, based upon some type of knowledge or theory, a one-tailed test is appropriate. On the other hand, if the researcher has no basis upon which to predict a directional outcome, a one-tailed test would be inappropriate. Thus, a logically consistent theoretical viewpoint resting upon past empirical work increases the power of the statistical test; that is, using a one-tailed test reduces the probability of a Type II error.

It should be noted that the issue of employing one-tailed tests is a controversial one. One argument against the use of one-tailed tests is that science should be objective and that such tests introduce a bias into the process by stating the outcome which the scientist believes should occur. A second argument is related to the question of whether one should ignore unpredicted rare outcomes (those in the unpredicted tail of the distribution) or whether, in actuality, it is even possible to ignore these outcomes. A third argument against the use of one-tailed tests is that, rather than decreasing the probability of Type II errors, they may actually increase their probability. If, for instance, the reasoning behind a particular one-tailed test is incorrect and the difference between means is in the unpredicted tail of the curve, the probability of not finding that difference, i.e., committing a Type II error, becomes 1.00. The use of a one-tailed test depends directly upon the adequacy of the theoretical rationale and the empirical grounding for that rationale. Since *(a)* much of psychological theory is based upon concepts which are not precisely defined in terms of their measurement and physical operations, *(b)* the concepts themselves are not linked in an exact mathematical manner, and *(c)* behavior is complex, variable, and multiply determined, the reasoning process which leads to a one-tailed test is often not totally clear. In other words, a prediction other than the particular one which generates a given one-tailed test may be possible, and if that alternative prediction is the appropriate one, the probability of a Type II error will have been increased rather than decreased. Some researchers have taken a strongly conservative stance in regard to one-tailed tests, arguing that, due to the above problems, they should not be employed. As I stated, the issue is controversial.

So far, we have spoken of two ways of reducing the probability of a Type II error: choosing a less extreme alpha level, which increases the probability of a Type I error, and employing a one-tailed test, which depends on the theoretical and empirical base for the prediction. Let us now discuss ways which do not depend on either changing alpha or the directionality of the test. Looking at Figure 7–3, it can be seen that if either the two curves were farther apart or they were less variable, they would not overlap as much and the probability of a Type II error would be reduced. The remaining methods of reducing the probability of a Type II error deal with reducing the overlap of the null hypothesis and two population curves.

Attempt to Maximize the Power of the Independent Variable

If the null hypothesis and two population curves were farther apart, the probability of a Type II error would be reduced. For example, if the escapable noise population mean was 19 and the inescapable noise population mean was 13, a 6 point difference, the null hypothesis and two population curves would look like those in Figure 7–5. Given an alpha level of .05 (two-tailed), the researcher would again need a difference between his sample means of 5.49 points in order to reject the null hypothesis. Anything to the left of 5.49 on the second curve of Figure 7–5 would produce a Type II error. This is approximately 43 percent of the curve, and thus there is a 43 percent chance that he will make a Type II error. Keep in mind that when the populations were only 4 points apart, an alpha level of .05 (two-tailed) yielded a probability of 70 percent for a Type II error. Thus, large differences between population means imply less probability of Type II errors. To put it another way, large differences between population means are more readily detected than small ones.

In terms of experimental research, larger differences between populations are represented by more powerful manipulations. For example, if subjects are given 100 trials with either escapable or inescapable aversive noise, this would be a more powerful manipulation than giving subjects only 25 such trials. Thus, greater exposure to a treatment may be a more

FIGURE 7–5

Sampling distributions of differences between means under the null hypothesis (one population: *M* = 0) and the alternative hypothesis (two populations: *M* = 6.0)

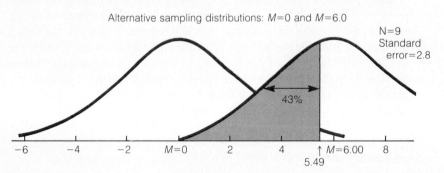

powerful manipulation and consequently reflect larger population differences. Subjects in both groups could be exposed to 110, as opposed to 85, decibel noise, with the assumption that the aversion would be greater under the 110-decibel level and would enhance the escapable versus inescapable noise differences. Stronger manipulations, then, also reflect larger population differences and increase the probability of rejecting the null hypothesis.

If the study is correlational in nature, where subjects are selected to be in groups, selection from populations which are divergent from one another enhances the probability of rejecting the null hypothesis. For example, assume that a researcher, interested in the relationship between creativity and performance on a problem-solving task, wanted to compare high and low creative subjects in terms of their problem-solving ability. If she gives a test of creativity and divides subjects into high and low creative groups by assigning those above the median of the distribution to the high creative group and those below the median to the low creative group, she will be investigating less diverse populations than if she created her high and low creative groups from the upper and lower quarters of the distribution. In other words, very high and very low creatives would represent more diverse populations than moderately high and low creatives.

Thus, investigating more diverse populations, whether that is reflected by more powerful manipulations or by more extreme selection, enhances the probability of rejecting the null hypothesis and consequently reduces the probability of a Type II error. The catch here is that it is not always possible or often not even desirable to investigate large population differences. In the case of experimental studies, larger population differences mean more powerful manipulations, which can be reflected in more exposure to or larger doses of the independent variable. Very high noise levels, while possibly enhancing the difference between the escapable and inescapable noise conditions, may be dangerous to subjects. So ethical considerations often limit our ability to increase the power of the manipulation. Prolonged exposure to the experimental conditions, while possibly producing more powerful results, may also not be economically feasible. That is, subjects may not be available for long time periods, or if subjects are paid for participating, it may be too expensive to pay them for extended periods of time. In terms of correlational studies, selection from extreme populations often limits the generalizability of the results.

One other possible problem with investigating extremely different populations is that the results achieved may be obvious. A couple of ludicrous examples may illustrate this phenomenon. Let us say that we are testing whether people hit on the hand with a hammer report more pain than those tickled with a feather. Ten subjects are randomly assigned to the hammer or feather condition. After being hit with the hammer or tickled with the feather, each subject rates their pain on a 10-point scale, and the means of the two groups are then compared. Obviously, the difference will be significant since the populations are so far apart, but the results, of course, are not only meaningless, they were totally obvious before the experiment. If one wanted to discover whether intelligence was related to problem-solving ability and compared subjects whose IQ was above 130 with those whose IQ was below 70, there is no doubt a significant difference would be found. There is also no doubt that everyone would have predicted that difference. The issue is then that extremely large population differences may reflect obvious and unimportant effects. Thus, while larger population differences reduce the probability of Type II errors, it is not always possible to produce powerful manipulations, and extremely large population differences may be so obvious that they are virtually meaningless.

Reducing Variability of Sampling Distributions

We stated that the probability of a Type II error would be reduced if either the population difference was large (as discussed above) or the variability of the sampling distribution curve of differences between means was small. The variability of sampling distribution is measured by its standard error. The standard error of the mean, the measure of the variability of a sampling distribution of means, is a function of two values: the standard deviation of the population and the size of the sample. The standard error of the difference between means is also a function of these same two values. In the initial discussion of sampling distributions, it was pointed out that as sample size increased, the standard error decreased. Thus, larger size samples are drawn from sampling distributions with less variability, and the sampling distributions of differences between means based upon larger sample sizes are also less variable.

Figure 7–6a depicts the same inescapable and escapable noise populations shown in Figure 7–2a. The inescapable noise population mean is 13, and the escapable noise population mean is 17. The standard deviations are both 6. Figure 7–6b depicts the sampling distributions of the mean from each population based upon sample sizes of 4. Thus, the standard error of each sampling distribution is 3, the population standard deviation (6) divided by the square root of the sample size (2). Figure 7–6c depicts the sampling distributions of the mean from each population based upon sample size 9. The standard error for each of these distributions is 2, the population standard deviation divided by the square root of 9, the sample size. As the sample size has increased, the two sampling distributions have become less variable and consequently overlap less.

Since the standard error of the difference between means is also a function of the population standard deviation and the sample size, it will decrease as the size of the samples increases. If the reader now examines Figure 7–7, the effect of increased sample size on the sampling distribution of differences between means can be seen. Recall that Figure 7–3a shows the sampling distribution of mean differences for the null hypoth-

FIGURE 7-6

Two populations *(a)*, with accompanying sampling distributions of the mean based upon sample size 4 *(b)*, and *(c)*

a. Population distributions

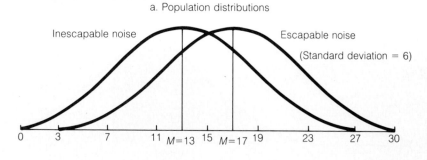

b. Sampling distributions of means

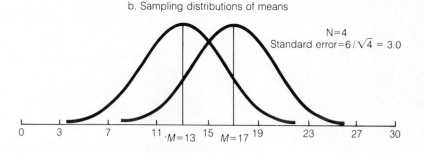

c. Sampling distributions of means

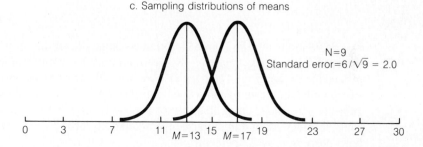

esis (one population) and for two populations whose means are 4 points apart. Figure 7–3 has been reproduced for purposes of comparison in Figure 7–7a. The standard error of each of the two curves in Figure 7–7a is 2.8, and the sample size is 9. Figure 7–7b shows the one and two population curves when the sample size is 18. The standard error is now 2, as opposed to 2.8. When the sample size was 9 and the standard error was 2.8, a mean difference of 5.49 points (1.96 × 2.8) was needed to reject the null hypothesis at the .05 level. Now with a sample size of 18 for each group and a standard error of 2.0, the difference needed to reject the null hypothesis is 3.92 points (1.96 × 2.0). The area to the left of 3.92 on the

FIGURE 7-7

Sampling distributions of differences between means under the null hypothesis (one population) and the alternative hypothesis (two populations) at sample size 9 (a) and sample size 18 (b)

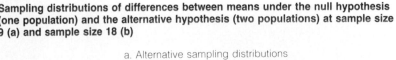

a. Alternative sampling distributions

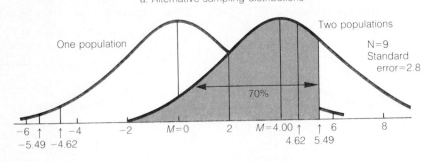

b. Alternative sampling distributions

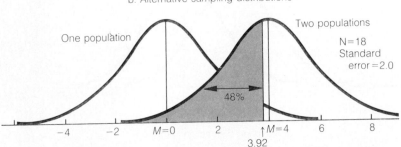

two population curve in Figure 7–7b indicates the probability of a Type II error, which is approximately .48. Keep in mind that with 9 subjects per group, the probability of a Type II error was 70 percent (the area of the two population curve to the left of 5.49 in Figure 7–7a), while with 18 subjects per group, the probability of a Type II error is now 48 percent. Thus, by increasing sample size, the probability of a Type II error has been decreased by 22 percent.

This seems to be a reasonable method for reducing the probability of a Type II error. The alpha level has not changed, a two-tailed test has been made, and the size of the difference between the two populations has remained the same. Unfortunately, there are practical disadvantages to increasing sample size. First of all, adding more subjects can be quite expensive. In some studies, subjects are paid for their participation, and thus increased sample size means increased financial costs. Additional subjects may also mean higher costs in the actual running of the study. In some studies, the treatments, which may be drugs or dosages of radioactivity to animals, may be quite expensive. In studies employing larger animals—nonhuman primates, for example—there may only be a limited number of animals available due to both cost and housing space available.

Another example of expensive treatment would be data gathered through interviews where each additional subject means a long interview carried out by a trained, paid interviewer. Finally, a great many psychological studies employ students from introductory psychology classes who participate as a course requirement. Students from these ''subject pools'' are often used by a number of people doing research, and thus, the number of subjects available for any one researcher may be limited. Therefore, while increasing sample size does reduce the probability of a Type II error, there are practical problems connected with employing large numbers of subjects.

The final problem with increasing sample size has to do with triviality. If the sample size is large enough, any difference in the population will be discovered, even a tiny and meaningless difference. For example, suppose a researcher randomly assigned 5,000 subjects to one speedreading technique, and 5,000 subjects to a second technique. At the end of the treatment period, treatment 1 subjects had a mean of 327 words per minute, while those in group 2 read at an average of 329 words per minute on a speedreading test. If the standard deviation of the speedreading test is 15, the standard error of the difference between means would be .30, and the probability that this 2-point difference could have occurred by chance would be less than 1 in 1,000. There is no question about it: Method 2 was more effective than method 1. The result would be significant but meaningless. With large enough samples, even trivial effects can turn out to be significant.

Remember that the effect of increasing sample size is to reduce the variability of the sampling distributions and, consequently, the overlap of the null hypothesis curve and the two population curve. The variability of the sampling distribution can also be reduced in another manner. Since the standard error of the mean and the standard error of the difference between means is a function of both the sample size and the population standard deviation, a reduction in the population standard deviation would also reduce the standard error.

The question is, how do you reduce the population standard deviation? Since the standard deviation represents the variability in the population, populations which have more homogeneous members will have smaller standard deviations. That is, populations whose members are very much alike will have less variability than populations whose members are very different from one another. Since the sample is a representation of the population, it follows that samples drawn from homogeneous populations will also be less variable than those drawn from heterogeneous populations. When working with nonhuman subjects, researchers often breed animals to be alike in certain ways, which makes these subjects less variable than nonselected animals. With human subjects, pretesting is often done to select subjects who score homogeneously. If the animals are genetically selected, or if the humans are selected by pretest for a characteristic which is related to the variable under investigation, then these subjects will be less variable than unselected subjects. These homogeneous populations with small variability will have sampling distributions with smaller standard errors.

✗ The problem with sampling from homogeneous populations is limited generalizability. Selected populations are by definition less diverse than unselected ones, and the generalization of results can only be made to these rather restricted populations. As an example, let us suppose that for the escapable versus inescapable noise study, the researcher wanted to increase his probability of rejecting the null hypothesis and decided to use only subjects whose IQs were between 95 and 105. He felt that since these subjects were alike on IQ, they would also probably be alike on anagram performance, the dependent variable. If he finds a significant difference between the mean anagram performances of his escapable and inescapable noise groups, he can now say only that for subjects whose IQs are between 95 and 105, inescapable aversive noise produces poorer performance than escapable aversive noise. This is a rather limited generalization since about 74 percent of the adult population have IQs less than 95 or greater than 105.

Sampling from homogeneous populations does reduce the variability of sampling distributions but has the drawback of limiting generalization. But there is another way to reduce standard errors by reducing the population standard deviations. This approach, rather than limiting the population by choosing only homogeneous populations, reduces the variability of unselected heterogeneous populations through statistical methods. Back in Chapter 2, the concept of components of variance was presented. It was stated that a total amount of variance could be broken down into a systematic component, which is related to another or other variables, and an unsystematic or error component, which is unrelated to other variables. The standard deviation of the population generally represents error variance since the individual differences it reflects are not shown to be related to any variable. If they could be related to another variable, then they would no longer be unsystematic. If this variance or part of it can be accounted for, that part can be removed, thereby reducing the population standard deviation, albeit statistically.

This statistical reduction in variability can be accomplished through a technique called matching. In this method, subjects are matched on a variable which the researcher feels will be related to the dependent variable. Let us use the example of IQ and anagram performance for contingent and noncontingent groups. In this case, instead of selecting from a homogeneous population, the researcher would use subjects with a wide range of IQs. After obtaining their IQs and before starting the treatments, he would match subjects by their IQs. If he had 20 subjects to assign to his two groups, he would produce 10 matched pairs. The first pair would consist of the two highest IQ subjects, the second pair the next two highest, etc., until the two lowest IQ subjects were assigned to the 10th matched pair. One member of each pair would then be randomly assigned to the contingent group and the other member to the noncontingent group. This should produce mean IQs for the two groups which are nearly equal and also large but nearly equal standards deviations. The correlation between the IQs in the two groups should be perfect since the highest IQ in one group is matched with the highest in the other, the second highest with the second highest, etc., down to the lowest with the lowest.

Following this matching, the subjects are treated with either the contingent or noncontingent aversive noise and then given the anagrams task. If IQ is related to anagram performance, anagram performance between the two groups should be correlated since the IQs of the two groups were perfectly correlated before the experiment. What this means is that the highest anagram performance in the contingent group should be paired with the highest in the noncontingent, etc. To the extent that the anagram performances between the groups stay in the same order as the IQs, IQ will account for some proportion of the variance in anagram performance. If we didn't have the IQ matching, we would only know that within each group subjects are quite variable in their anagram performance. With the matching, we can see that the variability is related to IQ.

In order to use this information, the test of differences between means is modified so that the standard deviations can be reduced by the amount accounted for by the matching. When the standard deviations are reduced, the standard error of the difference between means is reduced, the overlap of the null and two population curve is reduced, and the probability of a Type II error goes down. Matching can occur in other ways than by pairing subjects by tests scores. For example, identical twins are excellent for matching since they are genetically alike and usually experientially quite similar. One twin is assigned to each condition randomly in this case. Siblings also produce natural matched pairs as do litter mates in animal research.

If there are more than two groups, the matched sets are called blocks rather than pairs, but the same principles apply. With three groups, for example, three animals from the same litter can be randomly assigned to the groups, or the three highest IQ subjects could form the first block. Again, the statistical test is made by removing the variance accounted for by the blocking. In fact, the whole process of matching depends upon the proper statistical test being performed. If the statistical test is made without removing the effects of the matching or blocking, the probability of a Type II error may go up since by matching, the researcher has guaranteed the full range of scores within each group.

Just as there are problems with each of the other methods of reducing the probability of Type II errors, there are problems with matching. First of all, the researcher has to pick the correct variable to match on. That is, he has to pick one that will be related to the dependent variable. For example, if the researcher matched on height before the escapable-inescapable noise experiment, it is unlikely that anagram performances would bear any relationship to height. Sometimes, pretesting for the matching variable is carried out by giving subjects an alternate form of the dependent variable. Thus, the researcher, rather than using IQ on the matching variable, could have given subjects a sample of anagrams and matched them on this basis. This can sometimes alert subjects to the purposes of the experiment, or the pretesting can interact with the treatment to produce an effect which would not have occurred without pretesting. Often it is not possible to pretest and match subjects due to time considerations since pretesting must be completed for all subjects before the matching and the random assignment to treatments can ensue. Finally, in terms of natural matching, twins and even siblings often are not readily available.

Let us now summarize the ways in which a researcher can reduce the probability of a Type II error:

a. Increase the alpha level. Problem: This increases the probability of a Type I error.
b. Carry out a one tailed test. Problem: A strong basis in either theory or previous empirical work must exist. A finding opposite to that predicted cannot be employed to reject the null hypothesis.
c. Investigate larger population differences. Problems: Very strong experimental manipulations may be unethical. Very extreme groups in the population may be unrepresentative or may reflect obvious and trivial differences.
d. Increase sample size. Problems: Cost, both in time and money, may be too high. Large enough samples may allow one to find trivial phenomena.
e. Decrease population variability. Problems: Homogeneous populations limit generalizability. Matching entails picking the correct variable to match on; that is, one related to the dependent variable. Pretesting for matching can sensitize subjects to the manipulations. Natural matching by twins or siblings is difficult to achieve.

All of the approaches will reduce the probability of a Type II error, but all have disadvantages. In practice, the researcher generally attempts a combination of the above approaches. For example, in the case of the escapable versus inescapable noise groups, he may employ a one-tailed test, choose a level of noise high enough to have aversive effects, and carry out as many trials as possible in order to enhance the strength of the manipulation. He would employ the largest sample he could in light of the costs and subject availability, and finally he might possibly even attempt to match subjects on a variable related to anagram performance.

In the preceding discussion on Type II errors, the standard deviation of the population and consequently the standard error of the difference between means have been known. Therefore, the curves which we employed to calculate the probabilities of Type II errors under various circumstances represented normal distributions. In practice, the standard error of the difference between means is seldom known since the standard deviation of the population is seldom known. Therefore, in order to test the null hypothesis, the researcher has to estimate the standard error of the difference between means from the sample data. When matching has been employed, a special formula is used for the standard error which removes the effects of the matching. Whenever the standard error is an estimate rather than the actual standard error, the normal curve cannot be used to evaluate the result. Instead, a distribution known as t is the correct one for evaluating differences between means when the standard error of the difference is an estimate. The t distribution is actually a series of distributions each based upon a different size sample. When the sample size is quite small, the t distribution differs considerably from the normal distribution in that larger values are needed to reject the null hypothesis on the t than on the normal distribution. For example, whereas a value of 1.96 is needed at alpha = .05 on the normal curve, a value of 2.10 is needed at alpha = .05 for a sample size of 20 on the t distribution. As the sample size increases, the values of the normal and t distributions become closer. Since one needs larger values to reject the null hypothesis on the t than on the normal distribution, it is more difficult to reject the null hypothesis using the t distribution. When matching has been employed, a special formula for t is employed which removes the effects of the matching.

Therefore, the usual state of affairs in research is to (1) calculate the means of the two groups, (2) estimate the standard error of the difference between means from the sample data, (3) divide the estimated standard error into the calculated difference between the means of the two groups yielding the t statistic, (4) look this calculated t value up in a table of t distributions for the appropriate sample size in order to see if the calculated value is large enough to reject the null hypothesis. The computational procedures for testing the significance of the difference between the means of two samples using the t statistic are demonstrated in section IV of the appendix.

HAS AN ERROR OCCURRED?

In practice, the scenario will be that the researcher will choose an alpha level, randomly assign subjects to groups either with or without matching, differentially treat the groups, test them on the dependent variable, and carry out either a one or two tailed statistical test. If the calculated value of the statistical test exceeds the value for the chosen alpha level, the null hypothesis is rejected. If the calculated value falls short of the value for the chosen alpha level, the researcher fails to reject the null hypothesis. How does the researcher know whether a correct decision has been made or an error has been committed? The answer is that he doesn't know. Let us say that he rejects the null hypothesis at alpha equal to .05. He has either made a correct judgment, that is, there are two populations, or he has made a Type I error. He doesn't know which, but he does know that his probability of an error is .05. On the other hand, let us say that he fails to reject the null hypothesis at alpha equal to .05. He has either made a correct judgment, that is, there is only one population, or he has made a Type II error. The problem here is that without knowing the size of the population difference, he cannot know the exact probability of a Type II error.

Since researchers do not know the size of the difference between means in the population, they can only guard against Type II errors through the methods outlined above. A nonsignificant result could be due to choosing too high a probability level, weak manipulations, small sample size, or large group variances. Whereas a significant result allows the researcher to reject the null hypothesis and conclude that there are two populations, knowing the probability of being wrong in that conclusion, a nonsignificant result does not allow the researcher to conclude that only one population exists. The reader may have noticed that the statement has always been "fail to reject the null hypothesis" rather than "accept the null hypothesis." In other words, a nonsignificant result means that the researcher has failed to conclude that there are two populations. It does not mean that there is only one population. Failure to find significance could result from the fact that only one population exists, but it could also result from using too small a sample size, choosing too high a significance level, or most importantly, carrying out the manipulations ineffectively.

Which is more dangerous, a Type I or Type II error? The answer to that question depends upon the type of research being carried out. Recall the earlier example of the cancer drug research. In this case, incorrectly rejecting the null hypothesis (a Type I error) would produce disaster: The ineffective drug would be used, people would forego other treatments, and they would die. A failure to reject the null hypothesis when it was false (a Type II error) would also have a monumental consequence: A cure for cancer would have been lost.

In this case of the drug, both errors are very dangerous. To guard against a Type I error, a very extreme significance level would be chosen, .001 for example. But, of course, this would increase the probability of a Type II error so the sample size would have to be greatly increased and the manipulation strengthened. Another possibility would be to replicate the study exactly. A failure to again find a significant result would then cast doubt upon the first finding being a nonchance occurrence. This process of exact replication is sometimes quite difficult in that the same subject population is not available or the procedures may not be completely specified. Also, the cost of a replication in certain cases may be prohibitive, although certainly in the case of the cancer drug, the cost of not replicating would be even greater. The consequences of each type of error are great and easily perceived in the case of the drug, but what about psychological research or any research of a less applied nature?

In most psychological research, the direct consequences of statistical errors are not readily apparent. A significant result generally means that some evidence has been found for a part of a theory. It seldom means that an application will take place which could have dire consequences. On the other hand, it does often mean that other researchers will follow up on the result, and if a Type I error has been made, they will waste time, effort, and money exploring a blind alley. It also means a published article whose results were chance taking up valuable journal space. If a significant result is not found and a Type II error committed, it means that possibly an interesting piece of evidence supporting a theory was lost. But often other researchers are also testing the theory, and the evidence may be found by one or more of them. Therefore, a Type I error is considered to be more dangerous than a Type II error in most psychological research. In order to guard against Type I errors, most journals require alpha levels of at least .05. Thus, rather than the researcher choosing the alpha level based upon direct knowledge of the consequences of a Type I error, the alpha level has been set arbitrarily at .05. It should be noted that the above is a general notion about Type I and Type II errors and that the seriousness of each type of error depends upon the type of research involved.

It is important for the reader to understand that the term, *significance* is short for *statistical significance,* which means only that an event is rare by chance. As in the case of the hammer and the feather, a difference can be very rare by chance, statistically significant, and be entirely unimportant. The previous example of the two point difference between the sample means of the speed-reading groups which was significant is another case in point. The significance which was due to the large sample size reflected a trivial population difference. Thus, saying that a finding is significant does not necessarily imply that it is important.

THE SIGNIFICANCE OF THE CORRELATION COEFFICIENT

The statistical question in the case of testing differences among groups in an experiment is whether the means of the groups were drawn from the same population. That is, we are asking if the difference between two means or the variability among a series of means is simply random fluctuation or is large enough so that it probably reflects something systematic. In the case of the correlation coefficient, the statistical question concerns the relationship between two variables in the population. If the two variables are unrelated in the population, then a correlation that is greater than zero for any sample drawn from that population would be a chance fluctuation from zero.

Thus, in the case of the correlation coefficient, the null hypothesis is that the correlation in the population is zero. The sampling distribution of the correlation coefficient under the null hypothesis would center at the population value of zero and would contain all of the sample correlation coefficients, for a given sample size, drawn from that population. Sampling distributions based on larger sample sizes would have smaller standard errors, that is, less variability, which means that the sample correlations lie closer to the population correlation. A large enough sample correlation would produce a rejection of the null hypothesis and a conclusion that the population correlation was greater than zero. To put it another way, a rejection of the null hypothesis would result in a conclusion that there is a relationship between the variables in the population. Just as in the case of differences between means, a large enough value is one that occurs rarely by chance, for example less than 5 percent of the time. Therefore, a sample correlation which was large enough so that it would occur less than 5 percent of the time when drawn from a population where the correlation was zero would produce a rejection of the null hypothesis and a conclusion that the population correlation is greater than zero.

The logic then for the correlation coefficient parallels that for testing differences between means. We posit no relationship between the variables as our null hypothesis and then test to see if that hypothesis is untenable. If we reject the null hypothesis and conclude that the variables are related, we either have concluded correctly, the population correlation is not zero, or we have made a Type I error. If we fail to reject the null hypothesis, that is, our sample correlation is not large enough, we are either correct, the population value is zero, or we have made a Type II error. Just as in the case of testing mean difference, we can guard against a Type I error by choosing a more extreme significance level (.01 rather than .05). We can guard against a Type II error by increasing the size of our sample and thus increasing the chances of rejecting the null hypothesis. Since we are not manipulating, we cannot increase the power of the manipulation, and since there is no assignment of subjects to conditions, we cannot take advantage of matching. Thus, there is less direct control over Type II errors with the correlation coefficient than with the testing of differences between means.

Chapter 8

Validity of
Experimental Evidence

It was previously stated in this text that the question of validity was central to psychological research. Cook and Campbell (1979) employ the definition of the concepts of *validity* and *invalidity* to "refer to the best available approximation to the truth or falsity of propositions, including propositions about cause." The propositions in question are the hypotheses researchers have about how the world is organized. Whether the propositions deal with only the relationships among a series of variables examined through the correlational method or with the causal connections between variables studied through the experimental method, they are, for psychologists in particular, beliefs about the organization of behavior. Being beliefs or conjectures, they are open to the question of whether those beliefs are supported by the evidence.

Thus, researchers state their beliefs and then carry out studies and draw conclusions about those beliefs from the data gathered. We will see that it is the conclusions about the beliefs that are valid or invalid—true or false. In the present chapter, following Cook and Campbell (1979), we will distinguish between two types of validity relevant to experiments: *internal and external validity*. Internal validity refers to conclusions drawn about the effects of the operations employed in an experiment. External validity refers to the generality of the conclusions. A third type of validity, *construct validity,* which deals with conclusions about theoretical concepts and is relevant to both correlational and experimental studies, will be discussed in Chapter 12. We will begin with a discussion of internal validity.

INTERNAL VALIDITY

When researchers manipulate an independent variable and a significant result occurs for the dependent variable, they hope a conclusion can be drawn which states *(a)* that the independent variable is related to the dependent variable and *(b)* that the differences in the levels or conditions of the independent variable caused the differences in the dependent variable. It is the second conclusion for which internal validity is a concern. If a variable or variables other than the independent variable could have produced the effect, then these other variables are a threat to the validity of the conclusion that the independent variable was the cause. What this implies is that we establish validity by ruling out sources of invalidity. This means that we cannot precisely state that a conclusion is valid; only that it is more or less valid. In the original definition of validity, the phrase "approximation to truth or falsity" was used. To the extent that we are able to rule out or dismiss variables other than the independent variable as causes of a result, the truth of our conclusion that the independent variable is the cause of the differences in the dependent variable is more closely approximated.

Independent variables are defined by an operation or series of operations, and it is the conclusions about these operations to which the term internal validity applies. A researcher interested in the effect of motivation upon imagery might first pretest subjects' motivation by having them tell stories in response to Thematic Apperception Test (TAT) cards. The TAT is a projective technique which involves showing pictures of scenes to individuals and then having the individuals tell stories about what is happening in the scenes. The rationale behind the TAT and other projective techniques is to gather evidence about the motives of individuals through their fantasies; that is, through the stories they tell. He would then deprive subjects for either 2 or 16 hours (the operational definition of motivation, the independent variable) and then posttest them on the TAT. The number of references to food-related themes in the stories would be the dependent variable. If the two deprivation groups began the same and showed significant differences in the number of food-related themes in their posttest stories, could we draw the conclusion that the independent variable produced these differences? If we could eliminate the plausibility that a variable other than the two deprivation levels produced the differences, the experiment would be internally valid; that is, we could state that the difference in number of food-related themes was caused by the difference between being deprived for 2 versus 16 hours. The validity question here would only deal with the effect of the difference between 2 and 16 hours deprivation and not about motivation in general. In other words, internal validity would apply only to the effect of the specific operations employed in the study and not to the theoretical concept which is represented by those operations.

Up to this point, we have referred to variables other than the independent variable which could be plausible causes of an effect and which would render a conclusion internally invalid. The other variables which are threats to internal validity can be specified as falling into eight categories: history, maturation, testing, statistical regression, instrumentation, subject selection, subject attrition, and what I'll term leakage. The first five are related to situations where repeated measurement occurs, usually in the form of pre- and posttesting, whereas the last three can occur in either pre- and posttest or posttest only situations.

Let us take a situation and see how the threats to internal validity could affect the conclusions drawn. Assume the following research problem: A therapist is interested in the effects of success experiences on the alleviation of depression. The therapy consists of giving clients suffering from depression weekly tasks graded in difficulty for a period of 10 weeks. Each task is followed by feedback indicating that the client has performed successfully. Before being seen by the therapist, all prospective clients are given a number of questionnaires to fill out, including a 20-item depression inventory. Scores above 10 on this inventory indicate severe depression, and thus clients who score above 10 are chosen for the success therapy treatment. Each client in the study then has a pretest depression score somewhere above 10, and each is given the success therapy. The average pretest score is 16.5, and the average posttest score, that is, the depression score after the 10-week success therapy, is 11.3, and this difference between the pre- and posttest scores is significant. The depression scores have dropped significantly following the therapy.

What conclusion can the therapist draw in this study? Well, the only conclusion which can be drawn unambiguously is that the posttest scores are significantly lower than the pretest scores. Unfortunately, the reason for the drop in the depression scores from pre- to posttest is not at all clear. It could be the therapy that caused the drop, but the drop could also be due to other factors such as history, maturation, testing, and statistical regression. Let's examine these factors in order to see how each could rival the therapy as a cause for the drop in depression scores.

History

History refers to an event other than the treatment which occurs between the pre- and the posttest and thus rivals the treatment as a causal agent. In the above therapy study, an event that intervened between the pre- and post-depression tests could have produced the drop in depression scores. For example, let us say that the economy in the area had been rather sluggish at the time of the pretest with a high number of workers unemployed and that, during the period between the pre- and posttest, a new industry announced plans to open a large plant. The plant opening not only has the direct effect that many of the unemployed people in the area will now have jobs, but also the indirect effect that business and professional people in the area will gain from the increased prosperity. So, the plant opening will have an effect throughout the community. Now at the time of the posttest, depression scores are significantly lower, but is it due to the therapy or to the brighter economic outlook for the area? History has intervened to produce a quite plausible rival explanation for the results.

In the early 1970s, my students and I were carrying out a research project on attitude change. We had chosen to try to change attitudes toward student activism since at that time, this was a central topic on college campuses. We had measured students' attitudes toward the topic in February and had chosen as subjects for our study only those students who were strongly favorable toward student activism. At a later point in the semester, the students who had been selected were called in, were given the treatment which was designed to make them less positive toward the topic, and were then remeasured on their attitudes toward student activism. Statistical analysis showed that, following the treatment, the subjects were significantly less favorable toward student activism then they were before the treatment. Could we conclude from these pretest-posttest differences that our treatment had worked to change attitudes?

Well, unfortunately, during the period between the pre- and posttests, a number of violent incidents by protesting students had occurred throughout the country and received wide news coverage in the media. It would seem quite plausible that this violence may have been repugnant to students or even frightened them, causing them to reassess their previous support for student activism and consequently producing less favorable attitudes on the posttest. History intervened in the study to challenge our conclusion that our treatment had produced the change in attitudes. Fortunately, the study was designed in such a manner that we could directly examine the effects of history as a rival explanation. If it had not been so designed, history would have directly challenged the internal validity of our conclusions.

Maturation

Maturation refers to ongoing processes of growth or decline which occur between the pre- and the posttest. Young subjects might gain intellectual skills or older subjects might lose them through natural aging processes; education might provide formal knowledge; or physical development might change over time so as to make subjects stronger or weaker. Whereas history refers to a single event which intervenes between the pre- and the posttest to change responses, maturation refers to a rather continuous change in physical or psychological processes of the subjects. Subjects in the therapy study may have been gradually becoming less depressed, so that over the 10-week period of the study, scores continued to drop until they reached a point at the posttest where they were significantly different than they were at the pretest. Thus, the drop in depression scores may have been due to an ongoing maturational trend rather than the therapy. Also, the longer the time span between the pre- and the posttest, the greater the likelihood that maturation can threaten internal validity.

Consider the case of a treatment designed to facilitate sharing among fourth-grade school children. At the beginning of the school year, the children are observed by judges and scored in terms of the amount of sharing of school supplies that occurs. Following this, children read stories once a week in which the characters help each other and share their belongings. This story reading continues throughout most of the year until May when the children are again observed by the raters and scored for sharing. Comparison of the pre- and postsharing scores shows a significant increase in sharing. Has the exposure to the stories raised the level of sharing? It is possible, but certainly not clear in that another variable was operating alongside the stories. That variable is maturation. The children are now almost a year older, which means that they are more mature. Since sharing has been shown to increase with age, especially in the range of 9 to 10 years of age, the increase in sharing may be due to the natural maturation of the children and not to the stories.

Testing

Testing refers to the effects of repeated measurements upon responses in that taking a test the second time can change responses. Test items are often remembered along with the errors made, and thus performance may increase. In the case of the therapy study, subjects depression scores may drop simply as a function of taking the test a second time and being familiar with the items.

Regression

Statistical Regression refers to the fact that extreme scores tend to regress toward (get closer to) the population mean on a second testing. Due to the unreliability of the test, low scores on a first testing are likely to have been depressed, and high scores are likely to have been inflated. That is, a very high obtained score on a test lies close to the top limit of the test, and so the true score cannot vary as far upward from the obtained score as it can downward. The reverse is true for very low obtained scores. The true score cannot vary downward as far as it can vary upward. On a second testing, the chance factors that produced the depression or inflation of the scores will probably not occur; as a result, the high scores will be lower and the low scores higher than on the first testing. The less reliable the test and the more extreme the pretest scores, the greater will be the effect of statistical regression. In the therapy study, subjects were selected who were high on depression, and thus on a second testing, scores would be expected to move downward simply as a result of statistical regression due to the unreliability of the test.

Statistical regression could also have affected the results of the study involving changing attitudes toward student activism in that subjects were selected who were being favorable toward student activism. Due to the unreliability of the student activism measure, their scores would be expected to become less favorable on a second testing. Thus, the pretest-posttest difference could have been a function of a regression effect rather than a function of the treatment. Again, fortunately, due to the design of the study, we could draw a clear conclusion about the effect of the treatment. Whenever subjects are preselected on the basis of their extreme scores, regression will occur at the time of the posttest.

Instrumentation Error

The fifth threat to internal validity in pretest-posttest studies is instrumentation error. Instrumentation error refers to a systematic change in the measuring instrument over time which could have produced the pretest-posttest difference. This does not refer to a change in scores due to statistical regression produced by the unreliability of the measurement. Rather, it refers to scores being either higher or lower on a second measurement due to an actual change in the measuring instrument. These changes in the measuring instrument usually occur when judgments are required for scoring. For example, raters of behaviors often become better over time at judging relevant behaviors, and scores on a second testing may increase or decrease in accordance with this change. In the therapy study, an objective depression inventory was given, and thus little change in instrumentation would have been expected over time. If clinical ratings or judgments of depression had been used instead of the objective measure, changes in judgments over time would be likely. Subjects could have been judged as less depressed on the posttest simply because as the raters become more familiar with the rating scheme, they became more discriminating in judging depressed from nondepressed behaviors and consequently judged less depression overall on the posttest.

Instrumentation error could also have affected the results of the study on the sharing behavior of fourth graders since sharing was scored by three raters. It is certainly true that, at the time of the first ratings of sharing (the pretest), the raters were less experienced in observing the behavior of the children than at the time the second ratings were carried out. It is quite possible that this increased experience would make them more sensitive to various instances of sharing behavior, and thus more sharing behavior would be picked up by the raters on the posttest. The sensitivity of the instrument itself, that is, the raters systematically improving over time, may have resulted in the higher posttest ratings of sharing, thus making instrumentation error a plausible rival cause to that of reading the stories about sharing.

Thus, any or all of the above—history, maturation, testing, statistical regression, and instrumentation—can occur between the pre- and the posttest and produce differences between the pre- and the posttest scores. The question is, how do we know if the difference between the pre- and the posttest scores is due to one of these intervening events or to the factor in which we are interested? Specifically, how could we know if the lower scores on the depression measure given at the posttest was due to the therapy or to one or more of the other factors which could have affected the posttest scores. In the case of the studies described, we could not know. That is, we could not rule out history, maturation, testing, statistical regression, or instrumentation error as plausible causes of the pretest-posttest differences. The simple pretest-posttest design leads to internal *invalidity* and is therefore inadequate.

Employing Controls

The answer to the problem is to use designs which appropriately control for the above threats to internal validity and which consequently allow for clear conclusions to be drawn. There are a number of choices of designs in this regard, each having certain advantages and disadvantages. The designs differ in that a pretest may or may not be employed, a pretest condition and a no pretest condition may both be employed, and matching of subjects on some variable may or may not occur. All of these designs have two aspects in common: *(a)* all involve one or more nontreated groups, and *(b)* all involve the random assignment of subjects to conditions.

Table 8–1 depicts four designs which control for the threats to internal validity. The top row of each design is a listing, in temporal order, of the events occurring in the experiment. The entries in the table indicate whether or not each of the events occurs for each of the two groups in the experiment. Designs A and B are both pretest-posttest control group designs. They differ only with respect to whether or not matching occurs.

In design A, subjects may or may not be matched on some variable. If they are matched, one member of each matched pair will be randomly assigned to each group. If matching is not employed, subjects will simply be randomly assigned to the two groups. Following random assignment, a pretest assessment of the dependent variable is carried out for all subjects. The pretesting is then followed by implementation of the treatment for group 1 only (the experimental group); group 2 receives no treatment during this period (the control group). Both groups are then posttested on the dependent variable either with the same form of the test as used on the pretest or with an alternate form.

Design B differs from design A in that matching is done on the pretest itself. Thus, all subjects are pretested, matched on their pretest scores, and then randomly assigned to the two groups in matched pairs. Group 1 is then given the treatment, while group 2 receives no treatment during this

TABLE 8–1

Designs controlling for threats to internal validity

		Matching	*Random Assignment*	*Measure Time 1*	*Treatment*	*Measure Time 2*
A.	Group 1	Optional	Yes	Yes	Yes	Yes
	Group 2	Optional	Yes	Yes	No	Yes

		Measure Time 1	*Matching*	*Random Assignment*	*Treatment*	*Measure Time 2*
B.	Group 1	Yes	Yes	Yes	Yes	Yes
	Group 2	Yes	Yes	Yes	No	Yes

		Random Assignment	*Treatment*	*Measure Time 1*
C.	Group 1	Yes	Yes	Yes
	Group 2	Yes	No	Yes

		Random Assignment	*Measure Time 1*	*Treatment*	*Measure Time 2*
D.	Group 1	Yes	Yes	Yes	Yes
	Group 2	Yes	Yes	No	Yes
	Group 3	Yes	No	Yes	Yes
	Group 4	Yes	No	No	Yes

period. All subjects are then posttested on the same or on an alternate form of the dependent measure.

Both of these designs control for or account for the sources of internal invalidity. History, maturation, testing, statistical regression, and instrumentation can all occur in both designs A and B, but since subjects are randomly assigned to the two conditions, these factors occur equally for both groups. Thus, any posttest differences will be due to the only factor on which the two groups differed—whether or not the treatment was given.

Let us return to the depression therapy study to see specifically how the threats to internal validity can be controlled. Assume that, rather than using a simple pretest-posttest design, subjects have been randomly assigned to either a therapy or no therapy control condition, pretested on the depression inventory, given the therapy or given no therapy for identical time periods, and finally posttested on the depression inventory. Let us first assume that history acted by brightening the economic picture between the pre- and posttest. Since the economy would be affected similarly for both groups, this historical event could not rival the therapy as an explanation of posttest differences. Maturation also occurred between the pre- and the posttest in that, at least to some extent, subjects learned new facts, had new experiences, processed information, and grew older. Again, these maturational processes should be similar for both groups, and thus maturation would be ruled out as a rival causal agent. Also both groups are pretested and posttested on the depression inventory, and thus no differential testing or instrumentation effects could have occurred. Finally, although subjects are high on depression at the pretest and will show statistical regression on the posttest, the two groups will regress equally, ruling this factor out as a plausible rival cause.

Recall that when the study on changing attitudes toward student activism was discussed, it was mentioned that due to our design we could draw a clear conclusion about the effect of the treatment. The design employed an attitude change treatment group and a no treatment control group to which subjects selected as to being pro-student activism on the pretest were randomly assigned (design A). Thus, even though history intervened between the pre- and the posttest in the form of national violence by radicals, it intervened for both groups. Also, since the subjects selected on the basis of their favorable pretest scores were randomly assigned to the two groups, both groups would have been composed of extreme scorers. This means that statistical regression would have affected the groups equally. Thus, the difference in the means of the posttest scores must have been due to something beyond history and regression; namely, the treatment. By employing a control group to which subjects were randomly assigned, both history and maturation could be ruled out as threats to internal validity.

In both designs A and B, all of the above threats to internal validity are controlled. The choice between the two designs is one of matching or not on the pretest. Matching on the pretest in design B ensures that both groups start out the same on both their average pretest scores and on their group variance. The matching also makes possible removal of variance on the posttest scores through the appropriate statistical test, thereby decreasing the probability of a Type II error. The problem is that in order to match on the basis of the pretest, all of the subjects must be pretested prior to their assignment to the groups. Very often, this procedure is not possible. That is, subjects are often pretested and assigned to conditions at the time they arrive for the experiment. In the case of the depression therapy, it would probably be the case that depressed patients would arrive at the clinic continuously over a period of time, rather than all at once. Thus, it would be impossible to have all of the pretest depression scores available for matching before any treatment begins. Therefore, when there are practical limitations to matching, design A would have to be used.

Both design A and B control and account for the sources of internal invalidity. Design C, on the other hand, controls for but does not account for the sources of invalidity. Design C is a posttest-only design; that is, subjects are not pretested but are simply randomly assigned to the two groups, treated or not, and then posttested. Just as in the previous two designs (A and B), the threats to internal validity are controlled. Two threats to internal validity in the pretest-posttest designs, testing and instrumentation, are completely ruled out in the posttest-only design. First, since subjects in the posttest-only design are measured only at one point, there can be no threat to validity from repeated testings. Second, since only one measurement occurs, there cannot be systematic changes over time in the measuring instrument. History, maturation, and statistical regression can occur but are controlled for in the posttest-only design. Any historical events intervening between the point in time of random assignment and posttesting would affect both groups equally, and maturational changes during this period would also occur equally for both groups. Also, even though subjects are not pretested, high or low scores would have regressed toward the mean on a second testing, but this regression would occur for both groups. Thus, history, maturation, and statistical regression are all controlled in the posttest-only design by random assignment to the groups. These factors are controlled in this design, but they are not accounted for. Although both groups should experience history, maturation, and regression effects equally, since there is no pretest, we cannot determine the magnitude of the influence of these effects. In both of the pretest designs, we not only know that these effects influence the groups equally, but we are also able to tell the degree of influence of these factors by examining the change from pre- to posttest in the nontreated group. Since there is no pretest in the posttest-only design, the degree of influence of history, maturation, and regression cannot be assessed. It should be noted that although one can examine the degree of influence of the effects of history, maturation, and regression with the pretest, one cannot determine which variable or variables is operating.

There is a second even more important problem with posttest-only designs, and that is the question of which group changes. Returning again to the depression therapy example, assume that subjects, judged clinically to be depressed but not actually pretested, have been randomly assigned to the therapy or no therapy conditions. All subjects are posttested, either following therapy or following an equivalent waiting period. Analysis of the posttest scores shows that the group receiving therapy scores significantly lower than the nontherapy group on the depression inventory. Since subjects were randomly assigned to the groups, the threats to internal validity cannot be plausible rival explanations for the effect. That is, the difference between the groups is due to the difference in the treatment they received. The problem is that since there was no pretesting, we don't know whether the therapy lowered that group's depression scores. It could be the case that the therapy caused depression scores to remain rather stable, not improving but also not declining, whereas receiving no therapy produced a worsening effect. For example, it is possible that being assigned to wait for treatment may be one more indication of worthlessness to a depressed person. This, of course, may make them even more depressed. Thus, it would be the case that the waiting condition was not a control condition, but rather it was itself a treatment. The point is that the difference would be due to the no therapy group becoming more depressed, rather than the therapy group becoming less depressed. If a pretest had been given, we could observe how subjects within each group changed from pre- to posttest. So, the advantage of using a pretest is that a clearer interpretation of the effects of the treatment is obtained.

You might now be asking why a pretest is not always employed since it allows the researcher to both account for the threats to internal validity and to examine the nature of the group differences. The answer is that pretesting may have the disadvantage of sensitizing subjects to the manipulation and thus may possibly produce a number of problems. These problems have to do either with conceptual validity or what is called external validity. A full discussion of both conceptual and external validity will occur later, but at this point, a brief definition and example of each will suffice. An experiment has conceptual validity if the researcher can draw the conclusion that the results occurred for the reasons posited. The conceptual validity problem in regard to pretesting is that subjects exposed to a pretest followed by a treatment may change as a function of that treatment, but for reasons other than those posited by the researcher. For example, pretested patients treated with the depression therapy may change more than their counterparts in the nontreated control group, but not directly because of the therapy. Subjects scoring quite high on the pretest depression inventory and then going through a number of therapeutic sessions may attempt to please the therapist by lowering their scores on the posttest. Even though they have not actually become less depressed, their posttest scores will be lower than those patients who have not undergone therapy. Is this change due to the treatment? Absolutely, but not because the therapy alleviated depression. Rather, it was due to the treatment producing an attempt by subjects to manipulate their scores so as to show a change. Subjects in the control group would have no one to please, and therefore they would have no reason to manipulate their posttest scores. The therapy would produce an effect, but not for the right reason. If a posttest-only design was employed, subjects receiving the therapy would have no pretest experience on which to base a deliberate change.

Another related problem would occur where the pretest may cause the subjects not to change on the posttest in spite of the treatment. Studies in the area of cognitive dissonance often run into this problem. The theory of cognitive dissonance posits that when individuals behave in a manner that is inconsistent with what they believe, they suffer dissonance. Dissonance is an unpleasant or aversive state which motivates the individual to reestablish consistency and thus reduce the dissonance. Further, the theory states that the more pressure or force that is employed to bring about the inconsistent behavior, the less the dissonance that will be suffered. In other words, inconsistent actions which are taken voluntarily or under a high degree of choice produce the strongest dissonance. One of the ways researchers have produced dissonance is by having subjects write counterattitudinal essays; that is, essays which contradict their presently held beliefs. If, after writing the essays, subjects' attitudes change toward consistency with the essay, this is taken as evidence for the dissonance effect.

With this rather superficial description of the theory of cognitive dissonance, let us examine how pretesting might affect a dissonance experiment. The scenario is as follows: In the fall of 1980, I decide to do an experiment on cognitive dissonance which involves having subjects write counterattitudinal essays. I have the students write an essay supporting the taking and holding of the American hostages by the Iranians. The dissonance is manipulated by randomly assigning subjects to either a condition where they are given no choice in the matter or to a condition where they are told they are free to write either an essay supporting the Iranian action or to write one against the Iranian action. In order to persuade the high-choice subjects to write the counterattitudinal essay, I tell them that we have a lot of anti-Iranian essays already and that we really need pro-Iranian essays, but that the choice is up to them. After the subjects write the essays, they complete a scale designed to measure their attitudes toward the Iranian action. The results show that, as expected, the high-choice group is significantly more positive toward the Iranians than the low-choice group.

You may have noticed that the above description of the procedure did not include a pretest of subjects on their attitude toward the Iranians. A pretest was not given in our study because it may have robbed the results of construct validity. Assume that we had given a pretest to all subjects, instituted the choice manipulation, followed with the essay writing, and then administered the posttest. It is quite possible that subjects, having been tested on their attitude toward the Iranians and then given a choice, may have attempted not to appear inconsistent in their pre- and posttest attitudes. If this occurred, the pretest would have wiped out the effect of the choice manipulation. In fact, that is exactly why we chose the topic of the Iranians. It could be pretty well assumed that most subjects would not agree with the action of taking and holding the hostages, and thus an essay supporting the Iranian action would be incongruent with the subjects' attitudes. Thus, the strategy of many cognitive dissonance studies is to choose a topic where subjects' attitudes can be safely assumed, avoiding the problems of a pretest.

External validity refers to the generalizability of the results of an experiment. If a manipulation works only when subjects exposed to that manipulation are pretested, then the generalizability of the manipulation is restricted. Thus, even if a manipulation works for the reason posited by the experimenter but only works when pretesting is done, the effect is certainly less general than when the manipulation works with or without a pretest. Let us take an example from the area of imitation of aggression. Children are put in a room containing a number of toys including the ever popular Bobo doll, a large plastic clown which is designed to take almost unlimited abuse from children. Judges, surreptitiously watching the children, rate their aggressiveness. The children are then shown a film of a model who is either rewarded or punished after aggressing against the Bobo doll. The child is then returned to the room with the Bobo doll and the other toys and the behavior is rated again. The children in the two groups score equally on the aggression pretest, but those children exposed to the rewarded model score higher on the posttest than their punished model counterparts. Let us assume for the sake of the present discussion that the effect was due to the fact that the children imitated the rewarded and not the punished aggressive model; that is, assume that the experiment has internal validity.

Even so, the study may lack external validity. If the study was rerun with no pretest and the rewarded model effect did not occur, then the effect of reward would be limited to only those situations in which children are pretested. For example, it may be that children will imitate rewarded aggressive models only if they can aggress to some degree, previous to seeing the model, in a situation which is identical to the one in which the model performs. Since most aggressive models appear on television in situations totally unlike those the children find themselves, these results would have little generality.

If pretesting can threaten the conceptual and external validity of an experiment and if using a posttest-only design leaves us with less clarity as to the direction of results, what is the answer? Well, the answer is design D in Table 8–1, which is termed a *Solomon four-group design* (not named after the wise king). This design combines the advantages of both the designs employing a pretest and the posttest-only design. In this design, subjects are randomly assigned to four groups. Groups 1 and 2 are then pretested; groups 3 and 4 receive no pretest. Treatment then occurs for groups 1 and 3 only, and all groups receive a posttest. Control for the threats to internal validity are found in the posttest comparisons between groups 1 and 2 on the one hand and groups 3 and 4 on the other. Accounting for the threats to internal validity is possible by way of the pretest-posttest comparisons between groups 1 and 2. The effects of pretesting on the results can be found by comparing the posttest difference between groups 1 and 3. If the two are significantly different, it means that the treatment works differently with a pretest than it does without one.

Thus, design D covers all the discussed threats to validity and seems to be the design of choice. The problem is that in order to use design D rather than a simple pretest-posttest control or posttest-only design, many more subjects are needed. In the simple treatment-versus-no-treatment situation, twice as many subjects are needed for design D as for the other designs in Table 8–1. As experiments become more complicated, either because more levels of an independent variable are used (e.g., success therapy, drug therapy, or no therapy) or because of the use of more than one independent variable, the Solomon four-group design becomes more unwieldly. In choosing a design, there are not only questions of validity to consider, but also questions of cost and feasibility. In a more applied setting, such as that involving the depression therapy, there may be a limited number of subjects (depressed patients) to assign to conditions. Also, when the time involved in administering the treatment to each subjective is extensive, using a large number of subjects may make the total time for the experiment too long. Thus, although a design such as the Solomon four-group design is the ideal, reality often forces researchers to compromise.

There are three remaining threats to internal validity which have not yet been discussed: subject selection, subject attrition, and leakage. All three can act to threaten the ability to draw clear conclusions about the independent variable as a causal agent. These three threats are not a function of events which intervene between the pre- and the posttest and therefore would apply to all of the designs in Table 8–1.

Subject Selection

Whenever subjects are assigned to conditions on a nonrandom basis, the validity of the conclusions are threatened. Subject selection as a threat to internal validity then occurs when the groups which comprise the various levels or treatments of the independent variable are not composed on a random basis. If groups are not composed on a random basis, then they must be composed on some systematic basis. That systematic basis can then act as a factor which competes with the independent variable as an explanation for the results of the study. Employing the depression therapy example again, assume that the therapist decides to treat the depressed patients who come to her clinic with the graded task followed by feedback therapy. As a control group, she employs the depressed patients who go to another clinic across town and who are treated with antidepressive drugs. Both groups are pretested with the depression inventory, treated for the same amount of time, and then posttested.

The therapist finds that the two groups do not differ on the pretest, but that her group scores significantly less depressed on the posttest than the group receiving group therapy. Can she conclude that her graded task therapy is more effective than the drug therapy? Unfortunately, she cannot since there is a competing explanation for the result. Not only do the two groups differ in terms of type of therapy, they also differ in terms of selection. Patients arrived at the two clinics on some systematic basis and not via random assignment. Even though they start out alike on the depression inventory, they may differ at the outset on many other variables. For example, if the drug therapy clinic is in a poorer section of town, the economic differences between the patients at the two clinics would be a possible rival cause of the posttest depression differences. If the two clinics were in the same part of town, but patients were referred to the drug therapy clinic by a physician and chose the graded-task-therapy clinic on their own initiative, those patients who are aware of and concerned about their problem enough to seek help may be better candidates for any type of therapy than patients whose problem is diagnosed by a physician. Thus, the difference in posttest scores may be due to a personality variable related to their choice of or referral to a clinic, rather than the difference between the two therapies.

Assume that the therapist had decided to use only patients at the clinic employing the antidepressive drug. Before drug treatment, all patients must be informed of any side effects, and some of them then refuse the drug therapy. These patients are then placed into the graded-task-feedback therapy condition. Both groups, the control group receiving drug therapy and the experimental group receiving graded-task-feedback therapy, are now from the same clinic patient population. If the experimental group scores less depressed than the control group, can the therapist conclude that her therapy was effective? Again, she cannot since the patients who refused the drug treatment may be different than those who didn't refuse. For example, refusers may be those who show more initiative and thus may have better prognoses for depression alleviation. Again, posttest differences may be due to a personality variable related to their accepting or rejecting the drug therapy.

Let us take one final example of selection. Suppose that a researcher decides to study the effect of instructional set on memory. In this study, all subjects are told that they will see a series of adjectives which describe a student, and then they are either told that they will be asked to transmit their impressions of this student to other people or that they will receive more information about this student from other people. All subjects are then asked to recall as many of the adjectives as they can, the average number of adjectives recalled by each group (transmitters and receivers) being the dependent variable. The researcher decides that, in order to save time, he will use two sections of the introductory psychology course as his treatment groups. He then randomly chooses the 10:00 A.M. section for the receiving set group and the 2:00 P.M. section for the transmitting group. The results show that the receiving set group, as predicted, recalls significantly more adjectives than the transmitting set group. Can he conclude that the difference is due to the different sets? Again, unfortunately, he cannot since selection is also a rival causal agent in this case. Students sign up for different sections for various reasons. For example, early classes may indicate more motivated students, or the two classes may be selected for the professors who teach them; that is, the early class may be more rigorous and thus have better students. Finally, even if students are randomly assigned to the classes initially, the time of day that the class is taught and consequently the time of day that the experiment is run may have produced the difference in recall; students are probably more alert at 10:00 A.M. than at 2:00 P.M.

The point of these examples is that nonrandom selection of subjects introduces a rival causal agent into the experiment. Very often there is an attempt to match two groups on one or a number of variables related to the dependent variables in order to compensate for the fact that random assignment has not occurred. This procedure, although better than no attempt to produce equivalency between the groups, cannot rule out selection on some variable other than those variables chosen for matching. Even when the selected subjects are alike initially on the pretest, as in the case of the depression scores from the two clinics, there is no guarantee that the two groups do not differ on other variables which may be related to the dependent variable. Thus, in the long run, the only guarantee of equivalency is random assignment.

Subject Attrition

Subject attrition refers to a differential loss of subjects among the treatment groups. If the drop-out rate is greater from one group, the advantage of random assignment is lost in that the groups may no longer be equivalent. Going back to the original depression therapy design where subjects are assigned randomly to the therapy group or to a group that receives no treatment, assume that one third of the subjects in the therapy group have terminated the therapy before the end of the full 10 weeks of treatment. On the other hand, all of the waiting group subjects are available at the end of 10 weeks. Comparison of the posttest depression scores shows the therapy group to be significantly less depressed than the nontherapy group. Can we clearly identify the therapy as the causal agent here? Again, the answer is no. It is quite possible that those patients who dropped out were either more depressed or less motivated, leaving either the less depressed or more motivated patients in the therapy group. The nontherapy group contains the whole range of depression and or motivation, while the therapy group contains only a select group from the original random assignment. The factor which caused patients to drop out may also be the factor responsible for the posttest differences between the two groups. At least, this is a rival cause to the independent variable—the therapy.

If a pretest had been employed, one could actually see if those patients who dropped out had been more depressed, but the groups are still not equivalent at the time of the posttest. Subject attrition could also have worked in the opposite way, in that some subjects assigned to the nontherapy condition may have become tired of waiting and gone to other places for treatment. If these subjects had been less depressed or more motivated, then the nontherapy group would be left with less motivated or more depressed patients than the therapy group. In this case, the therapy group would show an advantage because the healthier patients dropped out of the nontherapy group. Finally, it could be the case that very depressed patients would lose the motivation to wait 10 weeks for therapy and drop out completely, seeking no other help. The nontherapy group would now consist of healthier patients, and this nonequivalence may wipe out the effect of the therapy. In this case, rather than attrition acting as a rival cause for the significant difference between the groups, it has acted so as to mask the effects of the independent variable and cause a Type II error to be committed.

Subject attrition refers not only to subjects actually dropping out of the experiment, but also to data from subjects being not usable. The cognitive dissonance study discussed previously illustrates this effect. That study was carried out in the fall of 1980, when the hostages were still in the hands of the Iranians. In the spring of 1981, a second study was undertaken on this same topic. One part of this second study involved a replication of the dissonance situation employed in the first study I described earlier; that is, a high- and a low-choice group writing essays favorable to the Iranians and then being tested on the attitude toward the Iranians scale. Unfortunately for us, but fortunately for the hostages, history intervened in the spring of 1981 in the form of a release of the hostages from captivity. The threat to validity was not due to history itself since both the high- and low-choice groups were exposed to the release of the hostages. The threat to validity from the release of the hostages came from the fact that it produced a differential loss of subjects from the two groups.

Although subjects were randomly assigned in equal numbers to the two conditions, there were 15 low-choice scores and only 10 high-choice scores at the end of the experiment. The reason is that five of the high-choice subjects took the option of writing an anti-Iranian essay, which made their behavior noncounterattitudinal and not useful for this research. The release of the hostages was accompanied by stories of their mistreatment at the hands of the Iranians, and these stories may have produced reluctance to write the pro-Iranian essay on the part of the high-choice subjects. In any case, these subjects were discarded, leaving a smaller sample size for the high- than for the low-choice condition.

The validity of this experiment was now threatened by subject attrition. Random assignment was the assurance of equivalence between the conditions at the start of the study, but since subjects had been discarded from one of the conditions, this equivalence could no longer be assured. It is quite possible, for example, that those subjects who refused to write the counterattitudinal essay were more strongly anti-Iranian to begin with. Since these extreme subjects were no longer included in the high-choice group, the groups were no longer equivalent in their initial attitudes; the low-choice group would contain more extreme anti-Iranians that the high-choice group. Thus, the attitude scores of the high-choice subjects would be more favorable to the Iranians at the end of the study not due to the dissonance effect, but rather to differential subject loss resulting in differential composition of the groups. If a pretest had been used, the initial attitudes of the discarded subjects could have been checked, but even if it had been found that they were no more extreme initially, attrition could not be ruled out as a rival cause. For example, these subjects could be less conforming in that they refused to write the counterattitudinal essay. This would mean that the low-choice group ends up being higher in conformity than the high-choice group, and this conformity difference could be the cause of the posttest attitude difference.

It should be made clear that the unequal group sizes do not in themselves threaten validity. If it could be determined that the loss of subjects was a random process, such as having the cards notifying them to come to the experiment be lost in the mail, having subjects not show up due to illness, or having the experimenter fail to show up due to illness, then a valid conclusion could still be drawn from the unequal size groups. Thus, it is only when the attrition is due, or at least could be due, to a systematic factor, that internal validity is threatened.

Leakage

The final threat to internal validity comes through a process that I term *leakage*. This threat occurs when knowledge about one of the treatments in an experiment becomes available to subjects in another treatment condition. Some of the effects of leakage can occur in both laboratory and applied or field settings, while others are pretty much restricted to applied research situations. One way in which leakage can threaten internal validity is when the treatment available for one group of subjects becomes available for other groups of subjects. For example, assume that in a class for gifted children, children are randomly assigned to either a problem-solving or a critical-reading-skills treatment. While the problem-solving group is receiving its training sessions, the critical-reading group is engaged in some other activity, and while the critical-reading group is receiving its treatment, the problem-solving group carries out some activity unrelated to critical reading. Since due to limitations of space both treatments are carried out in the same classroom, it is quite possible for each group to pick up treatment information designed for the other group. If the treatments are effective, we should find that the problem-solving group outperforms the critical-reading group on problem solving but is outperformed by the critical-reading group on the measure of critical reading. Assume that when the groups are tested at the end of the training period on both problem-solving and critical-reading skill, no differences appear. This finding may be due either to the fact that the training programs are not effective or to the leakage of treatments between the two groups which has provided both groups with both skills and thus eliminated any treatment differences.

A second way in which leakage can threaten internal validity is by producing rivalry between members of one treatment group and those of another group. Take the case of a program designed to produce effective parenting in a rural population. Parents within a number of rural communities who have been pretested on an inventory dealing with problems in childrearing are randomly assigned to either the effective parenting program or to a waiting control group. Since members of both groups come from the same small communities and may be friends and neighbors, communicaton about the treatment probably will occur. Those parents in the control group who learn that they have been excluded from this special program that is being offered in their community may compensate for this exclusion by trying to prove that they can enhance their own effectiveness without the benefit of the program. This rivalry on the part of the deprived control subjects, producing increased motivation, may wipe out the treatment effects. In a sense, we no longer have the effective parenting program being compared with a waiting control group, but rather we have a comparison between the effective parenting program condition and a high motivation or compensation condition produced through deprivation of the treatment.

A third way leakage can threaten internal validity is by producing demoralization in groups receiving less desirable treatments. In the above case of the effective parenting program, waiting control subjects who learn of the special program offered to their neighbors may become demoralized rather than highly motivated. That is, rather than attempting to compensate for their exclusion from the program, they may lose motivation to deal with their children and thus show higher posttest scores (more problems) on the childrearing inventory. Thus, the posttest difference between the treatment and control groups would be due not to the effectiveness of the parenting program, but rather to a worsening of the control group brought about by the leakage of knowledge about the treatment.

Both rivalry and demoralization occur most frequently when one group receives a desirable or beneficial treatment while the other group is deprived of that treatment (Cook and Campbell, 1979). This circumstance is most prevalent in applied settings and can be a direct threat to the internal validity of research or treatment programs. One way around this problem is to employ homogeneous blocks of subjects as the sampling units. Rather than randomly assigning subjects within a given area, for example a small town, to the various treatments, whole communities are assigned to a given treatment condition. At first glance, this would seem to introduce subject selection as a threat to internal validity, and indeed this would be the case if only two communities were compared. But if a number of towns can be sampled and these towns randomly assigned to the treatment conditions, then the problem of selection is avoided. The important point is that the problem of leakage is minimized since neighbors in the same town all receive the same treatment or no treatment, as the case may be. It should be noted that while communities have been used as the example here, the homogeneous blocks could be classrooms in a school, areas of a city, or small sections of a large college course. The choice of units is made on the basis of the availability of the units and the importance of the prevention of leakage.

Leakage can also be an issue both in studies where subjects are exposed only to their own treatment and in studies where differential desirability of treatments does not occur. Leakage of information about a treatment by subjects already exposed to that treatment to subjects who will subsequently be exposed may modify these latter subjects' behaviors. In many social psychological experiments, subjects are deceived as to the true nature of the treatment until the end of the experimental session, when they are fully debriefed. The first subjects, not knowing about the deception, may respond to the treatment as predicted, but subsequent subjects, having been informed about the deception, probably will not respond in the same way.

A recent study in our own laboratory, employing subjects selected from an introductory psychology course subject pool, is a case in point. In this experiment, which deals with similarity of attitudes and feelings of attractiveness, two same-sex subjects have been made to believe that they are attitudinally dissimilar to each other. They also have been told that there is a third subject of the opposite sex in another room who is highly attractive, 8.7 on a 10-point scale. Each subject has been shown the missing person's attitudes which indicate that the missing person is similar to one of them and dissimilar to the other. While the subjects are reviewing the attitudinal information, the experimenter takes the attitudinal information of the subjects down to the missing person. Upon returning, the experimenter informs the two subjects that ''we are actually studying people's perceptions of the dating process,'' and that the missing person will choose one of the two subjects as a partner for a short coffee date at the end of the hour. At this point the subjects are taken to separate rooms and are told that they have been chosen or not by the missing person. Both subjects then complete a series of scales designed to measure their judgments of their own attractiveness and their judgments of the other subject's attractiveness. At this point, the subjects are brought back together and fully debriefed.

The debriefing informs them that the attitudes that they studied were not the actual attitudes of the other subject or the missing person, but were bogus attitudes, completed by the experimenter, which were designed to create the perceptions of similarity and dissimilarity. They are also told that the missing person is actually missing; that is, he or she never existed. As part of the debriefing, the subjects are asked not to discuss the study with anyone. But let us assume that subjects disregard this plea and convey both the nature of the events of the study and the deceptions to other people who will also serve as subjects in the study. It is quite obvious that knowing about the illegitimacy of the attitudes and the nonexistence of the missing person will eliminate any actual effects of attitude similarity-dissimilarity and being chosen or not. Thus, the effect of leakage might be to eliminate the effects of the independent variables. The researcher can only act here to minimize the risk of leakage since it is very difficult to eliminate. Since the longer an experiment lasts, the greater are the chances for leakage to occur, researchers often try to run experiments as quickly as possible. While this is theoretically the optimum strategy, practical necessities often clash with brevity. For example, it may be impossible to physically schedule all the subjects in a short time span due to subject, experimenter, and/or equipment availability. A second possibility is to ask subjects not to discuss the study until after a specific date (when the study has been completed). Very often this plea for silence is accompanied by a description of the importance of the study in terms of its possible practical implications. Finally, subjects are often asked during the debriefing if they had any foreknowledge of the study and are subsequently omitted from further data analysis if they were informed beforehand. It should be noted that neither a plea for silence nor a question about foreknowledge guarantees an accurate response from subjects, and thus leakage is always a possibility.

In this section, the threats to the internal validity of experiments have been described. Each threat acts as a challenge or rival to the independent variable as a causal agent for the effects seen in a study. Some of these threats, such as history, maturation, and regression, can be directly controlled through random assignment or accounted for through pretesting, while others, such as certain types of leakage, can only be minimized through specific procedures, such as pleas for silence. If the threats to internal validity are indeed controlled, two other validity problems still remain. One is construct validity, which will be dealt with in Chapter 12, and the second is external validity, which is dealt with below.

EXTERNAL VALIDITY

     External validity refers to the degree of generalizability of the results of
a study. Given that an experiment is internally valid and that the independent variable can be identified as the causal agent for changes or differences in the dependent variable, a question of the generalizability of the
results arises. That is, once a cause-effect relationship has been determined between the independent and dependent variables, the question
arises as to how widely the finding applies. Thus external validity is
concerned with the question of inference or generalization which is the
process of moving from the specific to the more general. Specifically,
external validity deals with just how general an inference we can make
from our results. The concept of generalization here refers not only to the
population of subjects (such as college sophomores or white rats), but also
to stimulus conditions and situations. In other words, there is a question of
whether the results generalize to levels or conditions of the independent
variable other than the specific ones employed in the study and also
whether the results generalize to settings other than the specific one in
which the study took place. This last question often arises for studies
conducted in the laboratory and relates to whether the results would occur
in a more naturalistic setting. We will begin our discussion of external
validity with generalization to populations of subjects.

Subject Generalization

If the samples of subjects were randomly selected from a given target
population and differential mortality has not occurred, then the results can
be directly generalized to that target population. The process of random
sampling from a population, so widely employed in survey and opinion
polling research, is carried out through a number of different procedures.
The purpose of all of these procedures is to achieve samples which will
represent the populations from which they were drawn. In other words,
the purpose is to enable accurate inferences to be made about populations.
The most straightforward of these methods involves the *simple random
sample,* where each member of the population has an equal chance of
being selected. Most lotteries or drawings are based on the method of
simple random sampling. In this procedure, each member of the population must be identified, assigned a unique number, and the numbers must
be then drawn in a random manner through a table of random numbers or
by actually physically mixing them before they are drawn. A second
sampling procedure is *stratified random sampling,* where the population is
grouped into relevant strata (e.g., age, race, religion), and then random
sampling is carried out within these strata. This guarantees representation
of the members of the different strata within the final sample. Consider an
opinion poll dealing with the issue of unemployment. Since they are a
minority of the population, a simple random sampling procedure might

contain so few black respondents that their results would be of little use in representing black opinion on the issue. Since the opinion of blacks on the issue of unemployment may differ widely from that of whites, adequately representing their opinion may be quite important. On the other hand, if the pollster sampled randomly within each racial stratum, rather than from the population as a whole, an adequate sample of black opinion could be tapped.

A third procedure is *cluster sampling,* which is employed when it would be difficult or impossible to uniquely identify each member of the population for random selection. In this procedure, groups or clusters of the population are identified, and then these clusters are randomly sampled. For example, a city could be divided into neighborhoods and then blocks randomly sampled within each neighborhood. Houses could also then be randomly sampled within each block. In this process, the individuals do not have to be identified beforehand, and thus this is a useful method when populations are quite large and identification of all members would be an expensive and exhausting process.

This discussion of sampling procedures is intended to be simply an overview. The process of drawing adequate samples from a population is a complex and technical one, and is treated in more depth in texts dealing specifically with this topic. The reason that this text does not cover sampling in an in-depth manner is that most psychological research studies do not deal with samples drawn randomly from a target population, but rather they employ samples gathered in unsystematic ways. For example, much laboratory research is carried out on college students selected from an introductory psychology subject pool, and selection from even this limited population is usually done on a nonrandom basis. That is, someone distributes subjects to users of the subject pool based upon the availability of subjects, or subjects actually choose the studies in which they wish to participate. Even if subjects in the pool were selected randomly, a generalization to only this specific population of introductory psychology students would be of limited value.

Keep in mind that this lack of random selection does not affect the internal validity of the study. As long as the researcher randomly assigns subjects to conditions and differential attrition and leakage do not occur, the study will be internally valid. Thus, even if the subjects who volunteer are all females over six feet tall in height, the study will be internally valid if those tall females are randomly assigned to conditions and if differential attrition and leakage do not occur. The generality of the results may be severely limited since very tall females would make up only a small proportion of the population, but they would be internally valid.

If populations are seldom clearly defined and samples seldom drawn randomly from populations, how do psychological research studies achieve generalizability; that is, how do they achieve external validity? Most samples, although gathered in a nonsystematic manner, do represent broader populations. The breadth of the population to which results can be generalized depends partly on the questions being asked. It is true that in most basic research studies, the researcher isn't interested in the absolute values of responses of subjects, but in relative differences between treatment groups. In a memory study, the researcher may only be interested in whether one condition produces greater recall than another. Although the absolute amounts of recall may be different for various samples (e.g., college student samples versus samples from the general population), it would be assumed that any sample would produce significant differences between conditions in the same direction. This, of course, is an assumption, and unless studies are carried out on a variety of samples and the same general results are found, it remains only an assumption.

It should be kept in mind that generalizations are not only made from samples of college students to the general population, but also from nonhuman samples to the general human population. Most basic work on psychophysiology and psychopharmacology is carried out on nonhuman samples, such as rats and monkeys. Also, much of the research on basic processes of learning, such as drive, habit, and reinforcement, employed rats and pigeons as subjects. The results of these studies were then generalized to the human population. In fact, much of the applied work on behavior modification is directly derived from the research in the operant conditioning laboratories using pigeons as subjects. Again, the more basic the process, the more warranted is the generalization from nonhuman to human populations; and again the assumption of generality holds until evidence challenging that assumption is gathered.

Gathering the evidence that challenges an assumption of generality across species often takes time since it requires studies with samples from various populations. Sometimes the results from studies on different species show that generality holds only under certain conditions for some species, and thus the generality of the original findings must be modified. An example of this modification of cross-species generalization is the work on learned helplessness. The original studies showed that dogs who were exposed to uncontrollable shock showed later performance deficits when compared to dogs who were either exposed to controllable shock or not exposed to shock at all. The results were quite striking in that those dogs given uncontrollable shock in one situation failed to learn to escape shock in a different situation. The results were also shown to hold for a number of different nonhuman species and finally for human subjects exposed to uncontrollable noise.

At this point, the generality or external validity of the research appeared to be quite strong. As more researchers carried out studies on learned helplessness with humans, employing a number of different types of uncontrollable stimulus situations, negative results began to appear. Sometimes the uncontrollability did not produce helplessness, and in fact, in some studies, subjects in the uncontrollable situation responded better than their counterparts in the controllable situation. At least in certain types of stimulus situations, humans did not respond like nonhuman subjects. It is true that humans are much more complicated organisms than dogs or other nonhuman species, and thus their perceptions of an uncontrollable situation and their responses to that situation may be more complicated than those of nonhuman subjects. In order to take into account the increased complexity of the human subjects, the theory of learned helplessness was modified to include judgments made by the human subjects. Specifically, an attributional framework derived from social psychological research was woven into the learned helplessness model. Basically, the reformulated theory now stated that humans, upon being confronted with uncontrollability, make judgments or attributions about the cause of the negative outcomes they are experiencing. For example, they judge whether or not their failure to control is due to some external source or to something such as ability or effort which is internal to themselves. They also make judgments about the specificity of the phenomenon; that is, is this a single event or is it a general tendency? Thus, it would be expected that individuals who see their failure to control outcomes as due to their lack of general ability would show helplessness on a subsequent task. On the other hand, individuals who view their failure as a specific instance of bad luck should show no performance deficits on a subsequent task. In fact, results employing the attributional reformulation of the learned helplessness model have shown support for that model. So although the original model was limited in generality, a reformulation of that model designed to account for human complexity does seem to possess external validity.

As research moves from the study of basic processes to that of application, the assumption of generality becomes more tenuous. For example, let us consider a project aimed at increasing the verbal skills of deprived children by exposing them to special materials and directed discussions of those materials. The researchers, being situated in a rural area in the northeast, employ children at a local school as subjects for their study. These children come from economically deprived backgrounds. They randomly assign the children to either a normal classroom or to a classroom which employs the experimental reading program, and at the end of the year, they test both groups on reading ability. They find that the experimental group scores significantly higher than the control group in reading ability. If the researchers now try to generalize their results to deprived children in other locales, they may be on shaky ground. These rural children may be very different from both deprived rural children in other parts of the country and from deprived urban children. In other words, this program employing very specific techniques may not work for the other populations.

In an applied project such as this one, the researchers may not only be interested in whether the children receiving the special program outperform control group children, but also in the actual increases in verbal ability produced by the program. Whereas the focus of basic research is on discovering relative effects, applied research projects are often concerned with absolute levels of responding. In other words, the generalization would not only be that the program works for deprived children, but also that it will produce specific increases for these children. This type of generalization is even more tenuous than the simple generalization that a program works. Thus, when working on applied research projects, definitions of a target population and random sampling from that population become much more essential for generalization to be valid.

Treatment Generalization

A second question of external validity concerns the generalizability of the experimental treatments or conditions of the independent variables. In most experimental situations, the researcher chooses certain operations to represent the independent variable. Treatment generalization refers to how well the results can be generalized to treatments other than the specific conditions employed in a study. This question of representativeness of treatments is a complex one and involves two types of inference.

The first type of inference concerns situations where the conditions of the independent variable reflect various magnitudes or amounts of some variable. Here, the external validity question refers to whether the results can be generalized to magnitudes other than those employed in the study. For example, a study dealing with the relationship between deprivation and performance might involve depriving subjects of food for either two, four, or six hours, or not depriving them (zero hours deprivation) and then assessing their performance on a task. If it is found that as deprivation increases performance improves, are we able to conclude that, in general, increased deprivation will be accompanied by better performance? In other words, could we generalize to deprivation levels other than those used in the study. Can we say that at 10, 12, 14, and 16 hours deprivation performance will continue to improve? In other words, can we generalize from the hours of deprivation we actually employed to larger amounts of deprivation?

To answer this question, let us consider the nature of the process of inference. It consists of making judgments about populations from samples which are representative of those populations. In terms of levels of deprivation, the values chosen, zero, two, four, and six hours, are representative of levels of deprivation between zero and six. In other words, if we had employed levels of ½, 2½, 4½, and 6½ hours deprivation, the results in all probability would have been the same as for the 0, 2, 4, and 6 hour levels. On the other hand, levels of 10, 12, 14, and 16 hours are not representative of the same population of hours that the original levels represented. In fact, in the case of deprivation and performance, the generalization would not hold. Performance has been shown to have a nonlinear relationship to deprivation. As deprivation increases, so does performance, up to a point; and then, as deprivation continues to increase beyond this point, performance decreases. Thus, in this case, an inference to values beyond six hours deprivation would have been dangerous and quite possibly in error.

It is also true that when only a few values of the independent variable are used and these values are very different from one another, generalizing to values between these is a tenuous procedure. For example, if only two very divergent levels were employed, generalizations about less divergent levels, between the two employed, may be incorrect; that is, the effect may only occur at the extremes.

The point is that when the conditions of the independent variable are levels which reflect an interval scale variable, extrapolation to values or levels beyond those employed or interpolation to values between those employed in the study may be incorrect. The safest grounding for a generalization occurs when the values of the independent variable represent a random sample of the possible values in the population to which the researcher wishes to generalize. Also, the greater the number of randomly chosen values represented, the safer the generalization.

The second type of inference in regard to the independent variable concerns qualitatively different questions about the specific manipulations involved in the study. In other words, do the results occur only for the particular manipulation employed, or would they also work for other similar manipulations. If, for example, one was interested in the relationship of deprivation in general to performance in general, then the same pattern of results that occur with deprivation of food should occur with deprivation of water or air. This does not mean that the same values of the independent variable would apply for air and water as were used for food since deprivation of air for two, four, or six hours would certainly fail to relate linearly to performance. It does mean that at whatever values are appropriate deprivation levels for those substances, the relationship of deprivation to performance would have the same pattern as for food. The point is that a statement about a particular type of relationship between deprivation and performance is a more general statement then a statement about deprivation of food and performance. How does one make such a generalization? The only sure way is to see if the statement holds up empirically; that is, carry out the study using substances other than food.

It may have occurred to the reader that the same questions of generalizability which are asked about the independent variable, could also be asked about the dependent variable. Just as a particular experiment uses a certain operation to reflect the independent variable, it uses a specific operation to assess the dependent variable. In the case of the deprivation study, assume that the measure of performance was the number of correct choices made by subjects in a difficult discrimination task. Would deprivation also relate to performance in the same manner if performance had been assessed through a problem solving task or through a verbal analogies task?

In some ways, this can be an easier question to answer than that about the generalizability of the independent variable. For example, if previous

correlational studies had shown that the ability to make complex discrimi-
nations, skill in problem solving, and facility with verbal analogies were
all intercorrelated, this would be a good basis for a generalization about
the dependent variable. In fact, there often is independent correlational
evidence for the convergence of a number of different performance
measures, and this evidence allows for broader generalizations about the
dependent variable.

Situation Generalization

The third question about external validity relates to the specific situations in which studies are conducted. It deals with concerns about whether
the phenomenon reflects relationships among behaviors which actually
occur in the environment or whether it only reflects something that
uniquely occurs in the laboratory. This question arises more often in some
types of research than in others. Laboratory work on basic physiological
processes, short-term memory, or time discrimination is probably less
concerned with questions of external validity about situations than in
research dealing with helping behavior, the effectiveness of therapy, or
the aggressiveness of children. The more basic the research, that is, the
more the research deals with fundamental processes, the less often the
question arises as to the generalizability of the situation in which the
research is conducted. In contrast, the more the research attempts to
answer questions about complex behaviors which occur in the real world,
that is, outside of the laboratory, the more often the question of generality
arises.

In a sense, this question of the generality of situations is a question of
artificiality. Is it possible that a finding produced in the laboratory reflects
only something about subjects in the laboratory and nothing about the
behavior of people in the real world. Actually the term *real world* does not
exactly fit since the laboratory is a part of the real world. Therefore, the
term *field* is often used to refer to all of those environments which are not
laboratory environments. In order to show how a study done in the
laboratory might have questionable generality in the field, consider a
study in the area of helping behavior. This topic, which deals with
studying the conditions under which people will become involved in a
situation and come to the aid of another person, springs directly from
issues which have arisen in our society. The brutal slaying of Kitty
Genovese while neighbors looked on without lending aid and other similar
incidents stimulated questions about the nature of our society and the
causes of such seemingly apathetic behavior.

Consider a researcher who is interested in the effect of race on helping
behavior. Specifically, he asks whether people of one race will give aid to
persons of their own race who are in trouble more frequently than they
will give aid to victims of the opposite race? Specifically, will white and
black people show differences in helping behavior toward black and white

victims? Assume a study in which male and female subjects arrive at a laboratory individually and are given problems to solve. The experimenter, after telling the subjects that they have only one hour to complete the set of problems and that they should work diligently, leaves the room. Twenty minutes later, the subject hears a knock on the door, which is followed by a stranger entering the room. The stranger, who is actually a confederate of the experimenter, identifies him or herself as a fellow student who has a problem and needs help. The problem is that the stranger has an appointment with a professor whose office is two floors up, but the stranger has to return to his dormitory since he has just been told that his roommate has had an accident. The subject is then asked to help by going up two floors to the professor's office and notifying him of the emergency situation. The subject can either agree to the request or refuse the request. The stranger then leaves the room, presumably to return to the dormitory. At this point, the subject either can do the favor or continue to work on the problems. Half of the subjects are black and half are white, and half of the subjects in each of these groups receives their favor request from either a white or a black confederate.

Assume that in this situation, the results show that both black and white subjects helped the victim significantly more often than they refused to help, but that there were no significant findings connected with either the race of the subject or the race of the stranger. In other words, both white and black subjects treated white and black strangers equally. One would conclude from this study that neither whites nor blacks discriminate in terms of helping behavior. There is, of course, the possibility that these findings occur in the laboratory but would not hold in the field. First of all, the laboratory is situated within a university, and the stranger was a fellow student. Under these optimal circumstances, discrimination may not occur. Second, a subject called into a psychology laboratory may be suspicious about the "true" purposes of the study, and in this case correctly perceive that the stranger was part of the experiment. Subjects is an experiment, in a sense, are being evaluated, and their helping behavior may reflect a tendency to want to produce a positive image. This would be especially true if the subject believed that the stranger was a confederate of the experimenter. Any or all of these factors would act so as to produce results in the laboratory which would not parallel those in the field.

One way to deal with these problems is to actually conduct the experiment in the field. This means that, rather than having subjects come to a laboratory, the researcher moves into the natural environment (the "field") of the subjects and manipulates the variables. One advantage of field experiments is that subjects do not realize that they are being studied. This, of course, eliminates the possibility of suspicion on the part of the subject and attempts to respond in a manner that will please the experimenter. The other advantage is that since the study is carried on in the subject's natural environment, the results apply to that environment and not just to the rather restricted environment of the laboratory. The problem with field experiments is that they are often very difficult to carry out. The laboratory allows the experimenter to control for extraneous variables, but in the field, those variables operate fully. Measuring the dependent variable is also much more difficult in the field. It is very unlikely that in the field one could manipulate an independent variable and then gather responses through questionnaires. In fact, the design of field experiments including the assessment of the behavior in question is often an ingenious process.

In order to demonstrate the nature of field experiments, let us examine an actual field experiment done in New York City by Gaertner and Bickman (1971) dealing with the effects of race on helping behavior. In order to study this problem in the field, the authors developed what they called "the wrong number technique." In this paradigm, a subject is called on the telephone by a caller who has dialed the wrong number. In this particular study, the caller asked the subjects if he had reached "Ralph's Garage." The caller gave his name and said that his car was stuck and that he needed help from the garage. The subjects, of course, told him that he had not reached Ralph's Garage, but rather that he had dialed a wrong number. The caller then informed the subject that he had no more change and asked the subject to make the call to Ralph's Garage for him, giving the subject the number of Ralph's Garage.

Keep in mind that Gaertner and Bickman were interested in the effects of race on helping behavior; that is, the amount of help given by whites and blacks to members of their own and the opposite race. The advantage of this field experiment is that the subjects did not know they were being studied and thus their responses would reflect the behavior that occurs in their natural environment. The difficulty with using the wrong number technique is that, since the manipulation occurs on the phone, the caller is not seen by the subject, and the subject is not seen by the caller. Thus, identification of race by visual means is impossible for both parties.

First, if the subjects could not identify the race of the caller, it would be impossible to determine their differential reactions to black and white callers. In order to deal with this aspect, the authors employed seven black and seven white confederates as callers. The black confederates employed a "southern Negro" dialect and the white confederates employed a "typical New York" speech pattern. In order to make sure that the race of the callers was evident, practice phone calls were tape recorded and then played for a group of college students who judged the race of each caller. These judgments were correct 92 percent of the time. Thus, the researchers could be confident that the subjects who received the calls would correctly perceive the race of the caller.

The second problem in this study was correctly determining the race of the person who received the call. In order to optimize the chances of contacting a subject of a given race, sampling was done through the phone book on the basis of last names (certain last names were common among blacks in New York City) and then on the basis of residence. Only subjects who lived in an area indicated by the census as being almost totally black were classified as black. Finally, as a further check on the race of the subjects, the caller and his assistant, who were both unaware of any of the criteria on which the subjects were selected, independently judged the subject's race on the basis of voice characteristics. Only if both agreed was the subject included in the data analysis. Agreement occurred for 99 percent of the calls. Thus, in order for a person called to be classified as to race, their name and more importantly their residence had to have a high probability of belonging to a given race, and then two raters blind to both of these criteria had to agree on their race. On this basis, over 1,100 subjects were classified by race.

The final problem in this field experiment concerned the dependent variable, helping. If the subjects agreed on the phone to help, that is, to call the garage, this of course could be recorded, but this did not mean that they actually would help. In order for helping behavior to occur, the subject would actually have to call the garage. Therefore, black and white callers gave the subjects different numbers to call, and each caller changed the location at which he said he was stranded before making the next call. Thus, a call by a subject to a specific number indicated that the subject had obviously been contacted by a white caller, and when the subject reported the location of the car trouble, this identified which caller it had been and, consequently, the race of the subject. By the way, the calls from the subjects were answered by a confederate acting like a garage attendant, who assured the subjects that they would immediately send help to the stranded motorist.

One other interesting situation arose in this study. Subjects would sometimes hang up before hearing the request for the phone call, and in this case, subjects would not be scored as to helping or not helping. Rather, they were simply recorded as premature hangups. In fact, the data from the premature hangups were used in subsequent data analyses.

The results showed that white subjects helped white callers more frequently than they helped black callers, but that black subjects did not discriminate between black and white callers. The other interesting finding was that a greater number of white than black subjects hung up prematurely. The results in general showed discrimination by whites but not by blacks. This technique, although quite difficult to carry out, has some distinct advantages over more traditional methods which often involve either laboratory environments or surveys which gather attitudinal information. As Gaertner and Bickman state: *(a)* the method is nonreactive, which means that subjects do not respond as a function of knowing they are subjects in an experiment, *(b)* the method assesses overt behavior and not just opinions or intentions, and *(c)* it deals with more broadly based samples than the usual laboratory study based on college student samples.

In order to further illustrate the method, the advantages, and the problems of doing field experiments, let us consider a study by Langer,

Janis, and Wolfer (1975) dealing with the reduction of psychological stress. Laboratory studies have shown that tolerance for stressful events can be increased if the individuals who are stressed perceive that they can control the stressful stimuli. In the laboratory, stimuli such as electric shocks or loud noise are often employed as stressors. These stimuli are, of course, quite specific, easy to identify, and last a shorter time than many stressors found in everyday life. Even more importantly, their implications for the individual's well being are much less profound than stressors in the natural environment. Thus, subjects' responses to laboratory stressors may not parallel their responses to stressors occurring in the field. Therefore, a field experimental study of reactions to naturally occurring stressors would seem an appropriate test of the external validity of the laboratory findings.

Specifically, Langer, Janis, and Wolfer were interested in the use of two strategies for reducing stress. One strategy dealt with coping devices for aversive events, while the second strategy dealt with providing realistic information about the aversive events. Since it was felt that surgery was a stressor that certainly has implications for the future well-being of the individuals who experience it, the subjects selected were 60 adults who were about to undergo elective surgery. In the coping device condition, patients were given ways to control the stress they were feeling about the surgery, such as focusing upon the positive aspects (e.g., improved health, extra care and attention) and reinterpreting the negative aspects (e.g., time in hospital as a vacation from outside pressures). Patients in the information condition received information about what would happen to them in terms of preparation for the operation and postoperative experiences. A third group received neither the coping nor the information presentations, and a fourth combination group received condensed versions of both the coping and the information presentations. The 60 patients were matched on a series of background variables (sex, age, seriousness of the operation) and then randomly assigned to the four conditions.

The dependent variables consisted of nurses' pre- and postmanipulation ratings of the patients' anxiety and their ability to cope with stress, and the number of pain relievers and sedatives the patient requested after the operation. Thus, a number of behavioral measures were employed to assess the effect of the manipulation. The results showed that those patients who received either the copying strategy alone or in combination with the information were rated as less anxious and more able to cope after the manipulation than either the information only or the control group. This effect of the coping strategy also showed up in the number of sedatives and pain relievers the patients requested after surgery; that is, the subjects who received the coping device treatment requested significantly fewer pills than the subjects who did not receive this treatment.

Again, as in the Gaertner and Bickman study, this field experiment has distinct advantages. First, the sample consists of people actually undergoing a stressful event in their lives, rather than subjects exposed to an artificial laboratory stressor. Second, overt behaviors as rated by the nurses and as indicated by the number of sedatives and pain relievers, and not just patient opinions, were employed as the dependent measures. On the other hand, the advantage of nonreactivity which existed for the Gaertner and Bickman study did not exist for this study. These subjects were approached and presented with a treatment by an experimenter. Thus, in some senses, although possibly not knowing they were subjects in an experiment, they did know that they were being treated.

Both studies extended other findings out of the laboratory and into the field, thus providing external validation for previous work. It can also be seen that external validity is no all or none proposition. That is, findings have more or less generality, more or less external validity. In the race and helping area, other types of help, other procedures for soliciting help, and certainly other places than New York City could have been employed. Studies employing a number of different cities and/or a number of different types of helping behaviors, and/or a number of different procedures would have more external validity than the Gaertner and Bickman study. In the same vein, studies on control of stress using a number of hospitals or other types of stressors than surgery would also have more external validity than the Langer, Janis, and Wolfer study. In other words, a greater degree of external validity is always possible. At the same time, it is not always plausible due to logistical, ethical and financial problems.

THE ETHICS OF RESEARCH

In both the real and the hypothetical studies described in this book, very little has been said about ethical concerns. This is not because ethical issues are unimportant, but rather because the studies were employed as examples of various methodological problems. The question of research ethics is an important one which has been discussed extensively in the professional literature. The American Psychological Association has, in fact, adopted a code of ethics pertaining to research. The principles embodied in this code are an attempt to protect the rights and safety of participants in research projects.

Ethical practice begins before any subjects are run and continues through to the end of the study and sometimes beyond. The first stage involves the consideration of the ethical implications of the study by the investigators themselves. This means that in planning the treatments and procedures for the study, their possible effects on the subjects should be evaluated. Thus, on an individual basis, researchers should modify or even discard procedures which would possibly put subjects at risk. The second stage is to submit the proposal for the project to a committee which has responsibility for evaluating the ethical standards of research projects. This committee may be a university-wide committee or one consisting of members of the researcher's own department. The purpose is to bring outside scrutiny to bear upon the question of ethics. The committee may approve the project as is or with required modifications, it may seek more information about the procedures from experts, or it may simply not approve the project. The questions which the committee may address can deal with possible physical hazards from shock or noise stimulation, for example, or from faulty electrical equipment, or they may deal with possible psychological hazards resulting from the treatments proposed. There are also issues of informed consent, deception, debriefing, and follow-up which the committee considers. Any question regarding the rights and safety of subjects is open for consideration by the committee.

Once the research is approved in either the original or in modified form, the researcher has responsibility for seeing that the approved procedures are carried out. This means that the investigator is responsible for the ethical practice of any collaborators or assistants in the project. Thus, a professor's project being run by a graduate student must conform to ethical standards, and the professor carries the responsibility of seeing that it does conform.

The next stage is where subjects become involved. First of all, the subjects must be informed as fully as possible about the procedures involved in the study so that they can decide whether or not to participate. All subjects must be given the opportunity to withdraw from the study if they so desire. In many universities, students in introductory psychology courses participate in research as a requirement of the course, which limits the freedom of subjects in choosing to participate or not. In order to provide a choice, most courses will offer alternative ways of fulfilling the requirement so that students who do not choose to participate in research will not be penalized. It should be noted that the right to withdraw from any particular study still holds for those students who do choose to participate in research. The requirement of informed consent is sometimes quite difficult to carry out, in that many studies cannot inform subjects fully until after the subjects' data have been collected. Full information, in these cases, would often negate the impact of the variables being studied or at least strongly bias the results.

In the cases involving either deception or concealment, the ethical emphasis must occur at the end of the study. Where deception has occurred, subjects must be thoroughly debriefed as to the nature and purposes of the deception. Consider, for example, the very first study described in this book. In that experiment, subjects were given either positive or negative feedback about their performance on a test and then moved into an encounter with an attractive or unattractive female. The test feedback was bogus, and the female was a confederate of the experimenter—two types of deception. Subjects in this study needed to be debriefed as to both the bogus nature of the feedback (assuring them that it was not related in any way to their actual performance) and to the fact that the woman was planted by the experimenter. Further, the subjects should be told the purpose of the bogus feedback and the purpose of moving them into the encounter with the confederate.

As a further step, many experiments require not only an explanation of the procedures, but also direct measures to remove negative effects. For instance, consider an experiment where subjects receive a depressive mood induction; that is, a treatment where they either read sad statements or where they actually recount a sad instance in their lives. An elated mood induction often will be given at the end of the session along with a mood measurement in order to remove the effects of the depressive mood induction.

Many of these ethical considerations are a special problem in field research. In doing laboratory research, participating individuals know they are being studied and, in fact, usually sign a voluntary consent form. While it is true that in some types of research situations subjects are deceived as to the true nature and purpose of the manipulations, they are still aware that they are being studied. In many field experiments, such as the Gaertner and Bickman study, subjects are not even aware that they are involved in research. They do not arrive at a laboratory, they are not approached by an interviewer, and they do not volunteer to participate. It is also true that, unlike the procedure in most laboratory studies, subjects in field experiments are not debriefed as to the nature and purposes of the study. Subjects in the Gaertner and Bickman study who actually called the garage continued to believe that they had actually helped out the stranded motorist. Also, subjects who failed to call were never informed of the hoax, which possibly allowed any feelings of guilt over being "bad samaritans" to continue.

These are issues on the ethics of research and they are difficult issues with which to deal. Informed consent in many field experiments seems to be out of the question since the point is to observe the behavior of subjects in their natural environments who do not know they are participating in a research project. What about debriefing of subjects? Would it really have been feasible for the researcher to have contacted the 1,100 subjects in the wrong number study and explain the purposes and procedures to them? Even if it were feasible in terms of time and effort, could 1,100 explanations have been given so as to provide real understanding of the problem being studied? Finally, what about the effects of revealing the hoax to the "good samaritans" who gave help? Would this have made them less willing to help in the future? This last question especially is a study in and of itself.

There are costs associated with doing meaningful research, and there are benefits to be derived from the research. If the costs outweigh the benefits, then the research should not be done. The catch in this cost-benefit judgment is weighing the cost and benefits. They are often difficult to accurately determine, and thus the judgment of costs and benefits varies depending upon who is judging. The saving grace to this problem is

TABLE 8–2
Situations involving questions of ethics

1. A drug to counteract a serious disease is to be tested. Patients with the disease must be randomly assigned to drug and placebo conditions. In order for the results to be valid, the subjects cannot be informed as to whether they are receiving the drug or the placebo. The drug is found to be effective. Is it ethical to withhold a possible cure from patients without their consent to act as part of a control (placebo) group? What are the possible risks and benefits?

2. An investigator interested in the degree to which individuals will obey authority has subjects administer increasing levels of shock to other subjects under different levels of feedback from the victims. The recipients of the shock are confederates of the experimenter and are actually never shocked. Subjects under all conditions obey authority and deliver high levels of shock to the confederates although feedback from the victim significantly reduces obedience. Some subjects suffer deleterious psychological effects from their actions, becoming nervous, crying, physically shaking, etc. Is it ethical to deceive subjects as to the fact that they are not actually inflicting pain on another person? Is it ethical to put subjects in a situation where their obedient behavior produces psychological distress? What are the possible risks and benefits?

3. A researcher interested in the phenomenon of bystander apathy carries out a field experiment in which a confederate steals a six pack of beer from a grocery store under conditions of different levels of bystanders being present in the store. The customers' behavior is observed and recorded in terms of intervention—trying to stop the thief, reporting the theft to the owner, calling the police, etc. It is found that the more bystanders who are present, the less likely any of them is to take any action about the crime. Is the staging of a crime, even with the store owners' consent, unethical? Is the surreptitious recording of behavior in a field setting unethical? What are the possible risks and benefits?

4. A researcher is interested in the effects of personal space upon arousal. He conducts a field experiment in a public men's lavatory manipulating personal space at the urinals by hanging an "out of order" sign on either the middle of three urinals (subjects will be separated by one urinal from a confederate), on an end urinal (subjects will be adjacent to a confederate), or on two of the urinals (subjects will be alone). An observer in a stall, armed with a periscope, surreptitiously records the time taken for urination onset. Stronger invasion of personal space leads to longer onset times for urination. Is the manipulation of *very* personal space in this manner unethical? Is the surreptitious recording of this *very* personal behavior ethical? What are the risks and benefits?

that most reputable research is carried on in the context of institutions such as universities, and these agencies oversee research proposals through committees who judge the ethical implications of research projects. Thus, a number of individuals not connected with a study must judge the ethicality of the study before it can be carried out. No system dealing with the complex issues of ethics is foolproof, but this system does guarantee consideration of the ethical problems associated with a study before that study is actually carried out. Table 8–2 contains some research situations which involve ethical considerations. These situations are derived from actual studies which have been carried out. The reader is encouraged to think about these situations, considering the possible risks to subjects, the benefits of the knowledge derived from these studies, and possible alternative methods which would raise fewer ethical questions.

Chapter 9

Quasi-Experimental
Designs

The strength of an experiment lies in its capacity to reveal cause-effect relationships. This strength derives from the ability of the researcher to manipulate variables. In group research, as opposed to single-subject research, successful manipulation depends upon random assignment of the subjects to the conditions of the study. Unfortunately, there are situations in which random assignment is not possible. For example, randomly assigning subjects within an institution such as a school to different treatment conditions may be impractical. There are problems here of leakage as a threat to internal validity in that information about the treatment or lack of treatment will be passed between the groups. Also, treating some members of an institution differently from others may cause resentment on their part or on the parts of their families (parents of school children for example) and therefore may be "politically" impractical. If the treatment involves some sort of therapy, there may be questions as to the ethics of depriving subjects of its value. In other words, there are situations where the researcher wants to determine the effects of a treatment or compare different treatments, but due to ethical, political, or logistical considerations, he cannot randomly assign subjects. There are also situations where a researcher is interested in the effects of an event over which there is no possible control. For instance, wars, economic depressions, newly passed or repealed laws, or natural disasters are all variables or treatments over which researchers have no control, but which nevertheless may affect variables of interest to them. In other words, there are situations where random assignment is not possible, but there is a need to draw conclusions about the effects of variables. Techniques and approaches have been developed for these situations, which, although not as powerful as true experiments, can lead to accurate conclusions about the effects of treatments. These approaches are termed *quasi-experimental designs*.

NONEQUIVALENT GROUPS DESIGNS

When subjects cannot be randomly assigned to conditions, they must be assigned in some other manner. For instance, either the subjects select themselves into the conditions, or the researcher chooses a group of subjects to act as a control for those who are to receive a given treatment. In either case, the groups formed may differ before the treatment is imposed. Groups formed in any nonrandom fashion are termed nonequivalent groups. Quasi-experimental designs usually involve comparisons between nonequivalent groups. While comparisons between randomly assigned groups lead to the clearest causal statements and are thus the most preferred designs, some quasi-experimental designs lend themselves to stronger causal statements than do others.

As an example of a weak quasi-experimental design, consider the posttest-only design with nonequivalent groups. With random assignment to conditions, this design controls for threats to internal validity (history, maturation, etc.), but with groups formed in a nonequivalent manner, this design does not allow for valid causal inferences about the effect of the treatment. The primary threat in this design is subject selection. Since the groups are formed nonrandomly, posttest differences may be due either to the treatment or to initial pretreatment differences between the groups. In other words, the groups may have started out differently and posttest differences may simply reflect this beginning discrepancy. For example, suppose that a large company has introduced an employee morale-building program into one of its plants. At the end of the two-month treatment, employee morale is assessed through a questionnaire. For comparison, a second plant of the company is selected and employees at this plant are also given the morale questionnaire. This second plant is acting as an untreated control group. Now assume that the plant receiving the morale building program has higher scores on the questionnaire (higher morale) than the untreated plant. Since the two plants may have differed on variables other than the treatment, we are not able to conclude that the treatment, the morale building program, produced the higher scores. For example, if one plant was in the Sun Belt while the other was in the North, these climatic differences could affect morale. Therefore, having no information as to the pretreatment morale of the plants, we cannot attribute posttreatment differences to the morale building program. With only a posttest, the nonequivalent groups design does not lead to valid conclusions. In fact, due to the weakness of the posttest-only design with nonequivalent groups, it could be argued that this design should be classified as a nonexperimental or correlational rather than a quasi-experimental design.

Thus, one requirement with nonequivalent groups is a pretest. With a pretest, the nonequivalent groups design becomes more interpretable, although it never reaches the level of validity of designs employing random assignment. With a pretest given to both a treated group and a nonequivalent untreated control group and then a posttest given to both, we have a design which controls for a number of threats to internal validity. Since the groups receive pre- and posttests at the same time, the direct effects of history and testing are lessened; that is, both groups are pretested and both are subject to the same historical events which intervene between the pre- and posttest. It should be noted that these threats to internal validity are lessened but not eliminated. For instance, the nonequivalent groups may react differently to the pretest, and the same intervening events (history) may differentially affect the groups. Also, if the groups are geographically separated, the intervening events may differ for the groups. In other words, since the groups are formed in a nonrandom fashion, subject selection may interact with the pretest and/or history to threaten internal validity. Also, both groups are subject to maturation, although as we shall see, they may not mature at the same rate. Thus, the design is certainly better than either a simple one-group, pretest-posttest-only design or a posttest-only design with nonequivalent groups. Even so, it is still a design whose internal validity is threatened.

The advantage of the pretest with the nonequivalent groups design is that one can compare the treated with the untreated group in terms of pretest to posttest changes. The rationale is that even if the treatment and control groups differ on the pretest, an increase or decrease in this difference on the posttest will illuminate the effect of the treatment. Take the case where the treatment group scores higher than the control group on the pretest. If the treatment has a positive effect, we would expect the difference between the two groups to be even greater on the posttest. Consider a program to train critical reading skills in gifted children. The children are selected for the program on the basis of their scores on intelligence and achievement tests and teacher recommendations. Assume that it was decided to employ the children who were recommended but weren't selected for the gifted program as controls for the gifted children. Both groups would be pretested on the dependent measures, the gifted children would be given their special treatment to improve problem solving while the controls would receive no treatment, and both would be posttested. First of all, the groups would differ initially on the pretest of critical reading skills, with the gifted children scoring higher than the controls. Let us say that at the posttest, the control group posttest mean has changed very little from its pretest mean, but the gifted group's posttest mean has risen a significant amount above its pretest mean. In other words, the difference between the groups at the posttest is larger than at the pretest.

The above pattern of results makes it appear as though the treatment given to the gifted children has produced the enhanced posttest difference between two groups. Unfortunately, there is a plausible cause which rivals the treatment as an explanation for the effect. That cause in an interaction between subject selection and maturation. Since the groups are nonequivalent, that is, they are not formed through random assignment, they may mature at different rates. The gifted children may mature faster than the controls in terms of gathering knowledge relevant to critical reading. Thus, the larger difference between the groups at the posttest as compared to the pretest may not be due to the treatment, but rather to an accelerated cognitive development rate among the gifted children.

A second threat to validity concerns the interaction of subject selection and history referred to previously. Assume that in order to produce a more equivalent control group, gifted children are identified in another school. Pretesting shows them to be highly similar to the treatment group. After the treatment, posttesting shows that the treated group scores higher than the untreated controls. Since both groups are composed solely of gifted children, they should mature at the same rate, and thus, the subject selection-maturation interaction should not threaten validity. On the other hand, since the groups are in different locations, they are subject to differential historical forces which could rival the treatment as a plausible cause of the differences. For example, one of the schools might receive a grant which may raise teacher morale and generally produce more involved and effective teaching. If the treated school was the one receiving the grant, the grant would rival the treatment as a plausible cause of the posttest differences. Therefore, even in the case where the groups are initially equated on the pretest, the nonrandom assignment makes the design vulnerable to threats to validity.

There are also other threats to validity in the pretest-posttest nonequivalent groups design having to do with the effects of nonrandom assignment on statistical regression effects. The issues involved are complicated and are fully treated in other texts (Cook & Campbell, 1979). The quasi-experimental design, then, although useful if random assignment is not possible, does not eliminate all threats to internal validity. Because of this fallibility, other controls have been proposed which bolster internal validity in this quasi-experimental design. In other words, these procedures increase the researchers' ability to draw causal conclusions about the effects of a treatment.

Cohorts as Controls

One procedure, which is employed in order to more closely equate the treatment and control groups, is to use cohorts which are groups of individuals who travel through a system in a sequential ordering. In a school system, for example, students move continuously through the various grade levels. Therefore, the students in a particular grade one year will be followed by highly similar students in that grade the next year. Each succeeding group of students will be very similar to those students who preceded them in terms of social class, religious background, etc. Or consider a community mental health center which institutes a treatment program for its depressive patients. These patients can be compared as to their depression scores with previous depressive patients who have not undergone this treatment. Since the same staff would have treated both sets of patients within the same institution, these cohorts should be quite similar in terms of setting and background characteristics. Such a comparison would not be between a nontreated control and a treated group, since the previous patients would have received some treatment, but rather between the new treatment and the previous methods.

As a final example of cohorts as controls, consider the situation where the military tries out a new training method for its bootcamp which is designed to promote group cohesiveness among the soldiers. Since bootcamp lasts for six weeks, a cohort consisting of the next wave of recruits to enter bootcamp can be employed as the control group and their cohesiveness scores compared with the preceding recruits who received the new training method. Since the background characteristics of recruits entering a program within a six-week period should be very similar, these cohorts should be very much alike. Thus, employing cohorts within a system as controls usually ensures comparability of treatment and control groups on a broad variety of variables. This is especially true if there is not a great time lag in terms of the separation between the cohorts as they move through the system. A large time lag between the cohorts may mean that the populations have changed. Consider comparing recruits in 1970 with those given the special training in 1980. If the types of recruits had changed in 10 years in terms of intelligence, education, etc., the difference between the groups may be due to these background differences and not to the training method. On the other hand, a short delay would ensure comparability of the groups.

The one strong threat to internal validity in the cohort approach is history. Since the control and experimental cohorts are evaluated at different periods in time, they can be affected by different historical forces occurring at those particular times. Suppose, for example, that during the cohesiveness training program for recruits, an international incident arose in which the honor of the United States was threatened, such as an embassy being attacked or an attempted kidnapping of an ambassador. This may serve to motivate the cohesiveness training group but would probably not have much impact six weeks later when the control cohort arrives. Thus, a difference between the two groups in cohesiveness may be due to the historical event and not to the cohesiveness training. Even with this limitation, the cohort design, where the use of cohorts is feasible, is a useful alternative to random assignment.

Multiple Dependent Measures

A second procedure which promotes valid conclusion drawing with nonequivalent groups involves the use of multiple dependent variables. This strategy consists of choosing dependent variables which should be affected by the treatment and also ones which should not be affected by it. If history, maturation, or any other selection-related variable is producing the result on the dependent variable of direct interest, the one that is supposed to be affected by the treatment, then the other dependent variables should also be affected by these sources. On the other hand, if the treatment is responsible for the group differences, then the dependent variable hypothesized to be related to the treatment should be the only one affected. It should be noted that using multiple dependent variables does not totally eliminate history as a threat to internal validity since history as well as the treatment could affect the dependent variables differentially. It is just that with multiple dependent variables, it is less likely that history would affect the target variable only.

The problem in this design is to choose alternative dependent variables which will not be affected by the treatment along with the dependent variable of interest. In other words, the alternative dependent variable should not be correlated with the dependent variable of interest. This is sometimes easier to achieve in theory than in practice. Consider the cohesiveness training example. Assume that along with a comparison between the experimental and control groups on cohesiveness, the researchers also measured marksmanship and physical fitness. Now assume that the recruits who received the cohesiveness training outperformed the control recruits not only on the cohesiveness measure, but also on physical fitness and marksmanship. At first glance, since all of the dependent variables showed differences, this looks as though the differences are artifacts of the nonequivalent groups, such as selection interacting with maturation or history, rather than being due to the cohesiveness training. This may not be the case. All of the variables could have been affected by the treatment. For example, the cohesiveness training could have increased cohesiveness and thereby also increased motivation and commitment. This may have affected the diligence with which the recruits engaged in the riflery and physical fitness exercises producing higher scores on those variables. Thus variables which were chosen because they appeared to be unrelated to the cohesiveness training may in fact have been indirectly affected by it. On the other hand, if the two groups had differed on cohesiveness but not on riflery and physical fitness, this would have been strong evidence for the effectiveness of the treatment. When the control and experimental groups differ on all of the dependent variables, selection differences may be operating or the treatment may be having an effect.

TREATMENT REMOVAL

A third strategy employed with quasi-experimentation involves the case where no control group of any type is available. When there is no control group, we have a simple pretest-treatment-posttest design which ordinarily is internally invalid. This strategy improves upon the simple pretest-treatment-posttest design by removing the treatment and testing the subjects again. This is a procedure analogous to that employed in the single-subject ABAB design discussed in Chapter 5. Consider the national imposition of the 55-mile-per-hour speed limit. Did this measure have the effect of reducing traffic fatalities?

Since the speed limit was imposed universally across the country, it would not be possible to obtain a group to which the speed limit did not apply. In other words, there could be no untreated control group. On the other hand, statistics would be available on the number of fatalities before the 55-mile-an-hour speed limit was imposed, which would be akin to a pretest. Statistics gathered during the period in which the 55-mile-per-hour speed limit is in force might show a decline in fatal accidents. At this point, we simply have a pretest-imposition of the speed limit—posttest design, which is open to the usual threats to internal validity. But now assume that the oil shortage eases and that the 55-mile-per-hour speed limit is lifted. In other words, the treatment is removed. If fatalities rise again in the period following the removal of the speed limit, this would provide evidence for the effect of the speed limit in lowering fatalities. Historical forces might have lowered the fatalities coincidentally with the imposition of the speed limit, but it is improbable that they would have then acted in the opposite manner coincidentally with its removal. It is also unlikely, although certainly not impossible, that maturational processes would have produced this decreasing and then increasing pattern of results. In other words, because removal of the treatment has reversed the pattern found with the introduction of the treatment, a more plausible judgment about the causal nature of treatment is possible.

There is a problem with the above procedure. If the treatment is supposed to have a long-term or relatively permanent effect, then the treatment removal design is not appropriate. For example, therapies should have long-term effects. That is, they should have effects even after the person leaves therapy. Consider a therapy for the treatment of phobics. A test of the phobia during therapy will probably show a drop in the phobic behavior compared with the pretreatment level of the phobic behavior. A test after the treatment is concluded will probably not show a return to pretreatment level since an effective therapy is usually one which produces long-term changes that last outside of the therapy situation. In other words, therapy is generally supposed to free the individual from the need for therapy, and thus low levels of phobic behavior should continue even after the therapy is removed. Therefore, treatment removal procedures are useful when the effects of the treatment should occur only during the treatment period.

Another variation on the treatment removal design is to repeatedly introduce and remove the treatment. The point here would be that changes occurring each time a treatment is removed over a number of such institutions and removals would rule out the possibility of coincidental occurrence of threats to internal validity. As in the single treatment removal design, the treatment must be one which has only temporary effects. It is also difficult to find situations where it is practical to continuously insert and remove treatments. It is unlikely, for example, that the 55-mile-per-hour speed limit could be instated, removed, reinstated, etc. Even in a more controlled environment such as a classroom, the introduction, removal, and reintroduction of a treatment might produce side effects such as resentment or frustration. Thus, while this quasi-experimental design is useful, it is not always practical.

TIME-SERIES DESIGNS

The treatment removal and the repeated treatment introduction and removal designs both involve situations where subjects serve as their own controls. Inherent in both designs is the notion of multiple measurements, both pre- and posttest, in order to establish patterns that would occur only as a result of the treatment and not as a result of extraneous sources (history, motivation, etc.). Another design of this same nature is the interrupted time-series design. In this design, observations are made over an extended series of times both before and after some event or treatment has intervened. The rationale behind this approach is to determine whether or not the interrupting event had any effect on subsequent behavior. This interruption in the time-series could be either an unplanned event, such as a scientific discovery or a natural or manmade disaster, or it could be a planned treatment. In any case, this design requires that a large number of observations have been made before the interrupting event takes place and that a large number are made following the event. Then, if the pattern of observations following the event differs from that preceding the event, the interrupting event is viewed as the likely candidate for having produced the change in pattern.

Consider the passage by a state legislature of a tough drunk-driving law. Evidence of traffic fatalities could be gathered over a number of years prior to the imposition of the law, and then further evidence could be gathered following the event. Three interrupted times-series for hypothetical data from the drunk-driving law situation are shown in Figure 9–1. The numbers of traffic fatalities in the state have been plotted in one-year intervals from 1968 to 1982. The law was passed in 1976. The use of one-year intervals in this case would yield only 15 plotted points (1968–1982), which is actually too few for an adequate time series analysis since there are only 7 points before and 6 following 1976—the year when the law was passed. If monthly death rates had been plotted, there would have been 84 points before and 72 points following the interruption of the time-series. The present use of one-year periods was to illustrate different possible patterns in a times-series in a straightforward manner. Figure 9–1a shows that there has been an upward trend in fatalities previous to the passage of the law and then a downward trend after the law comes into effect in 1976. In this case, the pre- and postinterruption trends move in opposite directions. In other words, the slopes differ in sign.

Figure 9–1a depicts the simplest case, the one in which a trend in a time series is reversed through an interrupting event. There are, though, much subtler types of effects produced by interruptions. For example, Figure 9–1b portrays a situation where traffic fatalities are on the increase before the passage of the drunk-driving law but increase at a slower rate after the law comes into effect. In other words, the pre- and postinterruption slopes are of the same sign (both positive) but differ in magnitude; the preinterruption slope is steeper than the postinterruption slope. Part of the increase in traffic fatalities before the law was passed was due to drunk driving, but some of the increase may have been due to other factors since the fatalities are still increasing after the law is passed. Another outcome is shown in Figure 9–1c. Here the law has lowered the overall number of fatalities, but they continue to increase at the same rate as before the law was passed. In other words, the pre- and postinterruption slopes are the same, but the intercept for the postinterruption time series has been lowered.

FIGURE 9–1
Hypothetical interrupted time-series of traffic
fatalities showing change in: (a) the direction,
(b) the slope, and (c) the level of the series

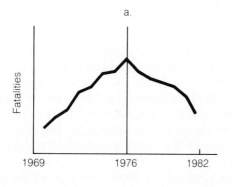

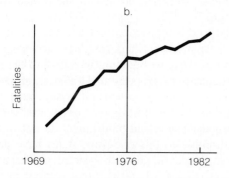

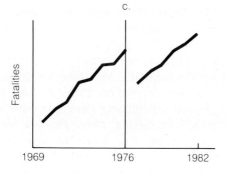

Traffic fatalities are still increasing at the same rate as before the law was passed, but the total number of fatalities or level of fatalities has been curtailed following the interruption.

Thus, the effects of a treatment or interruption in a time-series can be varied: reversing a trend, changing the slope, changing the level or intercept, or a combination of these. The effects of interruptions also vary as to whether or not they persist over time. For example, the law may drop the number of fatalities in the year immediately following its passage, but the fatalities may return to the old level and slope the next year. On the other hand, the law may produce a genuinely persistent decline in the number of fatalities. Also, the law may act immediately, producing effects soon after its passage, or the effects may be delayed for a period of time. For instance, if the number of prosecutions for drunk driving acted as a deterrent and took a period of time to accumulate, the law might not reduce fatalities for a number of years. This type of delayed effect of an interruption produces a threat to internal validity in the form of history. Since historical factors could intervene between the time the law was passed and the time at which the number of fatalities began to drop, these factors would act as a competing causal explanation for the change in the time-series.

A study by Mazur-Hart and Berman (1977) dealing with the passage of a divorce law will serve to illustrate an actual interrupted time-series quasi-experimental design. In 1972, the state of Nebraska passed no-fault divorce legislation. Prior to this legislation, divorce was based upon the notion of fault, with one spouse (the innocent party) accusing the other spouse (the guilty party) of some wrongdoing in regard to the marriage. Under this system, settlements of property and finances reflect punishment for the guilty party. Such an adversary arrangement has been criticized as being inappropriate for most divorce cases, in that clear guilt or innocence and consequent blame and punishment do not fit the usual divorce situations. In response to this criticism, states have passed no-fault divorce legislation. Under a no-fault system, marriages can be dissolved through mutual consent of the partners without questions of guilt or punishment involved. Critics of no-fault divorce legislation have argued that since divorce would seem to be easier to achieve under a no-fault system, divorce rates would increase.

In the case of no-fault divorce, the legislation, once passed, applies to the entire state, and therefore an adequate control group is not available. Therefore, an analysis of divorce rates over time for a period both preceding and following the implementation of the no-fault legislation would seem to be a useful quasi-experimental design; in other words, an interrupted time-series analysis of divorce rates. The first step was to choose the unit of time for the analysis. Since the state of Nebraska recorded divorces on a monthly basis, the month was chosen as the smallest unit of analysis, and the number of divorces per month over a six-year period were employed in the time-series analysis. This six-year period ran from January 1969 through December 1974; the passage of the no-fault divorce law occurred in July 1972. The month of July 1972 was not included in the analysis since the interruption occurred at this time and a classification of this month as being in the pre- or postinterruption period was impossible.

The basic idea was to relate each month in the time series to the number of divorces occurring in that month in order to see if the trend for the time-series before the no-fault divorce law was passed differed from the trend occurring after its passage. The authors examined the effect of the interruption, the no-fault divorce law, through a procedure known as *multiple regression*. The reader will recall that regression is a statistical procedure for predicting scores on a criterion variable from scores on a predictor variable. Multiple regression is an extension of this procedure, in that scores on a criterion variable are predicted from scores on a number of predictor variables.[1] In the present study, multiple regression was employed to predict divorces per month, the criterion variable, from a number of predictor variables. These predictor variables indicate: *(a)* any change in the level of the series (a pre- versus postinterruption intercept difference), *(b)* any change in the trend or slope of the series, and *(c)* the overall slope of the series. In this way, each variable could be assessed for significance. In other words, a series could show a significant overall slope but no significant change in level or slope from pre- to postinterruption, indicating that the interrupting event had no effect. Or the series might show a significant overall slope and significant change in slope but no change in level, indicating that the interruption changed the rate at which the criterion, number of divorces in this case, increased or decreased. It should be noted that in order to carry out this regression analysis, certain assumptions had to be tested. These assumptions relate to the problem of dependency among the observations which occur in time-series analyses. Regression procedures call for independent observations, which means that the observations on any variable are unrelated to each other. In the usual case where different individuals yield the different observations, this assumption of independence presents no problem. In a time-series analysis, on the other hand, the observations are made at sequential time periods which may not be independent. In other words, data from one time period may be affected by closely preceding time periods and may, in turn, affect data from closely following time periods. This dependency can be tested and, if it exists, can be removed before carrying out the regression analysis. The logic involved in these assumptions and the actual tests of them are beyond the scope of this text. Suffice it to say that the researchers carried out these tests before employing the actual multiple regression for the time series analysis.

Having tested and met the assumptions and carried out the multiple regression analysis, only the overall trend or slope was found to be significant. In other words, there was a general increase in the number of divorces per month from January 1969 through December 1974. Neither the change in slope or level of the time-series from pre- to postinterruption was significant. Thus, divorce increased over this period and kept increasing at the same level and rate after the no-fault divorce law was passed.

In order to more closely examine the data, a number of other multiple

---

[1] A more complete explanation of multiple regression procedures is undertaken in Chapter 11.

regression analyses were performed, this time breaking the data into subsets. The first analyses consisted of examining rural and urban counties in the state separately. Both rural and urban counties showed the same effects: an overall increase in slope but no changes in slope or intercept from pre- to postinterruption. The next approach consisted of separate analyses of husbands and wives between 30 and 50 and those over 50 years of age. When these analyses were performed, there was again an overall increase in slope for each of the groups, and for both husbands and wives over 50 years of age, there was a significant change in the level of the time-series following the passage of the no-fault law. For these older groups, the number of divorces per month rose after the law came into effect and then continued to increase at the same rate (slope) as before the interruption.

Two other breakdowns of the data were also carried out. One involved separate analyses for couples married 1–5, 6–10, 11–15, 16–20, 21–25, and 26 years or longer. For the first five groups, the usual pattern occurred; that is, a generally increasing trend over the entire series but no changes in slope or level of the series from pre- to postinterruption. For the last group, those couples married 26 years or more, the overall trend was significant as well as the change in slope and level of the series from pre- to postinterruption. In this case, the slope changed from positive before the law was passed to negative afterwards. The final analyses looked separately at black and white couples. Both groups show overall increasing trends. The black couples also showed an increase in level from pre- to postinterruption.

While the interruption seemed to have some effects, these effects seemed to be quite specialized; that is, they occurred for people over 50 years of age, people married 26 years or more, and black couples. It should be kept in mind that breaking the data into smaller groups and carrying out separate analyses on these groups means that each analysis is based upon a small number of cases and may be somewhat unreliable. The interesting aspect is the lack of findings showing change in slope or level of the series from pre- to postinterruption. In other words, divorce was increasing in general before the passage of the no-fault law and continued to increase at the same rate and at the same level after the law came into effect. If one simply examined two points, one before and one after the passage of the law, one would come to the conclusion that the law increased divorce. On the other hand, an examination of the time-series before and after the interruption leads to an entirely different conclusion. Since this examination allows one to examine the trends of the data before and after the interruption and not just two points, a clearer picture of the effect or lack of effect of the interrupting event becomes possible.

There are also variants of the time-series design. For example, one can compare the time series of a group with an interruption with a nonequivalent control group having no interruption. If, for example, a comparable neighboring state had not passed a no-fault divorce law, the time-series for

Nebraska could have been compared with that for the control state. A second approach is to collect data on a nonequivalent dependent measure to see if the interruption affected only the variable of interest. In general, time-series analysis is useful when an entire population of interest receives a treatment and archival data are available for extended periods before and after that treatment. As with all quasi-experimental designs, the purpose is to evaluate causal agents with as few threats to internal validity as possible.

QUASI-EXPERIMENTAL DESIGN AND EVALUATION RESEARCH

A look at most of the scholarly journals in the field indicates that they contain research articles on a variety of issues. Even within a specific journal, which deals with a limited area of content in psychology, the topics covered are many and varied. For example, a single issue of the *Journal of Personality and Social Psychology* may contain articles dealing with attitudes, interpersonal attraction, person perception, decision making, and a number of other topics. The authors of the articles seem to march to different drummers. This variety is at least in part a function of individual differences in the interests of the researchers themselves. Problems are investigated because the individual investigators have chosen those specific content areas to research. The purposes of the studies are to shed light on a particular issue and in doing so to enhance knowledge about that issue.

In recent years, another type of research endeavor has begun to gain attention. This is evaluation research or program evaluation, and its purposes and emphases are quite different from the research found in most scholarly journals. As the name implies, evaluation research is aimed at evaluating the effectiveness of specific programs. These programs are usually applied or practical ones, as opposed to basic research programs, and cover a wide range of areas. Such programs might be a treatment or treatments for mental health, an enhancement project for gifted children, or a television procedure for educational purposes. The idea for the specific program and the procedures employed in the program usually are developed by someone other than the researcher who carries out the program evaluation. Thus, unlike the research projects which appear in scholarly journals, the interest in the ideas investigated in the project usually do not originate with the researcher. Rather, the program evaluator acts as an outside expert in research methods who provides the proper research design and statistical tools for evaluating the program. This does not mean that the evaluator will only deal with design and analysis. In fact, more often than not, the evaluator will need to work with the program directors in order to help them conceptualize the program in terms of their goals and procedures.

Evaluation research has become more commonplace with increasing needs for government funds for new programs and decreasing funds being available. Thus, a need has arisen to evaluate the effectiveness of proposed programs, rather than to simply assume that they will be effective. As more and more emphasis is placed on the evaluation of the effectiveness of proposed programs and societal interventions, the need for tools to carry out these evaluations has grown. While there are times when evaluators of a proposed program are able to carry out a true experimental design involving random assignment, it is also the case that for many researchers involved in evaluation situations, only quasi-experimental designs are possible.

Designing a Rural Mental Health Program

A rural mental health program in which I was involved as a research design consultant will serve as a useful example of the processes and problems in program evaluation. My first meeting with the directors consisted of their outlining a program aimed at prevention of mental health problems in rural children through some sort of training procedure for parents. The program was not very clearly articulated in terms of the actual procedures which would be involved or even the goals of the program. My first question dealt with the purpose of the program. In other words, what was the prevention program designed to prevent. This may sound as though it was a rather simple and even naive question, but in fact it proved to be one which was most difficult to answer. The purpose of the program was to train parents to deal more effectively with their children and thus prevent mental health related problems in rural areas. In order to assess whether the goal worked, one would have to assess mental health related problems, a vast catchall category for a wide variety of disturbances. Thus, we needed to immediately specify which problems would be affected by the training procedure and then find ways to assess these particular problems. In order to do this, we had to look closely at the parent-training procedure itself. Unfortunately, the parent-training procedure was also an abstract concept which, at that point, was totally undefined in terms of specific techniques and processes. In other words, we had an undefined program which was to produce goals which were also undefined. The purpose was laudable, that is, to decrease mental health related problems in children, but the specifics were completely missing.

Therefore, we first needed to enumerate what types of mental health problems were of interest, to decide if these could be assessed, and then to design a training program which would have an impact upon these problems. One way of deciding which mental health problems would be targeted would be to review statistical evidence of the incidence of various problems and then to aim the program at those problems which have the highest incidence. In our case, for this geographical area, these statistics were not available. Therefore we relied upon the clinical experience of the project personnel to determine the target problems. Fortunately, a number of important behavioral problems could be identified, and instruments to assess many of these were available. We were able to find previously developed measures which had been shown to be reliable and for which evidence had been gathered as to their validity. Also, one of the staff at the medical center where the program was being planned had previously carried out research on a parent-training program. This individual had the expertise needed to design the specific program. If this person had not been available, an outside consultant would have been called in to design the actual parent-training sessions.

After many meetings and a great deal of work, a series of training procedure sessions was developed from previous work done on this topic. These sessions had to vary for parents of children of different ages. For example, the training procedure for parents of children two to four years of age would differ from those aimed at parents of children five to seven years old. Thus, the rather simple idea of parent training turned out to be a complicated and involved set of procedures. Along with the formal assessments of specific problems, a series of questionnaires dealing with the parents' feelings about the program and about specific parenting skills were also developed. In other words, we would have one level of evaluation which dealt with reduction of specific behavioral problems and a second level which dealt with more narrowly defined and more direct effects of the program on the parents themselves. Therefore, even before the actual research design question was discussed, a long and involved process of definition and specification occurred.

We were now ready to deal with the problems of implementing and evaluating the programs. The directors of the program wanted to simply administer the measurement instruments we had chosen as a pretest, implement the training program, and then readminister the instruments as a posttest. The reader will recall that simple pretest-posttest designs are generally invalid; that is, one cannot draw valid conclusions about the effects of the training from these designs. Therefore, I had to convince the directors that adequate control groups were needed and that random assignment of subjects was the best way to assure validity. Since the design would include nontreated control groups, objections were raised as to depriving individuals of the advantages of the parent-training programs. In other words, they made the assumption that the procedures were effective even before they were evaluated. I argued that, first of all, since these people had never had these treatments previously, we were not taking anything away from them, and second of all, since the program may not even be effective, we may not be depriving them of anything of value. After much debate, we agreed on a design involving random assignment of individuals to the training procedure and to nontreatment control groups. Once I had achieved their basic agreement to carry out random assignment, I was ready to explore the full design of the study in cooperation with the staff member who had developed the parent-training procedure.

At first we had decided to run parent-training sessions within each rural community and randomly assign subjects within the community to the training group or to the nontreatment control group. We rejected this idea since it was felt that the leakage problems discussed in Chapter 8 would challenge the validity of our conclusions. In other words, we felt that nontreated subjects might hear of the treatment and feel deprived of its "benefits," or they might discover information about the treatment and thus be indirectly affected by it. Therefore, we decided to randomly assign whole communities to the treatment and control groups. It is, of course, possible that a training procedure could leak from one community to another, but it certainly was less likely than leakage within a single community. The final design of the study contained groups which were put through all of the training programs while other groups received only one shot of training. In other words, some groups would receive training at each age level appropriate to their children over the span of the study, while others would receive training only once during the entire study. Finally, even within the nontreated groups, that is, those who would receive no training at all, some would receive pretesting and some would not. Thus the actual design turned out to be quite complex. The parent-training component had evolved from abstract and amorphous notions to a set of specified procedures and assessible goals with a design which would allow valid conclusions to be drawn.

It should be stated that not all evaluation situations are as initially amorphous and undefined as this one. Sometimes the directors are quite sophisticated and specific in terms of procedures and goals. One advantage in this particular situation was the ability to employ random assignment and thus achieve a true experimental design. This is often not possible in evaluation research situations. In any applied situation, there are difficulties involved which are not present in the laboratory, and thus ideal research designs are quite unusual in the area of program evaluation. Ideal designs would be those which allow for clear causal statements about the effects of the treatment or treatments. In other words, ideal designs are those which are internally valid. The basis of the true experiment, as we saw earlier, is the process of random assignment to conditions. Unfortunately, in many applied settings, random assignment is not feasible. For example, program directors often are not willing to withhold a treatment from individuals. As I alluded to previously, this hesitation is often based upon the assumption that the treatment is effective, even before it has been evaluated. There are also cases where a treatment occurs for all individuals. For example, consider the situation where a state legislature is considering the impact of passing a tough drunk-driving law on the accident rate. This law would, of course, apply to all citizens, and thus there would be no way of randomly assigning drivers to treated (the law applies) and untreated (the law does not apply) groups. Thus, any innovation which is available or applies to all members of a population is not a candidate for evaluation through random assignment procedures.

Finally, evaluators are often called in to evaluate the effect of a treatment after it has already occurred. In each of these cases, random assignment is not feasible. Therefore, nonequivalent control groups, time-series analysis, or combinations of these two often are the only plausible means of carrying out evaluations of programs or societal interventions. Although these approaches are never as powerful as true experiments in terms of drawing causal conclusions, they are still worthwhile alternatives to no evaluation at all. The techniques of design and analysis which have been developed for these quasi-experimental procedures have become more sophisticated and will probably tend to increase in sophistication in the future, allowing for more powerful judgments as to the effects of programs and interventions.

UNDERSTANDING
MORE OF
THE VARIANCE

Chapter 10

Multivariate
Experimental
Approaches

In order to clarify the basic nature of the correlational and experimental approaches, the discussion has been limited to the simplest cases of both: the two variable correlational situation and the single independent variable experimental situation. In both approaches, the simple cases are the building blocks of more complex research designs. In the case of correlation and regression, the basic logic for the two variable case can be expanded in order to examine the relationships among a series of variables through multiple correlation and regression designs and through a technique known as factor analysis. In terms of the experimental approach, the basic logic for the single independent variable experiment can be expanded to include two or more manipulated variables, or both manipulated and nonmanipulated variables simultaneously. In either case, the purpose for employing more complex designs is generally the same—to understand or account for more of the variation. In this chapter, we will deal with experimental designs, while the complex correlational approaches will be dealt with in the following chapter.

FACTORIAL EXPERIMENTS

Behavior is complex, and therefore, so are the causes of behavior. It is very seldom the case that a single variable acts so as to produce changes across a variety of circumstances. Usually the case is that variables produce effects only when they occur in specific situations or under certain circumstances. For example, an advertising program designed to increase the number of polio innoculations may work only if the public has become aware of a recent polio outbreak. In the same vein, programs designed to produce gasoline conservation may work only after a gasoline shortage has occurred. In other words, generally, behavior is multiply determined; that is, a number of causal agents acting together may be responsible for a given behavior. Thus, researchers often must manipulate more than one independent variable at a time in order to produce changes in a dependent variable. An experiment in which more than one independent variable is manipulated is called a *multifactor design*. If the independent variables are completed crossed, that is, if all possible combinations of the conditions exist, the experiment is called a *factorial design*. Consider the very first study described in this book where subjects are given positive or negative feedback on a test and then moved into an encounter with an attractive or an unattractive woman. One independent variable is feedback (positive or negative), and the other is attractiveness of the woman (attractive or unattractive). These variables were completely crossed providing four conditions: positive feedback–attractive woman; positive feedback–unattractive woman; negative feedback–attractive woman; and negative feedback–unattractive woman. Thus, this was a factorial design consisting of two completely crossed independent variables. The number of variables which can be simultaneously manipulated is limited only by the availability of subjects and time and the ability of the researcher to interpret the findings. Also, each variable manipulated can consist of two or more levels or conditions.

The size of a factorial experiment can be determined directly from the notation employed to describe it. Each independent variable is represented by a value which indicates the number of levels or conditions of that variable, and each number is separated from the preceding number by an x. Thus, a 2 × 2 factorial would consist of 2 independent variables, each with 2 conditions (this was the experiment described above); a 2 × 2 × 2 factorial would consist of 3 independent variables, each having 2 conditions; and a 4 × 3 × 2 factorial would consist of 3 independent variables, with 4, 3, and 2 conditions, respectively. The total number of conditions in the experiment can be calculated by simply multiplying the numbers together. Thus, the 2 × 2 design would include 4 conditions, the 2 × 2 × 2 design would have 8 conditions, and the 4 × 3 × 2 design would have 24 conditions. It should be obvious that as the number of independent variables increases and/or the number of levels of each gets larger, the total number of conditions in the experiment grows.

As an example of a factorial design, let us consider an experiment by Gold and Cowles (1973). In this experiment, the focus was on the effects of different instructional sets upon recall. Basically, the authors posited that when individuals are prepared or set to transmit information, they will process information differently than when they are set to receive information. Specifically, it was hypothesized that a set for transmission produces storage of each unit discretely, whereas a reception set produces a more global and connected type of processing. If the information to be processed was connected or interrelated, then a reception set should have an advantage over a transmission set in terms of recall. On the other hand, if the information was discrete, not interconnected, then a transmission set should work at least as well, if not better than, a reception set. In order to test these ideas, two independent variables were needed: one reflecting the set for transmitting or receiving and the other reflecting the interrelatedness of the information to be processed.

The interconnectedness of the information was varied by employing two lists of adjectives: a related list composed of 6 clusters of 5 highly related adjectives and a second list composed of 30 adjectives which were unrelated to each other. The different sets were instituted by telling subjects that after seeing a list of adjectives describing an individual, they would be asked to either transmit their impressions of the individual to other students or they would receive more information about the individual from other students. A third condition in which subjects were told that they would be neither transmitting their impressions to others nor receiving more information from others was included as a control. Thus, the design was a 3 (transmission-reception-no set) × 2 (related-unrelated list) factorial. In a complete factorial design, all combinations of the independent variables are represented. In this experiment then there were the following six combinations of conditions:

transmission-related list   reception-unrelated list

transmission-unrelated list   no set-related list

reception-related list   no set-unrelated list

The rationale and procedure for a factorial design is identical to that of the single independent variable experiments described earlier. Subjects are randomly assigned among the conditions, which means that the groups differ from one another only by chance before they are differentially treated. Thus, any differences after treatment which are very rare by chance, significant, would be due to the effects of the treatments. In the above experiment, this procedure was followed in that the subjects were randomly assigned among the six conditions. After being given either the instructional set to receive or transmit or the no set instructions, subjects were shown one of the two lists in a random sequence. Each adjective was presented on a single slide and shown for only 1½ seconds. Following the presentation of the final slide, subjects were simply asked to write down as many of the adjectives as they could remember, listing them down the page.

The results of the transmission-reception experiment are shown in Table 10–1a. The three conditions of the set variable (transmission-reception-no set) are listed across the top or columns of the table, and the two list conditions (related-unrelated) are listed on the rows of the table.

TABLE 10–1

Actual outcome (a) and hypothetical outcomes (b) and (c) of the tuning set experiment

a.

	Transmission	Reception	No Set	
Related	1.3123	1.4811	1.4925	1.4286
Unrelated	1.3156	1.2956	1.3495	1.3202
	1.3140	1.3884	1.4210	

b.

	Transmission	Reception	No Set	
Related	1.3123	1.4811	1.4925	1.4286
Unrelated	1.1452	1.2956	1.3195	1.2634
	1.2268	1.3884	1.4060	

c.

	Transmission	Reception	No Set	
Related	1.3123	1.4811	1.4925	1.4286
Unrelated	1.4824	1.2956	1.3495	1.3758
	1.3974	1.3884	1.4210	

Thus, each cell of Table 10–1a represents a specific combination of the two independent variables. The values in the table are the average recall scores for each experimental group. The recall scores were calculated as proportions of the list recalled by each subject, and these proportions were then transformed to meet certain statistical requirements. The important point here is that higher scores reflect more words recalled.

Main Effects and Interactions

Analysis of the data from a factorial experiment allows for the examination of two types of phenomena: main effects and interactions. Main effects refer to the effects of each independent variable, and interactions refer to the joint effects of the independent variables. In Table 10–1a, the main effects are shown by the numbers outside of the double lines. The main effect for the list type is reflected in the two row scores outside the vertical double lines. These two scores were found by averaging the scores for all subjects who received each list, regardless of their set condition. Thus, 1.4286 is the average recall score for all subjects who received the related word list, and 1.3202 is the average recall score for all subjects who received the unrelated word list. The main effect for set is reflected in the three column scores below the horizontal double lines. These three scores were found by averaging the scores for all subjects in each set condition, regardless of the type of list they received. Thus, 1.3140 is the average recall score for all subjects who received a transmission set, 1.3884 is the average recall score for all reception set subjects, and 1.4210 is the average recall score for all no set condition subjects. Both main effects were significant, indicating that: (a) subjects receiving the related list recalled more than those receiving the unrelated list, and (b) the three set conditions differed in the amount recalled, with the transmission group scoring the lowest.

An interaction, as the term implies, means that the independent variables act together in a manner that is different than either variable acting alone. The interaction between list type and set was significant, which means that the results differed depending on the particular combination of the two variables subjects received. For example, set had no significant effect on those subjects receiving the unrelated list, but for those who received the related list, subjects in the transmission condition recalled significantly fewer words than those in either the reception or no set conditions. Thus, set had quite a different effect depending upon whether or not the material to be recalled was discrete (unrelated) or could be organized (related). Specifically, reception had an advantage over transmission when the information was related but had no advantage when the information was unrelated.

In a sense, the interpretation of the significant main effects needed to be qualified because of the significant interaction. Although it was true that the main effect for list type is significant in that the related list group outperformed the unrelated list group, this overall effect is due entirely to the differences found in the reception and no set groups. The set main effect is also qualified by the interaction in that the overall differences among the three set conditions are due to the differences found only within the related word list condition. In order to show what the situation might look like if no interaction had occurred, fictitious data are shown in Table 10–1b. In this case, there is still a main effect for each independent variable but no interaction. The related word list has an advantage over the unrelated list in all three set conditions, and the reception and no set conditions have an advantage over the transmission condition in both types of word list conditions. The main effects in this case do not have to be qualified.

One way to depict results is through figures. The actual outcome of the set experiment is shown in Figure 10–1a and the hypothetical outcome in Figure 10–1b. It can be clearly seen from Figure 10–1a that the three sets differ at the related but not at the unrelated list condition, whereas in Figure 10–1b the three sets differ at both list conditions. The results depicted in Figure 10–1b are often described as representing additivity in that the three set conditions simply go up in value from the unrelated to the related list condition but hold their relative positions. In other words, the increase from the unrelated to the related list condition is a constant addition to each set group. The three lines for each set group between the two list conditions are almost parallel (that is, the slopes are equal), which is an indication that there is no interaction present. On the other hand, in Figure 10–1a, the line for the transmission condition certainly is not parallel to the other two lines. The slopes are quite different indicating the interaction effect.

Interactions thus occur when the effect of one of the independent variables differs depending on the effects of another of the independent variables. This can take place in a number of ways. For example, independent variable A shows no effect under one condition of independent variable B but a large effect under another condition of independent variable B. In the set experiment, transmission and reception acted similarly under the unrelated word condition but showed a large difference under the related word condition. A second type of interaction would occur where the conditions of independent variable A show opposite effects under the conditions of independent variable B. If, for example, recall for reception would have been higher than that for transmission in the related list condition but recall for transmission would have been higher than reception in the unrelated list condition, this second type of interaction would have occurred. Hypothetical results for this type of interaction are shown in Table 10–1c, and the graphic presentation is shown in Figure 10–1c. Inspection of Table 10–1c shows that the main effects for both set and list type are smaller than they are in Table 10–1a or Table 10–1b. Figure 10–1c shows that not only are the lines not parallel, their slopes are opposite in sign.

FIGURE 10–1

Graphic presentation of the actual outcome (a) and hypothetical outcomes (b) and (c) of the tuning-set experiment

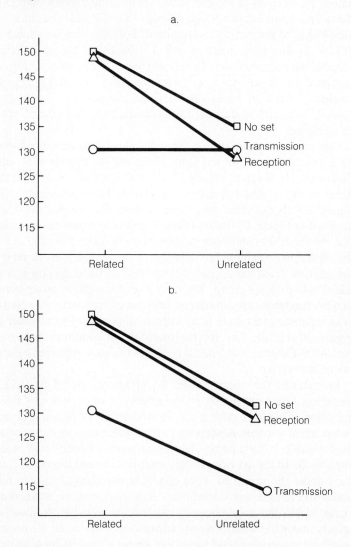

In order to gain a further understanding of factorial experiments and their resulting main effects and interactions, let us examine another study. This research by Russ, Gold, and Stone (1979) dealt with the effects of confusion and attitudinal similarity on interpersonal attraction. Past research had consistently shown that individuals showed high attraction to others with attitudes similar to their own and low attraction to others holding attitudes dissimilar to their own. Much of this research was based

FIGURE 10-1 *(concluded)*

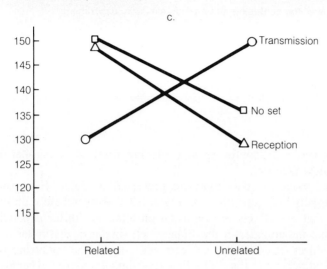

on a paradigm or model wherein subjects, after filling out an attitude scale, are provided with the attitudes of a stranger. These attitudes actually are completed by the experimenter and are made to appear either similar or dissimilar to the subjects' own attitudes. After studying the bogus attitudes, the subjects complete a measure of attraction toward the stranger. Again, the results of most of these studies have shown that subjects are highly attracted to the similar stranger and not attracted to the dissimilar stranger.

Russ, Gold, and Stone argued that in the situation where people were confused, the attraction to similar others would break down. Specifically, they hypothesized that subjects in a state of confusion would need to make sense of the confusion and would search for information which would provide understanding. They argued that others who were attitudinally similar, having a perspective like that of the confused individual, would be unable to provide information which would facilitate understanding. Dissimilar others, on the other hand, having a different perspective, would be able to provide information which might be useful in achieving understanding.

In order to test these ideas, two variables needed to be manipulated: confusion and attitude similarity. Confusion was varied by exposing subjects to either a highly surrealistic film or to a rather mundane control film. The two films were pretested in order to ensure that they were confusing and nonconfusing, respectively. Attitudinal similarity was manipulated, as in previous experiments, by providing subjects with bogus attitude scales that were either similar or dissimilar to their own positions. The dependent variable was a measure of the subjects' attraction to the stranger with the similar or dissimilar attitudes. Thus the design of the

TABLE 10–2
Results of the confusion and attitude similarity experiment

	Confusing film	*Nonconfusing film*	
Similar	8.41	10.66	9.53
Dissimilar	10.75	8.08	9.41
	9.58	9.37	

study was a 2 (confusing-nonconfusing film) × 2 (similar-dissimilar attitudes) factorial.[1]

The results of the study are presented in Table 10–2 and shown graphically in Figure 10–2. As Figure 10–2 shows, there is an interaction such that the effects of confusion on attraction differ depending upon whether the attitudes of the stranger are similar or dissimilar to those of the subject. Specifically, subjects who viewed the confusing film were more attracted to a dissimilar than to a similar stranger, whereas subjects exposed to the nonconfusing film were more attracted to a similar than to a dissimilar stranger. This is the second type of interaction discussed previously: the conditions of one variable show opposite effects under the conditions of the other variable. It can also be seen that with this type of interaction, there are no main effects. That is, the mean of the subjects in the similar condition (9.53) is very close to the mean of the dissimilar condition subjects (9.41), and the mean of the subjects exposed to the confusing film (9.58) is very close to the mean of the subjects in the nonconfusing film condition (9.37).

Although both the set experiment and the experiment discussed above employed two independent variables, experiments can employ more than two independent variables. The results become more complex in that there are more main effects and more interactions. For example, in a 2 × 2 × 2 factorial which has three independent variables with two conditions each, there are three possible main effects and four possible interactions. If we call the three variables A, B, and C, respectively, there are A, B, and C main effects, A × B, A × C, and B × C two-way interactions, and an A × B × C three-way interaction.

In order to demonstrate a three independent variable factorial design, let us consider a second experiment by Russ, Gold, and Stone (1980), a follow-up to the earlier study on confusion and similarity. Two of the variables were identical to those employed in the original study: confusion represented by the confusing and nonconfusing films and attitude similarity manipulated through the bogus technique. The third independent

---

[1] The actual study manipulated three confusion conditions, the third being a presentation of the confusing film preceded by a brief explanation. The role of this third confusion condition will be discussed later under the topic of construct validity. The results are presented here as a 2 × 2 factorial for the purpose of clarity in demonstrating a factorial experiment.

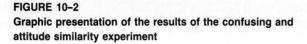

FIGURE 10-2
Graphic presentation of the results of the confusing and attitude similarity experiment

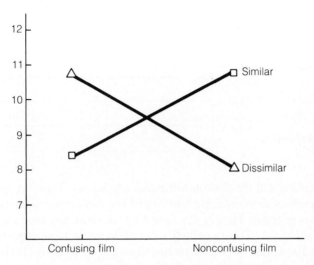

variable was whether or not subjects were given an opportunity to think about the film they had viewed. Russ et al. (1980) argued that if subjects had an opportunity to think about the confusing film after seeing it, they would be able to make sense of it and consequently would not need information from another person. Since the dissimilar strangers are the information providers, attraction to them should decrease when subjects are provided with the opportunity for thought about the film. On the other hand, opportunity for thought should have no effect on subjects exposed to the nonconfusing film since they presumably already understand it. Thus, the authors predicted an interaction among all three variables.

The procedure in this study followed that of the original experiment except that, following the presentation of the film, subjects were given either a brief period to think about the film or were engaged in a filler task of adding columns of numbers, which was designed to prevent them from thinking about the film. The results of the study are presented in Table 10-3 and shown graphically in Figure 10-3. Since the situation in which subjects are deprived of an opportunity to think about the film is nearly identical to that in the first study, we would expect the results to parallel those found in the first experiment. Examination of the lower half of Table 10-3 shows this to be the case. In the confusing film condition, subjects have greater attraction to dissimilar others than to similar others, but in the nonconfusing film condition, there is the usual finding of greater attraction to similar others.

On the other hand, when given an opportunity for thought, subjects showed greater attraction to the similar than to the dissimilar other in both

TABLE 10–3

Results of the confusion, attitude similarity and opportunity for thought experiment

Opportunity for thought	Confusing film	Nonconfusing film
Similar other	9.3	7.4
Dissimilar other	6.3	6.8

No opportunity for thought	Confusing film	Nonconfusing film
Similar other	8.1	9.6
Dissimilar other	9.3	6.1

the confusing and the nonconfusing film conditions. Thus, an opportunity to think about the confusing film wiped out the greater attraction to the dissimilar stranger. Figures 10–3a and 10–3b show the three way interaction graphically. The opportunity for thought and no opportunity for thought conditions have been plotted separately for clarity. It can be seen that Figure 10–3b parallels Figure 10–2, but Figure 10–3a shows almost the opposite effect. It should be pointed out that these results could have been plotted differently from the way they were plotted in Figure 10–3. That is, the confusing and nonconfusing film conditions could have been plotted separately, or the similar and dissimilar conditions could have been shown on separate graphs. The results would have remained the same; only the perspective would have been changed.

Just as in the case of a two-way interaction where the effect of one variable depends upon the conditions of a second variable, a three-way interaction means that the effect of one of the variables depends upon a particular combination of the other two variables. Three way interactions are more complicated and thus more difficult to interpret than two-way interactions. In general, the higher the level of interaction, the more difficult and complex the interpretation of the findings. Even if a complex interaction can be interpreted, it may mean that the finding is so qualified that it is meaningless. The bottom line might be that the effect occurs only if condition 1 of factor A combines with condition 2 of factor B, condition 3 of factor C, and condition 2 of factor D. Any other combination of the factors produces no effect. This would be analogous to a surgeon saying that he performs successful appendectomies if he operates on Tuesday mornings or Thursday afternoons, the patient weighs less than 110 pounds and is female or more than 210 pounds and is male, and he has not scored over 90 on the golf course the day before the operation; all other combinations will produce botched operations. So many qualifiers would exist that success could be predicted but only in a fairly trivial number of cases. Thus, interactions can be so complex, depending upon so many combinations of variables, that they may be meaningless. On the other hand,

FIGURE 10–3
**Graphic presentation of the results of the confusion attitude
similarity, and opportunity for thought experiment**

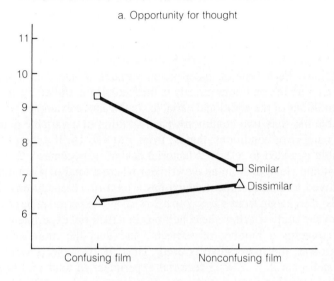

a. Opportunity for thought

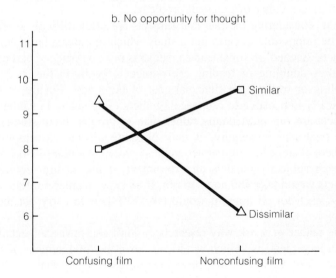

b. No opportunity for thought

higher-order interactions, although complex, may be meaningful. It is the
task of the investigator to discover interactions of variables and then
attempt, where feasible, to interpret them. In other words, interactions
involving a number of variables should not be avoided simply because
they are complex but should be examined in order to determine whether
any meaningful pattern exists. In fact, the simplest findings to interpret

are main effects, since only one variable is involved in the effect. Thus, while the logic of manipulating a large number of variables simultaneously is straightforward, the interpretation of the results of such a multiple manipulation is often anything but straightforward.

Another problem with factorial experiments which employ a number of independent variables is the number of conditions involved. A 2×2 factorial has 4, a $2 \times 2 \times 2$ has 8, and a 4-factor $2 \times 2 \times 2 \times 2$ has 16 conditions. Each time an independent variable is added to a study, the total number of conditions already in the study is multiplied by the number of conditions of the additional variable. In the above examples where each variable has only two conditions, each addition of a variable doubles the total number of conditions; that is, from 4 to 8 to 16. If a three-condition variable is added to a 2×2 factorial design, it becomes a $2 \times 2 \times 3$ design and changes from an experiment where a total of 4 conditions are employed to an experiment which has a total of 12 conditions. In other words, the change from a 2×2 to a $2 \times 2 \times 3$ experiment has tripled the size of the study. Each of the conditions in a factorial experiment, called a cell, contains a number of subjects, and thus the more cells in the experiment, the more subjects used. Thus, if 10 subjects were used in each cell of a $2 \times 2 \times 3$ factorial experiment, a total of 120 subjects would be needed for the study. Needing large numbers of subjects often produces a number of practical problems.

First, considering the fact that subjects are often difficult to recruit, it may be impossible to carry out a study which requires a large number of subjects. Second, in some studies, subjects must be paid for participating, and thus doubling or tripling the number of cells in the study means doubling or tripling the financial cost of the study. Finally, it may be physically impossible to run large numbers of subjects. In studies where subjects are run individually rather than in groups, or in studies where each treatment is lengthy, it may be quite difficult to employ large numbers of subjects. Sometimes studies involve 4 or more 1-hour sessions for each subject, and thus an experiment of this nature requiring 120 subjects would take 480 hours to run. If an experimenter ran four subjects a day, each for an hour, it would take 120 days to carry out the entire study.

The reader may ask why researchers don't use fewer subjects in each cell in large designs, which would cut down the total number of subjects needed. The answer is that researchers often do just that. Rather than eliminate an independent variable, researchers will often use fewer subjects in each of the conditions of the experiment. If, for example, only 60 subjects rather than 120 subjects were used in a study requiring 4 hours per subject, the total running time of the study would be cut from 480 to 240 hours—a substantial savings. If this was a $2 \times 2 \times 3$ factorial, rather than dividing the 120 subjects into 12 cells, giving 10 subjects per cell, 60 subjects would be split among 12 cells, yielding only 5 subjects per cell. This smaller cell size does bring problems. It will be recalled from

Chapters 6 and 7 that statistics based on small sample sizes are less reliable than those based on larger size samples. The variability of the sampling distribution curve increases as the sample size decreases resulting in larger confidence intervals for sample statistics. Thus, means or other statistics based upon 5 subjects will be less accurate than those based upon 10 subjects. Think of it this way. With only a few subjects in a condition, one or two discrepant scores can affect the statistic quite powerfully, but with larger numbers of subjects, a few discrepant scores will have less effect. Thus, researchers cannot simply avoid the increase in subjects that occur with larger designs by employing fewer subjects per condition. Their price will be less accurate estimates (statistics) in each condition of the study.

Testing Significance in Factorial Designs

In Chapter 7, we discussed only the case involving testing the significance of the means of two groups. Although the logic of the decision process, the commission of Type I and Type II errors, and the ways to control these errors apply to situations involving more than two groups, the process of testing for significance changes to some extent. To begin with, let us examine the situation where there is only a single independent variable with more than two conditions. Consider the situation where a researcher believes that the effects of various psychotherapeutic techniques are due mainly to the effort patients expend in those treatments. That is, patients often put a great deal of time, money, and energy into therapy and then may come to believe in the effectiveness of the therapy in order to justify their expenditures. Thus, the actual effectiveness of a given therapy in alleviating a problem would be due, at least in part, not to the type of therapy itself, but rather to the fact that patients expend a great deal of effort, justify that effort by believing in the effectiveness of the therapy, and act on those beliefs by showing improvements.

In order to test this belief, the researcher designs a study consisting of three conditions to which patients are randomly assigned. All of the patients are snake phobics, and a pretest measure shows that all of them will not approach a snake. Patients in condition 1 are systematically desensitized to snakes over the four-week period by relaxing them in the presence of images of snakes, pictures of snakes, etc. In condition 2, patients are told that physical exercise is related to fears, and thus they are put through a four-week exercise program in which they run, do calisthenics, lift weights, etc. Finally, condition 3 is a no-treatment control group who simply wait and are tested at the end of four weeks.

The dependent variable in the study is the distance in inches the patients will travel in approaching a snake in a cage at the end of a room. Now if the researcher wanted to compare the means of all of these conditions with each other, she would have to carry out three separate significance tests: condition 1 versus condition 2, condition 1 versus condition 3, and condition 2 versus condition 3. Not only is this a laborious process, but the probability of finding one of these differences to be significant by chance, if each is tested with a 5 percent risk, is unfortunately larger than .05.

Therefore a different statistical process is employed which guards against chance findings. This process is called an *analysis of variance* (ANOVA). The reader will recall that in discussing the concept of variance in Chapter 2, it was pointed out that the variance of any variable could be broken down or partitioned into a systematic and an unsystematic component. The systematic component was that part of the variance which was related to another variable or variables, while the unsystematic or error component was that part of the variance which was unrelated to another variable or variables. In the above study on effort justification, the total variance of the dependent variable—that is, the individual differences in degree to which the patients approached the snake—could be partitioned into a component which was related to the independent variable, the three different treatments, and a component which was unrelated to those treatments, the error component.

The systematic component would be reflected in differences among the means of the treatment groups. For example, assume that the hypothesis about effort justification was correct. In this case, we would expect to find that, on the average, patients in both the desensitization and exercise groups approached the snake more closely than the patients in the no-treatment control group. Thus, the means of the two therapy groups should diverge from the mean of the control group, and the greater the divergence of the treatment group means, the greater the variability of these means. This variability is obviously related to something systematic—namely, the different treatments. There is also another source of variability, and that is found within each group. Although the means of the two therapy groups are higher than the control group mean, not everyone in the therapy groups benefits equally from the therapies. For example, within the desensitization therapy group, some patients approach the snake very closely, while others still maintain a great deal of distance. These individual differences within the groups cannot be due to the treatments since within each group, all subjects receive the same treatment. To what is this within-group variance then due? The answer is that we don't know. We have an explanation and evidence for the variability of the group means (the treatments) but no evidence for the variability within the groups. We are in a state of ignorance as to the within-group variance, and ignorance is error.

If we compute a ratio of the variance between the group means to the variance within the groups, that is, a ratio of the systematic to the error variance, we can determine whether the variability in the group means is greater than that which would be expected by chance. This ratio generates a statistic called *F,* which can be interpreted as to its probability of occurrence by chance by employing the proper statistical table. In other words, just as a normal curve is tabled and we would employ this table to evaluate results that are normally distributed, variance ratios are distributed as a distribution called F, which is tabled and which we can use to evaluate our ratio of variances. If the ratio of systematic to error variance is large enough so that a ratio that large would occur rarely by chance, less than 5 percent of the time for example, we would reject the null hypothesis that the independent variable had no effect. This would be akin to rejecting the null hypothesis that the three group means were all drawn from the same population. The computational procedures for testing the significance of the difference among the means of three groups through the ANOVA are demonstrated in section V of the appendix.

This same logic can be extended to situations involving more than one independent variable. For example, in a 2×2 factorial design, there are 4 groups of subjects. Differences among the means of the four groups, i.e., the variability of these means, would reflect systematic variance. It would be systematic in that it would be a function of the different treatment combinations the groups received. Differences among the scores within the groups (i.e., the variability of the scores within the groups) would reflect error variance. In the case of the factorial design, the variance among all of the means can be broken down or partitioned into variance due to main effects and interactions. Consider the 2×2 factorial experiment on attraction discussed earlier. In this experiment, the variance among the means of the four conditions (the systematic variance) can be partitioned into variance due to the main effect of attitude similarity, variance due to the main effect of level of confusion, and variance due to the interaction between the two independent variables. Each one of these variances can then be tested as to significance through the F statistic. The F statistic in this case would consist of the ratios of each of the above variances to the within-group or error variance. In the case of a three independent variable experiment, the variance between the means of all of the groups can be partitioned into variance due to each of the three main effects, variance due to each of the three two-way interactions, the variance due to the three-way interaction. Again each of the above variances can be tested for significance through the F statistic. The computational procedures for a 2×2 ANOVA are demonstrated in section VI of the appendix.

When an effect is significant and involves more than two conditions, further analyses are required. For example, a main effect involving an independent variable with three conditions simply indicates that the differences among the means of the conditions are significant. It does not indicate which differences among the means are significant. The three means may all differ from one another, or two of them may not differ from each other but both differ from the remaining mean. In order to test where the significant differences occur, further statistical procedures, called multiple comparison tests, must be carried out. If the comparisons had been decided on before the study was run, planned or a priori tests are appropriate. On the other hand, if the findings were not expected and the comparisons were not determined beforehand, post-hoc or unplanned comparisons are used. The main difference between the two types of comparisons is that it is more difficult to reject the null hypothesis when post-hoc tests are employed since the differences between the means have to be greater than differences tested with a priori tests. Thus, post-hoc comparisons are more conservative than planned comparisons. The carrying out of multiple comparisons is not limited to situations where main effects are involved. A significant interaction means that at least 4 conditions will be involved (a 2×2 interaction, the simplest possible, involves 4 means). In order to determine where the significant effects have occurred, multiple comparisons, either planned or unplanned, are utilized.

The examples of factorial experiments given have all dealt with independent variables which were qualitative in nature. In other words, the conditions of the independent variables differed in kind rather than in degree. This is not always the case. Many experiments employ some or all independent variables which are qantitative in nature. When a main effect or interaction occurs which involves a quantitative variable, one in which the conditions can be ordered as to the level or degree of the independent variable, a trend analysis may be used to determine the nature of the relationship between the independent and dependent variables. This is a procedure which allows the researcher to determine whether the means of the conditions are a linear or a curvilinear function of the treatment levels and, if curvilinear, what type of curve best describes their trend. The use of a trend analysis following a significant effect for a quantitative variable is directly analogous to the use of multiple comparison tests described above.

COMBINING MANIPULATED AND NONMANIPULATED VARIABLES

Whereas factorial experiments consist of manipulating two or more independent variables simultaneously, a factorial design can employ both manipulated and nonmanipulated variables. Since designs which deal with nonmanipulated variables are correlational, employing both manipulated and nonmanipulated variables in the same design means blending the correlational and experimental approaches, and in fact, I will refer to such designs as *blended* designs. The essence of a blended design is that at least one of the variables is manipulated, and at least one is not. In the case of the manipulated variable, random assignment to the various conditions is the key. The nonmanipulated or correlational variable, on the other hand, involves classification or identification of subjects rather than assignment.

Thus, in a blended design, subjects are either *(a)* measured on some variable and then classified on the basis of their scores into distinct groups or *(b)* are identified as belonging to various groups by one or more ostensive or obvious characteristics. Within each of the groups formed either from the measurement or the identification process, subjects are then randomly assigned to the various treatment conditions of the manipulated variable. Assume that we want to study the effects of being chosen or not by an attractive member of the opposite sex on subjects' self-esteem. Further, assume that we are interested in whether males and females will respond to the choice in the same way. Therefore, a blended design is in order. The nonmanipulated variable is subject sex, and in this case, the two groups are formed simply by identifying whether or not the subjects are male or female. The manipulated variable consists of two conditions; the subject is chosen or is not by an attractive member of the opposite sex. The actual procedure then would be to randomly assign half of each sex to the chosen condition and the other half to the not-chosen condition. In the case of subject sex, the formation of the groups is a straightforward procedure based either on direct observation and identification of the subjects as male or female or on the subjects' own responses identifying their gender. Other variables, such as race or political party affiliation, are formed in this same manner. Thus, where the variable is of the nominal scale type discussed in Chapter 2, identification of the groups is relatively straightforward; subjects simply state their race or political preference which automatically categorizes them on that variable.

On the other hand, whenever the correlational variable is composed of a continuum, classification of subjects into groups becomes somewhat more complex. First of all, subjects must be measured on the variable of interest and then classified on the basis of this measurement as to the group or level of the variable to which they belong. The formation of the categories or levels of the variable is a rather arbitrary process on the part of the researcher since the groups can be formed in a number of ways. First of all, the researcher must decide the number of groups or levels desired. Second, the composition of the groups must be determined in terms of the scores which define the boundaries of the groups. In other words, one must be able to say that subjects whose scores fall between certain points would be classified into specific groups, such as high, medium, or low.

Sometimes this can be accomplished by consulting previously published information on the measured variable. If, for example, a variable such as self-esteem was assessed through a standardized scale, subjects could be classified as to being high or low in self-esteem on the basis of how their scores compared with the normative data for the scale. This type of classification based on normative standards can produce difficulties. If, for example, the norms for the scale were developed upon subjects from the general population but the subjects to be employed in the study are college students, the use of the scale norms for purposes of classification may produce groups or categories of quite divergent sizes. Assume, for example, that a researcher was attempting to classify college student subjects into liberal or conservative groups based on whether their scores fall above or below the population median on a standardized measure of liberal and conservative attitudes. Since most student populations are more liberal than the general population, most of the subjects in the study will fall above the general population median and thus will be classified as liberal. This means that the liberal category will contain many more subjects than the conservative category.

This unequal group size is further compounded when subjects in each group are then randomly assigned to the various levels of the independent variable. Assume that when 50 subjects are classified on the basis of comparing their liberalism-conservatism scale scores to norms for the scale, 80 percent, or 40, of the subjects fall above the median (liberal) and only 20 percent, or 10, of the subjects fall below the median (conservative). If the subjects in each of these groups are then randomly assigned between two conditions of a manipulated variable, the two liberal groups will consist of 20 subjects each, while the two conservative groups will each contain only 5 subjects. These very divergent group sizes will then make comparisons between means or other statistics quite unreliable.

One answer to this problem is to classify subjects into the categories, not on the basis of the generalized test norms, but upon their own distribution of scores. Thus, rather than comparing each subject's liberalism-conservatism scale score to the general population median, each would be compared to the median calculated from only the scores of the subjects in the study. As before, those subjects scoring above the criterion (the median) would be classified as liberal, whereas those falling below would be classified as conservative. This would guarantee that half of the subjects would be classified as liberal and half as conservative and that the further random assignment within each category would produce approximately equal conditions over the whole design.

Although this procedure of using the subjects' own distribution of scores as a basis for classification does guard against unequal group size, it may have two types of negative consequences. First, it may produce weak results in that the population difference being investigated may be quite small. In the case of the liberalism-conservatism variable, classifying on the basis of the median of the distribution of the sample of college students may produce samples which reflect very liberal and somewhat liberal populations rather than liberal and conservative populations. It then may be more difficult to find a difference on the dependent variable between two categories of liberals than between a liberal and a conservative category. Thus, the probability of a Type II error may be increased. Second, if a difference is found between these less extreme groups, the generalizability of the finding could be questioned. On the other hand, finding a difference between these less extreme categories may mean that the finding would be even more powerful if more extreme categories based upon the general norms had been used. In other words, if a highly liberal and a somewhat liberal group differ, then surely a liberal and a conservative group would differ to an even greater extent. This is certainly possible, but it is not a sure bet. It is sometimes the case that extremes from the two ends of the continuum perform alike, but each will differ from moderate scorers. This is a case of the nonlinear relationship between variables discussed previously. Thus, a generalization from the results obtained on less extreme groups to those which would be obtained on more extreme groups may be unwarranted.

In order to demonstrate a blended design with classification on a continuous variable, let us reconsider the study dealing with the effect of being chosen on self-esteem. This time, assume that we are interested in physical attractiveness rather than subject sex as the nonmanipulated variable. That is, we want to form groups that differ in physical attractiveness. Whereas, the categories for subject sex were obvious, attractiveness is a continuous variable not open to simple classification. Individuals differ in physical attractiveness by degree, and therefore, physical attractiveness must be assessed or measured in some manner.

One way to do this would be to have a group of judges independently rate each subject, and if there is interjudge agreement on the ratings, average the ratings to yield an attractiveness score for each subject. The next step is to determine categories for the physical attractiveness variable. This can be accomplished by using the data from the judges since normative data will probably not exist for ratings of this type.

A first decision must be made as to the number of groups which will be formed. That is, should there be only high and low physical attractiveness groups or possibly high, medium, and low groups? Once the desired number of categories or groups is determined, a second decision arises as to the definition of those groups. Employing the attractiveness scores of our subjects, we could compose the two groups by classifying those subjects falling above the median of the distribution as high and those falling below the median as low in attractiveness. This would ensure an equal number in each category since the median is the point which separates the top and bottom halves of a distribution.

The groups would then be composed of those subjects scoring above and those scoring below a given number. Since it would be highly unlikely that the measure of attractiveness was perfectly reliable, subjects' scores would contain some degree of measurement error. At scores close to the point where the split into groups was made, this measurement error might mean misclassification of subjects. For instance, subjects scoring just above the median and classified as being in the high attractive group might actually belong to the low attractive group, and vice versa for those subjects scoring just below the median. In other words, subjects close to the point at which the groups were formed may have fallen into the groups by chance alone. In order to deal with this problem, researchers often discard subjects with scores close to the cutting point. One way to do this would be to employ a statistical tool known as the standard error of measurement, which is a measure of the variability of the errors of measurement. The higher the reliability of a measuring device, the smaller the standard error of measurement. By discarding scores within one standard error of measurement above and below the cutting point, the chances of misclassification would be greatly reduced. Two standard errors of measurement in both directions would lessen the probability of a misclassification to an even greater extent. If the reliability is high and the standard error of measurement is small, then few subjects will be lost. But if the standard error of measurement is large, cutting down the threat of misclassification will cost the researcher a large number of subjects.

A second reason besides misclassification for not forming groups from those subjects above and below a single cutting point deals with the power of the effects. Even if unreliability were not a factor, subjects with scores around the cutting point are probably very much alike. For example, subjects just above and just below the median attractiveness score are probably not very different from each other in attractiveness. On the other hand, subjects in the top and bottom quarters of the distribution would certainly be expected to have a greater chance of differing. Therefore, researchers often choose more extreme scores as their classification points. In a sense, this is akin to increasing the strength of a manipulation, which as discussed in Chapter 7, increases the probability of rejecting the null hypothesis. Choosing extreme scores, on the other hand, does mean discarding more subjects, which in turn implies ending up with smaller size groups which thus lowers the chances of finding a significant result. The use of extreme groups also means more restricted generality for any findings; that is, the findings only apply to those extremes. Also, if the nonmanipulated variable is not linearly related to the dependent variable, then the two extreme groups may not differ, and thus the use of extreme groups could work against the researcher by obliterating a finding. If, for example, one employed extremely high and low anxious subjects in a complex task, it would be highly probable that no differences in performance would be found. Since anxiety and performance have often been found to be nonlinearly related, both high and low anxious subjects would show poor performance.

In order to deal with this problem of nonlinear relationships and extreme groups, multiple groupings are often employed. That is, subjects in the anxiety example above would be grouped into high, moderate, and low anxious categories, thus picking up the better performance of the moderately anxious subjects. This, of course, means more groups with fewer subjects per group. If the researcher also wants to separate the groups to reduce chances of misclassification between the high and moderate and low and moderate groups, this will mean even further reductions in group size.

Thus, decisions have to be made as to the number of categories or groups formed and to the method in which those groups are formed. More categories or levels means greater generality and the possibility of non-linearity. On the other hand, multileveling also means fewer subjects per group and possibly greater loss of subjects from guarding against mis-classification. Forming groups through a median split ensures group size equality but often does not produce highly distinct groups due to unreliability. The task of the researcher is to weigh these alternatives and form groups which fit the purposes of the research at hand. In the long run, any judgments about group composition become somewhat arbitrary in that many other compositions, beside the chosen one, are also possible.

Reduction of Error Variance

One reason for employing a blended design is to reduce unsystematic or error variance. When subjects are randomly assigned to groups, those groups are often quite heterogeneous. That is, subjects within each group may differ from one another on variables related to the dependent measure. By first separating or classifying subjects on a variable related to the dependent measure and then randomly assigning subjects within the classifications to the treatment conditions, greater homogeneity is achieved. Consider again the study on the effect of being chosen or not on subjects' self esteem. Assume that we had not employed a mixed design, but rather had simply randomly assigned subjects to the two conditions. Each condition would contain both males and females, and if males and females characteristically or chronically differ in self-esteem, then each of the experimental groups will be heterogeneous with respect to self esteem.

Table 10–4a shows hypothetical results for the two conditions. The mean and standard deviation for each group is shown at the bottom of each column of scores. Although the mean self-esteem score for the chosen group is greater than that for the not-chosen group (26.2 and 23.2, respectively), the variability within each group is so large that the difference between the means is not significant. The letters M and F beside the scores in Table 10–4a indicate males and females in each group. Table 10–4b contains the scores in Table 10–4a grouped as to subject sex. Inspection of Table 10–4b shows that within each of the experimental conditions, males score higher than females, and that within each sex, subjects in the chosen condition score higher than subjects in the not-chosen condition. Further, within each of the four conditions, there is less variability than there was within the two groups in Table 10–4a; the standard deviations for the conditions in Table 10–4b are quite a bit smaller than those in Table 10–4a.

By classifying subjects within each of the two experimental conditions by sex, a single independent variable design has been turned into a blended design. Since a blended design is a factorial, there are possible main effects and interactions. Analysis of the data in Table 10–4b reveals significant main effects for both the experimental variable (chosen–not-chosen) and subject sex but no interaction between the two variables. That is, the chosen condition shows significantly greater self-esteem than the not-chosen condition for both sexes. Since the scores for the main effect of experimental condition are identical to those in Table 10–4a, the finding of a significant difference for experimental condition in Table

TABLE 10–4

Hypothetical results for the total sample (a), and broken down by sex (b) for the self-esteem experiment

a.

	Condition	
	Chosen	Not-chosen
	33 M	21 F
	27 M	30 M
	20 F	19 F
	31 M	19 F
	22 F	24 M
	22 F	17 F
	29 M	28 M
	24 F	26 M
	29 M	26 M
	25 F	22 F
Mean	26.2	23.2
Standard deviation	4.28	4.28

b.

		Chosen	Not-chosen
		33	30
		27	24
		31	28
Male		29	26
		29	26
	Mean	29.8	26.8
	Standard deviation	2.28	2.28
		20	21
		22	19
		22	19
Female		24	17
		25	22
	Mean	22.6	19.6
	Standard deviation	1.94	1.94

10–4b must be due to the smaller amount of within-group or unsystematic variance. Thus, in this case, value of the nonmanipulated variable was to reduce error variance and increase the likelihood of a significant finding.

Generality of Findings

In order to circumvent the problem of increased within-condition variability due to sex differences, the study could have employed only one of the sexes. While variability would have been reduced, generality would have also been limited. On the other hand, showing that the manipulation works in the same manner for both sexes enhances the generality of the findings. In Table 10–4b, this is exactly what occurs. Although males score higher on self-esteem than females, the difference between the chosen and not-chosen conditions is the same for both sexes; that is, males in the chosen condition score three points above males in the not-chosen condition, and females in the chosen condition score three points above their not-chosen counterparts. The absence of any interaction also supports the generality of the experimental condition main effect, since without an interaction, the main effect does not have to be qualified.

Although the above logic about the generality of effects is compelling, a note of caution is in order. The evidence for generality was the failure to find a significant interaction between the manipulated and nonmanipulated variables. Thus, one could conclude that the effects of being chosen or not were the same for both sexes. Unfortunately, since evidence for generality is a nonsignificant interaction between the nonmanipulated and manipulated variables, this is identical to accepting the null hypothesis. The reader will recall that failure to reject the null hypothesis does not result in its acceptance. Thus, since we cannot accept the null hypothesis, technically we also cannot conclude that generality exists from a failure to reject the null hypothesis.

Differential Effects of the Manipulated Variable

Very often, the real strength of a blended design is that it shows that the effects of the manipulated variable are not general. That is, it shows that the manipulated variable has different effects depending upon the population of subjects to which it is applied. For example, a special program designed to increase problem-solving ability may work for students of high intelligence but not for students of average intelligence; or it may work for both but be more effective for the high than for the average students.

In order to demonstrate the differential effectiveness mixed designs can show, consider a study on attitude similarity and attraction by Thornton, Ryckman, and Gold (1981). The authors hypothesized that the usual findings of high attraction to attitudinally similar others and low attraction to attitudinally dissimilar others could be modified by concentrating on personality differences in preference for interesting and exciting experiences. Previous research had shown individual differences in a variable termed *sensation seeking,* which reflects differences in preference for arousing activities and novel situations. It was argued that high sensation seekers would see a situation in which they were to meet with a dissimilar other as exciting and challenging and thus would be attracted to that dissimilar individual. Low sensation seekers, on the other hand, in their attempt to avoid excitement and novelty, would see a dissimilar other negatively and would thus show low attraction. In order to test this idea, subjects were classified as being high and low sensation seekers on the basis of their scores on selected items from the sensation-seeking scale, which were related to interpersonal situations. Subjects within each sensation-seeking group were randomly assigned to either the similar or dissimilar attitude condition, which was manipulated by producing bogus attitude scales as described previously in the studies on confusion and attraction. Attraction to the stranger was also measured in a manner identical to that previously described.

Thus, there were two variables in this blended design: attitude similarity-dissimilarity (the manipulated variable) and sensation seeking (the nonmanipulated variable). Although there was a significant main effect for attitude similarity, with greater attraction expressed in the similar than the dissimilar condition, this was qualified by the sensation seeking x attitude similarity interaction. The means are shown in Table 10–5, and the interaction is depicted graphically in Figure 10–4. Although, as the results show, there was greater attraction to a similar than to a dissimilar other in general, high sensation seekers were more attracted to a dissimilar other than their low sensation seeking counterparts, whereas they were less attracted to a similar other than the low sensation seekers. In fact, the really large difference in attraction between similar and dissimilar others comes mainly from the low sensation seekers. Thus, the generality of the strength of the similarity attraction relationships were shown to need at least some modification based upon this personality variable.

A study by Bandura (1965) on imitation of aggressive behavior provides another demonstration of how a blended design can show the limits of the generality of a manipulation. Bandura was interested in the effects of different consequences of a model's aggressive behavior on subsequent imitation of that behavior. In order to investigate this problem, he videotaped adult models aggressing in novel ways against a Bobo doll, an adult-size plastic clown, which is designed for rough play by children. The manipulation consisted of three different conditions which appeared at the close of the videotape. In the model-rewarded condition, a second adult appeared on the scene, praised the model, and gave the model a treat. In the model-punished condition, the second adult verbally reproached and spanked the model with a rolled-up magazine. The no-consequences condition omitted the appearance of the second adult.

The nonmanipulated variable in the study was subject sex. Equal

TABLE 10–5

Results of the blended design study of attitude similarity and sensation seeking

	Similar	Dissimilar
High Sensation seeking	4.80	4.12
Low	5.38	3.01

FIGURE 10-4
Results of the attitude similarity and sensation-seeking study

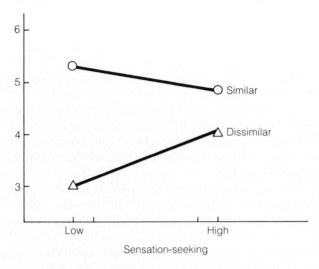

numbers of male and female children were randomly assigned to the three conditions of the manipulated variable. All subjects viewed the identical videotape of the model aggressing against the Bobo doll, followed by one of the three subsequent conditions: reward, punishment, or no consequence. Each child was then taken to a room containing the Bobo doll and other toys and observed by judges who rated the level of imitation performed. Examination and testing of the means revealed that when the model was punished, subjects gave fewer imitative responses than when the model was either rewarded or no consequences occurred for the model and that the reward and no consequences conditions did not differ significantly. Thus, punishment suppressed performance but reward did not enhance it over no consequences. In terms of subject sex, boys gave more imitative responses than girls. Finally, separate analyses of the treatment means for the two sexes showed that boys showed no significant differences among the conditions, but girls showed the pattern described above; that is, girls in the model punished condition produced fewer imitative responses than girls in either the model rewarded or no consequence condition, and these two conditions did not differ from each other.

Thus, in terms of performance of imitative aggressive responses, consequences to the model do have an effect in that punishment serves to suppress imitative aggressive performance. On the other hand, the effect of punishment seems to work only for girls. The study then, by including subject sex as the nonmanipulated variable, showed an important limit to the generality of the manipulated variable.

Testing Hypotheses about the Correlational Variable

In both the attitudinal similarity × sensation seeking study and the model consequences × subject sex study, the emphasis was primarily on the manipulated variable. That is, the primary interest was in the limits of the similarity-attraction relationship in the first study and the generality of the model consequences variable in the second study. The addition of the nonmanipulated variables helped to illuminate the workings of the manipulated variables by showing the situations under which effects do and do not occur, but the emphasis was upon the manipulated variables. This is not always the case. There are many research situations in which the primary variable of interest is the nonmanipulated variable, and in fact, the manipulated variable is employed to further the understanding of the nonmanipulated variable.

One such area where the nonmanipulated variable is the focus of interest is the study of sex differences. Subject sex, rather than being included to increase the generality of a manipulation or to reduce error variance, is the variable of primary interest in these studies. The manipulated variables are employed to shed light upon the nonmanipulated variable. A study by Lenney, Gold and Browning (in press) dealing with sex differences in self-confidence will show how a manipulated variable is employed to illuminate a nonmanipulated variable. Much of the literature on sex differences had shown women to be generally lower than men in self-confidence. This study tested the idea that sex differences in self-confidence were a function of social comparison. Specifically, the authors hypothesized that the self-confidence and actual performance of women would be lower than that of men when they compared their performance to others of high ability but that male and female self-confidence and performance would not differ when comparison was made to average or low-ability others.

In order to test this, male and female subjects were informed that they would meet with a partner at the end of their experimental session to cooperate on a problem solving task. Subjects were then provided with a brief portrait of their future partner which described the partner as either high, average, or low in ability. All subjects then completed an achievement test, rated their own performance, and estimated their future partner's performance on this test. We will only concentrate on the test scores since the other variables were subjected to rather complicated analyses. The means for these scores are shown in Table 10–6.

It can be seen that the largest sex difference, and the only significant one, occurs where comparison is made with a high-ability partner, and in fact, women score somewhat higher than men in the average-ability partner condition. Thus, the study sheds some light on the processes involved in sex differences in self-confidence. Since the manipulated variable interacted with subject sex, we are able to understand the circumstances under which the sex difference occurs. The focus here was not on

TABLE 10–6
Results for the blended design study of partner ability level and sex of subject

	Ability of Partner		
	High	Average	Low
Males	7.21	3.18	5.67
Females	2.47	4.94	4.60

social comparison level but rather on sex differences, and the manipulated variable was employed to shed light on what might be contributing to sex differences in self-confidence.

Often a theoretical approach emphasizes individual differences related to cognitive style or personality. For example, Rokeach (1960) postulated differences in cognitive style which he termed open- and closed-mindedness, and Rotter (1966) dealt with personality differences in belief in internal versus external control. Both of these researchers developed scales to measure these concepts: the dogmatism scale to assess open-closed mindedness and the IE scale to measure internal versus external control orientation. The testing of the theory often involves exposing high- and low-scoring individuals to various manipulated variables in order to determine differential performance by these individuals.

As a specific example, consider Rotter's work on internal-external locus of control. Rotter postulated that individuals differed in terms of whether they believed that control over outcomes was internal or external. According to Rotter, internally oriented people believe that outcomes are a function of factors within individuals, such as ability and effort, whereas externally oriented individuals believe that outcomes are determined by luck or powerful others. Thus internally oriented people believe that they control the events in their lives, whereas externally oriented people believe that events are outside of their control. The IE scale consists of a series of items designed to measure these orientations, and thus, individuals can be divided into internals and externals, based upon their IE scale scores. In order to test whether individuals who scored high and low on the IE scale actually showed differences in behavior consistent with these beliefs, Rotter and Mulry (1965) carried out a mixed design study.

Rotter and Mulry hypothesized that internals, believing that they could personally control outcomes, should find a task defined as demanding skill more involving, and a task defined as depending on chance less involving, than externals. Subjects were divided into internals and externals based on their IE scale scores and then randomly assigned to either a skill or chance condition. The task for all subjects was to match an angle with one of four alternative angles turned in various directions. In fact, all angles were equally close so that no correct answer was possible. Subjects in the skill condition were told that although the task was difficult, some individuals were skilled at picking the correct angle. Subjects in the chance condition were told that the task was so difficult, it was totally dependent on luck. Subjects in both conditions were then given a series of eight training trials on which they were told that their responses were correct on six of the eight trials. A series of 50 extinction trials, all of which were incorrect, then followed. The dependent measure was the time taken to respond; that is, pick an alternative on each trial.

Rotter and Mulry hypothesized that if internals do become more involved than externals in skill situations, their response times should be longer in these situations reflecting greater deliberation before choosing. Also, if they become less involved in chance situations than externals, their response times should be shorter under chance. This is indeed what they found. The authors calculated reaction times for both the first eight training trials where subjects received positive feedback on six of the trials and for the 50 extinction trials where subjects received no positive feedback. The results for both measures were parallel. Internals took significantly longer to choose an alternative under skill than under chance instructions. Second, their reaction times under skill instructions were significantly longer than those of the externals under skill instructions. The externals did show slight but not significantly longer reaction times under chance than under skill, which is consistent with the authors' hypotheses. Again, as in the Lenney, Gold, and Browning study on sex differences, the emphasis was upon the nonmanipulated variable. Rotter's interest was in the internal-external variable, and the manipulated variable of skill versus chance was only employed to further illuminate the workings of this personality variable.

Blended designs then can fulfill a number of purposes: *(a)* the reduction of error variance thereby decreasing the probability of a Type II error, *(b)* showing the generality of the finding for an experimental variable, *(c)* showing a differential or limiting effect of an experimental variable, and *(d)* testing hypotheses derived from a theory concerned with the correlational variable.

SAME SUBJECTS—DIFFERENT CONDITIONS: WITHIN-SUBJECTS DESIGNS

In all of the factorial designs discussed so far, each condition or combination of conditions has been represented by different subjects. That is, no subject has served in more than one condition. It is possible though, to have a subject serve in more than one condition, and in fact, designs can be employed in which a subject serves in all possible conditions. In that particular case, all of the results of the study would be within subjects effects in that the relevant comparisons would be between the responses of all of the subjects exposed to one treatment and the responses of those same subjects exposed to another treatment. In contrast, comparisons of conditions containing different subjects are termed between-subjects' effects.

One advantage of a within-subjects design is economy. To the extent that the same subjects can be used in more than one condition of the study, fewer subjects are needed to assign to the conditions. For instance, if a 2 × 3 × 2 between-subjects design was employed and the researcher wanted 10 subjects in each of the 12 conditions, a total of 120 subjects would be needed. On the other hand, this same 2 × 3 × 2 design run as a completely within subjects study would require only 10 subjects since each of the 10 would serve in all 12 of the conditions.

A factorial study then could either be a completely between-subjects design in which each condition contains different subjects, a completely within-subjects design in which every condition contains the same subjects, or a combination of the two. Thus, in a factorial experiment, one of the independent variables might be a between-subjects variable, while a second independent variable would be a within-subjects factor. Let us say that the 2 × 3 × 2 factorial above employed between-subjects factors as the first and second independent variables and a within-subjects factor as the third independent variable. If the researcher again wanted 10 subjects in each condition, a total of 60 subjects would be needed since the first two factors jointly contain six conditions each with different subjects. If only the first factor was a between-subjects variable, then a total of only 20 subjects would be needed, 10 assigned to each of the two conditions of that factor. Thus, the greater number of factors which are within-subjects variables, the fewer the total number of subjects needed for the study.

A second positive aspect of within-subjects designs resides in their ability to account for systematic variance, thereby reducing error variance. Since each subject serves in more than one condition, variance due to within-subject stability over conditions can be accounted for. That is, to the extent that subjects' responses across the repeated conditions are correlated, systematic variance due to subject differences can be calculated. This is very much akin to the effect of matching discussed previously, which was to allow the researcher to reduce error variance. This increased the probability of finding a significant result and consequently reduced the probability of a Type II error. Thus, matching or using repeated measurements allows one to account for subject differences which would ordinarily be unsystematic and relegated to error variance.

Since it can often be difficult to schedule and recruit subjects for an experiment and since it is likely that error variance will be reduced, it would seem to be advantageous to design studies with within-subjects factors. Unfortunately, there is an important drawback to within subjects designs. In some studies it is impossible to expose subjects to more than one condition of an independent variable without rendering the results of that variable useless. For example, in the Bandura study on modeling, it would have been quite difficult to expose the children to the model carrying out aggressive acts against the Bobo doll and then being rewarded, and then show them the same exact aggressive sequence followed by the same model being punished or no consequence occurring for the model. If different models carrying out different acts had been used for the two sequences, then both the consequences (reward, punishment, no consequence) and the sequences themselves would have differed in the two conditions, and a clear judgment about the effects of consequences would have been impossible. A between-subjects design allowed the researcher to produce treatments with differential consequences to the model but identical sequences of aggressive behavior preceding those consequences.

Even if subjects can be meaningfully exposed to more than one treatment, the order in which the treatments are administered may become an important factor. If receiving treatment A affects the subjects' responses to treatment B, then giving A first and then B will produce a different result than giving B first and then A. For the sake of argument, assume that in the Bandura study, subjects could be meaningfully exposed to identical aggressive sequences followed by either reward or punishment. Remember that in the original between subjects design, females exposed to the punished model showed lower levels of imitation than females exposed to both the rewarded model and the model who received no consequences. In the within-subjects design, all of the female subjects would be exposed to the rewarded, punished, and no consequence models.

Now assume that the subjects first see the punished model sequence, and imitative behavior is assessed, and then they see the rewarded or no consequence sequence each followed by assessment of their imitative behavior. Their level of imitative behavior on the first assessment should be similar to that of the subjects in the model-punished condition of the original between subjects study. On the other hand, their imitative behavior following exposure to the rewarded model may be quite different from that of the children in the between-subjects study. Once exposed to a punished model which has the effect of lowering imitative behavior, this effect may carry over into the model-rewarded sequence and continue to lower imitation. If this occurs, then the punishment and reward treatments will show about the same level of imitative behavior, and consequently the conclusion would be that reward and punishment do not act differently. The effect of one treatment would have carried over into a second treatment, which would obscure the differential effects of reward and punishment.

Now assume that the opposite order had been given; i.e., the model rewarded followed by the model punished sequence. Given that reward did not enhance imitative behavior in the original study (remember that reward and no consequences did not differ), it may be that in this order the subjects imitative behavior following the model punished sequence may be lower than that following the model rewarded sequence. Thus, in this within-subjects design, reward and punishment would differ in their effects when the model rewarded sequence occurs first but would not differ when the model rewarded follows the model punished sequence. The conclusions about the effects of reward and punishment would then differ depending upon the order chosen by the researcher.

The way around this dilemma is to employ both orders, randomly assigning subjects to each order. Half of the subjects would see the model rewarded followed by the model punished sequence while the other half would receive the model punished followed by the model rewarded sequence. The design would now consist of an additional between-subjects factor of order (along with subject sex) and the within-subjects factor or reward-punishment. An interaction between the order and reward-punishment factors would then show that the differential effects of reward and punishment occur only in the punishment followed by reward sequence. If the researcher wanted 10 subjects of each sex (20 subjects total) in both the reward and punishment conditions, dividing these into the two orders would leave only 5 subjects of each sex in each combination of order and reward-punishment condition. On the other hand, if the researcher wanted 10 subjects of each sex in each experimental condition, 40 subjects total would be needed for the study: 10 males and 10 females in one order and 10 of each sex in the other order. Thus, the creation of two orders, a between-subjects factor would entail doubling the number of subjects. Unless there was a particular interest in the order effect, this within-subjects design would not be more efficient than the original between subjects design.

In order to simplify the exposition of the discussion of carryover effects in a within-subjects design, the no consequences condition in the original Bandura study has not been discussed. Consider now a within-subjects design employing all three conditions: reward, punishment, and no consequences to the model. Remember, we are assuming here that the subjects could meaningfully be exposed to all three sequences. If order was now included with three conditions, the number of conditions would grow tremendously, since there are the following six possible orders:

reward-punishment-no consequences
reward-no consequences-punishment
punishment-reward-no consequences
punishment-no consequences-reward
no consequences-reward-punishment
no consequences-punishment-reward

If 10 subjects of each sex per experimental group was desired, 120 subjects total would be needed; 60 males and 60 females assigned to the six orders. The within-subjects design with three conditions and order included has become highly inefficient.

There are cases though, where the effects of order can be minimized, keeping the within-subjects approach efficient. These cases consist of situations where subjects can be repeatedly exposed to the various treatments. That is, rather than undergoing only a single exposure of a treatment, subjects can be treated repeatedly with the various treatment conditions. Each instance of a particular treatment is then a replication, and the replications of all of the treatments can be randomly interspersed so as to minimize any order effects.

Consider a classic study by Collins and Quillian (1969) dealing with the way memory is organized. The authors were interested in testing a model which posited that memory is structured as a hierarchy with larger superordinate categories at the top of the hierarchy, smaller classes under these larger categories, and finally, specific examples of the smallest class or category stored at the bottom of the hierarchy. For example, animal might be a large superordinate category, and under animal would be stored smaller classes such as birds and fish; under birds would be stored the specific examples such as canary, robin, crow, etc. One implication of this model is that some concepts are stored closer to each other in memory than they are to other concepts. For instance, canary would be stored closer to bird than to animal since it is stored directly under bird but only indirectly under animal. A second aspect of the model was that properties of objects are stored within the hierarchy in an economical fashion in that they are stored at the highest level of the hierarchy to which they apply. Eating is a characteristic of animals in general, and thus the property of eating would be stored with animal. Flying, on the other hand, does not apply to all animals but does apply to birds and would thus be stored with bird. The color yellow is specific to a canary and not to all birds and thus would be stored with canary. Thus the propery yellow would be stored closer to canary than would the property flying, and flying would be stored closer to canary than eating.

In order to test this structural model, Collins and Quillian ran an experiment in which subjects were given sentences which they had to judge as true or false by pressing an appropriate button. The sentences referred either to the name of an object (''a canary is a bird'') or to a property (''a canary flies''). Within each type of sentence (name or property), three different levels of relationships were presented. Zero-order relationships for names of objects would simply be a repeat of the item, ''a canary is a canary''; first-order relationships would deal with concepts which are one step apart on the hierarchy, ''a canary is a bird''; and finally, second-order relationships would deal with concepts two steps apart, ''a canary is an animal.'' The property statements followed this same logic with zero-order statements dealing with properties stored directly with objects, ''a canary is yellow''; first-order statements dealing with properties one step removed, ''a canary flies''; and second-order statements dealing with properties and objects two steps apart, ''a canary eats.'' Half of the sentences were true ''a canary is yellow,'' and half were false, ''a canary has fins.'' The dependent measure was the reaction time taken to correctly judge each sentence recorded in milliseconds. If the hierarchical model was correct, then lower-order statements should show faster reaction times than higher-order statements. Since "yellow" is stored closer to canary than "flies," judging "a canary is yellow" should be faster than judging "a canary flies." In the same vein, judging that "a canary is a bird" should take less time than judging that "a canary is an animal."

Thus, the study was a three independent variable factorial design consisting of type of statement (property or name), truth of statement (true or false), and level of statement (zero, first, or second order). Many different statements were developed for each combination of the independent variable. For instance, "a salmon is pink" and "a shark is dangerous" both would be examples of true property statements at the zero-order level, along with "a canary is yellow." "A salmon is a fish" would be a true name statement, while "a shark is a bird" would be an example of a false name statement. By having a large number of statements reflecting replications of each combination of the independent variables and by interspersing the statements randomly, subjects could be exposed to all of the combinations of the independent variables. In fact, different subjects could receive different orders of the sentences which would further control for any carryover effects due to the order in which the sentences were presented. Thus, the study was run as a completely within-subjects design, each subject receiving all of the combinations of the independent variables, and since each subject received all combinations, only eight subjects were employed in the experiment.

The results of the study for just the true statements are presented in Table 10–7. An example of each type of statement is given under each reaction time. The data are approximate average reaction times since they have been read from a graphic presentation from the original article and represent results from three studies which differed only slightly. It can be seen that in line with the predictions for both name and property statements, as the level of the statement increases from zero to second order, the reaction time to correctly answer or judge the statement also increases. Thus, employing a within-subjects design results were achieved which

TABLE 10–7
Results of the semantic memory study

		Type of Statement	
		Name	Property
	Second Order	1240 (a canary is an animal)	1475 (a canary has skin)
Level of Statement	First Order	1175 (a canary is a bird)	1385 (a canary can fly)
	Zero Order	1000 (a canary is a canary)	1310 (a canary is yellow)

strongly supported a hierarchical model of memory. The design could be employed because of the ability of the researchers to give subjects a series of exposures to the treatments, thereby controlling for order or carry over effects.

COMBINING BETWEEN- AND WITHIN-SUBJECTS DESIGNS

So far, the discussion of within-subjects designs has centered upon situations where each subject is exposed to all combinations of the independent variable. As it was stated earlier, studies which use both within- and between-subjects variables are possible and employed quite frequently. In fact, the pretest-posttest control group design discussed previouly in relation to internal validity is such a combination of between- and within-subjects design. The between-subjects factor consists of the experimental and control conditions to which subjects are randomly assigned, while the pre- and posttest on which all subjects are measured is the within-subjects factor. Analysis of the data from this design would yield main effects for both the between- and within-subjects factors and an interaction between the two types of factors.

In the situation where the experimental group of subjects receives the treatment, while the control group does not, we would expect to find the interaction of the between- and within-subjects factors significant if the treatment is effective. Since the experimental and control groups should start out fairly close together on the pretest, discrepancy between them should occur on the posttest if the treatment is effective. Thus, the between-subjects factor should behave differently at one level of the within-subjects factor (the pretest) than at the other level (the posttest), and this is the definition of an interaction. Thus, one prominent use of combining within- and between-subjects factors is in studies which employ pre- and posttesting.

Combinations of between- and within-subjects designs also occur in situations other than those which involve pre- and posttesting. Studies which involve a series of measurements after the various treatments have been given to groups of subjects are between- and within-subjects designs. Assume that the subjects in the first Russ, Gold, and Stone study on the effect of confusion on attraction to a similar or dissimilar stranger had answered not only the attraction items, but also an equal number of items dealing with the value of the stranger's viewpoint in understanding the film. Thus, each subject would have had an attraction toward the stranger score and a score indicating how valuable the stranger was as a viewpoint provider. We could now enter those two scores in our analysis as a within-subjects variable.

Thus the design of the study would now be a 2 (similar-dissimilar other) × 2 (confusing film–nonconfusing film) × 2 (attraction-viewpoint) factorial, with the first two factors being between subjects factors and the third being a within-subjects factor. Hypothetical results for this study are

TABLE 10–8

Hypothetical results of combining between-subjects factors (attitude similarity and confusion) and a within-subjects factor (attraction-information)

		Attraction	Information
Confusing Film	Similar	8.41	8.27
	Dissimilar	10.75	10.86
Nonconfusing Film	Similar	10.66	8.66
	Dissimilar	8.08	8.12

presented in Table 10–8. The first column of the table contains the attraction item scores, which have been reproduced from Table 10–2, while the second column contains hypothetical results for the viewpoint items. When the film is confusing, subjects are more attracted to dissimilar than to similar strangers and also feel that the viewpoints of the dissimilar strangers would be of greater value than the viewpoints of similar strangers. These results would, of course, fit quite well with the reasoning behind the study. Subjects are confused by the film, seek to understand it, feel that dissimilar others can provide a new viewpoint, and are thus attracted to them. This also is consistent with the rationale of the study in that subjects exposed to the nonconfusing film and thus not being at all confused would see neither the viewpoint of a similar or a dissimilar stranger as particularly useful. Thus, in this hypothetical case, the inclusion of the attraction and viewpoint scores as a within-subjects factor would shed more light on the issues and processes connected with confusion and attraction.

It should be noted that since all subjects first answered the attraction items and then the viewpoint items, this would not be an experimental variable. In other words, we don't know if subjects exposed to the confusing film actually saw the dissimilar stranger's viewpoint as valuable and then were attracted or if they were attracted and then decided that the viewpoint was valuable. On the other hand, if half of the subjects answered the attraction items followed by the viewpoint items while the other half answered in the reverse order, the within-subjects factor would be an experimental variable. This would mean, of course, that order of responding (attraction-viewpoint, viewpoint-attraction) would be another between-subjects variable and would consequently enlarge the study to a $2 \times 2 \times 2 \times 2$ design. For this reason, many studies forsake order as a variable and employ the within-subjects factor as a nonmanipulated variable.

In order to further examine the nature of between- and within-subjects designs, let us examine an actual study on memory processes and the maintenance of stereotypes by Rothbart, Evans, and Fulero (1979). Stereotypes are categorical judgments about groups of people, the most well known ones applying to racial, national, and religious minorities. The hallmark of stereotypes is the prejudgment or expectancy that all members of the group that is the object of the stereotype, fit the stereotype. It has been noted that once formed, the stereotype seems to endure, resisting evidence which would disconfirm it. For instance, presented with a member or members of a group, individuals holding a stereotype about that group may fail to remember behaviors which do not fit the stereotype and only remember confirming behaviors, thus further solidifying the stereotype. Rothbart, Evans, and Fulero were interested specifically in how such expectancies act to bias the recall of events which confirm or disconfirm the stereotype.

In order to investigate the manner in which evidence is distorted as a function of expectancies, the authors carried out a between- and within-subjects design consisting of two between- and two within-subjects factors. The first between-subjects factor consisted of two different types of expectancies: *(a)* an expectancy that a group of men was friendly and sociable and *(b)* an expectancy that a group of men was intellectual and scholarly. The second between-subjects factor was the time that the above expectancies were given: *(a)* before observing a set of 50 behaviors and *(b)* after observing the 50 behaviors. Subjects then were randomly assigned among the following four conditions produced from the two between subjects factors:

friendly expectancy-before behaviors,

friendly expectancy-after behaviors,

intellectual expectancy-before behaviors,

intellectual expectancy-after behaviors.

The 50 behaviors consisting of 17 confirming and three disconfirming behaviors for each expectancy, and 10 behaviors unrelated to either expectancy were shown to subjects on slides. Subjects were then given the following five category labels: intelligent, friendly, unintelligent, unfriendly, and unrelated; they were then asked to recall the behaviors that they had seen that fit into each of the five categories.

Four of the five categories (intelligent, friendly, unintelligent, unfriendly) actually comprise a 2 × 2 within-subjects factorial design. One factor is the type of behavior recalled (intelligent or friendly), and the second factor is whether the behavior recalled confirms or disconfirms the stereotype.

Thus, the design was a 2 (expectancy: friendly-intelligent) × 2 (time behaviors shown: before-after expectancy) × 2 (types of behavior recalled: friendly-intelligent) × 2 (confirming-disconfirming instance recalled) factorial with the first two factors as between-subjects and the last two factors as within-subjects factors. The mean number of items recalled

TABLE 10–9

Results for the expectancy study combining between-subjects factors (time of expectancy and type of expectancy) and within-subjects factors (confirmation and type of behavior)

Between-Subjects Factors	Within Subjects Factors			
	Confirming Behaviors		Disconfirming Behaviors	
	Intelligent	Friendly	Nonintelligent	Unfriendly
Expectancy before items Intelligent expectancy	4.83	4.05	1.33	1.21
Friendly expectancy	4.02	4.74	1.42	1.19
Expectancy after items Intelligent expectancy	3.18	3.64	.87	.95
Friendly expectancy	3.38	3.49	1.03	1.08

is given in Table 10–9. The within-subjects factors are depicted as the columns, and the between-subjects factors as the rows of the table. If expectancies about groups cause individuals to recall a high number of behavioral instances which confirm that expectancy, then subjects with an intelligence expectancy should recall more behaviors related to intelligence than friendliness, and subjects with a friendly expectancy should recall more friendliness than intelligence-related behaviors. Keep in mind that the subjects were actually shown 17 friendly and 17 intelligence-related behaviors.

The means for the first two rows and the first two columns of the table reflect the two types of confirming behaviors recalled (intelligent and friendly) as a function of the expectancy subjects had been given before seeing the behaviors. It can be seen that subjects given an intelligence expectancy before seeing the behaviors do recall more intelligence than friendliness related behaviors.

Inspection of the last two columns of Table 10–9 shows that the expectancies didn't work quite as neatly for the disconfirming behaviors. Although subjects given a friendly expectancy did recall fewer unfriendly (disconfirming) behaviors than nonintelligent behaviors, the intelligence expectation subjects recalled more rather than fewer nonintelligent opposed to unfriendly behaviors. Thus, the tendency to overinclude instances which confirm a stereotype seems to be stronger than the tendency to exclude instances which challenge the stereotype.

A look at the bottom two rows of Table 10–9 shows that the effect does not occur when the expectancy is given after the behaviors are seen. These results for the expectancy-after condition are as expected in that the stereotype comes first and information is processed on the basis of it. This lack of findings, of course, lends further substantiation to the notion of expectancies or stereotypes acting so as to process information in a biased manner.

By employing both between- and within-factors, the authors were able to simultaneously examine two types of behaviors and two types of instances of those behaviors. Thus, when a researcher hypothesizes that the manipulations will differentially affect different behaviors, a between- and within-design allows for a test of that hypothesis.

Chapter 11

Multivariate
Correlational
Approaches

Events in the world are often complicated and depend on a great many factors. Consider, for example, the landing of the space shuttle. In order to be able to predict and control this event, many variables must be considered. The NASA scientists must understand the effects of variables such as temperature, wind velocity, barometric pressure, and fuel consumption, as well as a host of factors related to human performance. Knowing all of these and many more factors, the landing can be fairly well predicted and controlled. The same is true for behavior. Very seldom are we able to account for much of the variability in behavior through only a single factor. Behavior is complex, and in order to account for that complexity, many factors have to be considered.

Just as the simple experimental design can be expanded into more complex designs involving a number of independent variables, the simple two variable correlational design can be expanded to include the analysis of many variables. In the present chapter, we will discuss a number of the different forms that these multivariate approaches can take. We will begin with the direct expansion of the simple regression and correlation situations into the multiple regression and correlation cases and then proceed through the concepts of partial correlation and factor analysis. Although the actual statistical analyses connected with these techniques are rather involved and sophisticated, the concepts behind the techniques can be understood without resorting to mathematics. We will therefore present the conceptual rather than the mathematical bases of these approaches.

MULTIPLE REGRESSION AND CORRELATION

It will be remembered from Chapter 4 that regression is a technique for predicting one variable (the criterion) from another variable (the predictor) through an equation for a straight line. The reader will also recall that, employing linear regression, we are able to determine the amount of variance in the criterion variable which can be accounted for by the predictor variable. The basic logic behind the determination of variance was to calculate the variance of the errors of prediction (the differences between the actual criterion scores and the scores predicted from the best fitting straight line), and subtract this error variance from the total variance in the criterion variable. This leaves the variance in the criterion variable which can be accounted for by the predictor variable; that is, the systematic variance. It was also shown that the ratio of the systematic variance to the unsystematic variance produced a statistic called F, which tested the significance of the relationship between the predictor and the criterion variables. Finally, it was pointed out that the ratio of the systematic to the total variance in the criterion reflected the proportion of the variance of the criterion variable which could be accounted for by the predictor variable and which was also the square of the correlation coefficient.

This same logic extends directly to the case of multiple regression, except that rather than predicting a criterion variable from a single predictor variable, the criterion variable is predicted from a number of predictor variables. Most behavior is complex, which means that a single predictor variable generally will account for only a part of the variance in a criterion variable, just as a single independent variable in an experiment will determine only part of the variance in a dependent variable. The factorial design is an experimental approach for dealing with behavioral complexity and multiple regression is an approach to this same complexity problem which can be used in nonexperimental situations.[1] The logic is that since a single predictor variable can usually only account for part of the variance in a criterion variable, other predictor variables may account for or predict some of the variance in the criterion variable not accounted for by the first predictor. In other words, other predictor variables may account for some of the unsystematic or error variance which remains; that is, they may account for variance which is not accounted for by the first predictor.

In the case of multiple regression, rather than a predicted score being generated from a single predictor, a predicted score is generated from a weighted linear combination of a number of predictors. A linear combination is simply a sum of the scores on a number of variables. A weighted linear combination then is a sum produced by weighting or multiplying each score by some value before adding up the scores.[2] The reader will recall that in the single predictor situation, the values of the slope of the line and the intercept are chosen so as to produce a best fitting straight line, where *best fitting* is defined as that line which produces the smallest errors of prediction. In the multiple regression case, the weights that multiply each of the predictor scores are chosen on this same basis. That is, they are chosen to produce from the linear combination predicted scores which will be as close to the actual scores as possible. In other words, they are chosen so as to produce the smallest possible errors of prediction.

One way to depict multiple regression and multiple correlation graphically is through the use of Venn diagrams, which are curved figures (circles, ellipses, etc.) that can be shown to overlap to various degrees. Each figure represents the variance of a variable, and the overlap of any two figures represents the amount of variance shared by the two variables. Figure 11–1 depicts the relationship between a criterion variable (Y) and a single predictor variable (X). The figure with the broader border repre-

---

[1] Actually, multiple regression is a statistical procedure which can be used to analyze data in both experimental and nonexperimental situations. The emphasis in this chapter is on the conceptual basis of multiple regression as it applies to nonexperimental situations.

[2] If the criterion variable is qualitative in nature, a variant of multiple regression, called discriminant function analysis, is employed. In this case, rather than predicting a score on the criterion variable, a number of predictors are employed to predict the probability of membership in one of the categories of the criterion variable. For example, a series of predictor variables might be used to predict membership in categories of pathology such as schizophrenic, depressive, phobic, etc.

FIGURE 11-1
Venn diagram depicting a single predictor situation

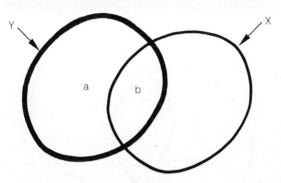

sents the criterion (Y) and the finer bordered figure represents the predictor (X). The distinct areas within the criterion figure are represented by lower case letters. First of all, one can see that the predictor and criterion overlap, indicating that they are related. The shared or predicted variance is represented by area *b* within the criterion figure, while the variance in the criterion not accounted for by the predictor is represented by area *a*. Thus, area *a* is the variance of the errors of prediction, and area *b* is the systematic variance in the criterion.

Since the square of the correlation coefficient is the proportion of variance in the criterion variable accounted for by the predictor variable, in this diagram r^2 would be equal to the ratio of area *b* to areas *a* plus *b*. In other words, $r_{yx}^2 = b/a + b$. Also, since the significance of the relationship between the predictor and criterion variables is evaluated through the ratio of systematic to error variance, the ratio of area *b* to area *a* would test whether the *X* variable accounts for a significant amount of the variance in the *Y* variable.[3]

Now examine Figure 11-2. This diagram represents the situation where three predictor variables (X_1, X_2, and X_3) are used to predict the variance in the criterion variable (Y). As in Figure 11-1, the various areas within the criterion variable are represented by lower case letters. The numbers in parentheses reflect the size of each lettered area. We can see that each of the predictor variables is related to the criterion to some extent, since each overlaps the criterion variable. Thus, X_1 accounts for area *b*, X_2 for area *c*,

---

[3] Since it is the concept of regression and not the actual calculations involved in the technique that is important for our purposes, the author has taken certain liberties in expressing the above relationships. These liberties are in the use of the term *variance*. In the case of the testing of significance of the relationships between two variables, the two variances involved in the ratio are called *mean squares*. They are estimates of variance as opposed to the descriptive measures of variance, which are calculated by finding the average of the squared deviations around the mean. A thorough discussion of how these measures are calculated is beyond the scope of this text and is not necessary for an understanding of the concepts involved.

FIGURE 11-2
Venn diagram depicting three unrelated predictors

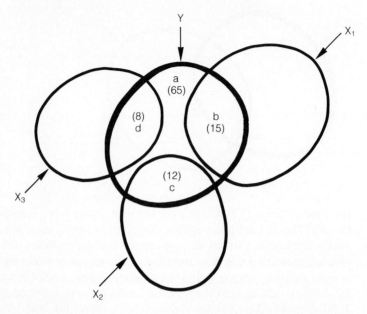

and X_3 for area d within the criterion variable. It is also true that since none of the predictor variables overlap each other, none of them are interrelated; that is, they are all independent of each other.

We can see that the total area of the criterion which is systematic variance would be area b plus area c plus area d, leaving area a as the unsystematic or error variance. If we divide the sum of areas b, c, and d by the total area of Y, we would have the proportion of the criterion variable which can be accounted for by the three predictor variables. Keeping in mind that the square of the correlation coefficient is the proportion of variance in the criterion variable accounted for by the predictor or predictors, then the ratio of the sum of areas b, c, and d to the total area of Y would be a squared correlation coefficient. A correlation coefficient which involves more than one predictor is called a multiple correlation, and is symbolized as R. Thus, $R^2yx_1x_2x_3 = b + c + d/a + b + c + d = (15 + 12 + 8)/(15 + 12 + 8 + 65) = .35$. The squared correlations between each of the predictor variables and the criterion variable can also be represented by dividing the area in the criterion variable accounted for by each predictor by the total area in the criterion variable. Thus, $r^2yx_1 = b/a + b + c + d = .15$, $r^2yx_2 = c/a + b + c + d = .12$, and $r^2yx_3 = d/a + b + c + d = .08$. If we sum these three square correlation coefficients, we get the multiple correlation coefficient: $b/a + b + c + d \,(.15) + c/a + b + c + d \,(.12) + d/a + b + c + d \,(.08) = b + c + d/a + b + c + d \,(.35) = R^2yx_1x_2x_3$. Thus, in the case depicted in Figure 11–2, the squared multiple correlation is equal to the sum of the three squared single variable correlation coefficients. We will see that this is only true for cases such as that depicted in Figure 11–2 where the predictor variables are not interrelated.

Another multiple predictor situation is depicted in Figure 11–3. Again, the numbers in parentheses indicate the size of the lettered areas. This case is somewhat more complicated than the one depicted in Figure 11–2 due to the overlap of X_1 and X_2. In other words, in Figure 11–3 not only are each of the three predictor variables correlated with the criterion variable, but in addition two of the predictors are correlated with each other. If we consider the total area in Y that is accounted for by the three predictor variables, we have area b plus area c plus area d plus area e, leaving area a as error variance. Again following the rule that the squared correlation is the proportion of variance accounted for, we have $R^2yx_1x_2x_3 = b + c + d + e/a + b + c + d + e$. In other words, $R^2yx_1x_2x_3 = (15 + 5 + 30 + 10)/(15 + 5 + 30 + 10 + 4) = .60$. The single variable squared correlations are: $r^2yx_1 = b + c/a + b + c + d + e$ (.20), $r^2yx_2 = c + d/a + b + c + d + e$ (.35) and $r^2yx_3 = e/a + b + c + d + e$ (.10). If we sum these as we did for Figure 11–2, we have $b + 2c + d + e/a + b + c + d + e$ (.65) which is not equal to $b + c + d + e$ (.60), the squared multiple correlation, $R^2yx_1x_2x_3$. In summing the three squared single variable correlations, we have accounted for area c twice; that is, through X_1 and again through X_2. When the predictor variables are intercorrelated, we cannot obtain the squared multiple correlation through a simple addition of the individual squared single variable correlations.

FIGURE 11–3
Venn diagram depicting a situation with two related and one unrelated predictors

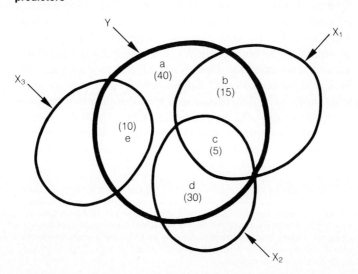

How then is the multiple correlation obtained when the predictor variables are intercorrelated? In order to answer this question, let us examine more closely the variance in the criterion variable accounted for by X_1 and X_2. We see that the variance accounted for by X_1 consists of two parts, b and c, and that the variance accounted for by X_2 consists of two parts, c and d. Area b accounted for by X_1 and area d accounted for by X_2 are the unique contributions those variables make in predicting Y. Area c which both variables account for is the nonunique contribution of each variable, in that this variance would have been accounted for by the other variable. If area c was divided between X_1 and X_2, then all of the variance in Y could be accounted for without accounting for area c twice. In fact, that is what is done. The weights given to the variables in the linear combination take into account the overlap among the predictors in such a way that all of the systematic variance in the criterion variable is accounted for, but not redundantly.[4]

Unique Contributions

In choosing predictor variables, it is important to be able to see what each variables adds or brings uniquely to the prediction process. In order to understand how we evaluate the contribution of each predictor variable, consider the situation depicted in Figure 11–4, which is more complex than that depicted in Figure 11–3. In this case, all three of the predictor variables are intercorrelated and each is correlated with the criterion variable. Again, let us begin with the total amount of the Y variance that is accounted for, which is $b + c + d + e + f + g$, and that which is not amounted for, which is a. If we now wanted to see how much each predictor variable adds to the prediction scheme, we could calculate the unique contributions of each of the predictor variables. On the diagram, we are able to directly identify these areas. Beginning with X_1, we see that although it accounts for areas $b + c + d$, only area b is accounted for uniquely. That is, area c is also accounted for by X_2 and area d is accounted for by both X_2 and X_3. Looking at X_2, we see that only area e is accounted for uniquely since areas c, d, and f are also accounted for either by X_1, X_3 or both X_1 and X_3. Finally, X_3 accounts for area g uniquely, while areas d and f are accounted for by the other two predictors. Thus, X_1 contributes area b, X_2 area e, and X_3 area g uniquely. These areas are the respective losses that would occur if the variables were eliminated from the regression equation. On this basis, it would seem clear that not much

---

[4] The weights are called regression coefficients and are analogous to the slope of the line in the simple regression situation. The slope of the line represents the predicted change in the criterion variable (y) from a unit change in the predictor variable (x). In the multiple regression situation, each regression coefficient represents the predicted change in the criterion variable from a unit change in a given predictor variable, holding all of the other predictor variables constant. This idea of holding variables constant will be explained in more detail in sections of this chapter dealing with partial correlation.

FIGURE 11–4
Venn diagram depicting a situation with three related predictors

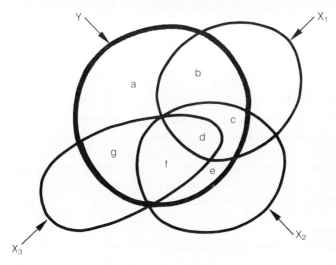

would be lost with the elimination of X_2, since area e is such a small amount of the criterion variable.

One way of choosing predictors for a regression equation is to calculate the unique contribution of each predictor and then either retain or eliminate each predictor on the basis of the size of its unique contribution. One criterion for judging the size of the unique contribution is statistical significance. If the variance of the unique contribution is divided by the error variance, we have a test of the significance of that contribution. In choosing predictors, those variables which make significant unique contributions to the prediction of the criterion would be retained.

Although the Venn diagrams are useful tools for understanding the concepts of multiple regression, it is the mathematical and statistical calculations employed which actually provide the information about unique contributions, multiple correlations, and error variance. These calculations are quite complex and involved, especially as the number of variables increases. The tool that has opened multiple regression and the other correlational techniques to wide use is the high-speed computer. The complex and tedious calculations involved can be carried out in short order through computer programs. A researcher now is able to employ many predictors in a prediction scheme, testing each for its contribution to the prediction of the criterion variable.

This availability of data processing for large amounts of data collected from many subjects on many variables has brought on problems related to decisions about the contributions of predictor variables. For example, if 10 predictor variables were entered into a regression equation to predict a criterion variable, the overlap or relationships among various combinations of the predictors might be so great that no single predictor may account for much unique variance in the criterion variable. Therefore, methods have been produced which, rather than entering all of the predictors into the equation simultaneously, enter the predictors one at a time. These methods are called *stepwise procedures,* since the variables are entered one step at a time.

Stepwise Procedure

In order to see how a stepwise procedure works, let us examine Figure 11–5. There are five predictor variables in this diagram and a single criterion variable. Each of the predictor variables is related to the criterion variable, and there are also relationships among the five predictor variables. A nonstepwise procedure would first calculate the total variance accounted for by the five predictors $(b + c + d + e + f + g + h + i +$

FIGURE 11–5
Venn diagram depicting a four-predictor situation

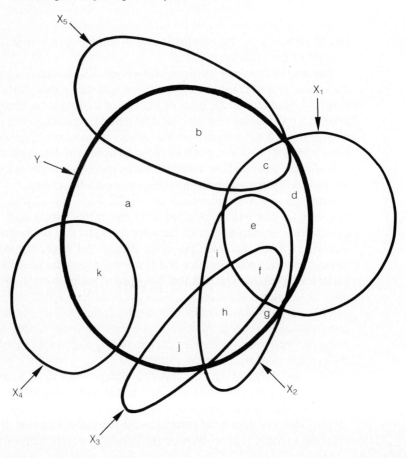

$j + k)$ and then calculate the unique contribution of each predictor to this total systematic variance. Thus, X_1 would contribute uniquely area d, X_2 areas g and i, X_3 area j, X_4 area k, and X_5 area b. The stepwise procedure on the other hand, would enter the predictor variables one step at a time. The bases for whether one predictor enters before another are given below.

Step 1: All of the predictors are compared as to their total contributions to the criterion.

$$X_1 = c + d + e + f$$
$$X_2 = e + f + g + h + i$$
$$X_3 = f + h + j$$
$$X_4 = k$$
$$X_5 = b + c$$

That variable with the largest area is chosen, which is X_5.

Step 2: All of the predictors except the one chosen on the first step are compared as to their contributions to the criterion which do not overlap with X_5.

$$X_1 = d + e + f$$
$$X_2 = e + f + g + h + i$$
$$X_3 = f + h + j$$
$$X_4 = k$$

That variable with the largest area is chosen, which is X_2.

Step 3: All of the predictors except those chosen on the first two steps (X_5 and X_2) are compared as to their contributions to the criterion which do not overlap with X_5 or X_2.

$$X_1 = d$$
$$X_3 = j$$
$$X_4 = k$$

That variable with the largest area is chosen, which is X_4.

Step 4: The two predictors not chosen on the first three steps (X_1 and X_3) are compared as to their contributions to the criterion which do not overlap with X_5, X_2, or X_4.

$$X_1 = d$$
$$X_3 = j$$

Since both of these areas are quite small, neither may be statistically significant, and therefore both variables may be excluded from the equation (not entered).

This solution has provided a different picture than the one obtained when all of the predictors were entered simultaneously and each tested for its unique contribution. In relationship to all of the other predictors, X_2

had only a small unique contribution, area $i + g$, and thus may have been eliminated. On the other hand, its unique contribution only in relationship to X_5 in the stepwise procedure, was area $e + f + g + h + i$, a healthy contribution. In fact, in a nonstepwise solution, the testing of the unique contributions may have eliminated X_1, X_2, and X_3 since their unique contributions were only area d, areas g and i, and area j, respectively. If this had occurred and only X_5 and X_4 had been retained, these two predictors together would only account for area $b + c + k$. On the other hand, using the stepwise procedure, X_5, X_2, and X_4 would be retained accounting together for area $b + c + e + f + g + h + i + k$, a substantial gain. In practice, both types of procedures could be applied and compared in order to accurately interpret the interrelationships among the predictors and their contributions to the criterion variable. When predictors overlap, the judgment of which predictors to include in an equation is not clear-cut and obvious. Whether or not a predictor is useful depends not only on its relationship to the criterion, but also on its relationship to the other predictors. Therefore, examining the contributions of predictors in a number of ways is often essential.

Choosing Predictors

As it was stated previously, one criterion for judging whether or not to retain a predictor is statistical significance. The criterion of statistical significance can be used in either the stepwise or nonstepwise procedure, and it certainly is a useful way of making decisions. It is not the only basis on which judgments about predictors can be made. In fact, there are situations in which predictors that make significant unique contributions will still be eliminated. For example, with very large size samples, even small amounts of unique variance accounted for will be statistically significant. In these cases, the judgment of whether or not to retain a predictor variable is made not on the basis of whether the unique contribution of the predictor variable is significant, but rather on the basis of whether the actual size of the contribution is large enough to warrant including the predictor. For example, a predictor variable which only uniquely accounts for 2 percent of the criterion variance may not be retained as a predictor due to considerations such as the cost of using the predictor or the time taken to gather the data on the predictor.

These cost and time considerations generally arise in applied situations where actual decisions about individuals will be made on the basis of predicted scores on the criterion variable. In basic research situations, questions of cost and time are not as important since the purpose of multiple regression in basic research is to discover relationships between a criterion variable and a set of predictors, and not to actually employ multiple regression as a predictive procedure. In order to more fully understand this difference between applied and basic research uses of multiple regression, let us consider an example of each, beginning with an applied situation.

Assume that a large company needs to hire a great many managerial level employees. The policy has been to consider all of the applicants for these managerial positions. The company subjects each potential manager to an intensive three-month training program which ends with an evaluation of the candidate. In the past, many of these candidates have received low evaluations and consequently were not hired for the positions. This, of course, means that a great deal of time (the three months) and expense (the cost of the training program which includes housing, meals, and expenses, as well as the actual training cost) has been wasted on the washed-out candidates. In order to improve their efficiency, the company has decided to try to predict which candidates will be successful and to then select candidates in the future.

Researchers for the company choose the following four predictors variables: *(a)* intelligence, as measured by an individually administered two-hour test, *(b)* leadership potential, as measured by a short (15-minute) questionnaire, *(c)* problem-solving ability, as measured by a three-problem, 30-minute test, and *(d)* college grade point average. For two years, all applicants who apply are given the three tests, and their college transcripts are collected. In other words, just as in the past, the company admits all of the applicants to the training program, except that the predictor variable information is now collected at the beginning of the program. Three hundred people are trained during the two-year period.

At the end of this two-year period, the company has 300 evaluations (the criterion variable) and 300 each of the intelligence, leadership, and problem solving test scores, plus 300 college grade point averages. A multiple regression is then computed between the criterion scores and the predictor scores. The hypothetical results are shown in Figure 11–6. First of all, the total amount variance in the evaluations that can be predicted by the combination of the four predictor variables is significant. The squared multiple correlation is $R^2yx_1x_2x_3x_4 = (b + c + d + e + f + g + h + i + j)/(a + b + c + d + e + f + g + h + i + j)$ which represents about 50 percent of the variance in the evaluations. Each of the unique contributions of the variables *(b, d, f,* and *j)* is also significant.

Even though each of the predictor variables contributes to the equation, should the company use all of them to predict evaluations? After intensive consideration of the results, the decision is made to retain college grade point average, problem solving, and leadership, and to eliminate intelligence from the prediction equation. The basis of this decision is that intelligence testing, although significantly improving the prediction of evaluations, is costly. A two-hour test given by a trained examiner is just too expensive in terms of time and money for the amount of unique variance that is accounted for by that variable to be worthwhile. Thus, the decision is a practical one based on the cost effectiveness of including

FIGURE 11-6
Venn diagram depicting the prediction of training program evaluations from four
predictors (leadership, college GPA, intelligence, and problem solving)

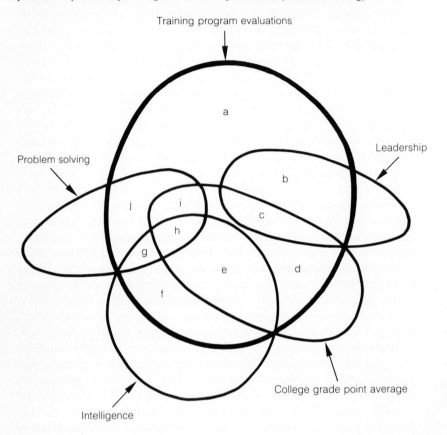

intelligence in the prediction scheme and not on the statistical significance
of its contribution. The next step is to employ the information gathered on
these 300 candidates to predict the evaluations of future applicants to the
training program. Thus, the company will find the weights to be given to
these three retained predictor variables (grade point average, problem
solving, and leadership) that produce the smallest errors of prediction.
These weights will then be applied to each new applicant's scores on the
problem solving and leadership tests and to their grade point averages, and
a predicted evaluation score will be generated for each applicant. If the
predicted evaluation score is one indicating success, the applicant will be
accepted to the program, and if the predicted score indicates failure, the
applicant will be turned away. Therefore, only applicants with a high
probability of success will be taken, and consequently very few failures
should occur, saving the company a great deal of time and money in
training costs.

The second use of multiple regression is in basic research situations. Here the aim is not to actually generate predicted scores and select individuals, but rather to discover the relationships between a criterion variable and a set of predictor variables. In order to demonstrate this process, consider a study by Ryckman, Robbins, Thornton, and Cantrell (1982) dealing with physical self-efficacy. The authors were interested in the ways in which individuals perceive their own physical states in terms of their physical abilities and their physical presentations. They developed a measure assessing perceived physical self-efficacy which they called the Physical Self-Evaluation Scale. The authors reasoned that if this scale was tapping aspects of physical self-efficacy, it should be related to actual behaviors such as sports involvement and physical powers. They also reasoned that if their measure assessed a unique construct, it should account for more of the variance in physical behavior than previously developed measures.

In order to test these ideas, subjects were given the physical self-efficacy measures, the Tennessee Physical Self-Concept Scale, which was a previously developed measure of physical self-concept, the Health Locus-of-Control Scale, which was a measure tapping perceived control over health-related matters, a questionnaire tapping information about sports involvement, and a dart-throwing task. First, using the sports involvement measure as the criterion variable, the Tennessee Physical Self-Concept Scale was entered as the first predictor variable, followed by the other two scales. This process of predetermining the order of entry of predictor variables is called hierarchical regression analysis. In this study, the rationale for entering the Tennessee Physical Self-Concept Scale on step 1 was to determine the amount of variance which could be predicted by the Physical Self-Evaluation Scale beyond that accounted for by the previously developed measure. On step 1, the Tennessee Physical Self-Concept Scale was significantly correlated with the sports involvement measure. On step 2, the Physical Self Evaluation Scale was entered, and it showed a significant, unique contribution. This means that it accounted for a significant amount of variance beyond that already accounted for by the Tennessee Physical Self-Concept Scale. Finally, the Health Locus-of-Control Scale was entered on step 3, and it did not show a significant unique contribution. In fact, when all three variables were included in the regression equation, only the Physical Self-Evaluation Scale showed a significant unique contribution. In other words, the significant amount of variance the Tennessee Physical Self-Concept Scale accounted for in the criterion on step 1 was not unique; that is, it also could be accounted for by the Physical Self-Evaluation Scale.

When dart-throwing performance was used as the criterion, the results paralleled those found for sports involvement in that the Physical Self-Evaluation Scale showed the highest unique contribution. Thus, not only was the Physical Self-Evaluation Scale able to predict actual sports involvement and dart performance, but it also was able to account for more of the variance in these variables than a previously established measure, the Tennessee Physical Self-Concept Scale. Multiple regression was not employed here in order to actually predict scores, but rather to test hypotheses about the scale the authors had developed. This use of multiple regression relates to construct validity, the topic dealt with in Chapter 12.

PARTIAL CORRELATION

In experimental situations, control is achieved through use of random assignment. In other words, random assignment assures that on average any differences between group means on the dependent variable must have been caused by the differences in the levels of the independent variable since the groups are equated on all other variables before the manipulation occurs. Since random assignment does not occur in correlational research, the relationship between two variables may be influenced by one or more other variables. In other words, a variable other than the two variables being correlated might be affecting or confounding the relationship. In order to take a simple example, assume that there is a strong positive relationship between the number of down-filled jackets sold and the amount of heating oil used each January for the last 30 years in Bangor, Maine. This is a case where another variable is probably producing this relationship in that both variables are directly related to temperature and only indirectly related to each other.

If the effect of temperature on each of the variables could be controlled, we could see the influence of temperature on the relationship between the variables. Controlling temperature would mean holding it constant over the 30-year period, which is obviously physically impossible to do. An alternative would be to select those years where the average January temperature was the same or at least nearly the same, and then correlate the number of down jackets sold and the amount of heating oil used for only those years. If the correlation remained high, then temperature could not be the variable responsible, since it would be constant, that is, it would not vary, for these selected years. On the other hand, if the correlation dropped or disappeared, then it might be that temperature was the confounding variable.

Although the logic of this approach of selecting the years having similar average temperatures is quite appropriate, this method of gaining control has serious practical limitations. First of all, the average temperatures may vary a great deal, and thus the years selected as being similar in temperature may in fact not be all that similar. This, of course, means that temperature would be less variable than if no selection occurred, but it certainly would not be constant. Second, selection of very similar years in terms of average temperature may mean ending up with a sample based on only a small number of cases. This, of course, means a less reliable sample. Thus, the method of control through selection of cases which are similar on a possible confounding variable is not a useful one.

On the other hand, if it could be achieved without selecting cases, the logic of equating subjects or cases on a possible confounding variable and then examining the correlation between the original variables does have merit. Rather than selecting only those cases which are similar on a possible confounding variable, all cases can be made to be identical on a confounding variable through statistical procedures. It will be recalled from the discussion of regression that a predicted score can be generated for each subject or case through the regression equation. The difference between this predicted score and the actual score represents the part of the actual score that is not related to the predictor variable; that is, it is a residual or error component. The logic of partial correlation is to correlate the residual scores of the two variables of interest. In other words, each of the variables is predicted from the confounding variable, the predicted scores are subtracted from the actual scores, and these residuals are then correlated. Thus, the correlation that is calculated is between two variables, each of which is free from or equated on the confounding variable.

Let us return to our example of jackets, oil, and temperature in order to more correctly demonstrate the procedure. Keep in mind that we want to examine the correlation between the number of down-filled jackets sold and the amount of heating oil used with the effects of temperature held constant. We would first predict the number of down jackets sold from the average temperature. Thus, for each of the 30 years in our sample, we would have both the actual number of down jackets sold and the number of down jackets sold which we predicted from the temperature in that year. If, for each of the 30 years, we took the difference between these two figures, we would have 30 scores each of which represents the number of down jackets sold in a given year which is not related to the temperature of that year. This same process would then be carried out predicting the amount of oil used in each year from the average temperature in that year, and subtracting the predicted from the actual scores. If we then correlate these two sets of difference scores (actual number of down jackets minus predicted number of down jackets and actual oil used minus predicted oil used) we would have the relationships between the number of down jackets sold and amount of oil used with the effects of temperature removed or held constant. This correlation would be the partial correlation between these two variables.

In order to more fully illuminate the use of partial correlation in relation to a psychological research example, let me present an actual example of a research problem. Data have been collected on children who have been treated for psychological problems at a psychiatric nursery school. These data include measures of the level of pathology of both the children and their parents and whether or not the parents have had counseling. A fairly high positive correlation is computed between the measure of the level of pathology of the children and whether or not their parents have had counseling, indicating that the more pathological the child, the more likely their parents are to have had counseling. Since this is not an experimental study, no cause-effect relationship can be drawn between the two variables. In fact, there are a number of possible explanations for the relationship. One possible explanation is that parental counseling leads directly to the child's emotional problems. In other words, something inherent in the counseling itself produces behavior in the parents which is detrimental to the child. A second possibility is that more pathological children are hard to deal with and thus produce emotional problems in their parents, resulting in the parents seeking psychological help. A third possibility is that parents who themselves have problems and are thus more likely to receive counseling also have poorer relationships with their children, producing a higher rate of pathology in those children. In the latter case, it is not the counseling which produces the childs pathology, but rather the level of the parents' emotional problems.

In order to determine the degree to which the relationship between the child's level of pathology and whether the parents have had counseling is due to the confounding variable of the level of the parents emotional problems, a partial correlation would be computed between the variable of the child's level of pathology and the variable of whether the parents had counseling with the variable of the parents' level of emotional problems or pathology held constant. Specifically, the child's level of pathology score would be predicted from the parents' level of pathology score and this predicted score subtracted from the actual score. Then parent counseling would be predicted from the parents' level of pathology score, and this predicted score would be subtracted from the actual score. Each difference score (child's level of pathology and parent counseling) would then be unrelated to the parents' level of pathology, and these two scores would then be correlated producing a partial correlation. If the partial correlation did not drop substantially from the original correlation, the parents' level of pathology would not be a reasonable explanation for the original correlation. On the other hand, if the original correlation decreased or vanished, then it is quite possible that the parents level of pathology was the variable producing the original correlation.

The reader will note that I used the phrase *quite possible* rather than unequivocally stating that the original relationship is due to the parents' level of pathology. This is correlational research, and as such, definitive causal statements are not possible. As I stated, if the original correlation did not decrease substantially when the parents' level of pathology was held constant, then it can definitely be stated that this correlation was not due to the parents' level of pathology. In other words, in this case, the parents' level of pathology can be ruled out as the variable responsible for the relationship. A drop in the original correlation is only suggestive of the fact that the parents' level of pathology is moderating the relationships between the variables of the child's level of pathology and whether or not the parents had received counseling. It is also possible that all three variables are related to a fourth variable, such as socioeconomic level, which might be the determiner of the relationship among all three of the variables.

Table 11–1 depicts a number of possible interconnections among the variables where arrows reflect direct causal relationships. In *A*, the two original variables are shown to be directly causally related. The child's pathology causes the parents to seek counseling. In *B* the parents' level of pathology causes both the child's level of pathology and their seeking psychological help. Here the child's level of pathology and the parents' seeking of counseling are not related directly, but only through their common link to the parents' level of pathology. In *C*, the child's level of pathology produces the parents' level of pathology, which in turn causes the parents to enter counseling. In *D*, the socioeconomic level of the family produces pathology in both the parents and the child, and the resultant parental pathology causes the parents to enter counseling.

TABLE 11–1
Possible causal paths for the child pathology study

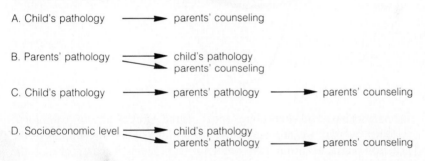

Each of these diagrams in Table 11–1 represents an hypothesis about the relationships among the variables. The partial correlation, if it was substantially lower than the original correlation, would only tell us that the parents' level of pathology was in some way involved. It would not tell us which of the hypotheses in Table 11–1 is more plausible. There are methods which are beyond the scope of this text for testing the plausibility of these alternative hypotheses. For our purposes, it is important to note that relationships between variables can be quite complex in that two variables may be directly causally related or related only indirectly through complicated causal networks with other variables.

Partial Correlation and Regression

Partial correlation can be examined through regression analysis and depicted through Venn diagrams. Figure 11–7 shows a situation in which two predictor variables (X_1 and X_2) are predicting a criterion variable (Y). Assume here that Y is the child's level of pathology, X_1 is whether or not

FIGURE 11–7
Venn diagram depicting the relationships among three variables: parent counseling, parent pathology, and child pathology

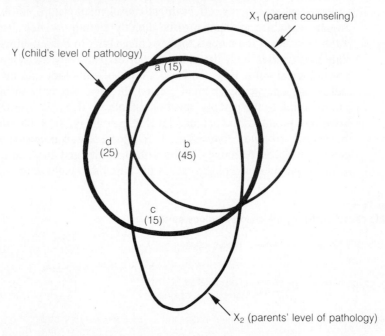

X_1 (parent counseling)

Y (child's level of pathology)

a (15)

d
(25)

b
(45)

c
(15)

X_2 (parents' level of pathology)

the parents have had counseling, and X_2 is the parents' level of pathology. In other words, we are predicting the child's level of pathology, the criterion variable, from two predictor variables—whether or not the parents have had counseling and the parents' level of pathology. The variance accounted for in the criterion variable by X_1 would be areas a and b. The proportion of variance in the criterion accounted for by X_1, would then be $(a + b)/(a + b + c + d)$. Since the square of the correlation coefficient indicates the proportion of variance in one variable accounted for by a second variable, the square root of the above ratio would be the correlation between the child's level of pathology and whether or not the parents had counseling.

A partial correlation is the correlation between two variables with a third variable removed or held constant. Thus, if we remove X_2 from both Y and X_1 and then correlate X_1 and Y, we would have the partial correlation between Y and X_1. Removing X_2 takes out area b from X_1 and areas b and c from Y. This leaves only area a in X_1 overlapping Y, and only areas a and d in Y itself. The proportion of variance in Y accounted for by X_1 when X_2 is removed from both Y and X_1 would be $(a)/(a + d)$. Area a is X_1's unique contribution to Y, and area $(a + d)$ is the total variance left in Y after X_2 is removed. Again, since the square of the correlation coefficient is the proportion of variance in one variable accounted for by a second variable, the square root of $(a)/(a + d)$ would be the correlation between X_1 and Y with X_2 removed from both—the partial correlation between X_1 and Y.

In this particular case, we see that much of the area of overlap of X_1 and Y is also overlapped by X_2, leaving X_1's unique contribution, area a, quite small. Thus the systematic variance in Y accounted for by X_1 when X_2 is held constant or removed is small compared to the total amount of systematic variance in Y accounted for by X_1. In this case, the partial correlation between X_1 and Y will be smaller than the original correlation.

On the other hand, since X_2 is removed from Y as well as from X_1, the ratio of the unique contribution of X_1 (area a) to the variance remaining in Y after X_2 is removed from Y, (area a + area d) may still be quite substantial. Assume that the numbers in parentheses represent the size of each of the areas. The original correlation between X_1 and Y would be the square root of $(15 + 45)/(15 + 45 + 15 + 25)$ or .77, the square root of $(a + b)/(a + b + c + d)$. The partial correlation would be the square root of $15/(15 + 25)$ or .61, the square root of $a/(a + d)$. The partial correlation is lower but not a great deal lower than the original correlation. Thus, the size of a partial correlation sometimes can be misleading.

In regression analysis where we are predicting a criterion variable rather than simply examining the relationship between two variables, the aim is usually to see the degree to which the variance accounted for in the criterion variable that is accounted for by a given predictor variable overlaps with another predictor variable. Thus, the interest is in comparing the original proportion of variance accounted for by a particular predictor variable to the proportion of unique variance accounted for by that predictor. In the case of Figure 11–7, we would compare the original correlation which is the square root of $(a + b)/(a + b + c + d)$ to the square root of $a/(a + b + c + d)$. This last value is called a part or semipartial correlation since the effects of X_2 are removed only from X_1 but not from Y. The original correlation between X_1 and Y in Figure 11–7 was .77. The semipartial correlation would be the square root of $15/(15 + 45 + 15 + 25)$ or .38. Since the original correlation and the partial correlation are based upon the same denominator, the total variance in Y, they are readily compared.

In the case where there is a criterion variable to be predicted, the semipartial correlation between the criterion variable and a predictor with another variable held constant is the appropriate measure to use. When there is not a clear criterion variable but rather simply two variables which are related to each other, the appropriate method is to remove the effects of a confounding variable from both of the original variables; that is, to calculate the partial correlation.

FACTOR ANALYSIS

In many research situations, rather than the interest being in predicting a specific criterion variable from a set of predictor variables or seeing the relationship between two variables when a third confounding variable is held constant, the aim is to examine the interrelationships among a set of variables. Factor analysis is a technique for achieving this aim.

To the extent that any two variables are correlated, they share common variance; that is, they have something in common or are alike in some way. In fact, in a sense, we could say that a perfect correlation between two variables means that they are the same thing. Let us return to our earlier example of the relationship between the number of down jackets sold and the amount of heating oil used, assuming this time that the relationship is perfect, that is, the correlation is 1.00. According to my philosophy, down jackets sold and heating oil used are the same things. Obviously they do not look alike, feel the same, or smell the same, and thus the senses certainly wouldn't perceive them as being the same thing. On the other hand, since they are perfectly related, they apparently act the same way; that is, as one increases, so does the other. As we stated previously, they are both probably related directly to temperature and as such are different looking but identical manifestations or reflections of the same underlying variable. In a sense, we would be measuring temperature through two different indicators.

Just as a perfect correlation indicates that two variables are the same thing, a correlation that is less than perfect indicates that although two variables have something in common, in the sense that part of each of the variables manifests the same underlying process, each variable also has something not shared with the other. If we considered the interrelationships of three variables (V_1, V_2, V_3) we would see that there are three possible correlations: V_1 with V_2, V_1 with V_3, and V_2 with V_3. Figure 11–8 depicts such a three-variable situation. Areas a, c, and g represent the parts or variance of each of the variables that has nothing in common with the other variables. Some of this unique variance is due to measurement error, i.e., unreliability, and as such cannot relate to any other variable, while other parts of this unique variance are reliable but specific to that variable alone. The remaining areas, b, d, e, and f represent common variance; that is, variance shared by two or by all three of the variables.

If we examine this common variance, we see that area e represents common variance shared by all three variables. Area b is the common variance of V_1 and V_2, area f is the common variance of V_1 and V_3, and area d is the shared or common variance of V_2 and V_3. With only two variables, there is only one common variance easily identified by the correlation between the variables, but with more than two variables, there are usually different common variances, and the identification of these becomes more complex. The point is that any variable contains variance which is unique, unrelated to the other variables, and variance held in common with the other variables. This common variance is divided into that shared by all of the other variables and that shared by only some of

FIGURE 11–8
Venn diagram depicting common and specific variance among three variables

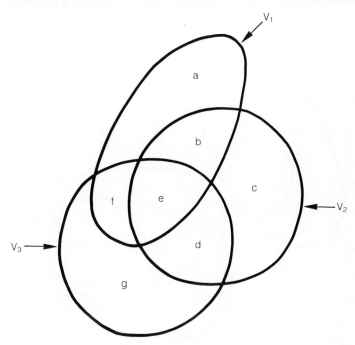

the other variables. The question is how do we identify these different common components.

Let us take the case depicted in Figure 11–9. There are four variables, X_1 through X_4, which have been intercorrelated. This situation, which is rather straightforward, could be easily interpreted in terms of common or shared variance. There are two definite clusters of variables, X_1 and X_2 on the one hand and X_3 and X_4 on the other. Area a, a relatively large overlap, is shared by X_1 and X_2, and area c, again a large overlap, is shared by X_3 and X_4. Thus, X_1 and X_2 are measuring something in common as are X_3 and X_4, and the two clusters are unrelated to each other. Only the small area b would be shared between the two clusters and this only between X_1 and X_4. Thus, we would identify two clusters or common factors in this figure by simply examining the clear overlap of X_1 and X_2 and X_3 and X_4 and the lack of overlap between these two sets of variables. The reader will see that if we increased the number of variables to six or more, the diagrams would become rather messy, and therefore Venn diagrams will not be useful from this point on.

We can convey the ideas here by examining the hypothetical correlation matrix in Table 11–2. This table contains all of the intercorrelations

FIGURE 11–9
Venn diagram depicting two clusters of variables

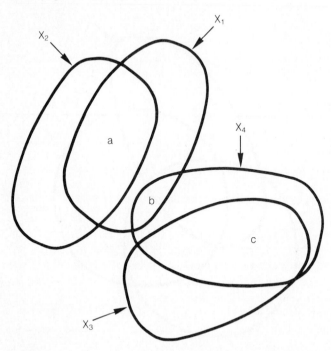

among the variables. The 1.00s in the diagonal represent the correlations
of each of the variables with themselves, and the values which are not on
the diagonal represent the correlations between pairs of variables. The
elements below the diagonal have been omitted since they are identical to
those above the diagonal; that is, the correlation between X_1 and X_2 is the
same as that between X_2 and X_1. Inspection of Table 11–2 reveals two
district clusters made up of X_1, X_2, X_3 on the one hand and X_3, X_4, X_5 on
the other. The first three variables are highly related to each other but have
little in common with the last three. The last three variables are also highly
interrelated but show little relationship to the first three which are highly

TABLE 11–2
Hypothetical correlation matrix for six variables

	X_1	X_2	X_3	X_4	X_5	X_6
Vocabulary X_1	1.00	.75	.82	.10	.13	.20
Reading comprehension X_2		1.00	.68	.05	.11	.18
Information X_3			1.00	.15	.08	.09
Speed X_4				1.00	.59	.84
Strength X_5					1.00	.70
Skill X_6						1.00

interrelated. Let us say that X_1, X_2, and X_3 are measures of vocabulary, reading comprehension, and information, respectively, and that X_4, X_5, and X_6 are measures of speed, strength, and physical skill, respectively. You now would not only see that there are two distinct clusters but that they can be conceptually identified as verbal intelligence and physical prowess. In other words, you would group highly correlated variables together as reflecting a common property and then, through knowledge of those variables, interpret the meaning of the common property.

In a sense, you would have carried out a nonmathematical factor analysis, searching for clusters of variables and interpreting their common properties. In fact, if every correlation matrix was as clear as that depicted in Table 11-2, there would be no need for a formal factor analysis. Unfortunately, most correlation matrices are complex, consisting of high, moderate, and low correlations among the variables. Also, correlation matrices can be quite sizeable since researchers often examine the relationships among a large number of variables. Even in the relatively small matrix in Table 11-2, there are 15 correlation coefficients to examine. A 10-variable matrix would entail the examination of 45 correlations, and a 20-variable matrix would produce 190 correlations to examine. Thus, it is easy to see that the eyeball method becomes unwieldly and that a tool is needed to identify common clusters of variables.

Factor analysis is the formal mathematical tool which is employed to group and identify common clusters of variables. While the specific calculations are complex and involved, the logic behind the technique is relatively straightforward. First of all, assume that large numbers of individuals have been measured on the six variables discussed in relation to Table 11-2: vocabulary, reading comprehension, information, speed, strength, and physical skill. Each person has a score on each of the six variables. The scores on one of the variables do not look like the scores on any of the other variables since each variable is measured in different units. Therefore, in order to make the scores comparable, they are converted to standard scores. It will be recalled that standard scores vary between approximately positive and negative three. We now have a situation where each of a large number of individuals has six scores all in the same units. Some of the scores will be positive and some negative and might look like those depicted in Table 11-3.

If we added the six scores for each individual, we would produce a new seventh score which would be the sum of the six. This is, of course, very much akin to the procedure employed with tests; the items on a test are summed producing a total score. Thus, each individual now has the six original scores plus a seventh score which is a composite of the first six. This new composite or sum score is the score for an individual on the first factor. Therefore, the first factor simply consists of the sum of the original variables. If we now correlate each of the original six variables with the new seventh variable, we will determine how strongly each of the original variables relates to the first factor. These correlations between the vari-

TABLE 11–3
Hypothetical matrix of standard scores for N subjects for six variables

Individual	Z_1	Z_2	Z_3	Z_4	Z_5	Z_6
			Standard Scores			
1	− 1.25	− 1.41	− 1.26	.02	.09	.33
2	.37	.09	.55	− .19	− .06	.10
3	2.17	1.99	1.46	− 1.20	− 1.55	− 2.10
4	.06	− .01	.17	1.73	1.06	1.56
5	.19	.23	− .15	− 2.31	− 1.58	− 1.47
6	1.65	1.73	1.91	− .09	.10	.55
7	− 2.22	− 2.12	− 1.58	− .15	− .02	− .46
8	− 1.54	− 1.01	− 1.46	− 1.20	− .87	− 1.12
9	− .38	.21	.30	− 1.60	− 1.53	− 1.87
10	.82	.48	.61	1.47	1.31	.99
N	− .46	− .33	.06	2.41	2.12	1.96

ables and the factor are called factor loadings and indicate the degree to which each of the variables contributes to the factor. The first factor will explain some of the relationships or common variance among the variables. The higher the correlations among all of the variables, the more of the common variance that will be explained. At this point, unless all of the variables are very highly intercorrelated, we will want to find a second factor in order to explain more of the common variance among the variables. Therefore, the process must begin again by adding up the six scores for each individual. Obviously, if we again add the original scores, we will simply duplicate the first effort. Therefore, the scores must be changed before adding them.

Keep in mind that we want to find a second factor which will explain the relationships or common variance among the variables which the first factor has not already explained. Thus, we must remove the effects of the first factor from each of the six variables. In order to do this, employing regression, we simply calculate a predicted score for each individual on each variable using the score on the first factor as the predictor variable. The difference between the individual's original score and the score predicted from the first factor would be the score on that variable with the first factor removed. This sounds quite similar to the procedures discussed in the partial correlation section, and it is. We now have six scores for each subject which are unrelated to the first factor. A summation of these scores will produce a seventh score, which will be the second factor, and the correlations of this second group of scores with the score on the second factor will be the loadings of the variables on the second factor.

This process is repeated; that is, each factor is removed from the scores, a new factor is calculated by summing, and the factor loadings are then obtained. Each successive factor will contain lower factor loadings, meaning that less and less of the common variance is explained by each. The optimum situation is to explain as much of the variance as possible with as few factors as possible. Thus, if 10 variables are factor-analyzed and most of the variance is accounted for by the first two factors, most of the relationships among the 10 variables can be explained through these two factors. It is certainly more parsimonious to deal with two things than with 10 things, and since one criterion of the goodness of scientific ideas is parsimony, this criterion would be met.

It should be noted that there are a number of different methods of factor analysis most of which are variations of the above procedure. They differ in terms of the sophistication of the mathematical techniques used. For example, in one widely used factor analytic technique, the scores are weighted before being added up to produce a factor. The weights are chosen so as to maximize the common variance accounted for by the factor. Nevertheless, the basic procedure is the same: the scores are summed to produce a new variable; the correlations between each of the original variables and the new variable, the factor loadings, are determined; the effects of the first factor are removed from each score; and the process repeats itself to find the next factor. In actuality, rather than operating on the scores themselves, the process is carried out by working with the correlations between the variables. This is mathematically simpler and yields identical results.

The aim of factor analysis is to cluster variables together into factors. The purpose is to reduce the number of variables, and in fact, the techniques described above are called methods of condensation. They are the first stage of a factor analysis. Once the factors have been computed, a second stage, called *rotation*, occurs. Again, if a researcher finds that the first two factors in a 10-variable factor analysis account for most of the variance and subsequent factors account for only small amounts of variance, only the first two factors will be used. These first two factors will then be subjected to rotation.

Rotation of Factors

What is rotation and why is it necessary? Rotation is a technique for producing a higher degree of clarity in the results of the first stage of a factor analysis. Due to the mathematics involved in the condensation stage, the reduction of the variables by extracting as much common variance as possible, the factors achieved are not usually clear; that is, they are not easily interpreted. Many of the variables will substantially load on or correlate with all of the factors extracted. This means that the interpretation of the meaning of the factors becomes difficult. In order to clarify the interpretation of the factors, rotation is carried out. Rotation is a way of putting a different perspective on the results without changing the basic nature of those results.

Consider a situation where you are standing on a corner and observe an accident where a truck hits a car totally demolishing it. Let us say that you had been standing on a balcony above the street corner and had observed the same accident. Given that you described the accident under each condition, standing on the ground and up on the balcony, your descriptions would probably differ at least to some degree based upon your differing perspectives. The facts would be exactly the same under both circumstances, but your description of those facts would change depending upon your viewing position. Comparison of the factors and their loadings before and after rotation is akin to comparing your report of the accident from the street-level and balcony-level perspectives.

Just as changing positions for viewing the accident does not change the objective happening of the accident, rotating the factors does not change the amount of variance extracted by the factors; that is, the rotated and unrotated factors explain the same amount of the relationships or common variance among the variables. They do explain it differently. Keep in mind that the purpose of a factor analysis is to reduce the number of variables to a few factors which can be interpreted as to their psychological meaning. The interpretation would be simplified if each variable only loaded on one of the factors. For instance, if a factor analysis of 10 variables resulted in two factors, a clear interpretation would occur if five of the variables loaded highly on the first factor and five on the second factor. We would then know that the first factor clearly represented whatever those first five variables had in common, while the second factor represented the common variance of the remaining five variables. This would be a simple situation in that interpretation of the factors would be quite clear. This clarity is exactly the criterion of rotation. It is termed simple structure. The aim of rotation is to produce a pattern of loadings such that variables that load highly on one factor will have low loadings on remaining factors. Thus, each factor will consist of both high and low loadings.

In order to see the results of the two stages of a factor analysis, the unrotated and rotated loadings for a factor analysis of the six variables shown in Table 11–2 are presented in Table 11–4. The reader will recall that a simple inspection of the correlations in Table 11–2 showed variables 1 through 3 to be highly intercorrelated and variables 4 through 6 to

TABLE 11–4
Factor loading of six variables on two rotated (a) and rotated (b) factors.

Variable	Unrotated Factors (a)		Rotated Factors (b)	
	Factor I	Factor II	Factor I	Factor II
Variable vocabulary	.73	.59	.92	.10
Reading comprehension	.67	.60	.89	.00
Information	.69	.60	.90	.05
Speed	.66	−.63	−.10	−.90
Strength	.63	−.56	.00	−.85
Skill	.73	−.59	.05	−.94

be highly intercorrelated. The left hand side of Table 11–4 shows the unrotated factors which result from the actual factor analysis of these variables. The picture is unclear since all six variables have substantial loadings on both Factor I and on Factor II, although variables 4 through 6 do load negatively on Factor II. Still, all in all, this is not the clear picture one would expect from the original correlations among the variables. Figure 11–10 is a graphic representation of the loadings of the six variables on the two factors. The solid lines represent the two factors, the numbers in parentheses represent the variables, and the tips of the short arrows are the loadings of the variables on the two factors. Each variable is plotted with respect to both of the factors. For instance, variable 1 loads .73 on Factor I, and a line perpendicular to the Factor I axis from the point for variable 1 would intersect that axis at .73. A line from this same point perpendicular to Factor II would intersect Factor II at .59, which is the loading of variable one on the second factor.

The broken lines represent the axes for the rotated factors, which are labeled as Factor I and Factor II. The longer arrows indicate the direction of rotation, and the reader can see that the original axes have been rotated approximately 45 degrees to their new positions. The rotated axes have

FIGURE 11–10
Graphic representation of two unrotated and rotated factors

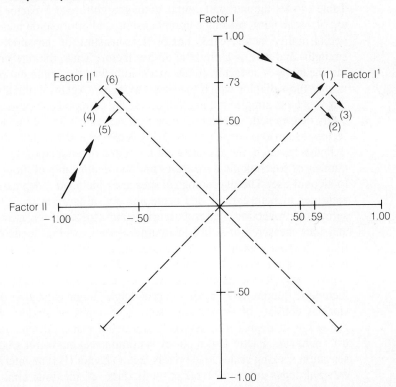

quite a different relationship to the points than the original axes. Factor I cuts through the center of the cluster of points representing variables 1 through 3, and Factor II cuts through the cluster of points representing variables 4 through 6. In other words, variables 1 through 3 lie directly on or very close to Factor I, and variables 4 through 6 lie on or close to Factor II. This state of affairs produces a much clearer picture than that produced by the unrotated factors since any point which lies on or close to an axis will have a substantial value (loading) on that axis but will have a value (loading) of zero or near zero on the other axis. Thus, variables 1 through 3 load substantially on Factor I but close to zero on Factor II, while variables 4 through 6 load highly on Factor II but almost zero on Factor I.

The rotated loadings are shown in Table 11–4b and present a clear picture of the relationships among the six variables. Keep in mind that in the present case of only six variables that show the clear patterns of correlations depicted in Table 11–2, a formal factor analysis would not have been needed. On the other hand, with a large number of variables and high, moderate, and low correlations, a simple examination of the correlation matrix would not be sufficient. In this case, a factor analysis would provide a picture of the clusterings of variables that would be difficult to achieve through an examination of the correlation matrix.

Once the rotated factors have been calculated, a third step takes place which involves the interpretation of the meaning of the factors. In terms of Table 11–4b, the interpretation is quite straightforward. Factor I, consisting of vocabulary, reading comprehension, and information measures, is a verbal ability factor, while Factor II, consisting of measures of speed, strength, and skill is a physical ability factor. Thus, the interpretation of the meaning of a factor comes from inferring the common component among the variables which load on that factor. Again, in the above case, this was quite simple, but in other cases, the common component is not so easily determined. In order to show how interpretations of the meaning of factors are made, consider a study by Kulberg and Cantrell (1980).

In this research, the authors were interested in the relationships among a number of psychological measures and the relationship of these measures to alcohol use. The psychological measures included a depression scale, measures of both chronic and acute anxiety, a neurosis scale, two measures of extroversion, scales measuring four aspects of sensation seeking, and four measures of belief in internal versus external locus of control (IE). The four rotated factors are presented in Table 11–5, and the first two factors are presented graphically in Figure 11–11. For purposes of clarity, only factor loadings above .40 are presented. How can these factors be interpreted? Factor I is probably a factor indicating depression since it consists of depression itself, both types of anxiety which are symptoms of depression, neurosis, and belief that a difficult world controls behavior. Factor II is a purely sensation-seeking factor since all four sensation-seeking scales load on this factor. Factor III is an internal versus external locus of control factor with three of the four control scales

TABLE 11-5
Factor loading for 16 variables on four rotated factors in the alcoholism study

Variable	Factor I	Factor II	Factor III	Factor IV
Alcohol use	.50	.45		
Depression	.86			
Chronic anxiety	.81			
Acute anxiety	.69			
Lie				
Neurosis	.78			
Extroversion 1				.64
Extroversion 2				.51
Sensation seeking 1		.67		
Sensation seeking 2		.63		
Sensation seeking 3		.55		
Sensation seeking 4		.44		
IE 1	.41		.61	
IE 2				
IE 3			.79	
IE 4			.47	

FIGURE 11-11
Graphic representation of two rotated factors in the alcoholism study

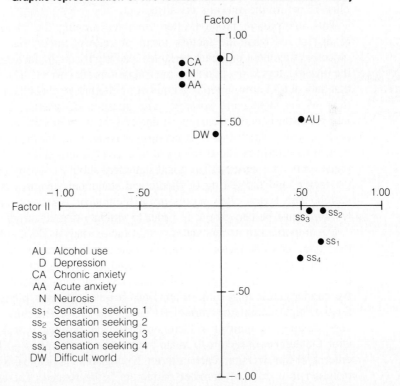

AU	Alcohol use
D	Depression
CA	Chronic anxiety
AA	Acute anxiety
N	Neurosis
ss_1	Sensation seeking 1
ss_2	Sensation seeking 2
ss_3	Sensation seeking 3
ss_4	Sensation seeking 4
DW	Difficult world

loading on this factor. Factor IV contains only the two extroversion scales and thus seems to be an extroversion factor.

Alcohol use loads on both Factor I and Factor II. Thus, the use of alcohol seems to be related to two quite different clusters of variables. On the one hand, it seems to be connected with depressive orientations, and on the other hand, it is also connected with stimulation-increasing tendencies (sensation seeking). This makes sense intuitively since the use of alcohol can be connected with either drowning one's sorrows and reduction of emotional pain or decreasing inhibitions and allowing oneself to engage in sensual activities.

Factor analysis is a powerful tool which allows researchers to analyze complex relationships among many variables. It can be employed as a discovery or exploratory technique whereby an investigator searches for meaningful clusters of variables, or it can be used as a method of confirming hypotheses about the interrelationships of variables. As a method of exploration, it enables large groups of variables to be condensed into more parsimonious clusters. These clusters of common variance can then be logically interpreted as to their meaning; that is, what is common among the variables which load together on a factor can be figured out. This interpretation in the case of exploratory factor analysis is done after the fact. In other words, investigators put their interpretations on the factors after they see the evidence, rather than predicting the clusters before the analysis is carried out.

This interpretive process often involves naming the factors and a discussion of what the factors mean or reflect, rather than a simple objective statement of which variables load highly on the factors. How do the investigators know that their interpretations are correct? The answer is that they don't know. Usually a number of alternative plausible interpretations of the factors are possible. The question of whether a particular interpretation is correct cannot be decided from the results of the factor analysis from which the interpretation was derived. Further studies are needed to determine the correctness of a given interpretation. Any interpretation is, in a sense, a theoretical statement about a concept reflected in the factor, and the testing of theoretical statements requires further research. The factor often represents a theoretical construct, and future research must be carried out in order to validate that construct.

It is important to understand also that factor analysis does not produce the "one" possible factor structure. In other words, there are a number of possible factor structures in most sets of data. If, for example, one decides to rotate the first three factors rather than the first five factors produced in the condensation stage, one often finds a quite different picture of the relationships among the variables. Thus, the factor structure achieved depends upon the number of factors rotated. The problem is that deciding upon the number of factors to rotate is a rather arbitrary process. There are criteria for this decision, each criterion having some logical basis and each resulting in a different number of factors being rotated. Therefore, the

factor structure achieved and consequently the interpretation of that structure is complicated and variable; that is, it is not a fixed process.

On the other hand, rather than employing factor analysis as an exploratory tool, it can be used to gain confirmation for theoretical perspectives.
If, for example, Kulberg and Cantrell has posited that there are two
independent sets of conditions associated with alcohol use—one reflecting sensual behaviors and the other neurotic behaviors—and then factor
analyzed both sensation-seeking and neuroticism-related variables and
found the factor pattern confirming these predictions, this would have
been an example of a nonexploratory factor analysis. Confirming a given
prediction is always more powerful or persuasive than interpreting after
the fact.[5]

---

[5] It should be noted that there is a procedure called *confirmatory factor analysis* which is
employed for testing hypotheses about factor structure.

UNDERSTANDING
PSYCHOLOGICAL
CONSTRUCTS

Chapter 12

Construct
Validity

In the preceding chapters, we have discussed both simple and complex correlational and experimental methods of psychological research. At this point, we will try to show how these methods can be employed to gather evidence for testing theoretical ideas. The testing of theory is a central aspect of construct validity and is carried out using both the experimental and the correlation method. The term *construct validity* has been used to refer to theory testing through both experimental and correlational approaches (Cook & Campbell, 1979) but also has been used in a more restricted sense to refer to the testing of theory related to individual difference constructs (traits, abilities, etc.). I have decided to term all types of theory testing research as construct validation.

The reader will recall from the discussion in the first chapter that theory serves an important function in psychological research. First of all, it organizes discrete facts, and second of all, it provides an interpretation of those facts. Since theory states the connections between the events which occur in the world, providing an explanation for the way in which the events are related, it is the interpretation aspect of science. Most scientific differences of opinion are not over what events occur, but rather the controversies concern the meaning of those events. A psychological theory is a particular interpretation by an individual of a series of events. The term *particular* here implies that this is only one of a number of possible plausible interpretations of the events. Each of these interpretations serves as a rival explanation to the other interpretations for the events. The testing of these rival interpretations is what construct validation is all about.

Since theories are never true or false only more or less probable, construct validation is not an all-or-none process. Rather, it is usually a gradual process where each consecutive piece of evidence which is consistent with the theory and inconsistent with a rival theory enhances the plausibility of the theory as a reasonable interpretation of reality. In other words, theories become more or less probable with each bit of evidence collected.

In previous chapters, we have already discussed validity which is empirical rather than theoretical in nature. Calculating the predictive efficiency of a measure, that is, the amount of variance the measure accounts for in a criterion variable, is often a test of the predictive validity of the measure. The question here is frequently a practical or applied one of whether or not the measure works as a predictor; it does not involve its deeper theoretical meaning. For example, if we wanted to predict college grades and we found that the physical attractiveness of students predicted 75 percent of the variance in college grades, then we would have a predictively valid measure of the criterion variable, college grades. The important aspect would be to find a predictor variable which worked rather than to test a theoretical construct. The rational for how or why the measure worked would be much less important than simply finding that it did work. In the case of college grades and physical attractiveness, the high relationship between the two variables might cause us to question the use of grades as a valid measure of college achievement. But if grades were taken as a valid indicator of college achievement, then physical attractiveness would be a predictively valid measure of grades.

The point is that if the question being addressed deals only with establishing an empirical relationship between variables and does not concern the theoretical basis of the relationship, then the question of construct validity is not at issue. This distinction applies not only to correlational situations, such as the predictive validity case described above, but also to experimental investigations as well. For instance, consider the situation where a company wants to choose between two training procedures for new employees. In order to find out which procedure is most effective, they carry out a simple experiment in which new employees are randomly assigned to one of the two procedures, trained, and then evaluated on their on-the-job performance. It is found that the two treatments differ significantly from each other. The company can now choose and implement the more effective of the two. Since these were the two training procedures they were choosing between and since the purpose of the research was only to find the more effective of the two, theoretical questions were not involved, and thus construct validity was not at issue here. Thus, there are research questions which are purely empirical in nature, and in these cases, questions of a theoretical nature may not arise.

Most research situations are not purely empirical in nature. Rather they involve variables which represent theoretical notions. These studies involve theory testing, which means that they involve construct validation. In order to understand the nature of construct validation, let us turn first to the construct validity of experiments.

In Chapter 8, we discussed the internal validity of experiments. The questions raised in regard to internal validity were technical as opposed to theoretical in nature. Specifically, it was stated that an experiment was internally valid if it could be concluded unambiguously that the independent variable produced the differences in the dependent variable. To the extent that there were other plausible rival causes for the effects, such as history, maturation, regression, etc., the experiment was not internally valid. Controlling for these rival causes and thus producing an internally valid experiment is largely a function of the manner in which subjects are assigned to conditions and the use of adequate control groups. In other words, if *(a)* subjects are randomly assigned to the conditions, *(b)* either a pretest-posttest control group or a posttest-only control group design is employed, and *(c)* differential attrition of subjects does not occur, the study will be internally valid.

If the study is internally valid, then a clear conclusion can be drawn that the differences between the groups on the dependent variable are produced by the independent variable. Actually, the conclusion is that the operations used to represent the independent variable produced the effect. If we are only interested in the specific operations employed in the study, then the experiment is valid, since internal validity would be the only type of validity at issue. On the other hand, if the operations represent a theoretical variable, then the issue arises as to the construct validity of the experiment. Most research is not concerned with the specific operations employed in an experiment. Rather, the interest is in a broader theoretical variable. The operations are chosen by the investigator either on an intuitive basis or on the basis of past research on the topic to represent the theoretical variable. Internal validity is only a question of whether the specific operations employed in an experiment produced the observed effects. In a study involving theoretical issues, a further question arises as to whether the effects produced by the manipulation were produced for the reasons stated in the theory. Obviously, if an experiment is not internally valid, we can not determine whether it has construct validity. In other words, if regression, history, maturation, etc. are plausible causes for the outcome, then we can't be sure that the manipulation produced the outcome, and consequently, we can't determine if it was produced for the reasons stated by the investigator. The bottom line of all of this is that there must be internal validity before there can be construct validity. On the other hand, internal validity alone does not guarantee construct validity. Internal validity then is a necessary but not a sufficient condition for construct validity in experiments.

CONCEPTUAL VALIDITY IN EXPERIMENTS

The central issue of construct validity as it pertains to experiments is whether the independent variable produced the results for the theoretical reasons posited by the researcher. The alternative to this question is whether the results were produced by a plausible reason other than that posited by the experimenter. Again, it is not a question of whether the operational independent variable produced the effects, but rather by what mechanism the effects were produced.

As an example, consider the famous study on the effects of fluoride on tooth decay. The design was to randomly assign subjects to either the fluoride toothpaste group or to a group that used the same toothpaste sans fluoride. Both groups brushed three times per day for the same length of time and avoided between meal treats. At the end of the test period, both groups were checked for tooth decay, and it was found that the fluoride group had significantly fewer cavities. Since random assignment to the two conditions was employed and given that differential attrition had not occurred, the experiment was internally valid.

Assuming that the element fluoride was not chosen from the periodic table of elements on a whim, it would be logical to posit that there were compelling reasons for the choice of fluoride as a decay-fighting agent. In other words, there were theoretical notions of how fluoride would act so as to reduce the occurrence of cavities. Let us say that the investigator believed that the fluoride was absorbed into the enamel of the teeth making the teeth impervious to decay. The finding of significantly fewer cavities in the group that used fluoride would only show that fluoride reduced cavities but not that it worked by hardening the tooth enamel. If fluoride had not hardened the enamel, but rather had neutralized the decaying effects of food, the same results, in terms of fewer cavities, would have occurred. Thus, the experiment would lack construct validity. If the investigator had taken steps to design the study so as to discriminate between the two different explanations, the alternative explanation could have been eliminated as a rival. For example, if not only the number of cavities but also measures of enamel hardness had been collected, a judgment could have been made about the plausibility of the two explanations.

An experiment provides construct validity to the extent that the results *(a)* support the predictions of the theory under investigation and *(b)* discriminate between the explanations of the theory under investigation and other plausible rival explanations. In order to more fully comprehend the nature of construct validation as it applies to experiments, let us consider studies in four different areas of psychology: *(a)* work on the theory of learned helplessness, *(b)* research on cognitive dissonance theory, *(c)* studies on children's memory, and finally *(d)* the research by Russ et al., discussed previously, on attraction to a dissimilar other.

Learned Helplessness

Let us begin with the initial work on the theory of learned helplessness (Seligman, 1975). The basis of the theory is that experience with uncontrollable aversive events leads to a perception of uncontrollability which results in learned helplessness, a state characterized by lowered response initiation. Specifically, Seligman found that dogs that had been exposed to uncontrollable shock failed to learn to escape shock in a subsequent task by jumping a hurdle. In order to test whether it was the experience with uncontrollability or merely the exposure to the shock which produced the subsequent performance decrements, a simple but elegant experiment was carried out employing yoked controls.

In this design, one group of dogs received shock but could control that shock by learning a specific response (pressing a panel with the nose). Thus, for this group, the cessation of shock was contingent upon the correct response of the dog. A second group of dogs was exposed to the same shock as the first group but could not control the shock. For this group, the cessation of shock was not contingent upon a particular response of the dog. In order to ensure that the dogs from both groups were exposed to the identical shock durations, the dogs were run as yoked pairs. What this means is that the cessation of shock for the dog in the second group would occur when the dog in the first group pressed the panel. Thus, shock began simultaneously for both animals and ceased at the identical time for both animals. The only difference being that cessation of shock was systematically connected to a given response for group 1 (panel pressing), but was connected to no specific response for group 2. A third group received no experience with shock. Of course, the dogs were randomly assigned to the three groups.

All of the dogs were then placed in a new situation called a shuttlebox. A shuttlebox is a walled pen with two compartments separated by a hurdle. Both compartments have metal floors which can be electrified by the experimenter. The task for the animal is to escape from the shock in the compartment in which it has been placed by jumping the hurdle into the nonelectrified compartment. Dogs that were either given no exposure to shock or were exposed to controllable shock learned to jump the hurdle and escape from shock in the shuttlebox. Dogs in group 2, those that were exposed to uncontrollable shock, failed to learn the escape response. Since the dogs in groups 1 and 2 were treated identically in terms of receiving the same amounts of shock, the difference between them must have been due to the fact that the dogs in group 1 were treated with contingent shock in the previous task, while those in group 2 were treated with noncontingent shock. While this certainly seems to be support for the notion of control as the critical factor, alternative explanations existed which called into doubt the construct validity of the experiment.

The strongest alternative explanations were based upon the idea that the dogs treated noncontingently learned a response which competed with hurdle jumping in the shuttlebox. In other words, it was not that these dogs, exposed to noncontingency, learned that they had no control. Rather, they learned some response such as freezing which, although useful in the noncontingent situation, competed with the appropriate response of hurdle jumping in the subsequent test situation. In order to eliminate this plausible rival hypothesis of a competing response, Maier (1970) carried out a passive escape experiment. Whereas the usual escape situation entails an active response on the part of the organism (bar pressing, hurdle jumping, etc.) which terminates the aversive stimulation, the passive escape situation entails having the organism remain immobile in order to terminate the aversion. Employing the triadic design, one group of dogs was trained to escape shock by remaining passive. A second group was yoked to the first and received shock noncontingently. The third group was untreated. All groups were subsequently run in the shuttlebox. Maier reasoned that if response competition was a viable alternative hypothesis, the group trained to escape by remaining passive should show response deficits in the shuttlebox as compared to the nontreated group. On the other hand, if control was the central issue, only the noncontingently treated group should show deficits. In fact, this latter result was the case. The group trained to escape by being passive escaped in the shuttlebox by jumping the hurdle; the noncontingent shock group did not. Thus control and not response competition received further support in this experiment.

Each of the above two experiments increased the construct validity of the theory of learned helplessness. In other words, each added credence to Seligman's theoretical position that experience with noncontingency or noncontrol leads to a perception of noncontrol and consequently to help-lessness as evidenced by response deficits. Neither study definitively proves that the theory is correct, but each eliminates plausible rival explanations and thus increases the construct validity of the theory. Thus, construct validation is an ongoing process in that, as each study gathers more evidence consistent with the theory and eliminates plausible rival hypotheses, the theory gains in credibility; that is, it becomes more probable as an explanatory mechanism.

Cognitive Dissonance

A series of studies by Zanna and Cooper (1976) dealing with cognitive dissonance are a second example of experiments designed to establish construct validity. The reader will recall that cognitive dissonance is hypothesized to be a state of aversive or noxious arousal which arises as a result of inconsistency between behavior and attitudes. This aversive arousal then produces a change in attitude in order to bring about con-sistency with the behavior and thereby reduce the arousal. Research has generally supported the notion that behavior which is discrepant with an individual's attitudes and which occurs under relatively low pressure (high choice) results in a change in attitude toward consistency with the behavior.

Although these studies produced results consistent with the predictions of the theory of cognitive dissonance, they did not provide evidence showing that aversive arousal following behavior which was inconsistent with attitudes produced the attitude change which occurred in these studies. In fact, others (Bem, for example) argued that subjects in these studies merely observed their own behaviors and from these behaviors inferred their attitudes. This position predicted the same outcomes as those predicted by cognitive dissonance theory but for different reasons. This plausible rival to cognitive dissonance theory stated that arousal played no part in the attitude change process. In order to demonstrate whether or not arousal was a necessary component of the attitude change which occurs in the typical cognitive dissonance study, Zanna and Cooper carried out a series of clever experiments designed to provide validity for the theory of cognitive dissonance.

They first borrowed a technique called misattribution of arousal which had been successfully employed in other research contexts. The basic notion of misattribution is that a particular emotion is a function of autonomic arousal and a label given to that arousal. If the label changes, the emotion experienced also changes. Thus, if the arousal experienced by an individual is attributed to some external source rather than to something within the individual, the emotion experienced by the individual is changed. Zanna and Cooper reasoned that if the arousal associated with cognitive dissonance could be misattributed to some other source, the resulting change in emotion should greatly modify the usual attitude change associated with cognitive dissonance. If, on the other hand, the critics of cognitive dissonance theory were correct and arousal was not involved in the attitude change found in the typical cognitive dissonance study, misattribution should have no effect upon attitude change. In other words, if arousal is not there in the first place, it cannot be misattributed.

In one experiment, after taking a drug which was alleged to have an effect on memory but in actuality was a placebo, subjects were told that the drug had side effects which produced a reaction of tenseness, a reaction of relaxation, or that the drug had no side effect. While the subjects waited for the drug to take effect, a period of 30 minutes according to the experimenter, they were told about another study dealing with opinion research. Half of the subjects in each of the side effect conditions were given a choice of participating, while the remaining subjects were given no choice; that is, they were forced to participate in this second study. This second study consisted of writing an essay supporting a position the students were known to be against. The students' attitudes toward this topic were assessed at the end of the experiment. The results are shown graphically in Figure 12–1.

The typical cognitive dissonance experiment finding would be that under high choice, writing the counterattitudinal essay would result in

FIGURE 12–1
Graphic presentation of the results of the choice and misattribution experiment

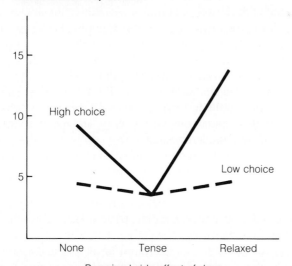

Perceived side effect of drug

Note: Higher scores indicate greater agreement with the attitude discrepant essay.

more favorable attitudes toward the essay topic than writing the essay under low choice. In the no side effect condition this is what Zanna and Cooper found. In the tense side effects condition, if subjects misattributed the arousal resulting from engaging in the attitude discrepant behavior under high choice to the effects of the pill, this should limit the attitude change which occurs as a function of the arousal. In fact, this is exactly what the results reflected. Whereas high and low choice subjects differed in the no side effects condition (the typical finding), this difference disappeared in the tense side effects condition. In the relaxed side effects condition, the subjects could not misattribute their arousal to the pill since the pill was supposed to have the opposite effect; that is, it was supposed to relax them. Being a placebo, of course, the pill had no such effect. Thus, subjects believing that the pill should relax them and still feeling aroused in spite of the pill should label their emotional state even more intensely than the typical dissonance-experiencing subjects. This in turn should produce even stronger attitude change toward the essay topic. In fact, this is also what happened. The difference between the high and low choice subjects in the relaxed side effects condition was even greater than that in the no side effects condition.

Cognitive dissonance theory posits that the arousal experienced when one engages in attitude discrepant behavior is aversive or noxious in nature. Although this first study then showed that arousal is necessary for attitude change in the cognitive dissonance situations, it did not provide evidence that the arousal was aversive. In order to address this question of the specific nature of the arousal, a second study was carried out. As before, subjects were given a memory drug (actually a placebo) and told of the side effects. As in the first study, one group was given the tense side effects instructions, a second group was told that the drug has no side effects, and a third group was told that the drug produced a side effect of pleasant excitement. All subjects were then given the choice of participating in an essay writing study while they waited for the drug to be absorbed. The essay was again counterattitudinal. Thus, in this study, all subjects were in a dissonant situation. Finally, the subjects filled out a scale measuring their attitude toward the essay topic. All subjects had been pretested on this topic in our earlier study, and therefore the investigators could measure attitude change.

Comparison of the tense and no side effects conditions showed that the attitude change toward the essay was greater in the no side effects condition. In other words, as in the first study, the misattribution worked. If the pleasant excitement side effect condition lowered the amount of attitude change in the same way as did the tense side effect condition, then the position that dissonance is an aversive state would be untenable. In fact, the attempt to misattribute the arousal to the pill under the pleasant excitement side effect condition did not work. These subjects changed their attitudes as much as those in the no side effect condition. Thus, the arousal experienced must have been aversive and therefore could only be misattributed to another aversive source, the pill with the tense side effect.

In order to supply even stronger evidence that dissonance is arousing and that the arousal is necessary for the resultant attitude change, a third experiment was carried out. Misattribution is a redirecting of arousal from one source to another; in this case, from the dissonance to the pill. The investigators asked in this case what would occur if arousal, rather than being redirected, were actually suppressed. They reasoned that in the case where arousal was suppressed, attitude change should also be suppressed. Again the procedure closely followed that of the previous two studies with one exception. In this study, the subjects were told that the researchers were testing groups with the memory drug containing either a small dosage of a stimulant or a small dosage of a tranquilizer, or a placebo. All subjects were told that they were in the placebo condition. In actuality, subjects were randomly assigned to receive either the stimulant, the tranquilizer, or a placebo. As in the first study, during the absorption period, subjects were either forced to participate in writing a counterattitudinal essay (low choice) or were asked to volunteer to write the essay (high choice). As usual, attitudes toward the essay topic were tapped at the end of the experiment. The results are presented graphically in Figure 12–2.

If arousal is necessary for attitude change to occur, as cognitive disso-

FIGURE 12–2
Graphic presentation of the results of the choice and drug type experiment

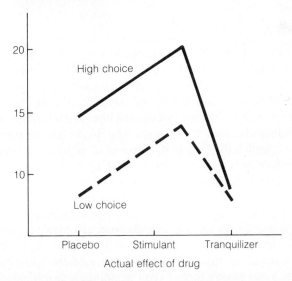

Note: Higher scores indicate greater agreement with the attitude discrepant essay.
This figure is taken from Cooper and Zanna (1976).

nance theory predicts, then the tranquilizer should lower arousal and wipe out the difference between the high and low choice groups. In fact, this is exactly what occurred: subjects given a placebo showed the usual dissonance effect, that is, high choice subjects were more favorable toward the essay topic than low choice subjects, but in the tranquilizer condition no differences were found between the high and low choice conditions. Thus, the tranquilizer eliminated the typical attitude change. In the stimulant condition, high choice subjects were more favorable toward the essay topic than low choice subjects and were more favorable than even the high choice placebo subjects. The stimulant served to intensify the arousal resulting from the dissonance manipulation.

These three studies, the first demonstrating that misattribution of arousal eliminates the usual attitude shift which follows attitude discrepant behavior, the second showing the specific nature of the arousal produced by attitude discrepant behavior, and the third showing the effects of actually modifying arousal through drugs, provide strong conceptual validity for the cognitive dissonance position. As the reader can tell from the above work, construct validation is a continuous process in which more and more evidence is gathered which supports a theory and at the same time challenges plausible rival theoretical positions. Is cognitive dissonance theory now the "proven" explanation for the attitude change that occurs following attitude discrepant behavior? The answer is no. It has certainly become a more probable explanation as a result of the above experiments, but these studies have not eliminated all rival explanations. A theory is not true or false, it is only a more or less probable explanation of reality than some other theory.

Children and Rhyming

As a third example of conceptual validation, we will examine the work of Hayes, Chemelski, and Palmer (1982) dealing with the effects of prose and verse materials on children's memory. The authors were interested in how rhyme affects the acquisition of new information by preschool children. Previous investigators had posited that rhyme facilitates learning in young children because it increases their liking for the material and therefore the attention they pay to it. Hayes et al. argued that, according to some information processing theories, rhyming might actually interfere with initial learning of material. According to these models, processing of semantic features of verbal material produces greater retention than processing of phonetic characteristics. Given that rhyme increases attention to the phonetic over the semantic features of verbal material, rhyme will actually interfere with learning of that material. In other words, presenting material in rhyming format may interfere with learning in young children by causing them to pay attention to the phonetic features which are irrelevant to semantic comprehension. In order to determine the effect of rhyme upon young children's retention of verbal material, Hayes et al. carried out a series of studies.

In the first experiment, two stories written in verse form were chosen from books of children's nursery rhymes. Each story rhyme consisted of four stanzas. A prose version was produced for each story by moving lines between different stanzas which eliminated the rhyming nature of the material, but still left a meaningful story. Thus the prose and verse versions contained exactly the same verbal materials but in different orders. The two forms of each story were then tape recorded for presentation to the children, a group of preschoolers. The children were randomly assigned to either a prose or rhyme condition and within each of these to one of the two stories. A stanza was played for the child, and then a recognition question was asked about the content of the stanza. Following the last question, the children indicated how much they liked the story by pointing to a smiling, neutral, or frowning face.

Consistent with the information processing approach and contrary to the position advocating rhyme as an effective method for increasing retention, the performance in the prose condition, across both stories, was better than that in the verse condition. At the same time, a greater number of children liked the verse rather than the prose versions of the stories. Thus, verse does increase liking for the material but does not facilitate retention of that same material.

In order to ensure that their findings in the first experiment were not due to the two stories chosen, a second study was carried out employing the original two stories plus an additional two stories, each produced in a prose and rhyme version. This time each child heard, in prose or verse form, both of the original stories or both of the new stories, answering a recognition question after each stanza. Again, better retention occurred for the prose versions regardless of which stories were presented, and again the children showed greater liking for the rhymed versions. Thus, the finding seemed to be a general one, not limited to specific stories. This second experiment, as the reader may have noticed, was more of a test of external validity than of construct validity since it examined the generality of the stimulus materials. In the third study, a further probe into the memory process was undertaken.

In the first two studies, all of the recognition questions dealt with nonrhyming aspects of the stories. It could be argued that if the questions had related to the rhymed words of the stories, the children in the verse conditions may have showed greater retention. In order to test this notion, children were presented with two stories, both in prose or both in verse form, and again asked questions following each stanza. This time, half of the questions dealt with rhymed words and half with nonrhymed words in the stories. The results showed an interaction as depicted in Figure 12–3. The children again showed greater retention for the prose than for the verse form stories but only when the questions dealt with nonrhyming

FIGURE 12-3
Graphic presentation of the rhyming experiment

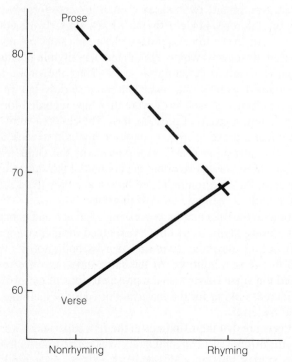

words in the stories. When the questions referred to rhymed aspects of the stories, the verse and prose conditions did not differ. Questions about the rhymed aspects of the stories seemed to lower the retention associated with the prose version more than they raised the retention of the verse form condition. Thus, the lower retention rate for verse form stories in the first two studies does not seem to be a function of the wrong questions being asked, that is, nonrhyming questions. Thus, one alternative explanation can be eliminated or at least declared implausible.

In order to provide even a more sensitive test of the effects of rhyme versus prose material, a fourth study was conducted. This experiment examined recall of the content of the stories rather than recognition, assuming that since recall is a less structured procedure, it might be the place where the advantage of rhyming would occur. Also, rather than presenting the stories one stanza at a time and then questioning the child, two stanzas were presented by the child's preschool teacher followed by open-ended questions about those stanzas. As with the recognition questions in the three previous studies, recall was better for the prose than for the verse conditions. Interestingly, 82 percent of the story events correctly recalled by the subjects in the verse condition were related to rhyming aspects of the stories. Thus, rhyme does seem to promote children's attention to rhyming elements but with negative effects in terms of nonrhyming elements.

A fifth study was carried out by Hayes et al. in order to verify that the negative effects of rhyme are a function of the children's age and to make sure that the difficulty of the prose and verse forms of the stories was equivalent. In order to test this, they employed adult subjects since previous literature has shown that adults employ rhyme to enhance recall. Rhyme is used as a tool for adults and does not act at the expense of semantic comprehension. Therefore, adults should actually perform better with verse. Adult subjects heard either the prose or verse form of one of the stories and were then given a free recall test of the content of the story. Following recall, the subjects were also given transcripts of both versions of the story and asked to indicate which would be the most difficult for preschool children to learn. Unlike the children, the adults, as predicted, showed better recall in the verse than in the prose condition. Subjects in both conditions judged the prose to be more difficult for preschoolers. Thus, the material in the verse condition certainly was not harder for adults and in fact was judged by them to be easier for the preschoolers.

The results of the five studies do seem to support a levels of information processing model and to be evidence against the facilitating effects of rhyme in young children. First of all, all four of the studies with children showed a clear advantage of the prose over the verse condition. Second, this effect occurred with different stories and with both recall and recognition questions. Finally, adults, as expected, showed exactly the opposite effect; that is, better recall with verse than with prose. All of these results seem to be in clear support of the information processing approach and in opposition to the facilitation of rhyme notion. At the same time, there is little direct evidence for the causal agent behind the poorer performance in the verse conditions. In other words, although the data are consistent with the effects posited to occur at the level of processing of phonetic features, the results do not clearly show that rhyming predisposes children to a more superficial type of learning. It is true, however, that liking for the story was higher in the verse condition, and if this is directly correlated with attention to the rhyming features, this would enhance phonetic processing. Also, in the recall study, children in the verse condition did recall a large amount of material connected with rhyming, supporting the notion that rhyme does focus attention on the phonetic aspects of the material over the semantic aspects.

Attraction to a Dissimilar Other

As a final example of construct validation through the experimental method, we will return to research discussed in Chapter 10; that of Russ et al. dealing with attraction to a dissimilar other. In order to refresh the reader's memory, let us restate the theoretical underpinnings of the research. Previous investigators had consistently found that individuals were more strongly attracted to a similar than to a dissimilar stranger. The basic experimental design for these studies consisted of measuring subjects' attitudes toward a series of topics and then showing the subjects the attitudes of a stranger who was either similar or dissimilar to them. The attitudes of the stranger were bogus; that is, they were manipulated by the experimenter to either agree or disagree with the subjects. Russ et al. argued that under normal circumstances, individuals who hold beliefs will be attracted to similar others who will validate or support those beliefs; but that under circumstances where they are confused, individuals will be attracted to dissimilar others who will provide new viewpoints and end the confusion.

It will be recalled that the actual study they undertook to test this hypothesis consisted of *(a)* exposing subjects to either a highly confusing film or to a mundane control film and *(b)* the manipulation of attitude similarity through the bogus attitude technique. In Chapter 10, the study was presented as a 2 × 2 factorial design; that is, two levels of attitude similarity (similar and dissimilar) and two levels of film (confusing and nonconfusing). This was done in order to demonstrate the nature of an interaction. In actuality, there were three film conditions rather than two. As depicted in Chapter 10, subjects did see the confusing or the nonconfusing film, but in addition, a third group of subjects saw the confusing film accompanied by a clarifying explanation. The authors argued that since the confusing and nonconfusing movies were two different films, they would vary not only on confusion but also on many other aspects as well; e.g., quality, interest, etc. Since the issue was that the confusing film caused subjects to seek understanding which dissimilar others could provide, if some understanding of the film was provided before the film was shown, subjects would not need dissimilar others and attraction to them would decrease.

The explanation, which was fabricated by the authors, should provide some strucure or understanding and render the confusing film less confusing. Since subjects in both confusing film conditions would see the same film, any difference between them on attraction to the dissimilar stranger would be due to the explanation provided. This would provide validation of the authors' theory that dissimilar others are sought when one is confused and needs a different viewpoint. The attraction scores are shown in Table 12–1. The first two columns are a replication of Table 10–2, the confusing and nonconfusing film conditions, respectively, while the third column is the confusing film with the explanation condition. Inspecting the first two columns, the reader will recall that, as predicted, the usual greater attraction to a similar over a dissimilar other occurred in the nonconfusing film condition, whereas subjects showed greater attraction to a dissimilar over a similar other in the confusing film condition. The third column of Table 12–1 shows that the explanation with the confusing film wiped out the greater attraction to the dissimilar other found in the

TABLE 12–1
Results of the confusing and attitude similarity experiment

	Confusing Film	Nonconfusing Film	Confusing Film with Explanation
Similar	8.41	10.66	10.00
Dissimilar	10.75	8.08	6.66

confusing film alone condition. Subjects who received an explanation about the confusing film showed greater attraction to a similar than to a dissimilar stranger. In fact, the difference was even larger than in the nonconfusing film condition.

In order to gain further evidence for the validity of their theoretical explanation, the authors had included a questionnaire which subjects completed after rating their attraction to the stranger. These questions dealt with the information the subject wanted from the stranger. The item, dealing with the degree to which the subject would like to speak with the stranger about the film, showed that subjects had a greater desire to speak with the dissimilar than with the similar stranger about the film in the arousing film condition but showed no differences in the other two conditions. In other words, subjects actually indicated a desire to talk with the dissimilar stranger, again providing some theoretical support for the notion of a need for understanding.

In a previously published study by Byrne and Clore (1967), which had also employed confusing and nonconfusing films, the investigators had expected the usual greater attraction to a similar other to increase as a function of being exposed to a confusing film. Instead, it had decreased but not reversed as in the above study. These authors argued that the confusing film aroused and confused subjects to such a degree that they did not recall the stranger's attitudes accurately. That is, they recalled them as being less similar and less dissimilar than they actually were, which thus increased their attraction to the dissimilar and decreased their attraction to the similar other. Russ et al., of course, argued that the findings were the result of confusion causing attraction to the dissimilar other due to a search for understanding and not due to faulty memory. In order to rule out this alternative hypothesis of distorted memory, Russ, et al., asked their subjects at the end of the experimental session to recall the stranger's attitudes. If the rival explanation was correct, subjects in the confusing film condition should show less accurate recall. In fact, there were no recall accuracy differences among the conditions. Thus, subjects knew the attitudes of the strangers and were attracted on this basis.

All of the experiments discussed, whether dealing with learned helplessness, cognitive dissonance, children's memory, or similarity of attitudes and attraction, were attempts to gather evidence for a given theoretical idea. None of the investigations, including those containing a number of studies, provides proof positive for the theory. Each does show evidence supporting the theory, and each rules out at least some alternative explanations. Each theoretical notion becomes more valid as more confirming evidence is accumulated and as more plausible rival explanations are shown to be improbable. Thus, construct validation is a continuous process rather than on all-or-none proposition. We will see in the next sections, dealing with nonexperimental approaches to construct validation, that the continuous nature of the process also occurs.

CONCEPTUAL VALIDITY OF INDIVIDUAL DIFFERENCE VARIABLES

All of the previous examples, from learned helplessness to similarity of attitudes and attraction have dealt with theoretical processes. In other words, these studies have investigated, through experimentation, the effects of various stimulus situations on responses to those situations. For example, how do individuals respond to noncontingent events, and what is the process behind their responses? How do subjects deal with confusion in terms of their attraction to others, and what is the explanation for their responses to the confusion? Another way of approaching the study of behavior is to first develop a method of assessing individual differences on a theoretical variable. This entails first the successful construction of a test or scale to assess the variable and then relating that scale or test to other variables to which the theory predicts it should relate. Thus, theories about personality, creativity, or ability variables often begin with the assessment of those variables and then proceed to examine the hypothesized relationships of these variables to other variables. These theoretical variables are called *psychological constructs,* and their validity is established through construct validation.

In a sense, we have already discussed this approach in Chapter 11 in relationship to multiple regression. The topic focused on as an example in that section was perceived physical self-efficacy. The reader will recall that the authors developed a measure of Physical Self-Evaluation and then proceeded to use that measure and other previously developed scales to predict involvement in sports and to predict actual physical skill, as evidenced by dart-throwing ability. Although this research was not discussed in regard to construct validity, the study was an attempt to validate the construct of Physical Self-Evaluation.

Need for Cognition

In order to fully demonstrate the development and validation of a measure of individual differences, let us turn to the work of Cacioppo and Petty (1982) on the *need for cognition.* These authors were interested in the construct of need for cognition, which refers to a need to understand the world by structuring situations in meaningful ways. In other words, the authors posited that individuals differ in their need to think about and make sense of their experiences. The first step then was to produce a measure of the need for cognition. Sample items were ''I prefer complex to simple problems'' (high need for cognition) and ''Thinking is not my idea of fun'' (low need for cognition). These items were administered to two groups known to differ on this need: the high need for cognition group was composed of faculty at a large university, while the low need for cognition group consisted of factory assembly line workers. Any items which did not discriminate between the two groups were discarded, leaving 34 items in the scale.

The internal consistency reliability of the scale was calculated using a variant of coefficient alpha (see Chapter 3) and found to be quite high. These items were then factor analyzed to determine whether need for cognition could be considered a unidimensional construct or whether the authors would need to consider a number of different types of need for cognition. In other words, the factor analysis was a second step to ensure internal consistency. If one factor accounted for most of the variance, then the scale could be considered to tap a single construct. In fact, this was the result of the factor analysis with the first factor accounting for a large amount of variance compared with the amount of variance accounted for by any of the succeeding factors. This process of developing a measure that is internally consistent (i.e., reliable) is absolutely essential. One cannot test the validity of a construct with an instrument that is unreliable. Since the 34 items formed a homogeneous scale, they could be summed to produce a total score. The total scores for the faculty were then compared with those for the factory workers, and a highly significant difference was found; that is, as expected, faculty scored much higher on the scale. This finding is actually rather underwhelming since the items on the scale were originally chosen on their ability to discriminate between the two groups. At this point, the authors had developed a scale and checked it for internal consistency.

A second study was carried out employing a larger sample of subjects from a different area of the country. In this investigation, the 34 items of the Need for Cognition Scale chosen in the first study were administered to a sample of 419 university students along with two other measures: the Embedded Figures Test and the Test Anxiety Scale. The Embedded Figures Test is a measure of the degree to which individuals can separate figure from ground (background) or the degree to which they are able to differentiate among events. Since the ability to separate figure from ground and to differentiate among events may be related to the need to think about and examine aspects of stimuli in the environment, there should be some correlation between scores on the Embedded Figures Test and the Need for Cognition Scale. On the other hand, the Embedded Figures Test is a measure of cognitive style, whereas the Need for Cognition scale is a measure of the need to think about and examine events, and thus the correlation between the two measures should be low.

If the correlation was very high, then the two measures would be tapping the same construct, and one could not discriminate between cognitive style and need for cognition.

The items on the Need for Cognition Scale were factor analyzed to see if the same factors emerged as in the first study but with a larger and more homogeneous sample (all college students). The results of this factor analysis were consistent with those obtained in the first study; that is, the pattern of factor loadings for the items paralleled that found in the first study. The correlation between the Need for Cognition Scale and the Embedded Figures Test was significant but quite low ($r = .19$). Thus, although the measures share some common variance, they certainly are not tapping identical constructs. Finally, test anxiety and need for cognition were unrelated, showing that test anxiety was not producing biased results.

With the first two studies, the authors showed that the Need for Cognition Scale (a) was homogeneous, (b) discriminated between a group known to engage in highly cognitive activities (university faculty) and a group whose occupations were not highly cognitive (factor workers), (c) assessed a construct distinguishable from cognitive style, and (d) was unrelated to test anxiety.

The authors reasoned that since intelligent individuals should have experienced positive outcomes in connection with engaging in thinking about issues, there should be some relationship between intelligence and need for cognition. A second question they raised concerned the relationship between the construct of open- and closed-mindedness (dogmatism) and need for cognition. According to Rokeach (1960), individuals differ in the degree to which they tolerate inconsistencies within their belief systems and in the degree to which they actively consider and think about information they receive. These differences in open-closed-mindedness are tapped by an instrument called the Dogmatism Scale. Therefore, nondogmatic individuals, ones open to a broad range of issues and ideas, should be higher in need for cognition than individuals who are highly dogmatic. Again, the correlation between the two variables should be significant but not extremely high given that need for cognition is a separate construct. Third, the transparency of the Need for Cognition Scale was questioned. Since the items were fairly obvious in what they were tapping, it was possible that subjects simply responded to the scale in a socially desirable manner. In other words, subjects may have answered the items not in terms of their actual beliefs, but rather in terms of what would be "good" or desirable responses. In order to address these three issues, the third study involved the administration of the Need for Cognition Scale along with an intelligence test, the Dogmatism Scale, and a measure of social desirability.

The results showed that need for cognition was related to intelligence ($r = .39$) and to dogmatism ($r = -.27$). The negative correlation reflects the fact that high dogmatic subjects showed a low need for cognition. The correlation between social desirability and the Need for Cognition Scale was nonsignificant. Thus, need for cognition was related to both intelligence and open-mindedness as predicted and was unrelated to social desirability.

In a final study, the authors employed an experimental design which involved the random assignment of subjects to a complex or a simple task. It was hypothesized that subjects high in need for cognition would enjoy the complex more than the simple task, while those low in need for cognition would enjoy the simple more than the complex task. In fact a significant need for cognition by simple versus complex task interaction confirmed this hypothesis.

In summary, the results of the studies tended to support the validity of the construct of need for cognition. First of all, as predicted, the Need for Cognition Scale was correlated to some extent with cognitive style, dogmatism, and intelligence. On the other hand, the moderate size of the correlations showed that the Need for Cognition Scale was assessing a construct which was not identical to any of these other constructs. Second, subjects scoring high on the scale showed preference for a task involving more complex cognitive activities, while low need for cognition subjects preferred a simpler task. Further studies showing differences between subjects scoring high and low on the Need for Cognition Scale in other types of situations—as well as correlational studies showing that the construct differs from other theoretical notions about cognitive functioning—would continue to build the validity of the construct of need for cognition. In other words, as in the examples dealing with the conceptual validity of experiments, construct validation is a continuous as opposed to an all-or-none activity.

Liking and Loving

Let us examine another area of research dealing with an individual difference construct—the work of Rubin (1973) on the construct of love. A great deal of research had been carried out in the area of interpersonal attraction, but most of this research was concerned with liking rather than with love. Rubin posited that liking and loving were related but not identical concepts, in that liking was concerned with affection and respect, whereas loving was related to attachment, caring, and intimacy. In order to begin to distinguish between the concepts of liking and loving, a pool of items was developed reflecting attitudes toward a particular other person and administered to a large group of undergraduate students. Each item was responded to in terms of the student's boyfriend or girlfriend (if they had one) and also in terms of a platonic friend of the opposite sex.

The items were then factor-analyzed in order to see if two separate factors emerged which reflected liking and loving, respectively. In fact, this process led to two 13-item scales, one whose items related to attachment, caring, and intimacy; e.g., ''I feel that I can confide in _____ about virtually everything,'' and the other whose items dealt with affection and respect; e.g., ''In my opinion, _____ is an exceptionally mature person.''

Rubin now had two scales which appeared to reflect liking and loving, respectively. When scales appear to be measuring the construct of interest, they are termed *face valid;* however, it can be true that face valid measures have no other validity. In other words, to assume an instrument is valid simply because it appears valid is an assumption based upon faith and not upon evidence. In fact, face validity has been derisively termed faith validity. In order to move beyond face validity, Rubin collected more data.

This time he solicited his subjects with a campaign of posters and advertisements. Offering a monetary inducement for participation ($1), he requested couples who were dating, going together, or engaged but not married. The subjects were asked to show up together and fill out a questionnaire. The campaign proved highly successful in that 182 couples participated in the study. The questionnaire consisted of the liking and love scales completed with respect to the dating partner and to a close same-sex friend and a number of other questions about the subjects and their relationships.

Rubin could now examine the liking and love scores of the two partners and also compare each subject's ratings of their dating partner with their ratings of their close same-sex friend. Although there should be some correlation between the liking and love scores for the dating partners, this correlation should only be moderate if liking and love are two different constructs. This is in fact what Rubin found, although the correlations between the scales differed for the two sexes. The males' liking and love scores for their female partners were correlated .56, while the females' scores for their male partners were correlated only .36. Thus, males more than females tended to have more congruency between their liking and love for their partners. Both sexes did show the expected pattern of a moderate correlation between the two scales. The comparison of the average liking and love scores toward partners and close same-sex friends showed that whereas liking was high for both partners and friends, love scores were high for partners only. The results for the two sexes are depicted in Figure 12–4. Thus, the love scale was able to discriminate between romantic partners and close same-sex friends. As the reader can see from Figure 12–4, although the love scores for both sexes toward the same-sex friends are much lower than those same scores for their partners, women's love scores for their friends was quite a bit higher than men's. This may reflect a differential ability of the two sexes to establish intimate relationships with members of their own sex. In summary then, the scales acted as expected in that love and liking for partners showed a moderate relationship to each other and love for a partner was higher than love for a close friend, while liking was higher for both partners and friends.

One of the items on the questionnaire asked the subjects to respond to

FIGURE 12–4
Graphic presentation of the love scale study

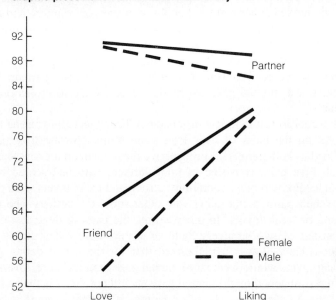

the item: "Would you say that you and _____ are in love?" by circling "yes," "no," or "uncertain." Scores on the love scale were quite strongly correlated with this item for both sexes: males $= .53$ and females $= .61$. On the other hand, the correlations of scores on the liking scale were quite a bit lower: males $= .36$ and females $= .29$. A second item asked the subjects to estimate the likelihood that they would eventually marry on a scale ranging between zero and 100 percent. Again, the correlations between the love scale scores and the probability of marriage were high: males $= .59$ and females $= .60$, whereas the correlations between liking scale scores and likelihood of marriage were much lower: males $= .35$, females $= .33$. Since love and marriage are seen to go hand in hand in our society, these patterns of correlations support the construct validity of the love scale.

As the next step in the process of construct validation, Rubin decided to move from questionnaire data to direct behavioral observation. In order to do this, he needed to find a behavioral variable which would be sensitive to differences in degree of love. The variable he chose was eye contact. In both the popular literature and the social science literature, eye contact is viewed as a means of establishing communication and intimacy. The notion of lovers gazing into each others' eyes has been amplified in story and song. Rubin invited dating couples who had filled out the love and liking scales to participate in a study. The strategy was quite simple. While the partners were waiting for the study to begin, they were viewed through a one-way mirror by two observers. One of the observers watched the male partner, and the other watched the female partner. Whenever the female looked at her partner, her observer pressed a button, and whenever the male looked at his partner, his observer pressed a button. Each button activated its own clock, and the simultaneous pressing of both buttons activated a third clock. Thus, the time each partner spent looking at the other was recorded as well as the time spent by the two partners in mutual gaze. It was mutual gaze which should be related to scores on the love scale.

In order to test this, Rubin separated the subjects into strong and weak lovers on the basis of their love scale scores. Strong love pairs were defined as both partners scoring above the median on the love scale, while weak love pairs consisted of both partners who had scored below the median. For two other conditions, strong and weak lovers were paired not with their partners but rather with other subjects' partners who were also strong or weak lovers. In other words, the pairs in these last conditions consisted of two strangers, both of whom were either strong or weak lovers. Thus, it was hypothesized that for the actual dating pairs, the strong lovers would have more mutual gaze than the weak lovers. For the paired strangers though, mutual gaze should not differ between the strong and weak lover pairs. In other words, if mutual gaze is a behavioral symptom of love, then it should only occur between two lovers.

Rubin's data supported these predictions. First of all, the amount of looking recorded on the third clock, that is, the clock reflecting mutual gaze, was higher for the strong than for the weak lover dating pairs. On the other hand, the total amount of looking as recorded on clocks 1 and 2 did not differ for these pairs. In other words, only mutual gaze varied as a function of the dating couple's scores on the love scale. If total amount of looking as well as mutual gaze had varied, then the difference in mutual gaze between the strong and weak lover pairs may simply have been a function of individual differences in propensity to look at others rather than in differences related to gazing at the loved one. Second, the strong and weak love strangers did not differ in their amount of mutual gaze. This also supports the idea that it is strong love toward a particular person that is reflected by mutual gazing, as opposed to a general tendency on the part of strong lovers to mutually gaze indiscriminately at any other individual.

The construct validation process for the love research consisted of a series of steps. It began with the conceptual definitions of love and liking and then moved to the development of scales to measure these constructs. In other words, the first step was to cross the bridge from the abstract theoretical definition into the real world of behavior. Finding only moderate correlations between the love and liking scales supported the notion of two related but still distinct constructs. The work with dating partners and the pattern of scores on the love and liking scale for the partner and for a friend lent further support to the validity of the construct, as well as the correlations of the two scales with questions about future prospects for the couple. Finally, the study on eye contact moved the research into the area of relationships between the love scale scores and directly observable behavior. In other words, love scale score differences became evidenced in differences in mutual gazing. Thus, in a series of studies, the construct of love was measured and its validation begun. It is a complex construct, and so any single study would supply only a small piece of validational evidence, and any series of studies would only begin a continuing validational process.

With both the need for cognition and the love research, the process began with the development of reliable measures of individual differences of the constructs and then proceeded to correlations of the measures with other variables. Another construct validational scheme based upon the correlational method is the multitrait-multimethod approach developed by Campbell and Fiske (1959).

MULTITRAIT–MULTIMETHOD

The logic underlying the multitrait-multimethod approach is quite straightforward: measures of the same construct should be highly correlated, while measures of different constructs should not be highly correlated. For example, in the research on liking and love, different ways of assessing love should be highly correlated, but these same measures should not show high correlations with measures of liking. If a measure of love was as highly correlated with a measure of liking as it was with a second measure of love, then the constructs of love and liking could not be differentiated from each other. Assume, for example, that Rubin had measured love and liking with his scales and had also assessed these constructs through behavioral measures such as hand-holding, hugging, kissing, etc., for love and through helping and favor-doing for liking. If the measures of physical affection were highly correlated with scores on the love scale, helping and favor doing were highly correlated with scores in the liking scale, and if the correlations between the loving and liking measures were low, the validity of liking and loving as two different constructs would gain support.

Basic to this method is the notion of at least two different types of assessments of at least two different constructs. In this approach, the different methods and the different constructs are completely crossed. In other words, if constructs X and Y are assessed through methods A and B, all possible combinations result: XA, XB, YA, and YB. Employing different kinds of measurements of a construct enhances the generality of the construct; that is, the definition of a construct is not limited to only a single specific operation. While it is true that Rubin's scale was the means by which he operationalized the construct of love, this was certainly not the only way it could be assessed. Other methods of measuring the construct could be developed, and if these methods correlated highly with

Rubin's scale, this would lend validity to the construct. This type of validity, which is based upon the correlation of different types of assessment of the same construct, is termed convergent validity. Convergent validity alone is not enough to determine construct validity; that is, it is only one aspect of the process of construct validation.

The second aspect is discriminant validity. Just as different measures of the same construct should converge, measures of different constructs should diverge. When measures of two different constructs do not correlate highly, we have evidence for discriminant validity. On the other hand, if measures of two different constructs correlate highly, the constructs do not have discriminant validity. For example, if Rubin, after having conceptually defined liking and love, had found the liking and love scales to be highly correlated, the constructs would have lacked discriminant validity.

In other words, the process is to measure two or more constructs in two or more ways and then examine all of the intercorrelations among the variables Table 12–2 shows the matrix produced when the constructs A and B each measured by methods I and II are intercorrelated. Each cell of the table is labeled in terms of whether or not the constructs are the same and whether or not the assessment methods are the same. Where both the

TABLE 12–2
Multitrait-multimethod matrix

| | Construct A | | Construct B | |
	Method I	Method II	Method I	Method II
Method I (Construct A)	1. C = same M = same reliability			
Method II	5. C = same M = different convergent validity	2. C = same M = same reliability		
Method I (Construct B)	7. C = different M = same	9. C = different M = different	3. C = same M = same reliability	
Method II	10. C = different M = different	8. C = different M = same	6. C = same M = different convergent validity	4. C = same M = same reliability

C = construct
M = method

method and the constructs are the same, as in the diagonal cells of the matrix (cells 1 through 4), we have reliability; either the internal consistency or the stability of a given measure. The utility of including reliabilities in the matrix is that they give an upper boundary to the rest of the correlations in the matrix. The reader will recall that reliability reflects the accuracy of measurement and two measurements can only correlate with each other to the extent that each is reliable. Thus, knowing the reliability of each instrument in the matrix tells us the possible extent that each instrument could correlate with the other instruments. The nondiagonal cells contain validity information. Where the constructs are the same and the methods are different (cells 5 and 6), we gather evidence of convergent validity.

In the remaining cells (7, 8, 9, and 10), we gather evidence of discriminant validity. The reader will recall that the correlation between two variables is a measure of their shared or common variance. That common variance may reflect the fact that the two variables measure some of the same content, but it may also reflect the fact that both variables were measured by the same method. In other words, two variables may correlate to some degree simply because the same measurement technique was used to assess both of them. Consider, for example, the correlation between love and liking. Some of their shared or common variance may have been due to the fact that both variables were measured by the same type of scale as well as to the fact that love and liking had components of content in common. The correlations in cells 7 and 8 of Table 12–2 reflect this situation where two constructs are measured by the same method. If these correlations are substantial, it is not clear whether the constructs are similar or simply the methods by which they are measured are similar. In other words, content and method are confounded in cells 7 and 8.

Cells 9 and 10 reflect two constructs measured by two different methods. If the correlations in cells 9 and 10 are compared with those in cells 7 and 8, we are able to determine the degree to which the relationship between the variables is due to common content versus common method. In other words, if the correlations in cells 7 and 8 were substantially higher than those in cells 9 and 10, we would know that much of the commonality between the variables was due to method variance and not to the similarity of the constructs. Since the relationship between the variables would drop when common method variance was controlled, the constructs would have discriminant validity. Low correlations in cells 9 and 10 would reflect the fact that the two constructs are distinct, at least from each other. On the other hand, if the correlations in cells 9 and 10 remained as high as those in cells 7 and 8 and all were substantial, the relationship between the constructs could not be due to method variance. Rather, it must be due to the fact that the same content is being assessed. Therefore, one could not conclude that A and B are distinct constructs; that is, they would not have discriminant validity.

In order to examine the multimethod-multitrait approach more closely, consider a study by Moskowitz and Schwarz (1982). Although the authors were interested in the convergence of two methods rather than in the validation of constructs, their research will serve to demonstrate the multimethod multitrait approach. For our demonstration purposes, we will treat the research as an attempt to show convergent and discriminant validity for the constructs of dependency and dominance in young children. Each of the constructs, i.e., dependency and dominance, were assessed by two separate methods.

One method was the use of actual counts of behaviors reflecting each of the constructs. This technique consisted of having trained observers watch each of the children a number of times. Specifically, observations on 56 children were carried out three hours per day, five days per week, for a period of eight weeks. This resulted in each child being observed for 30 minutes per week or a total of 240 minutes over the entire study. An individual observation period was 4 minutes long and was divided into a series of 10-second intervals. Thus, observers watched a given child for 10 seconds and then coded the child's behavior. Coding consisted of five categories of behavior for each construct. Examples of the coding categories for dependency were "seeks instrumental help" (e.g., the child requests someone to tie their shoe) or "being near" (e.g., the child stays within six inches of another person). Examples of the coding categories for dominance were "verbal command" or "threat." Gathering these counts of dependency and dominance behaviors was obviously an involved and tedious process.

The second method for assessing the constructs was the use of ratings of the children by individuals who knew them: the teacher and a graduate and two undergraduate assistants in the preschool. These raters independently rated each child on a seven-point scale in terms of the likelihood that the child would perform each of the categories of dependence and dominance behaviors used in the behavioral counts.

There were then two constructs, dependency and dominance, each assessed by two methods, behavioral counts and ratings by knowledgeable informants. From these data the researchers could calculate a number of measures: *(a)* reliability coefficients for each measure of each construct, *(b)* correlations between the two methods for each construct (convergent validity), *(c)* correlations between the two constructs for each method, and *(d)* correlations between the two constructs for different methods (discriminant validity). The multimethod-multitrait matrix is shown in Table 12–3. The correlations in this table are for all weeks and all raters. The values in parentheses are generalizability coefficients, a variant of reliability coefficients. These are quite high except for the behavioral counts of dependency. Thus, the measures are fairly consistent. The values in brackets are convergent validities, both of which are significant, showing that each of the constructs can be assessed with two different methods. The evidence for discriminant validity comes from the comparison of the four correlations between the two constructs. Two of these correlations,

TABLE 12-3

A multitrait-multimethod matrix for two traits (dependency and dominance) and two methods (behavior counts and ratings)

Construct:	Dependency		Dominance	
Method:	Behavior Count	Rating	Behavior Count	Rating
Behavior count	(.38)			
Dependency rating	[.37]	(.83)		
Behavior count	.11	.03	(.76)	
Dominance rating	.14	.16	[.59]	(.92)

.11 and .16, reflect both method and content in common, while the remaining two, .14 and .03, reflect only common content. In this study, all of these correlations were nonsignificant, which shows evidence for discriminant validity.

In general, the results support the validity of the two constructs. First, all of the measures are reliable, although the reliability of the assessment of dependency through behavioral counts is quite a bit lower than the reliabilities for the other measures. Second, each construct has convergent validity in that the behavioral counts and the informant ratings are correlated for both dependency and dominance. Finally, the constructs have discriminant validity since the correlations between the constructs are all nonsignificant.

The evidence for convergent and discriminant validity involves relative judgments. In other words, evidence for convergent and discriminant validity involves comparisons among the correlations in the multimethod-multitrait matrix. In the present study, the correlations reflecting discriminant validity were nonsignificant, but this is not always the case; that is, the correlations between the two constructs may be significant. In this case, it is first necessary to compare the same method correlations with the different method correlations. If the correlations between the constructs when measured by different techniques are much lower than the same method correlations, then the observed relationships between the constructs is due to common method and not common content. On the other hand, if the different method correlations are substantial and are not much lower than the same method correlations, the constructs are actually related. The process now is to compare these different method correlations between the constructs with the convergent validity correlations. If they are much lower and the convergent validity correlations are high, there is evidence for discriminant validity. On the other hand, if the correlations between the constructs measured by different methods as well as those within the constructs are quite high, there is convergent but not discriminant validity. What this means is that the constructs are not able to be differentiated from each other, which in a sense means that they are the same construct. Whatever that construct is, it can be assessed reliably through different methods. The question remains though as to what the construct actually reflects.

The point is that the multimethod-multitrait approach as a method of construct validation is not an all-or-none process. The choice of a construct to validate against, that is to show discriminant validity, is a crucial issue. If a construct is picked which conceptually has nothing to do with the one for which validation is being sought, low correlations between measures of the two constructs is almost guaranteed, but it is also conceptually meaningless. For example, if one is trying to provide construct validation for the construct of physical self-evaluation, the lack of correlation with creativity, although technically providing evidence for discriminant validity, actually lends little to the validation of the construct. On the other hand, if the researcher has theoretically distinguished the construct of physical self-evaluation from the construct of personal control, then the lack of correlation between measures of the two constructs—as compared with strong convergent validity for the construct of physical self-evaluation—does provide validation for the construct of physical self-evaluation.

This process of showing that conceptually similar things go together and that conceptually different things diverge is what the process of construct validation is all about. Very often, evidence for the validity of a construct accumulates. Various studies show convergence or similarity of results employing different methods, while other studies rule out rival explanations or show lack of correlation with measures of other constructs. Constructs are theoretical entities. They are explanations or theoretical descriptions of events and not the events themselves. This means that they must be mapped into the world, and the mapping process is an imperfect one. Whether or not a theoretical explanation or description is valid depends on the adequacy of the methods employed including the design of the study and the measuring instrument. When evidence from many sources using different methods consistently supports the explanation provided by the construct while rival explanations gain little support, the validity of the construct increases.

Chapter 13

The Research
Process:
A Personal
Journey

Most undergraduate students are exposed to psychological research in two ways. First they are told about research findings in the psychology courses they take, either by their instructors or by reading the textbooks in the courses. These accounts usually present rather sketchy descriptions of the designs and procedures employed and rather superficial descriptions of the results of the studies. After reading a textbook description of a study, one has a general idea of what occurred, but the actual details are usually omitted. This rather superficial approach is a reasonable one since the purpose of most textbooks is to summarize the findings on a given topic in order to present a conceptual view of that topic.

PSYCHOLOGICAL JOURNALS

The second manner in which students become exposed to psychological research is through reading articles in psychological journals. This type of exposure usually occurs when term papers are required in courses. These scholarly journals are the primary places where the results of research become public. Some of the journals are published under the sponsorship of professional organizations, such as the American Psychological Association, while others are under independent sponsorship. The great majority are refereed in that the manuscripts submitted to them are carefully reviewed for acceptance in the journal by at least two professionals who are competent in the content area of the submitted paper.

The form in which the articles are presented is similar in most journals and follows a logical sequence: *(a)* abstract, *(b)* introduction, *(c)* method, *(d)* results, and *(e)* discussion. The abstract, which is a single paragraph or short statement of the problem and the findings, is presented at the beginning of the article in order to provide the readers with an overview. This allows the readers to decide whether or not the research is relevant to their interest. The first actual section of the article is the introduction, which presents the general issues which were investigated, providing references to other published research which bears on the topic. The purpose of the introduction is to clearly state the rationale of the study so that the reader will understand the predictions made by the author and the reasons for the methods employed to test those predictions.

The method section, which follows the introduction, provides the details relating to the manner in which the study was carried out. Often this begins with a brief overview of the design and sequence of events. This is followed by a subsection which is labeled subjects that describes the makeup of the sample employed, in terms of variables such as sex and race, as well as information as to the manner in which the sample was obtained. Thus, the description might be something like: "Subjects were 60 male and 40 female students from the introductory psychology course at the University of Maine who participated in partial fulfillment of their course requirement."

The next subsection, which may be labeled in various ways, describes the instrumentation employed in the study. In some studies, this includes specification of the mechanical and electrical equipment involved, as well as the physical environment in which the research was carried out. Thus, in studies dealing with perception, physiological responses, or memory, technical information relating to aspects such as the manner in which stimuli were presented (for example, by slides or on a cathode ray tube) and the devices through which responses were assessed (counters, printers, multichannel recorders) are described in detail. In studies which do not employ highly technical equipment, the materials may involve different stimulus configurations given to subjects. For instance, subjects may have read paragraphs which vary systematically, and these paragraphs are given in detail in this section. This subsection also includes descriptions of scales and questionnaires which are employed to assess subjects' responses. The third subsection deals with the design and procedure of the study. The entire sequence of events in the study is laid out in a step-by-step fashion. Each event in the study is detailed in terms of the role of both the experimenter and the subject.

The results section explains the type of statistical analyses employed and the actual findings of those analyses. Each hypothesis being tested is discussed in turn as to whether or not the findings support or fail to support that hypothesis. This section also often includes tables of statistics, such as means, standard deviations, correlation coefficients, factor loadings, etc., and figures which graphically depict the outcomes. Very little interpretation is included in the results section; rather, it is a straightforward presentation of the findings.

The final section is the discussion, which is the author's interpretation of the results. This section generally includes a restatement of the theoretical position and a summary of the evidence supporting that position. The author will also attempt to show how the data do not support rival positions. In complicated studies, some of the hypotheses are not supported, and the discussion section often includes a rationale for this lack of support. This section usually concludes with a brief statement of the implications of the findings for future research. In other words, the author usually proposes some possible directions for future studies.

Although journal articles contain much more detailed and informative presentations of research than textbooks, due to limitations on space, they are still condensations of the actual occurrences in a research project. For example, only a limited amount of background information relating to the rationale of the study can be included in the introduction. Thus, studies which bear on the issues in a tangential manner often must be omitted from this section, leaving only room for the most directly relevant background research. The method section, although fairly detailed, still omits many details of the actual procedure since a full moment-by-moment transcript would be much too cumbersome to include in the article. This means that many of the individual events are lost from the article. The results section usually includes only summary data of the most relevant findings. The individual scores of subjects are not included in this section. Also, a number of different types of data analyses may have been carried out but only some of them reported.

The point is that even the most comprehensive of journal articles must summarize the study in such a way as to produce a coherent readable presentation of the investigation and its findings. Many ideas, events, and analyses are omitted in order to achieve this concise final product. What very often appears in the journal article to be aclear, orderly, and logical sequence of events is the result of a series of false starts, modifications, and rethinking to which the reader has not been a party. In other words, the presentation of a study in a journal contains plastic surgery; that is, the warts on the investigation have been removed. In fact, the actual complete study usually contains a great many imperfections. In order to give the reader a better understanding of the actual happenings in a study, I will try to present some studies in which I have been involved complete with their warts.

COGNITIVE DISSONANCE AND ATTRACTION

The research project which I will discuss dealt with the effects of cognitive dissonance upon attraction to similar and dissimilar others. The grounding for this research came from previous work on interpersonal attraction. First of all, previous research had shown that, by and large, individuals tended to prefer others who were similar to themselves in attitude over dissimilar others. The basis of this attraction was posited to be reward. That is, attitudes similar to our own consensually validate our views of the world and are thus rewarding, whereas dissimilar attitudes threaten our perceptions of the world and consequently are aversive. The exception to this general finding of attraction to similar others seemed to occur when individuals are in a confused state. The study by Russ, Gold, and Stone (1980), which was discussed in a previous chapter, provided evidence that in a confusing situation consisting of the showing of an ambiguous film, individuals became more strongly attracted to a dissimilar than to a similar other. The argument of the authors was that in a state of confusion, one needs information which will provide clarity and end the confusion, rather than consensual validation of one's existing attitudes. Dissimilar others, since they view the world differently from oneself, might provide perspectives which would be useful for alleviating the confusion.

Following the original study, we decided to attempt to provide further validity for its theoretical basis. Unfortunately, the confusing film employed in that study was no longer available, and thus we had to search for a new film. This new film had to be not only confusing, but also quite brief since we only had an hour of each subject's time for the entire experiment—including the presentation of the film. After viewing a large number of films, a few were chosen for pretesting with samples of subjects. Most proved to be not very confusing and, even worse, to be boring.

Since confusion was the essential ingredient for attraction to a dissimilar other, we began to search for other methods of creating confusion. This is where we arrived at the use of a cognitive dissonance manipulation. In a typical cognitive dissonance experiment, subjects engage in a behavior which is discrepant with what they believe. They engage in this behavior under either strong or weak pressure; that is, they are given either a high degree of choice or no choice at all. As in the Zanna and Cooper studies discussed in Chapter 12, subjects are either told to write an essay or they are given a choice of whether or not to write an essay which is inconsistent with their beliefs. According to cognitive dissonance theory, attitude discrepant behavior undertaken with little or no pressure results in cognitive dissonance, a state of aversive arousal, and then a consequent attitude change which reduces the dissonance.

We felt that when subjects engage in a behavior that is discrepant with what they believe under high choice conditions, this would produce a state of confusion. High choice, which is characterized by little pressure on the individual, means that in the cognitive dissonance situation there is insufficient justification for the behavior. In fact, this is the basis of the choice manipulation. Low choice produces sufficient justification for the behavior, but high choice does not, and consequently attitude change toward consistency with the behavior is the result. In other words, individuals who do something they do not believe in, with only minimal pressure exerted upon them, cannot explain the discrepant behavior; that is, they are confused about why they engaged in the behavior. We reasoned that the creation of cognitive dissonance should act as a confusing state. Unfortunately for our purposes, the confusion is terminated through the shift in attitude toward consistency with the behavior; that is, individuals end the confusion by changing their attitudes so as to make them consistent with the behavior in which they have engaged.

At this point, it seemed as though the cognitive dissonance situation which should produce confusion would not be of use to us since the attitude change which follows the arousal of cognitive dissonance will quickly end the confusion. Keep in mind that we were looking for a situation, like the ambiguous film condition, which would confuse subjects and raise their attraction to a dissimilar other. Our examination of the effects of the cognitive dissonance situation then moved us to consider the effects of the attitude shift itself on attraction to a dissimilar other. In other words, rather than concentrating directly upon the confusion created by the cognitive dissonance manipulation, we began to concentrate on the known results of that manipulation—the attitude change.

When individuals engage under high choice in a behavior which is discrepant with their beliefs, they change their beliefs toward that behavior. That is, they take on a new attitude which is inconsistent with their old attitude. Since attitudes tend to be interrelated, it would seem that the new attitude would also be inconsistent with many of their old attitudes. In other words, they have changed an attitude in order to bring about consistency with a behavior and in doing so now hold an attitude which is not congruent with their other attitudes. Ordinarily, individuals seek similar others in order to gain consensual validation of their attitudes. In the case where an individual has experienced cognitive dissonance and an attitude change has occurred, similar others would not be likely candidates to provide consensual validation of the changed attitude. Rather, they would threaten this new belief. On the other hand, others who are generally dissimilar in attitude would be more likely to agree with the changed attitude and thus provide consensual validation. Our position then was that individuals who engaged in a behavior that was inconsistent with their attitudes under high choice would (a) experience cognitive dissonance, (b) change their attitudes toward consistency with the behavior, and (c) show greater attraction to a dissimilar other than individuals who engaged in the attitude-discrepant behavior under low choice.

An idea which began with the effects of confusion upon attraction developed into the issue of the relationship of cognitive dissonance to attraction. The search for a method of producing confusion led to the cognitive dissonance situation which upon close examination seemed not to be appropriate for instigating confusion and consequent attraction to a dissimilar other but did seem relevant to producing attraction to a dissimilar other for the purpose of attaining consensual validation.

We now had a specific problem. The next stage was to begin to design a study to test this problem. Rather than follow the methodological sequence which would be presented in a journal article (subjects, instrumentations, and procedure), the present discussion will attempt to follow the sequence of events as they actually unfolded for us. First, in order to see the effect of cognitive dissonance upon attraction, we had to be able to institute or produce a state of cognitive dissonance. We borrowed the basic paradigm or model for this from previous research in the area of cognitive dissonance. The reader will recall from the discussion in Chapter 12 on construct validity that the studies on cognitive dissonance employed a design which entailed having subjects write counterattitudinal essays under conditions of high and low choice. We employed this same procedure.

Choosing the Essay Topic

In order to carry out this procedure, subjects are either told to or are given a choice of writing an essay which is counter to or against what they believe. One approach is to measure subjects' attitudes toward a topic a period of time before the actual essay writing occurs and then at a subsequent time, knowing their attitudes, ask them to write an essay counter to those attitudes. The subjects we were going to use were students enrolled in the introductory psychology course. These students participated in four hours of research projects in order to fulfill their course requirement. Brief descriptions of the research projects were posted on a centrally located bulletin board with the specifications of how many subjects of each sex were needed. The students then signed up for the projects which seemed to be of interest to them. Pretesting subjects would have entailed having students sign up for two hours of research. The first hour would have been devoted purely to pretesting and the second hour to the actual cognitive dissonance study. Since we would want a reasonable interval between the two hours, subjects would have to be individually contacted after the pretest in order to schedule their second hour. This posed three problems. First, since a large number of research projects were being carried out, subject hours were in short supply, and the pretesting would double the number of subject hours needed for our study. Second, it sometimes proved quite difficult to contact students, and this meant possible attrition of subjects. Third, since subjects were signing up for two hours of the same project, they may have connected the pretesting of their attitudes in the first hour with the cognitive dissonance manipulation in the second hour. In other words, having them write an essay which is counter to the attitudes we had assessed in the pretest may raise their suspicions and consequently invalidate the research. Thus, the pretesting seemed to have more disadvantages than advantages, and we chose to follow another strategy. The second approach is to pick a topic with which subjects are uniformly known to disagree and then, with no premeasurement of their attitudes, have them write an essay favorable to that topic. We then had to choose a topic which subjects would be strongly against and have them write essays favorable to this topic.

The choice of a topic can prove to be a delicate problem. First of all, the topic should be one towards which subjects hold strong beliefs since the purpose of the cognitive dissonance manipulation is to change those beliefs. On the other hand, if the topic is too extreme, to the point of absurdity, high choice subjects may refuse to write the essay or may become totally skeptical about the whole experience. If, for example, we chose an essay supporting the killing of all people over 56 years of age, I suspect that most people would disagree with the topic, but also most would either refuse to write the essay or simply take the whole experience as a joke. On the other hand, if the topic is highly controversial, then we cannot be sure of the opinions of subjects on the topic. For example, an essay supporting a mandatory retirement age of 65 may not be counterattitudinal for many subjects. Therefore, the aim is to choose a topic which subjects are known to be against but on which they could realistically write a favorable essay.

The topic that was chosen was the Iranian hostage crisis. The reader will recall that in 1980, the Iranian government, having overthrown the old ruler, the Shah, had taken a large group of American citizens hostage in the American embassy in Tehran. We believed that sentiment for the release of the hostages was very high, and therefore an essay supporting the Iranian action would be uniformly counterattitudinal. We decided to have subjects write essays, under high or low choice conditions, supporting the taking and holding of the hostages. The topic fitted all of our needs in that subjects would feel strongly about the issue but that at the same time some arguments could be made in support of the Iranian position. We also knew that this choice of a topic could prove to be hazardous since the hostages were still being held at the time of the study. For example, if the hostages were released unharmed or if other evidence in support of the Iranians surfaced, for example that the hostages were spies, attitudes toward the Iranian action might change very quickly, possibly turning a counterattitudinal task into an attitude congruent task, and thereby ruining the dissonance manipulation. Despite these possibilities, we decided to employ the hostage crisis as our topic.

Designing the Study

The topic for the essay was now settled upon and the remaining steps in the study could be designed. Keep in mind that we needed to find out if the cognitive dissonance manipulation worked, that is, if subjects under high choice become more favorable to the Iranians than those under low choice, and then to determine if these high choice subjects become more strongly attracted to a dissimilar other than the low choice subjects. We needed a measure of attitude toward the Iranians. One way of developing such a scale would be to write a pool of items and administer them to a large pilot group of subjects. An item analysis would then be carried out, correlating each item with the total score on the scale and discarding those items which do not correlate with the total score. The selected items would constitute the final scale, and coefficient alpha would be calculated as a measure of the internal consistency of the scale. In this manner, the scale would be developed before the actual study was carried out. Our procedure, due to lack of time, was to administer the items, without pretesting, to the subjects in the experiment and then carry out the item analysis after the fact. Although this procedure worked for us in that an internally consistent scale was achieved, it should be noted that this is not the most desirable approach to developing a scale. The scale we employed consisted of 11 items, each item followed by a strongly agree to strongly disagree response format. This scale is reproduced in Table 13–1.

The Manipulation of Attitude Similarity

For the similarity-dissimilarity part of the study, we employed the same procedure used in previous studies, such as the Russ, Gold, and Stone research discussed previously. This procedure consists of first measuring subjects' attitudes on an Attitude Survey dealing with a series of topics. The first four items from the Attitude Survey are shown in Table 13–2. The remaining items followed this same format and dealt with the topics

TABLE 13-1
Attitude toward the Iranians Scale

For each item circle the response category that most closely reflects your opinion.

SA	If you strongly agree
A	If you agree
MA	If you mildly agree
N	If you are neutral
MD	If you mildly disagree
D	If you disagree
SD	If you strongly disagree

1. Our government should not have allowed the Shah into the U.S.

    SA   A   MA   N   MD   D   SD

2. The Iranians had a right to demand the return of the Shah's wealth in exchange for the hostages.

    SA   A   MA   N   MD   D   SD

3. The Iranians had a right to demand the return of the Shah in exchange for the hostages.

    SA   A   MA   N   MD   D   SD

4. Iran should not be forgiven for seizing the hostages.

    SA   A   MA   N   MD   D   SD

5. The Iranians were justified in taking the hostages.

    SA   A   MA   N   MD   D   SD

6. Iran's behavior in the hostage situation is inexcusable.

    SA   A   MA   N   MD   D   SD

7. The Ayatollah's rule seems to be a better alternative for the Iranian people than that of the Shah.

    SA   A   MA   N   MD   D   SD

8. The U.S. would not have been morally wrong to use force in response to the embassy seizure.

    SA   A   MA   N   MD   D   SD

9. All nations should have completely ceased relations with Iran following the embassy takeover.

    SA   A   MA   N   MD   D   SD

10. It is plausible that the embassy personnel were actually spies.

    SA   A   MA   N   MD   D   SD

11. Given past U.S. involvement with Iran's affairs, it is not surprising that the embassy was seized.

    SA   A   MA   N   MD   D   SD

TABLE 13-2
Four items from the survey of attitudes

Directions: The following are a number of topics about which people usually hold opinions or attitudes. Following each topic are six possible attitudes. You are to choose the one attitude for each topic which is closest to your own. Indicate your choice next to the particular item you endorse.

Please answer every item. Your responses will be strictly confidential

1. Belief in God (choose one)

    _____ I strongly believe that there is a God.

    _____ I believe that there is a God.

    _____ I feel that perhaps there is a God.

    _____ I feel that perhaps there isn't a God.

    _____ I believe that there isn't a God.

    _____ I strongly believe that there isn't a God.

2. Birth Control (choose one)

    _____ I am very much in favor of most birth control techniques.

    _____ I am in favor of most birth control techniques.

    _____ I am mildly in favor of most birth control techniques.

    _____ I am mildly opposed to most birth control techniques.

    _____ I am opposed to most birth control techniques.

    _____ I am very much opposed to most birth control techniques.

3. American Way of Life (choose one)

    _____ I strongly believe that the American way of life is not the best.

    _____ I believe that the American way of life is not the best.

    _____ I feel that perhaps the American way of life is not the best.

    _____ I believe that the American way of life is the best.

    _____ I strongly believe that the American way of life is the best.

4. Sports (choose one)

    _____ I enjoy sports very much.

    _____ I enjoy sports.

    _____ I enjoy sports to a slight degree.

    _____ I dislike sports.

    _____ I dislike sports very much.

of premarital sex, the importance of money, student needs, drug laws, war, social aspects of college life, differences between the sexes, and regulation of big business. The second step is to create a bogus Attitude Survey which is similar or dissimilar to that of the subjects. This created or bogus attitude survey supposedly comes from a subject in another room. We decided first of all to modify the initial attitude survey slightly to include an item dealing with the degree of interference by the United States in the affairs of other nations and an item dealing with whether or not terrorism was justified. These items were added in order to pick out subjects who might be initially favorable to the Iranian position. We did not want to directly tap attitude toward the Iranians at the beginning of the study, since this might alert subjects to our purposes or cause them to try and be consistent on the measurement of their attitude toward the Iranians after the essay.

We then had to decide what constituted similarity and dissimilarity. This is a rather arbitrary decision since attitude similarity is a continuous variable running from exact similarity, which is perfect agreement on every single item, to complete dissimilarity, which is disagreement on all items. We decided upon 10 of 14 items of the attitude survey in agreement or disagreement for similarity and dissimilarity, respectively. Since the items varied in the degree to which each would be endorsed, we needed to also decide whether or not each similar item would match the subject's response exactly and each dissimilar item would exactly mirror the sub-ject's response. In order not to raise suspicion through an exact match, we varied the responses. Some of the similar items were exact matches while others were one step more or less extreme than the subject's response, with the constraint that similar items always stayed on the same side of the neutral point as the subject's response. Dissimilar items were varied in degree in the same way. Thus, even the seemingly straightforward idea of producing bogus attitude scales which were similar or dissimilar to the attitude scales of the subjects was a rather involved and complicated affair.

Assessing Attraction

We now had the initial survey of attitudes, which included the two extra items, and the scale measuring attitude toward the Iranians. We still needed to assess subjects' attraction for their bogus partners. We decided to carry this out in two ways. First we employed the Interpersonal Judgment Scale (IJS), a scale widely used in previous work on interper-sonal attraction. The IJS contains six items dealing with judgments as to another person's intelligence, knowledge of current events, morality, adjustment, liking for the person, and liking to work with the person in an experiment. Each item varies along a six-point continuum from positive to negative. For example, the intelligence item varied from 1, very much above average in intelligence, to 6, below average in intelligence. For half of the items, the most positive end of the continuum was scored 6, and the most negative end was scored 1, while the scoring was reversed for the remaining items. The last two items are summed to produce the measure of attraction.

In order to determine the possible motive for attraction to the other person, we included two additional items in the same format as the IJS items. One tapped how interesting the subject felt the other person's viewpoint on the essay topic would be, and the second dealt with the degree to which the subject was looking forward to discussing the essay topic with the other person. We believed that these items might indicate whether or not consensual validation was involved in the attraction response. The scale is shown in Table 13–3.

In order to assess attraction to the other person in another manner, we included seven bipolar adjective dimensions on which the subjects rated their partners. These included: interesting-boring, intelligent-unintelligent, complex-simple, likeable-unlikeable, mature-immature, pleasant-unpleasant, and closed-minded–open-minded. Each pair of adjectives was rated on a six-point scale with the positive end of the scale being scored six for four of the pairs and the negative end scored six for the other three pairs. The scale is shown in Table 13–4.

All of the measuring instruments were developed for the study, and therefore we now moved to considerations of the details of the procedures. The process was to think through the entire experiment from the advertising of the study to the debriefing of the subjects as to the purpose of the research. Many of the steps involved choices as to the exact procedure and each choice needed to be carefully considered. Our first choice dealt with whether or not to employ subjects of both sexes. The use of both male and female subjects had advantages and disadvantages. First of all, it would enable us to generalize the results to both sexes or, if the sexes responded differently, to describe those differences. At the same time, since we were not expecting sex differences, the finding of an interaction of sex with other variables would be difficult to explain. Also, if both sexes were employed, an approximately equal number of each sex would be needed in each experimental condition so as to be able to uncover any sex effects. This meant running a larger number of total subjects. Therefore, we chose to sacrifice generality and to employ only female subjects. Female subjects were chosen simply because they tended, in our experience, to be somewhat more dependable. That is, they tended to show up for experiments more regularly than males. Our second choice centered upon the number of subjects which would be treated at each session. We could either run one subject at a time, or we could run subjects in groups. Most of the past research on cognitive dissonance had employed single-subject sessions. The advantage of this approach is control over the experimental situation. The subject, being alone, receives all of the experimenter's attention and in return generally responds with full attention. Also, any skepticism on the part of the subject is not reinforced by other subjects

TABLE 13–3
Six IJS items plus two additional items dealing with the essay topic

Below are a number of items dealing with the characteristics of the person whose attitudes you have just seen. Indicate your judgment of the individual for each item by simply *circling* the appropriate number on the scale which follows each item. Please answer all items. Your judgments will remain strictly confidential.

1. *Intelligence:* I believe that this person is (circle one)

| 1 | 2 | 3 | 4 | 5 | 6 |

very much above
average in
intelligence

below average
in intelligence

2. *Knowledge of Current Events:* I believe that this person is (circle one)

| 1 | 2 | 3 | 4 | 5 | 6 |

below average in
his (her) knowledge
of current events

very much above
average in his
(her) knowledge of
current events

3. *Morality:* This person impresses me as being (circle one)

| 1 | 2 | 3 | 4 | 5 | 6 |

extremely
moral

extremely
immoral

4. *Adjustment:* I believe that this person is (circle one)

| 1 | 2 | 3 | 4 | 5 | 6 |

maladjusted

extremely
well adjusted

5. *Personal Feelings:* I believe that I would probably (circle one)

| 1 | 2 | 3 | 4 | 5 | 6 |

like this person
very much

dislike this
person very much

present. Testing subjects in groups breaks this control down in that experimenters must divide their attention among the subjects, and an adverse reaction from one subject in the group can change the tone of the entire session. The advantage of group testing lies in its economy. If each session takes one hour, for example, and if 50 subjects are needed for the experiment, it will take 50 hours to run the study. On the other hand, if five subjects are run in each session, only a total of 10 hours would be

TABLE 13–3 (concluded)

6. *Working Together in an Experiment:* I believe that I would (circle one)

1	2	3	4	5	6

very much dislike
working with this
person in an experiment

very much enjoy
working with this
person in an experiment

7. *Essay topic:* I believe that this person's viewpoint on the Iranian crisis would be (circle one)

1	2	3	4	5	6

extremely interesting
to me

not at all interesting
to me

8. I (circle one)

1	2	3	4	5	6

am not at all looking
forward to discussing
the Iranian crisis with
this person

am looking forward
very much to discussing
the Iranian crisis with
this person

TABLE 13–4
Seven bipolar adjectives for rating the discussion partner

Please rate the discussion partner you will be meeting with on each of the following traits by circling the appropriate number.

Interesting 6	5	4	3	2	1 Boring
Unintelligent 6	5	4	3	2	1 Intelligent
Complex 6	5	4	3	2	1 Simple
Likeable 6	5	4	3	2	1 Unlikeable
Immature 6	5	4	3	2	1 Mature
Pleasant 6	5	4	3	2	1 Unpleasant
Closed-Minded 6	5	4	3	2	1 Open-Minded

needed. The time factor is important in a number of ways. First, laboratory or room space may be available for only a limited period of time. Second, experimenters, who are usually graduate or advanced undergraduate students, often have very real constraints on their time in terms of classes, studying, etc. Finally, in experiments where deception is involved, longer time periods mean a greater chance for the procedure and purposes of the study to leak and contaminate the results.

After weighing all of these factors, we decided to run subjects in groups. Our main reason for this decision rested upon the available time of the experimenters and the leakage factor. Fortunately, in this study, the decision served us well; in subsequent studies, it proved a hardship. The question now was to decide upon how large the groups at each session would be. The larger the groups, the stronger the possibility of non-cooperation or skepticism occurring among the subjects in the group. Also, each subject had to be supplied with a bogus attitude scale which needed to be prepared individually. We discovered that with practice, six bogus scales could be prepared, and thus six subjects were run in each session. The point was then raised that if we employed two experimenters, each in a separate room, 12 subjects could be run in a one-hour period. This would also have the advantage that subjects would know that there is another group of subjects being run simultaneously, which would enhance the believability of the manipulation of the bogus attitude scales. The disadvantage of this procedure is that two different experimenters will often produce somewhat different effects, thereby introducing more error variance into the results. We decided that the advantages outweighed the disadvantages, and thus two experimenters were employed.

The Experimental Procedure

The sequence of events in the study was now mentally rehearsed. Female subjects would be recruited from the introductory psychology course subject pool. A brief title, a description of the study which indicated that subjects would be filling out questionnaires, and the times of running would be posted on the research sign-up bulletin board. The information describing the study would be kept purposefully vague in order not to alarm subjects as to the deception involved in the research but at the same time would be made to sound interesting enough for them to sign up. At the indicated times, up to 12 subjects would arrive at the location listed on the sign-up sheet. The two experimenters would meet them and would haphazardly divide them into two groups. The groups would then be taken by their respective experimenters to two different rooms.

Since, for the similarity manipulation, the subjects were later to believe that they had been paired with a subject from the other room, it was necessary for the subjects to believe that the two groups contained an equal number of subjects. Therefore, if an odd number of subjects arrived for the study, one of the experimenters would take the larger group ahead to one of the rooms and would ask the other experimenter to wait a few moments for stragglers before taking the remaining subjects to their room. Even if the two groups were actually of unequal size, the subjects in the first group would believe that the late subject had arrived, equalizing the groups; and the subjects in the second group would know that the first group was larger than theirs, allowing for the later pairing of subjects.

Once in the rooms, the experimenters would simply ask the subjects to begin the study by filling out the attitude survey described earlier. The subjects were to put only their initials at the top in order to ensure privacy. Upon completion of the attitude surveys, the essay writing would take place. At this point, we decided that a context or rationale was needed for the essay writing; that is, we needed a plausible story or reason for having the subjects write the essays. After an exchange in which a number of possible stories were suggested, we agreed to tell the subjects that the psychology and political science departments were jointly investigating students' ability to reason on current issues and that the topic this particular week was the justification of the Iranians in taking and holding the hostages. We also felt that we needed to ensure student' familiarity with the issues, and therefore a brief printed paragraph was prepared detailing the history of the crisis. This paper was to be given to all subjects in the study before they wrote the essay.

The next issue with which we dealt was the manipulation of choice. The subjects in the low choice condition would be told that they were to write an essay supporting the Iranian action, while those in the high choice group would be told that they could write either a pro- or anti-Iranian essay. This high degree of choice was a problem since most subjects would choose to write the anti-Iranian essay. Therefore, we also told the high choice subjects that we had a great many essays which were against the Iranian action, and thus we needed some on the other side; that is, supporting the Iranian position. We again stated that the choice was up to them but that we did need pro-Iranian essays. All of the subjects were then handed a sheet of paper to write on which contained the line: "I believe that the Iranians were justified in taking and holding the hostages." Subjects in the high choice condition were informed that these were the only sheets we had left and that they could cross out this line if they wanted to. Finally, the subjects were told to write the essays from a first-person point of view since pilot data had indicated that some subjects tended to objectify their essays. In other words, they would state that "the Iranians believed" they were justified in this or that act, rather than stating the beliefs in the first person.

While the subjects would write their essays, the experimenters would leave the room for a brief period with the completed Attitude Surveys. After returning, they would make up the bogus attitude surveys while the subjects completed their essays. Assignment of the subject to a similar or dissimilar bogus partner was done on a random basis by simply shuffling the subjects' Attitude Surveys and then alternately filling out the bogus surveys as similar and dissimilar. After the essays were collected, the subjects would be told that they had been randomly paired with a partner from the other room with whom they would be discussing the essay topic, and that in order for them to know something about their partner, they would be given their partner's Attitude Survey to look over. After examining the bogus survey, which was either similar or dissimilar to the one they had completed at the beginning of the experiment, the subject would complete the IJS, the attitude toward the Iranians Scale, and the list of bipolar adjectives.

At this point, the experiment would be completed, and the subjects were to be debriefed as to the nature and purpose of the study and asked whether their partner was similar or dissimilar to themselves following the explanation of the similarity manipulation. This would serve as a check on whether the manipulation of attitude similarity was perceived correctly.

The experimental design was a 2 × 2 factorial consisting of 2 manipulated independent variables, each with 2 levels or values: (1) the bogus attitude of the partner (similar or dissimilar) and (2) the degree of choice in writing the essay (high or low). The next step was to consider the manner in which the subjects would be randomly assigned to the four conditions. If the subjects were to be tested one at a time by only a single experimenter, then random assignment was a rather straightforward procedure of simply producing a random ordering of the four possible conditions. Each subject who arrived would be run in the condition which appeared in that position in the random ordering. Our use of two experimenters and groups of subjects made the random assignment somewhat more complex.

First of all, within any group of six subjects, only the similarity variable could be randomly assigned. Here, three of the subjects could be assigned a similar partner and three a dissimilar partner, since each subject would see only his own partner's Attitude Survey. The choice variable, on the other hand, would have to be constant for any particular group of subjects. In other words, all of the six subjects within a group would have to be given the same choice condition by the same experimenter. Therefore, it was necessary to randomly assign the two experimenters equally to the two choice conditions. When one of the experimenters was running a high choice condition with one of the sequences, the other was running a low choice with the other sequence. An illustrative sequence of four sessions for the two experimenters, Jim and John, is shown in Table 13–5.

The design of the study was now set along with the random orderings of the conditions. The scales were typed in final form, duplicated, collated, and placed into folders. Thus, a folder contained, in order, all of the materials needed by each experimenter for each session. For example, the folder for Jim for the first session contained: six Attitude Surveys; six sheets of paper, each headed ''I believe that the Iranians were justified in taking and holding the hostages''; six Attitude Surveys for the bogus

TABLE 13-5
Sample of four sessions for two experimenters

	Experimenter	
Session Number	Jim	John
1	Low choice	High choice
2	High choice	Low choice
3	Low choice	High choice
4	High choice	Low choice

partners; six IJS, Attitude toward the Iranians, and bipolar adjective scales. A number of rehearsals which were held in order to make sure that the experimenters acted in a parallel fashion and also to give them practice in producing the bogus scales were followed by the actual running of the study which was completed in a space of three weeks. This time period included extra sessions in order to make up for those sessions where either very few subjects signed up or very few subjects actually showed up.

ANALYZING THE DATA

The next stage was to assemble the data into a form which was amenable for statistical analyses. All of the information concerning the condition in which subjects served, their responses to the various dependent measures, and such items as session number and experimenter were entered into a computer file. It will be recalled that the sequence of events was the writing of the essay and the manipulation of attitude similarity, followed by completion of the IJS and information items, the attitude toward the Iranians scale, and the bipolar adjectives. Therefore, the data analyses followed the above sequence. In order to eliminate those subjects who might have been initially sympathetic to the Iranians, we discarded from the analyses any subjects who endorsed the item on terrorism in the Attitude Survey.

IJS and Information Items

In order to combine items into a simple total score, it was necessary to determine if they were intercorrelated. It will be recalled from Chapter 3 that the intercorrelations among a set of items indicates the degree to which they reflect the same domain of content and can be summed to produce a reliable measure. The correlation between the two IJS attraction items was .42. Therefore, the two attraction items were summed and an analysis of variance was calculated on these scores. There was a significant attitude-similarity main effect, with subjects generally being more strongly attracted to the similar than the dissimilar partner. This main

TABLE 13-6
Results of the choice and attitude similarity experiments for four dependent variables

		SCALES		
	Attraction	Information	Iranians	Adjectives
Similar	7.83	8.00	19.83	27.00
HIGH CHOICE				
Dissimilar	7.60	8.00	26.40	26.20
Similar	9.11	8.78	24.00	31.44
LOW CHOICE				
Dissimilar	6.14	7.14	22.29	23.29

effect was tempered or qualified by an interaction between attitude similarity and choice. The means for the conditions are shown in the first column of Table 13-6. At low choice, the usual finding occurred of significantly greater attraction for the similar over dissimilar other, but at high choice the difference disappeared. The similar partner has dropped in attractiveness, and the dissimilar partner has risen at the high as compared to the low choice condition.

The correlation between the two information items was .64, and therefore the next analysis we carried out was an analysis of variance on the sum of these two items. We found no significant effects, but the pattern of the means, as seen in column 2 of Table 13-6, parallels that for the attraction scores: at the high choice condition, the similar and dissimilar means are identical, but at low choice, the similar mean is slightly larger than the dissimilar mean.

Attitude Toward the Iranians

We examined the correlations among the 11 items and chose seven of the items which were intercorrelated for our measure of attitude toward the Iranians. As a further check on the homogeneity of this seven-item scale, we correlated each of the seven items with the sum of the other six items. These item-total score correlations ranged from .33 to .51. We also calculated coefficient alpha, the measure of reliability, which was .71. Therefore, an analysis of variance was calculated on their Attitude toward the Iranians Scale scores. Neither of the main effects (choice or attitude similarity) were significant, but the interaction of the two variables was significant. The means are shown in column 3 of Table 13-6. The pattern of this interaction was that for the subjects matched with a similar partner, the high choice group was less favorable to the Iranians than low choice group, but for the subjects matched with a dissimilar partner, the high choice group was more favorable to the Iranians than the low choice groups.

Thus, rather than the usual effect of high choice producing more favorable attitudes toward the essay topic than low choice, the degree of choice interacted with the similarity or dissimilarity of the partner's attitudes. Looking at the means in Table 13–6 from another perspective, within the high choice condition, the similar subjects are much less favorable to the Iranians than the dissimilar subjects. Within the low choice conditions, the opposite pattern occurs, but the size of the difference is quite small. Therefore, the effect of the similarity manipulation seemed to intensify the cognitive dissonance effect for dissimilar subjects but to reverse the effect for similar subjects.

Bipolar Adjectives

The item-total score correlations for the seven bipolar adjectives ranged between .40 and .78, and coefficient alpha was .86. The final analysis we carried out was an analysis of variance on the combined seven-item bipolar adjective scale. As on the attraction items of the IJS, we found a significant similarity of attitude main effect with the subjects being more positive toward the similar than the dissimilar partner. Also, as in the attraction items, there was a significant interaction between attitude similarity and choice. The means shown in column 4 of Table 13–6 reveal that the usual similar over dissimilar effect occurs at the low choice condition but at the high choice condition the similar and dissimilar partners are judged about equally. Again, as with the attraction items, it appears that the subjects are less positive toward the similar partner in the high than in the low choice condition, but more positive toward the dissimilar partner in the high as opposed to the low choice condition.

THE MEANING OF THE RESULTS

What did all of these results show us? Well, the experiment succeeded in some ways and failed in other ways. Subjects in the high choice groups who were paired with a dissimilar partner, showed more attraction to the partner, more positive attitudes toward the essay topic, and higher scores on the adjective scale than their low choice counterparts. On the other hand, the high choice subjects paired with a similar partner showed less attraction, less positive attitudes toward the essay topic, and less positive scores on the adjective list than the low choice subjects paired with a similar partner. Even the information items, although nonsignificant, showed this same pattern.

Although we had gained some insight into the relationship between cognitive dissonance and attraction, we were left with an unanswered question. We needed more direct evidence as to the nature of attraction differences. We had posited that once an attitude shift had occurred as a function of choice, subjects would become more strongly attracted to a dissimilar and less strongly attracted to a similar partner. Our rationale for this prediction was a need for consensual validation of the new attitude which would be more likely from a dissimilar than from a similar partner. Although the predicted pattern of results occurred, direct evidence for our rationale was missing. In other words, we needed evidence for the validity of our theoretical rationale; that is, we needed construct validity.

THE SECOND STUDY

Therefore, we designed a second study to attempt to answer the above question. We reasoned that if subjects who experienced cognitive dissonance and changed their attitudes needed consensual validation, they should be attracted to a dissimilar other only to the extent that they could receive consensual validation from that person. For example, if the interaction with the dissimilar other precluded any discussion of the topic of the changed attitude, attraction to the dissimilar other would be lower than if the interaction involved a discussion of the dissonance-related topic. In this same vein, an interaction with a similar other which did not involve the dissonance-related topic would be less aversive than one involving the changed attitude, and attraction to the similar other should be greater in the unrelated topic situation. We decided to tell the subjects, at the point of the attitude-similarity manipulation, that either they would be discussing the topic of their own essay with their partner or that they would be discussing a different unrelated topic. We predicted that in the high as compared to the low choice condition, attraction to the dissimilar partner would increase, and attraction to the similar partner would decrease only in the situation where the essay topic would be discussed.

Before we began to actually run the second study, an event occurred over which we had no control—the Iranians agreed to release the hostages. After a number of discussions about whether to now change the essay topic, we decided that an essay favorable to the Iranians would still be counterattitudinal and that we would stick with this original topic. In order to tap into this turn of events, we added another item to the Attitude toward the Iranians Scale: "The United States should not abide by its agreement with Iran."

As the study progressed, we found, to our surprise, that in the high choice condition the subjects actively resisted writing the essay. The experimenters then made their pleas to the subjects more strongly, stating over and over that we really needed pro-Iranian essays. With a high degree of pleading, a portion of the subjects in the high choice group did finally write the essays, but in a sense the extra pressure upon them by the experimenters was in essence eliminating their degree of choice. In fact, this is exactly what occurred. High and low choice subjects did not differ on their attitudes toward the Iranians, and therefore the dissonance effect did not occur.

In the first study, very few subjects had refused to write the counterattitudinal essay, but in the second study, mass resistance occurred. From the reports of the experimenters, it was as though extremely negative feelings had been controlled while the hostages were in captivity, and the release of the hostages also brought about the release of highly emotional anti-Iranian sentiment. Therefore, we chalked up our lack of success to the particular series of events surrounding the topic we had chosen.

THE THIRD STUDY

Since the basic paradigm or model for the second study was still of paramount interest to us, we decided to change topics and pursue the issue in a third study. In a sense, we had to begin again in our search for a topic. We needed a topic toward which an overwhelming proportion of students would disagree. The topic we decided upon this time, after much debate, was a 12:00 P.M. curfew for freshmen. Since most of our subjects were freshmen, we decided that this would be a topic with which they would uniformly disagree. Our cover story would be that the board of trustees of the university was considering this curfew due to a rise in late-night vandalism in which freshmen were involved. The high choice subjects would also be told that we were gathering arguments on both sides of the topic for the board of trustees, and that since we already had a large number of anti-curfew essays, we would appreciate if it they would write pro-curfew essays. The low choice subjects would simply be told to write the pro-curfew essays.

Again, we followed the same basic procedure as in the first study. To our surprise, we again ran into stiff opposition to writing the essay in the high choice group. The experimenters were told not to bring about high pressure since this would essentially equate the high and low choice conditions and wipe out any dissonance effect. Although we ended up with enough subjects who wrote the essay under high choice to carry out a data analysis, the differential attrition between the high and low choice subjects was a direct threat to the internal validity of the study. It is certainly quite possible that those subjects who wrote the essay were the ones who initially were less strongly opposed to a curfew. This would mean that the original equating of the high and low choice conditions through random assignment would have been altered, leaving the usable subjects in the high choice group more positive toward the curfew than those in the low choice group. We had given no pretest on subjects' feelings about a curfew since we felt that this would sensitize them to the manipulation. Therefore we could not directly check to see if the high and low choice subjects who wrote the essay were equal before the manipulation of choice occurred.

The only premanipulation measure we had was the Attitude Survey. Five of the items dealing with topics relevant to students (premarital sex, birth control, student needs, drug laws, and sex differences) were analyzed by a 2 (high-low choice) × 2 (correct-incorrect essay) ANOVA. There were no significant main effects or interaction on any of these items. Those subjects who wrote the essays supporting the curfew did not differ from those subjects who refused to write the essays. It should be kept in mind that the lack of differences on the Attitude Survey items does not rule out subject attrition as a threat to the internal validity of the study. Subjects in the high and low choice groups may have differed on other attitudes or most importantly on their pretest attitudes toward the curfew. The Attitude Survey items were, at best, an indirect assessment of the equality of the conditions after differential attrition had occurred.

Keeping in mind the threat to the internal validity of the study, we decided to analyze the results for those subjects who wrote the pro-curfew essays. Our first step was to determine if the choice manipulation had worked. In summary, the analyses showed *(a)* the high choice subjects responding more favorably toward the curfew than the low choice subjects, *(b)* higher attraction to the similar than to the dissimilar partner under low choice but very little difference under high choice, and *(c)* higher information value ratings of the dissimilar than the similar partner under high choice but the opposite pattern under low choice. The essay topic manipulation did not interact with either choice or similarity. We had again found evidence that the typical findings of high attraction for a similar and low attraction for a dissimilar other can be altered through a cognitive dissonance manipulation. Unfortunately, our rationale for this finding was not supported in that the topic of discussion with the partner had no effect upon the attraction scores. We had expected to find that only when the dissimilar partner could offer consensual validation of the subject's attitude—that is, when the topic of the curfew was discussed— would the subjects become more attracted to the dissimilar partner. Unfortunately for our logic, this finding did not occur. Subjects were more strongly attracted to a dissimilar partner under high than under low choice regardless of the discussion topic. Either our logic about consensual validation was incorrect, or possibly the strategy for testing the logic was inadequate. As we thought about the issue, a plausible flaw surfaced. In the condition where the curfew was to be discussed, subjects were told that they would present their essays to their partners, whereas in the gasoline tax discussion groups, the partners were to present their essays. Thus, not only were the topics of discussion different in the two groups, but so were the perceived roles of the subjects. In one condition, the curfew presentation, the subject took the active role of presenting, while in the other condition, the subject played the more passive role of an audience. These differences may have differentially aroused subjects and wiped out the predicted attraction differences.

The second problem in this study, and a major one, was the high attrition due to the resistance of the high choice subjects to writing the essay. Although we attempted to check on this by finding no significant differences in scores on the various attitude survey items for the subjects who wrote the essay and those who refused to write favorably about the curfew, the internal validity of the study was left in doubt. The large-scale resistance left us puzzled since on our first study we had encountered almost no resistance.

The purpose of the next study in the series was now quite clear. We needed to find a procedure which would eliminate or at least drastically reduce the attrition found in the last two experiments, and we needed a test for our consensual validation explanation which was not confounded. After consulting with a well-known researcher in the area of cognitive dissonance, we found out that the procedure we had employed differed somewhat from the one he had traditionally used. In our procedure, subjects in the high choice condition were asked to write an essay on a topic toward which they were unfavorable. They were told that they could write an essay either supporting or attacking the topic (the Iranian action or the curfew) but that since we already had a great many essays which were negative, it would help us if they could write a favorable one. In the design our consultant used, subjects in the high choice condition were asked if they would write an essay on a topic they disagreed with while waiting for a second part of the study. In other words, they had a choice in whether or not they agreed to participate in the essay writing but not in which type of essay they wrote—favorable or unfavorable to the topic. Thus, our giving them a choice in the type of essay may have produced the high refusal rate. We would attempt to design the next study so as to follow the procedure employed by our consultant. We decided to also make one further procedural change. The experimenters reported that it had seemed to them that when only a few subjects showed for a session, there was a greater occurrence of essay writing than when a large number showed. If, for example, only four subjects arrived for a session, each experimenter then had only two subjects. An obvious difference between our studies and other dissonance research became apparent. We had run the studies in groups, while they had run individual subjects. Therefore, we would run each subject individually.

The second problem, that of the consensual validation explanation, we decided to again test through the discussion topic manipulation. We felt that due to the confounding of the presenter-listener roles with the topics to be discussed, this manipulation had not received a fair test in the last experiment. In order to solve this problem, all subjects would have to have the same role, namely presenter, regardless of the topic discussed. Thus, one group would have to present to their partners a counterattitudinal essay, while the other group would present an attitudinally consistent essay. This would necessitate having subjects write essays on two topics, one consistent and the other inconsistent with their beliefs. Half of the subjects would be told that they would present the attitudinally consistent essay, while the other half would be told that they would present the attitudinally inconsistent essay. In this way, the roles for both would be the same, and only the topics would differ.

If the proposed study works, we will have a handle on at least part of the dissonance—attraction relationship—and hopefully these studies will lead to a published paper on this phenomenon. The modifications, reassessments, and reformulations along with the hours of discussion among those involved in the research will not appear in the article. What will seem like a rather straightforward path will have actually been a rather complicated series of twists and turns. The research process is one which is difficult and demands great effort, creative thinking, and some degree of good fortune. Hopefully, this personal journey has provided the reader with some insight into the complexity of this process.

Appendix

Statistical Procedures

This appendix is designed to provide an extension to the discussions of statistical issues contained within the text. More thorough and detailed explanations of the procedures can be found in textbooks which deal solely with statistics. The purpose here is merely to show the formulas and demonstrate the computations involved in the procedures discussed throughout the text.

I. In order to facilitate the following presentations, a few definitions of symbols are in order.
   (a) X : a raw score
   (b) $\bar{X}$: the mean of a sample group of raw scores; μ: the mean of a population.
   (c) $x : X - \bar{X}$: a deviation score
   (d) N : the number of cases
   (e) Σ : add the scores
   (f) S^2: sample variance; σ^2: population variance
   (g) S : sample standard deviation; σ: population standard deviation

II. Computation of the mean, sum of squares, variance and standard deviation for the following 10 scores from a sample group:

   53, 49, 62, 71, 83, 47, 45, 78, 55, 67

   (a) Mean: $\bar{X} = \Sigma X/N$
   $$\Sigma X = 53 + 49 + \ldots + 55 + 67 = 610$$
   $$N = 10$$
   $$X = 610/10 = 61$$

   (b) Sum of squares: $\Sigma(X - \bar{X})^2 = \Sigma x^2$
   $$\Sigma x^2 = (53 - 61)^2 + (49 - 61)^2 + \ldots + (55 - 61)^2$$
   $$+ (67 - 61)^2 = 1,606$$

   (c) Variance: $S^2 = \Sigma x^2/N = 1,606/10 = 160.6$

   (d) Standard deviation: S = square root of the variance
   $$S = \sqrt{\Sigma x^2/N} = \sqrt{160} = 12.67$$

III. Computation of the correlation coefficient, the slope (b) and intercept (a) of the regression line, predicted criterion scores, and systematic and unsystematic components of variance for the following 10 pairs of X and Y scores:

(1) X	(2) x	(3) y	(4) Y	(5) $\hat{Y}$	(6) $(Y - \hat{Y})$
15	−4	3	82	81.24	.76
25	6	−11	68	75.64	−7.64
10	−9	−2	77	84.04	−7.04
18	−1	12	91	79.56	11.44
22	3	6	85	77.32	7.68

28	9	−9	70	73.96	−3.96
13	−6	−1	78	82.36	−4.36
20	1	1	80	78.44	1.56
16	−3	5	84	80.68	3.32
23	4	−4	75	76.76	−1.76

(a) Correlation coefficient:

$$r = \Sigma(X - \bar{X})(Y - \bar{Y}) / \sqrt{\Sigma(X - \bar{X})^2 \cdot \Sigma(Y - \bar{Y})^2}$$
$$= \Sigma xy / \sqrt{\Sigma x^2 \Sigma y^2}$$
$$\bar{X} = \Sigma X/N = (15 + 25 + \ldots + 16 + 23)/10$$
$$= 190/10 = 19$$
$$\bar{Y} = \Sigma Y/N = (82 + 68 + \ldots + 84 + 75)/10$$
$$= 790/10 = 79$$
$$\Sigma xy = (-4 \cdot 3) + (6 \cdot -11) + \ldots + (-3 \cdot 5)$$
$$+ (4 \cdot -4) = -159$$
$$\Sigma x^2 = (-4^2 + 6^2 + \ldots + -3^2 + 4^2) = 286$$
$$\Sigma y^2 = (3^2 + -11^2 + \ldots + 5^2 + -4^2) = 438$$
$$r = \Sigma xy / \sqrt{\Sigma x^2 \Sigma y^2} = -159 / \sqrt{286 \cdot 438} = -.45$$

(b) Slope: $b = \Sigma xy/\Sigma x^2 = -159/286 = -.56$
Intercept: $a = \bar{y} - b\bar{x} = 79 - (-.56)(19) = 89.64$

(c) Predicted scores: $\hat{Y} = a + bX$.
For the first X score (15), $\hat{Y} = 89.64 + (-.56)(15) = 81.24$.
For the second X score (25), $\hat{Y} = 89.64 + (-.56)(25) = 75.64$.
All of the predicted scores are found in column 5.

(d) Total, unsystematic, and systematic variance. The total variance is the variance of the criterion variable (Y).

1. The first step is to calculate the total sum of squares (Σy^2) which was previously found to be 438.

2. The unsystematic or residual variance is that part of the total variance which is unrelated to the predictor X. The sum of the squared differences between the actual and the predicted Y scores is the unsystematic component:

$$\Sigma(Y - \hat{Y})^2 = [(82 - 81.24)^2 + (68 - 75.64)^2 + \ldots$$
$$+ (84 - 80.68)^2 + (75 - 76.76)^2]$$
$$= 349.60$$

The differences between the actual and predicted scores are found in column 6.

3. If the unsystematic component ($\Sigma(Y - \hat{Y})^2$) is subtracted from the total (Σy^2), the difference reflects the systematic or regression component; that part of the total which is related to X.

$$\Sigma y^2 - \Sigma(Y - \hat{Y})^2 = 438 - 349.60 = 88.40$$

If the systematic component is divided by the total, a measure of the proportion of the Y variance which can be accounted for through X is obtained. This is also r^2.

$$r^2 = 88.40/438 = .20$$
$$r = \sqrt{.20} = .45$$

4. The significance of the relationship between X and Y is tested through the F statistic, by dividing the systematic by the unsystematic variance. These variances are estimates of population variance and are the sums of squares divided by other degrees of freedom. The degree of freedom for the systematic component is one and for the unsystematic component is $N - 2$. The results are usually put into tabular form as shown below:

ANOVA REGRESSION

Source of Variation	Sum of Squares	Degrees of Freedom	Mean Square	F
Total	438	9		
Regression (systematic)	88.4	1	88.4	2.02
Residual (unsystematic)	349.6	8	43.7	

The table is called an analysis of variance of regression table (ANOVA). The first column identifies the sources of variation (total, regression, residual), the second column contains the sums of squares, the third column the degrees of freedom, and the fourth column the mean square or variance estimate associate with each source. The mean squares are found by dividing the sums of squares by their associated degrees of freedom. The fifth column contains the F value for testing significance.

F = (systematic sum of squares/1)/(unsystematic sum of squares/$N - 2$)

F = (88.40/1)/(349.60/8) = 88.40/43.7 = 2.02

The F ratio can be evaluated in a table of F values found in most statistics texts. It is evaluated at the convergence of the column of the degrees of freedom for the numerator and row of the degrees of freedom for the denominator (1 and 8 in this case). If the calculated F value is larger than the tabled F value, the result is significant—not a chance occurrence. The F value of 2.02 is smaller than the tabled value of 5.32 and therefore the relationship between X and Y is nonsignificant. The null hypothesis is that the population $r = 0$, the small F value produces a failure to reject the null hypothesis.

IV. Testing the significance of the difference between the means of two samples through the t statistic using the following two groups of scores:

Group A	Group B
72	56
55	32
68	28
47	50
50	35

$$t = (\bar{X}_A - \bar{X}_B) / \sqrt{S^2/N_a + S^2 / N_B}$$

1. $\bar{X}_A = \Sigma X_A / N_A = 292/5 = 58.4$

2. $\bar{X}_B = \Sigma X_B / N_B = 201/5 = 40.2$

3. $S_A^2 = \Sigma(X_A - \bar{X}_A)^2 / N_A - 1$

$$S_A^2 = [(72 - 58.4)^2 + (55 - 58.4)^2 + (68 - 58.4)^2 \\ + (47 - 58.4)^2 + (50 - 58.4)^2] / 4 = 122.3$$

$$S_B^2 = \Sigma(X_B - \bar{X}_B)^2 / N_B - 1$$

$$S_B^2 = [(56 - 40.2)^2 + (32 - 40.2)^2 + (28 - 40.2)^2 \\ + (50 - 40.2)^2 + (35 - 40.2)^2] / 4 = 147.2$$

$$t = (58.4 - 40.2) / \sqrt{122.3/5 + 147.2/5} = 2.47$$

4. The t statistic is evaluated in a table of t at the appropriate degrees of freedom ($N_A + N_B - 2$ or in this case 8). The calculated t value $= 2.47$ is greater than the tabled t value $= 2.31$, and therefore the difference between the means is significant—not a chance occurrence. The null hypothesis is that the two means are drawn from the same population. The t value $= 2.47$ produces a rejection of the null hypothesis and a conclusion that the means are drawn from two different populations.

V. Testing the significance of more than two means through the analysis of variance (ANOVA) using the following three groups of scores (the first two groups are identical to those employed in problem IV.)

Group A	Group B	Group C
72	56	84
55	32	92
68	28	76
47	50	67
50	35	90

The ANOVA breaks the total variance into systematic and unsystematic components and tests the significance of the differences through the F ratio.

(a) The total sum of squares is the sum of the squares of the deviations of each score from the grand mean of all of the scores $(\bar{\bar{X}})$.

1. $\bar{\bar{X}} = \Sigma X / N_{total}$

   $\bar{\bar{X}} = (72 + 55 + \ldots + 67 + 90) / 15 = 902/15 = 60.13$

2. Total: $(X - \bar{\bar{X}})^2 = [(72 - 60.13)^2 + (55 - 60.13)^2 + \ldots + (67 - 60.13)^2 + (90 - 60.13)^2] = 5855.73$

(b) The systematic or between groups component is the variation of the group means around the grand mean. This variation is a function of the treatment in an experiment.

1. $\bar{X}_A = 58.4; \bar{X}_B = 40.2$ (see problem IV).

   $\bar{X}_C = \Sigma X_C / N_C = 409/5 = 81.8$

2. Between groups: $\Sigma(\bar{X}_{group} - \bar{\bar{X}})^2 \cdot N_{group} = (\bar{X}_A - \bar{\bar{X}})^2 \cdot N_A + [\bar{X}_B - \bar{\bar{X}}]^2 \cdot N_B + (\bar{X}_C - \bar{\bar{X}})^2 \cdot N_C$

   Between groups $= (58.4 - 60.13)^2 \cdot 5 + (40.2 - 60.13)^2 \cdot 5 + (81.8 - 60.13)^2 \cdot 5 = 4348.93$

(c) The unsystematic or within-groups component is the pooled variation of the scores within the groups around their group means.

1. Within groups: $\Sigma(X_A - \bar{X}_A)^2 + \Sigma(X_B - \bar{X}_B)^2 + \Sigma(X_C - \bar{X}_C)^2$

   Within groups $= (72 - 58.4)^2 + (55 - 58.4)^2 +$
   $(68 - 58.4)^2 + (47 - 58.4)^2 +$
   $(50 - 58.4)^2 + (56 - 40.2)^2 +$
   $(32 - 40.2)^2 + (28 - 40.2)^2 +$
   $(50 - 40.2)^2 + (35 - 40.2)^2 +$
   $(84 - 81.8)^2 + (92 - 81.8)^2 +$
   $(76 - 81.8)^2 + (67 - 81.8)^2 +$
   $(90 - 81.8)^2 = 1,506.8$

2. Since the total sum of squares is composed of two additive components, between and within groups, the within-groups component could have been found through subtraction.

Total = between + within
Within = total − between
Total = 5855.73 (from part A)
Between groups = 4348.93 (from part B)
Within groups = 5855.73 − 4348.93 = 1506.8 (This result is identical to that found through the direct method used above.)

(d) As in the case of regression (problem III), the results are usually put in tabular form as below:

ANOVA

Source of Variation	Sum of Squares	Degrees of Freedom	Mean Square	F
Total	5855.73	14		
Between groups (systematic)	4348.93	2	2421.97	19.23
Within groups (unsystematic)	1506.8	12	125.57	

Significance is evaluated through the F value which is a ratio of the between to the within mean square. This value, 19.23, is evaluated in a table of F values at the convergence of the column of the degrees of freedom for the between groups component and the row of the within groups component (2 and 12 in this case). The calculated F value of 19.23 is larger than the tabled F value of 3.89, and the groups are judged to be significantly different.

VI. Testing significance in a factorial design through ANOVA using the following groups of scores where A_1 and A_2 are two conditions of one independent variable and B_1 and B_2 are two conditions of a second independent variable.

	A_1	A_2
	17	20
B_1	22	16
	15	18
	19	21
	23	27
B_2	25	25
	20	26
	21	22

The total variation is broken into systematic (between groups) and unsystematic (within groups components) as in problem V. In the factorial design, the between groups component can be further broken into main and interaction effects.

(a) Total: $\Sigma(X - \bar{\bar{X}})^2$

   1. $\bar{\bar{X}} = \Sigma X/N_{Tot}$
      $\bar{\bar{X}} = (17 + 22 + \ldots + 26 + 22) / 16 = 21.62$

   2. Total: $\Sigma(X - \bar{\bar{X}})^2 = (17 - 21.62)^2 + (22 - 21.62)^2$
      $+ \ldots + (26 - 21.62)^2 + (24 - 21.62)^2 = 181.75$

(b) Between groups: $\Sigma(\bar{X}_{group} - \bar{\bar{X}})^2 = (\bar{X}_{A_1B_1} = \bar{\bar{X}})^2 \cdot N_{A_1B_1} +$
      $(\bar{X}_{A_1B_2} - \bar{\bar{X}})^2 \cdot N_{A_1B_2} + (\bar{X}_{A_2B_1} - \bar{\bar{X}})^2 \cdot$
      $N_{A_2B_1} + (\bar{X}_{A_2B_2} - \bar{\bar{X}})^2 \cdot N_{A_2B_2}$

   1. Below are the means for the groups:

	A_1	A_2
B_1	19.00	18.75
B_2	23.75	25.00

   2. Between groups $= (19.0 - 21.62)^2 \cdot 4 + (23.75 - 21.62)^2$
      $\cdot 4 + (18.75 - 21.62)^2 \cdot 4 + (25.0 - $
      $21.62)^2 \cdot 4 = 124.25$

(c) A main effect: $[(\bar{X}_{A_1B_1} + \bar{X}_{A_1B_2})/2 - \bar{\bar{X}}]^2 \cdot (N_{A_1B_1} + N_{A_1B_2}) +$
      $[(\bar{X}_{A_2B_1} + \bar{X}_{A_2B_2})/2 - \bar{\bar{X}}]^2 \cdot (N_{A_2B_1} + N_{A_2B_2})$
   A main effect: $[(19.0 + 23.75)/2 - 21.62]^2 \cdot 8 + [(18.75 +$
      $25.0)/2 - 21.62]^2 : 8 = 1.0$

(d) B main effect: $[(A_1B_1 + A_2B_1)/2 - \bar{\bar{X}}]^2 \cdot (N_{A_1B_1} + N_{A_2B_1}) +$
      $[(A_1B_2 + A_2B_2)/2 - \bar{\bar{X}}]^2 \cdot (N_{A_1B_2} + N_{A_2B_2})$
   B main effect: $[(19.0 + 18.75)/2 - 21.62]^2 \cdot 8 + [(23.75 +$
      $25.0)/2 - 21.62]^2 \cdot 8 = 121.0$

(e) $A \times B$ interaction is found through subtraction. When the two main effects are subtracted from the between-groups component, the remaining systematic variation is due to the interaction.

   $A \times B$ interaction: Between groups—$A - B$

   $A \times B$ interaction $= 124.25 - 1.0 - 121.0 = 2.25$

(f) Within groups or unsystematic component is as previously defined: Total − between groups. Within groups $= 181.75 - 124.25 = 57.5$

The ANOVA table following shows the results:

ANOVA

Source of Variation	Sum of Squares	Degrees of Freedom	Mean Square	F
Total	181.75	15		
Between groups	124.25	3		
A main effect	1.0	1	1.0	<1.0
B main effect	121.0	1	121.0	25.26
A × B interaction	2.25	1	2.25	<1.
Within groups	57.5	12	4.79	

As previously discussed, the calculated F values are compared to the tabled F values at the intersection of the column (numerator) and row (denominator) degrees of freedom. Each main and interaction effect mean square is divided by the within group mean square to produce the F value. Both the A main effect and the $A \times B$ interaction are less than one, resulting in a failure to reach significance. The B main effect F value $= 25.26$ is greater than the tabled F value $= 4.75$ and is therefore significant.

REFERENCES

Abramson, L. Y., Seligman, M. E. P., & Teasdale, J. D. Learned helplessness in humans: Critique and reformulation. *Journal of Abnormal Psychology,* 1978, *87,* 49–74.

Alford, G. W., Webster, J. S., & Sanders, S. H. Covert aversion of two interrelated deviant sexual practices: Obscene phone calling and exhibitionism. A single case analysis. *Behavior Therapy,* 1980, *11,* 15–25.

Azrin, N. H., & Lindsley, O. R. The reinforcement of cooperation between children. *Journal of Abnormal and Social Psychology,* 1956, *52,* 100–102.

Bandura, A. Influence of models' reinforcement contingencies on the acquisition of imitative responses. *Journal of Personality and Social Psychology,* 1965, *1,* 589–595.

Brock, T. C., & Balloun, J. L. Behavioral receptivity to dissonant information. *Journal of Personality and Social Psychology,* 1967, *6,* 413–428.

Byrne, D., Nelson, D., & Reeves, K. Effects of consensual validation and invalidation on attraction as a function of verifiability. *Journal of Experimental Social Psychology,* 1966, *2,* 98–107.

Byrne, D., & Clore, G. L. Effectance arousal and attraction. *Journal of Personality and Social Psychology, Monograph,* 1967, *6* (Whole No. 638).

Cacioppo, J. T., & Petty, R. E. The need for cognition. *Journal of Personality and Social Psychology,* 1982, *42*(1), 116–131.

Campbell, D. A., & Fiske, D. W. Validation by the multitrait-multimethod matrix. *Psychological Bulletin,* 1959, *56,* 81–105.

Collins, A. M., & Quillian, M. R. Retrieval time from semantic memory. *Journal of Verbal Learning and Verbal Behavior,* 1969, *8,* 240–247.

Cook, T. D., & Campbell, D. T. *Quasi-experimentation, design and analysis issues for field settings.* Chicago: Rand McNally, 1979.

Ferguson, G. A. *Statistical analysis in psychology and education.* New York: McGraw-Hill, 1971.

Festinger, L. A. *A theory of cognitive dissonance.* Stanford, Calif.: Standford University Press, 1957.

Gaertner, S., & Bickman, L. Effects of race on helping behavior: The wrong number technique. *Journal of Personality and Social Psychology,* 1971, *20,* 218–222.

Gold, J. A. *Attraction to a dissimilar other as a function of cognitive dissonance.* Paper presented at a meeting of the Eastern Psychological Association, Baltimore, Maryland, 1982.

Gold, J. A., & Cowles, N. L. Effects of tuning sets on free recall of clustered and unclustered word lists. *The Journal of General Psychology,* 1973, *88,* 211–220.

Gold, J. A., Ryckman, R. M., & Rodda, W. C. Differential responsiveness to dissonance manipulations by open- and closed-minded subjects in a forced compliance situation. *Journal of Social Psychology,* 1973, *90,* 73–83.

Hastorf, A. H., & Cantril, H. They saw a game: A case study. *Journal of Abnormal and Social Psychology,* 1954, *49,* 129–134.

Hayes, D. S., Chemelski, B. E., & Palmer, M. Nursery rhymes and prose passages: Preschoolers' liking and short-term retention of story events. *Developmental Psychology,* 1982, *18*(1), 49–56.

Jones, E. E., & Gerard, H. B. *Foundations of social psychology.* New York: John Wiley & Sons, 1967.

Kazdin, A. E. *Single-case research designs: Methods for clinicial and applied settings.* New York: Oxford University Press, 1982.

Kerlinger, F. N., & Pedhazur, E. J. *Multiple regression in behavioral research.* New York: Holt, Rinehart & Winston, 1973.

Kiesler, S. B., & Baral, L. "The search for a romantic partner: The effects of self-esteem and physical attractiveness on romantic behavior. In K. J. Gergen & D. Marlowe (Eds.), *Personality and social behavior.* Reading, Mass.: Addison-Wesley, 1970.

Kulberg, G., & Cantrell, P. Alcohol use and personality variables. Unpublished study, 1978.

Langer, E. J., Janis, I. L., & Wolfer, J. A. Reduction of psychological stress in surgical patients. *Journal of Experimental Social Psychology,* 1975, *11,* 155–165.

Latané, B., & Darley, J. M. Bystander apathy. In E. P. Hollander & R. G. Hunt (Eds.), *Current perspectives in social psychology* (4th ed.). New York: Oxford University Press, 1976.

Lenney, E., Gold, J., & Browning, C. Sex differences in self-confidence: The influence of comparison others' ability level. *Sex roles,* in press.

Levine, G. *Introductory statistics for psychology: The logic and the methods.* New York: Academic Press, 1981.

Maier, S. F. Failure to escape traumatic shock: Incompatible skeletal motor responses or learned helplessness? *Learning and Motivation,* 1970, *1,* 157–170.

Mazur-Hart, S. F., & Berman, J. J. Changing from fault to no-fault divorce: An interrupted time series analysis. *Journal of Applied Social Psychology,* 1977, *7*(4), 300–312.

McNemar, Q. *Psychological statistics.* New York: John Wiley & Sons, 1969.

Middlemist, R. D., Knowles, E. S., & Matter, C. F. Personal space invasions in the laboratory: Suggestive evidence for arousal. *Journal of Personality and Social Psychology,* 1976, *33*(5), 541–546.

Milgram, S. Behavioral study of obedience. *Journal of Abnormal and Social Psychology,* 1963, *67,* 371–378.

Moskowitz, D. S., & Schwarz, J. C. Validity comparison of behavior counts and ratings by knowledgeable informants. *Journal of Personality and Social Psychology,* 1982, *42*(3), 518–528.

Neale, J. M., & Liebert, R. M. *Science and behavior: An introduction to methods of research.* Englewood Cliffs, N.J.: Prentice-Hall, 1980.

Newcomb, T. M. *The acquaintance process.* New York: Holt, Rinehart & Winston, 1961.

Nunnally, J. C. *Psychometric theory.* New York: McGraw-Hill, 1978.

Rokeach, M. *The open and closed mind.* New York: Basic Books, 1960.

Rothbart, M., Evans, M., & Fulero, S. Recall for confirming events: Memory processes and the maintenance of social stereotypes. *Journal of Experimental Social Psychology,* 1979, *15,* 343–355.

Rotter, J. B. Generalized expectancies for internal vs. external control of reinforcements. *Psychological Monographs,* 1966, *80* (Whole No. 609).

Rotter, J. B., & Mulry, R. C. Internal versus external control of reinforcement and decision time. *Journal of Personality and Social Psychology,* 1965, *2,* 598–604.

Rubin, Z. *Liking and loving.* New York: Holt, Rinehart & Winston, 1973.

Russ, R. C., Gold, J. A., & Stone, W. F. Attractions to a dissimilar stranger as a function of level of effectance arousal. *Journal of Experimental Social Psychology,* 1979, *15,* 481–491.

Russ, R. C., Gold, J. A., & Stone, W. F. Opportunity for thought as a mediator of attraction to a dissimilar stranger: A further test of an information seeking interpretation. *Journals of Experimental Social Psychology,* 1980, *16,* 562–572.

Ryckman, R. M., Robbins, M. A., Thornton, B., & Cantrell, P. Development and validation of a physical self-efficacy scale. *Journal of Personality and Social Psychology,* 1982, *42*(5), 891–900.

Seligman, M. E. P. *Helplessness: On depression, development, and death.* San Francisco: W. H. Freeman, 1975.

Sidman, M. *Tactics of scientific research.* New York: Basic Books, 1960.

Thornton, B., Ryckman, R. M. & Gold, J. A. Sensation seeking as a determinant of interpersonal attraction toward similar and dissimilar others. *Journal of Mind and Behavior,* 1981, *2*(1), 85–91.

Zanna, M. P., & Cooper, J. Dissonance and the attribution process. In J. H. Harvey, W. J. Ickes, & R. F. Kidd (Eds.), *New directions in attribution research* (Vol. 1). Hillsdale, N.J.: Lawrence Erlbaum Associates, 1976.

Index

This book has been set Linotron 202, in 10½ Times Roman, leaded 2 points. Part numbers and titles are 24 point Times Roman and chapter numbers and titles are 24 point Times Roman. The overall type area is 30 by 48 picas.